IBM Microcomputers:
A Programmer's Handbook

Ranade IBM Series

IBM Microcomputers:
A Programmer's Handbook

Julio Sanchez
Northern Montana College

Maria P. Canton
Skipanon Software Co.

McGraw-Hill, Inc.
New York St. Louis San Francisco Auckland Bogotá
Caracas Hamburg Lisbon London Madrid Mexico
Milan Montreal New Delhi Paris
San Juan São Paulo Singapore
Sydney Tokyo Toronto

Library of Congress Cataloging-in-Publication

Sanchez, Julio.

    IBM microcomputers: A programmer's handbook by Julio
Sanchez, Maria P. Canton.
    p.   cm.
    ISBN 0-07-054594-4
    1. IBM microcomputers — Programming.   I. Canton, Maria P.
II. Title.
QA76.8.I1015S264   1990   90-5870
005.265 — dc20   CIP

1 2 3 4 5 6 7 8 9 0 DOC/DOC 9 5 4 3 2 1 0

ISBN 0-07-054594-4

*The sponsoring editor for this book was Theron Shreve, the editing
supervisor was David E. Fogarty, the designer was Naomi Auerbach, and
the production supervisor was Dianne L. Walber.*

Printed and bound by R. R. Donnelley & Sons Company.

Several trademarks appear in this book. The companies listed here are
the owners of the trademarks following their names: Compaq Computer
Corporation (Compaq); Hercules Computer Technologies (Hercules);
Hewlett-Packard Company (Hewlett-Packard); Intel Corporation (Intel);
International Business Machines Corporation (IBM); Lotus
Development Corporation (Lotus); Microsoft Corporation (Microsoft,
MS-DOS); Motorola, Inc. (Motorola); Tandy Corporation (Tandy-Radio
Shack); Zilog, Inc. (Zilog).

LIMITS OF LIABILITY AND DISCLAIMER OF WARRANTY

The author and publisher have exercised care in preparing this book
and the programs contained in it. They make no representation,
however, that the programs are error-free or suitable for every
application to which a reader may attempt to apply them. The
author and publisher make no warranty of any kind, expressed or
implied, including the warranties of merchantability or fitness for a
particular purpose, with regard to these programs or the documentation or theory contained in this book, all of which are provided "as
is." The author and publisher shall not be liable for damages in an
amount greater than the purchase price of this book, or in any event
for incidental or consequential damages in connection with, or
arising out of the furnishing, performance, or use of these programs
or the associated descriptions or discussions.
    Readers should test any program on their own systems and
compare results with those presented in this book. They should then
construct their own test programs to verify that they fully understand the requisite calling conventions and data formats for each of
the programs. Then they should test the specific application
thoroughly.

Contents

Preface

The Programmer's Handbook was conceived and designed in the conviction that technical information relative to the IBM microcomputers is dispersed, difficult to interpret, and costly. In composing this Handbook the authors have made a selection of useful technical data for programming the IBM microcomputers and compatible machines. The material is presented in three different forms:

1. Descriptive text

2. Code samples

3. Programming data (mostly included in figures and tables)

The text descriptions aim at providing the background information that makes the code samples, as well as the raw data presented in the illustrations, easier to understand and to apply. The programs, code fragments, and routines included with the text, and in three appendices, will hopefully save programmers from wasting efforts in *re-inventing the wheel*.

The plan for a reference book usually implies a compromise; all the technical data and the programming problems that relate to the dozen or more models of IBM microcomputers would fill many volumes. In fact, the collection of Technical Reference Manuals published by IBM takes up several feet of shelf space and costs over $1300. In this project we have chosen the word *handbook* as part of our title to indicate that the material has been selected so as to keep this work compact and portable. Also, that it has been our aim to collect the information that an IBM microcomputer programmer would like to keep *at hand*. The selection criteria for the material included in the Handbook has been based on the following points:

Standard equipment. We have limited our discussions to the hardware components that form part of a standard system. Most peripherals and other optional devices, such as printers, plotters, digital tablets, streaming tape drives, and optical drives are not discussed or only sparingly considered.

General usefulness. The material included in the Handbook is that which the authors believe to be of general use. Specialty subjects and components have been excluded.

Hardware and firmware.   The Handbook is limited to the hardware and firmware components of the IBM microcomputers. The treatment includes the BIOS software and services, since these are part of the machine. The various disk operating systems (DOS, OS/2, UNIX, and others) are not part of the subject matter.

In addition to the selection of the book's material contents, the authors have had to make other technical decisions. For example, subject often mandates a specific numerical base; addresses are almost universally expressed in hexadecimal and bit masks in binary form. But, in other cases, a number system preference has not been as evident. For instance, BIOS interrupt 10H provides 28 functions. In this case, there seems to be little justification for the practice of using hexadecimal numbers to list these services. Following what we consider to be the most reasonable method, we have used decimal numbers except in those cases where hexadecimal or binary are more meaningful or are technically preferable.

The authors would like to thank the friends and associates who provided advise, support, and assistance in this project. Jay Ranade, the series editor, has been very helpful at every stage of this book. At McGraw-Hill,Theron Shreve, David Fogarty, Kay Magome, and Naomi Auerbach were always available when we needed help. Kevin Carlson, Assistant Vice-President for Academic Affairs for Northern Montana College, Great Falls, enthusiastically supported this project from its start. Our thanks to Dr. Jerry Brown, Dr. Ron Talmage, Roger Stone, and Bob Cooper, also from Northern, for moral support and technical assistance. We are also grateful to Sharon Lowman who spent many hours helping produce the manuscript. And a very special thanks to our friend Chet Harris for his continued optimism and encouragement.

Great Falls, Montana   Julio Sanchez
                                                                                       Maria P. Canton

Abbreviations and Conventions

μs	microsecond	APA	all-points addressable
Bd/s	Baud per second	bps	bits per second
CGA	Color Graphics Adapter	cps	characters per second
DOS	Disk Operating System	EGA	Enhanced Graphics Adapter
EIA	Electronic Industries Association	Hz	hertz
in	inch	I/O	input/output
K	kilobyte	kHz	kilohertz
LAN	local area networks	LSB	least significant bit
Mbytes	megabytes	MCGA	Multicolor Graphics Array
MDA	Monochrome Display Adapter	MHz	megahertz
MSB	most significant bit	NMI	nonmaskable interrupt
ns	nanosecond	PCjr	PC Junior
POST	Power-On Seft-Test	PS/2	Personal System/2
RAM	random-access memory	ROM	read-only memory
s	second	tpi	tracks per inch
VGA	Video Graphics Array	W	watt

Typographical symbols in tables and figures:

->   Pointer, as in ES:BX -> video buffer

⇒ ⇐ ⇔   Direction of data flow

Number Systems:

Hexadecimal numbers are postfixed with the uppercase letter H, for example, 7E23H. Binary numbers are postfixed with the uppercase letter B, for example, 00011001B. Numbers written without the H or B postifix are in decimal notation.

A diskette containing the programs and source code fragments listed in this book is available for $18.00 (price includes shipping and handling). Please send check or money order to:

SKIPANON SOFTWARE CO.
Programmer's Handbook diskette
P.O. Box 6231
Great Flalls, MT 59406

Please specify 5¼-in diskette or 3½-in microdisk.

IBM Microcomputers:
A Programmer's Handbook

1

Systems Description

1.0 Historical Note

On August 12, 1981, IBM announced their first Personal Computer. The machine was a conservatively designed desktop computer that used the Intel 8088 microprocessor. The standard model sold for under $3000. It came with 64K of random-access memory (RAM) on the motherboard, which could be expanded to 256K on the system board, as well as 40K of read-only memory (ROM). Most of this ROM was assigned to a system support program called the basic input/output system, or BIOS. The original PC had one single-side, double-density disk drive. Formatted diskettes had a storage capacity of 180K. The original operating system software furnished by IBM for the Personal Computer was DOS version 1.0, developed by Microsoft Corporation. The features of the different IBM microcomputer models are listed in Table 1.1. Some important landmarks in the history of these machines appear in Table 1.2.

1.1 Overview of the PC Line

The design concept used in developing the original IBM Personal Computer called for a modular structure that could be configured according to the user's needs or desires. The motherboard contained five expansion slots, used for installing display drivers, serial and parallel communications ports, and other options.

IBM adopted an open-door policy regarding the Personal Computer hardware and software. Instead of closely guarding the technological secrets of the PC, IBM released extensive documentation in regard to the hardware and published a listing of the BIOS source code. Furthermore, the Personal Computer was equipped with several important components that were not produced by IBM, although the company could have easily furnished them. The most

Table 1.1. Machine Features

| | PC line | | | | | PS/2 line | | | | | |
	PC & PC XT	PCjr	PORTABLE PC	CONVERTIBLE PC	PC AT & XT 286	MODELS 25/30	MODEL 30-286	MODELS 50/50 Z	MODEL 60	MODEL 70	MODEL 80
Processor	8088	8088	8088	80C88	80286	8086	80286	80286	80286	80386*	80386
Speed (MHz)	4.77	4.77	4.77	4.77	6/8	8	10	10	10	16/25	16/20
NDP	8087	No	8087	No	80287	8087	80287	80287	80287	80387	80387
ROM	40K	64K	40K	64K	64K	64K	128	128K	128K	128K	128K
Maximum RAM	640K	512K	640K	640K	16 Mbytes	640K	16 Mbytes	16 Mbytes	16 Mbytes	16 Mbytes	16 Mbytes
Slots (8-bit)	5/8	0	8	0	2	2/3	0	0	0	0	0
Slots (16-bit)	0	0	0	0	6	0	3	3	7	3	7
Slots (32-bit)	0	0	0	0	0	0	0	0	0	2	3
DOS version	1.x/2.x	2.x	2.x	2.x	2.x/4.x	3.x/4.x	3.x/4/x	3.x/4.x	3.x/4.x	3.x/4.x	3.x/4.x
OS/2	No	No	No	No	Yes	No	Yes	Yes	Yes	Yes	Yes
Diskette	180K+	360K	360K	720K	1.2 Mbytes	720K	1.4 Mbytes	1.4 Mbytes	1.4 Mbytes	1.4 Mbytes	1.4 Mbytes
Hard disk	No/Yes	No	No	No	Yes	No/Yes	Yes	Yes	Yes	Yes	Yes
Color graphics	CGA	PCjr**	CGA	CGA	EGA	MCGA	VGA	VGA	VGA	VGA	VGA

* Model 70-A21 can be upgraded to the Intel 80486 CPU.
** The PCjr color graphics system is named the Video Gate Array.

notable of these were the floppy disk drives, manufactured by Tandon Corporation, and the operating system software, which was developed by Microsoft Corporation.

Table 1.2. *Landmarks*

OPERATING-SYSTEM SOFTWARE	YEAR	HARDWARE
DOS Version 1.0	1981	Personal Computer
DOS Version 1.1	1982	COMPAQ Portable
DOS Version 2.0	1983	PC XT
DOS Version 2.1	1984	PCjr PC Portable
DOS Version 3.0	1985	PC AT COMPAQ Deskpro 286
DOS Version 3.2	1986	PC Convertible COMPAQ Deskpro 386
DOS Version 3.3	1987	PC XT 286 COMPAQ Portable III PS/2 Models 25/30/50/60
OS/2 Version 1.0 DOS Version 4.0	1988	PS/2 Model 80 COMPAQ 386/25 PS/2 Model 70/50Z
Presentation Manager OS/2 Version 1.1	1989	PS/2 Model 55 and P70
	1990	80486 upgrade for Model 70-A21

1.1.1 The Original IBM Personal Computer

The most important hardware features of the IBM Personal Computer are listed below and in Table 1.3.

1. Intel 8088 microprocessor on the system board; an empty socket is provided for the optional installation of the Intel 8087 mathematical coprocessor.
2. Five expansion slots for attaching different options to the main system.
3. Read-only memory chips containing the basic input/output system (BIOS) software.
4. 64K of random-access memory in computers made before May 1983 and 256K thereafter; RAM can be expanded to 512K in the original systems and to 640K in the later models.
5. 83-key keyboard driven by an 8048 controller chip.
6. 8259 interrupt controller chip.
7. 8255 programmable peripheral interface chip.
8. 8253 timer and counter chip.
9. 8237 direct memory access chip.

Table 1.3. *IBM Personal Computer Hardware Summary*

DEVICE	SPECS	DESCRIPTION
Processor	8088	8-bit bus, 16-bit registers, 1 Mbyte address space; Intel microprocessor
NDP	8087	Optional Intel math coprocessor
Memory	ROM RAM	40K BIOS software; includes BASIC Original:16K minimum, expandable to 256K Upgrade: 64K, expandable to 640K
Power	63.5 W	Protected
Display	MDA CGA	Monochrome, 80 by 25 lines, alphanumeric Color, 640 by 200 pixels, APA graphics
I/O ports	Serial Parallel Mouse	Optional RS-232C serial port Optional, used as printer output Optional, requires hardware and software
Storage	Floppy (original) (upgrade) Hard disk	160K ,5¼-in drive under DOS 1.0, single-side, double-density, 40 tracks, 512 bytes per sector 360K, 5¼-in drive under DOS 1.1 or later, double-side, double-density, 40 tracks, 512 bytes per sector No hard disk support
Keyboard	83 keys	Typematic; uses Intel 8048 controller

1.1.2 The IBM Personal Computer XT

The IBM Personal Computer XT (extended technology) was introduced in March 1983. The most important new features of the XT were hard disk support and a new version of MS DOS. In addition, the XT was furnished with more memory, and the number of expansion slots was increased from five to eight. The power supply was also enlarged to 130 W. In all other respects the XT was identical to its predecessor, the PC. Externally the machines are indistinguishable; they use the same keyboard and can be connected to the same video display adapters. Table 1.4 lists the principal features of the IBM PC XT.

1.1.3 The IBM PC Junior

The IBM PC Junior (also spelled PCjr) was announced in November 1983 as a home version of the Personal Computer. Although IBM claimed that the machine offered a high degree of compatibility with its predecessors, it was inspired by radically different design concepts. Some of these ideas were not to resurface until the introduction of the Personal System 2 (PS/2) line in 1987.

The most noticeable difference between the Personal Computer and the PCjr is in the implementation of hardware options. In the Personal Computer, the video display and communications cards can be selected and installed by the user, while the PCjr comes equipped with several standard components over which the buyer has no choice. For instance, the PCjr includes color graphics display hardware and a serial port as part of the base system. On the other hand, the diskette drive, which can be considered standard equipment in the Personal Computer, is furnished as an option in the PCjr. The parallel port is optional in both systems.

Table 1.4. *IBM Personal Computer XT Hardware Summary*

DEVICE	SPECS	DESCRIPTION
Processor	8088	8-bit bus, 16-bit registers, 1 Mbyte address space; Intel microprocessor
NDP	8087	Optional Intel math coprocessor
Memory	ROM RAM	40K BIOS software, includes BASIC 256K, expandable to 640K
Power	130 W	Protected
Display	MDA CGA	Monochrome, 80 by 25 lines, alphanumeric Color, 640 by 200 pixels, APA graphics
I/O ports	Serial Parallel Mouse	Optional RS-232C serial port Optional; used as printer output Optional; requires hardware and software
Storage	Floppy Hard disk	360K, 5¼-in drive under DOS 2.0 or later, Double-side, double-density, 40 tracks, 512 bytes per sector 10- or 20 Mbytes
Keyboard	83 keys	Typematic; uses Intel 8048 controller

Features of the PCjr are listed below and in Table 1.5.

1. Integral color graphics video hardware
2. Built-in serial port compatible with RS-232C
3. Complex sound system
4. Cordless keyboard with infrared link
5. Two slots for 64K ROM cartridges
6. Optional joystick
7. No 8087 mathematical coprocessor socket

IBM and other manufacturers have made available several options and attachments for the PCjr, for example:

1. Memory expansion up to 768K
2. One or more 360K diskette drives
3. Parallel printer attachment
4. Joystick and light pen attachments
5. RGB color monitor and TV connector
6. PC-type keyboard and cord
7. Hard disk drives

Table 1.5. *IBM PCjr Hardware Summary*

DEVICE	SPECS	DESCRIPTION
Processor	8088	8-bit bus, 16-bit registers, 1 Mbyte address space; Intel microprocessor
NDP	No	No socket for coprocessor
Memory	ROM System RAM Extra RAM ROM	64K BIOS software; includes BASIC 64K, expandable to 128K In memory sidecar; expandable to 768K 2 cartridges, 64K each
Power	33 W	Three voltage levels, two-stage, protected
Display	Monitor TV	4-color, 640 by 200 pixels, APA graphics Optional connector for TV receivers
I/O ports	Serial Parallel Joystick Modem	Built-in RS-232C serial port Optional parallel printer attachment Optional attachable joysticks Optional internal modem
Storage	Floppy Hard disk	360K, 5¼-in drive under DOS 2.1 or later, double-side, double-density, 40 tracks, 512 bytes per sector Non-IBM second diskette drive available No hard disk support by IBM Non-IBM hard disk drive available
Keyboard	62 keys	Infrared, cordless, with optional cord

Table 1.6. *IBM Portable Computer Hardware Summary*

DEVICE	SPECS	DESCRIPTION
Processor	8088	8-bit bus, 16-bit registers, 1 Mbyte address space; Intel microprocessor
NDP	No	No socket for coprocessor
Memory	ROM RAM	40K BIOS software, includes BASIC 256K, expandable to 640K
Power	130 W	Protected
Display	Special	Monochrome, composite monitor
I/O ports	Serial Parallel Mouse	Optional RS-232C serial port Optional; used as printer output Optional; requires hardware and software
Storage	Floppy	360K, 5¼-in drive under DOS 2.0 or later, double-side, double-density, 40 tracks,
Hard disk	No	No hard disk support
Keyboard	83 keys	Typematic; uses Intel 8048 controller

1.1.4 The IBM Portable Computer

The Portable PC, introduced in March 1984, is quite similar to the PC XT, except that the Portable lacks hard disk support and uses an IBM Color Graphics Adapter as a standard video card. The low resolution of its video display, as well as its incompatibility with some monochrome software developed for the PC and the PC XT, was surely one of the causes for the Portable's demise.

Note that the PC Portable weighs 30 pounds, which explains why this microcomputer is thought of more as a *transportable* than as a *portable* machine. Table 1.6 lists the principal features of the IBM Portable PC.

1.1.5 The IBM Personal Computer AT

The IBM Personal Computer AT (advanced technology) was introduced to the marketplace in August 1984. In contrast with the XT, the AT implemented some substantial technological advances; for instance:

1. The use of Intel's 80286 microprocessor
2. Optional 80287 mathematical coprocessor
3. 16-bit input/output bus and a 16-Mbyte memory space
4. Built-in 20-Mbyte hard drive
5. Nonvolatile clock and calendar
6. 1.2-Mbyte capacity diskette drives
7. DOS version 3.0
8. Redesigned case with lock and 84-key keyboard
9. New 64K BIOS software in ROM

Table 1.7. *IBM Personal Computer AT Hardware Summary*

DEVICE	SPECS	DESCRIPTION
Processor	80286	16-bit bus, 16-bit registers, 16 Mbytes address space; Intel microprocessor
NDP	80287	Optional Intel math coprocessor
Memory	ROM RAM	64K BIOS software, expandable to 128K 256K, expandable to 16 Mbytes
Power	192 W	Protected
Display	MDA CGA EGA	Monochrome, 80 by 25 lines, alphanumeric Color, 640 by 200 pixels, APA graphics Color, 640 by 350 pixels, APA graphics
I/O ports	Serial/ parallel Mouse	Optional serial/parallel adapter provides RS-232C and printer ports Optional, requires hardware and software
Storage	Floppy Hard disk	5¼-in by 160/180K, 360K, and 1.2-Mbyte drives 20-Mbyte (upgraded to 40-Mbyte)
Keyboard	84 keys 101 keys	Original keyboard Upgraded keyboard. Both models have programmable delay and typematic rate

The Intel 80286 central processing unit of the Personal Computer AT contained an implied promise of multitasking that was not realized during the system's life span. The OS/2 operating system became available in late 1987, while the PC AT was dropped in July of that year with the introduction of the PS/2 line. Nevertheless, OS/2 can be used in the AT. Table 1.7 lists the principal features of the IBM PC AT.

1.1.6 The IBM PC Convertible

In April 1986 IBM introduced the PC Convertible, which represented a new effort at a portable PC (see Section 1.1.4). By this time, technological advances had made it possible to reduce the machine's weight to approximately 13 pounds and its dimensions to those of a small typewriter. The name *PC Convertible* relates to *converting* the machine into a desktop model by connecting it to the ac power line and using standard displays. The adapters and monitors necessary for this conversion are available from IBM. The monitor bases are designed so that the machine can slide under the display. Small, portable computers, like the PC Convertible, are also called *laptops*.

Some hardware components used in the PC Convertible are not identical to those of the IBM desktops. Consequently, some of the BIOS routines in the Convertible are different from those of the PC and AT. This explains why some programs that access the hardware directly are incompatible with this machine.

Table 1.8. *IBM Convertible Computer Hardware Summary*

DEVICE	SPECS	DESCRIPTION
Processor	80C88	8-bit bus, 16-bit registers, 1Mbyte address space; CMOS version of Intel's 8088
NDP	No	No socket for coprocessor
Memory	ROM RAM	2 ROMs, 32K each; Includes BASIC 256K, expandable to 512K
Power	AC adapter Battery Automobile	Standard 90 to 265 V 50/60 Hz Nickel-cadmium cells for 6 to 10 hours service. Optional charger Optional adapter for cigarette lighter
Display	LCD Monochrome Color	25 lines by 80 characters CGA emulation. Optional backlit model available. Both LCD displays are removable Optional CRT adapter and 9-in monitor Optional CGA-compatible 13-in monitor
I/O ports	Serial/ parallel Modem	Optional serial/parallel adapter provides RS-232C and printer ports Optional internal modem, 300/1200 bps
Storage	Microdisk Hard disk	2 microdisks, 3½-in by 720K each, under DOS 3.2 , double-side, double-density, 80 tracks, 512 bytes per sector, 135 tpi No hard disk support
Keyboard	78 keys	Typematic, with 10 function keys

Note that the PC Convertible is the only model of the PC line that continued to be manufactured and marketed after the introduction of the PS/2 line in April 1987. Table 1.8 lists the principal features of the IBM Convertible.

1.1.7 The IBM PC XT Model 286

The IBM PC XT 286, introduced in September 1986, is a version of the XT machine that is equipped with an Intel 80286 microprocessor (like the one used in the AT) and updated with some other AT-like features. In addition to the CPU, other significant improvements are an 80287 math coprocessor socket, high-density floppy drives, a battery-powered clock, and an AT-type keyboard. One of the inconveniences of the Model 286 is that the adapter cards used in this machine cannot be as high as those used in the AT. This has created some compatibility problems. Table 1.9 lists the principal features of the IBM PC XT Model 286.

Table 1.9. *IBM Personal Computer XT Model 286 Hardware Summary*

DEVICE	SPECS	DESCRIPTION
Processor	80286	16-bit bus, 16-bit registers, 16 Mbytes address space; Intel microprocessor
NDP	80287	Optional Intel math coprocessor
Memory	ROM RAM	40K BIOS software; includes BASIC 640K, expandable to 16 Mbytes
Power	157 W	Protected
Display	MDA CGA EGA	Monochrome, 80 by 25 lines, alphanumeric Color, 640 by 200 pixels, APA graphics Color, 640 by 350 pixels, APA graphics
I/O ports	Serial Parallel Mouse	Optional RS-232C serial port Optional; used as printer output Optional; requires hardware and software
Storage	Floppy Hard disk	5¼-in by 160/180K, 360K, and 1.2 Mbyte drives 20-Mbytye
Keyboard	101 keys	AT-type keyboard; programmable delay and typematic rate

1.2 Overview of the PS/2 Line

The first major change in the IBM Personal Computer line came in April 1987 with the introduction of the Personal System 2 microcomputers. The most interesting feature of the PS/2 line is its diversity; it includes an assortment of models and options that range from the 8086-driven Models 25 and 30, with

XT-compatible slots, to the Models 70 and 80, equipped with the Intel 80386 CPU and 16-bit slots of a radically new design.

The advent of the Personal System 2 computers also marked the discontinuation of most models of the PC line. The only exception was the PC Convertible (see Section 1.1.6). PS/2 brought several technological innovations as well as some changes in the design concepts of the PC line, for example:

1. PS/2 microcomputers come equipped with serial, parallel, and pointing-device (mouse) ports.
2. All models contain video systems with alphanumeric and graphic capabilities.
3. Diskette drives have been standardized to the 3½-in size.
4. All PS/2 models support hard disk storage devices.
5. System configuration is performed through software; this technology, called Programmable Option Select, or POS, makes mechanical switches unnecessary in PS/2 systems.

In addition, the PS/2 Models 50, 60, 70, and 80 use a new bus arrangement called the Micro Channel. The Micro Channel expansion slots are incompatible with cards developed for the XT and AT, and vice versa. Micro Channel uses a unique bus arbitration scheme, as well as eight DMA channels. This allows the system to move data between memory, disks, video, and ports without assistance from the CPU. Micro Channel interrupts are level-sensitive and allow interrupt sharing on all levels. It is discussed in Chapter 6.

Table 1.10. *IBM PS/2 Model 25 Hardware Summary*

DEVICE	SPECS	DESCRIPTION
Processor	8086	8-MHz Intel microprocessor with 16 Mbytes address space and zero wait states
NDP	8087	Optional Intel math coprocessor
Memory	ROM RAM	64K BIOS, includes BASIC Standard model: 512K, expandable to 640K Collegiate and LAN: 640K
Power	90 W 115 W	Units with monochrome display Units with color display
Display	MCGA	Monochrome or color, 640 by 480 pixels, APA graphics
I/O ports	Serial Parallel Mouse	Built-in RS-232C serial port Built-in bidirectional parallel port Built-in pointing device port
Storage	Microdisk Hard disk	1 or 2 720K 3½-in drives 20-Mbyte
Keyboard	84 keys 101 keys	Standard model Collegiate and LAN models

1.2.1 The PS/2 Model 25

The Model 25 is the simplest machine in the PS/2 family. It is furnished in three different models, named Standard, Collegiate, and LAN (Local Area Network) Station. Each is equipped with different standard equipment. Since this machine does not implement the Micro Channel standard, the Model 25 expansion slots are compatible with many cards and adapters for the PC line. Micro Channel adapters cannot be used.

The Model 25 can be easily identified because the system case and the monitor form a single unit. The machine can be furnished with either a monochrome or a color display, but, because of this single-unit design, it is not possible to change monitors or display adapters. Table 1.10 lists the principal features of the PS/2 Model 25.

1.2.2 The PS/2 Model 30

The original IBM PS/2 Model 30 was introduced in April 1987, along with several other PS/2 models. The basic machine design is directed toward compatibility with the PC line. As in the Model 25 (see Section 1.2.1), the expansion slots of the Model 30 are PC-compatible. This machine does not use the Micro Channel standard and will not accept Micro Channel cards or adapters, neither will it accept PC AT adapters.

The internal hardware used in the Model 30 is quite similar to that of the Model 25. Externally, the Model 30 case and monitors are separate components, in contrast with the Model 25's single-unit design. Nevertheless, both models use the Multicolor Graphic Array (MCGA) video standard (see Chapter 4). Table 1.11 lists the principal features of the Model 30.

Table 1.11. *IBM PS/2 Model 30 Hardware Summary*

DEVICE	SPECS	DESCRIPTION
Processor	8086	8-MHz Intel microprocessor with 16 Mbytes address space and zero wait states
NDP	8087	Optional Intel math coprocessor
Memory	ROM RAM	64K BIOS; includes BASIC 640K, expandable to 2 Mbytes
Power	70 W	Protected
Display	MCGA	Monochrome or color, 640 by 480 pixels, APA graphics Monitors: Monochrome display, Model 8503 Color displays, Models 8512, 8513, and 8514
I/O ports	Serial Parallel Mouse	Built-in RS-232C serial port Built-in bidirectional parallel port Built-in pointing device port
Storage	Microdisk Hard disk	1 or 2 720K 3½-in drives 20-Mbyte
Keyboard	101 keys	PS/2 standard keyboard with programmable delay and typematic rate

In 1989 IBM released a new version of the Model 30 equipped with an Intel 80286 processor, VGA graphics, a 1.44-Mbyte diskette drive and an optional hard disk. The machine, designated as the Model 30 286, retains the PC line compatibility of the original Model 30. Table 1.12 shows the characteristics of the Model 30 286.

Table 1.12. *IBM PS/2 Model 30 286 Hardware Summary*

DEVICE	SPECS	DESCRIPTION
Processor	80286	10-MHz Intel microprocessor with 16 Mbytes address space and one wait states
NDP	80287	Optional Intel math coprocessor
Memory	ROM RAM	128K BIOS, includes BASIC 1 Mbyte, expandable to 16 Mbytes (4 Mbytes maximum on system board)
Power	90 W	Protected, with voltage selection
Display	VGA	Monochrome and color alphanumeric and 640 by 480 pixels, 16-color APA graphics Monitors: Monochrome display Models 8503, 8506, 8507 and 8508 Color display Models 8512, 8513, and 8514
I/O ports	Serial Parallel Mouse	Built-in RS-232C serial port Built-in bidirectional parallel port Built-in pointing device port
Storage	Microdisk Hard disk	1.44-Mbyte, 3½-in drive 20- or 30-Mbyte
Keyboard	101 keys	PS/2 standard keyboard with programmable delay and typematic rate

1.2.3 The PS/2 Model 50 and Model 50 Z

The Model 50 is the simplest PS/2 model that implements the technological advances characteristic of this line, namely:

1. Micro Channel architecture

2. VGA graphic standard

3. 1.4-Mbyte diskette storage

4. Multitasking capabilities under OS/2

The use of Micro Channel makes the Model 50 incompatible with adapters developed for the PC line. This means that PC, XT, and AT cards cannot be plugged into a Model 50, or any other PS/2 model with a higher model number. The Model 50 is considerably more compact than the PC AT, which it supersedes. Table 1.13 lists the principal features of the Model 50 and 50 Z.

The Model 50 Z, released in June 1988, comes equipped with a 10-MHz 80286 microprocessor that operates at zero wait states. According to IBM, this feature improves the performance of the Model 50 Z by 35 percent.

Table 1.13. *IBM PS/2 Model 50 and 50Z Hardware Summary*

DEVICE	SPECS	DESCRIPTION
Processor	80286	10-MHz Intel microprocessor with 16 Mbytes address space. One wait state in Model 50 and zero wait state in Model 50 Z
NDP	80287	Optional Intel math coprocessor
Memory	ROM RAM	128K BIOS; includes BASIC 1 Mbyte, expandable to 16 Mbytes
Power	94 W	Protected, autosensing
Display	VGA 8514/A	Monochrome and color alphanumeric and 640 by 480 pixels, 16-color APA graphics Monitors: Monochrome display, Model 8503 Color displays, Models 8512, 8513, and 8514 Optional high-resolution graphic system; 1026 by 768 pixels, 256-color APA graphics
I/O ports	Serial Parallel Mouse	Built-in RS-232C serial port Built-in bidirectional parallel port Built-in pointing device port
Storage	Microdisk Hard disk	1.4-Mbyte 3½-in drive 20-, 30-, or 60-Mbyte
Keyboard	101 keys	PS/2 standard keyboard with programmable delay and typematic rate

1.2.4 The PS/2 Model 60

The most visible feature of the Model 60 is that the machine's main case is designed to stand, vertically, on the floor instead of sitting on the user's desk. The advantages of the Model 60 over the Model 50 are four additional Micro Channel slots, a faster hard drive, and 2K of battery-backed CMOS RAM.

The more roomy case and the additional slots are due to IBM's plan to allow this machine to be used as a base for small multiuser systems. The space inside the Model 60 case is sufficient for an additional diskette drive and a second hard disk drive. Table 1.14 lists the principal features of the Model 60.

1.2.5 The PS/2 Model 70

The Model 70 was announced in June 1988 as the first IBM desktop computer equipped with the Intel 80386 microprocessor. The only other member of the PS/2 family equipped with this chip is the Model 80 (see Section 1.2.5).

Externally, the Model 70 resembles the Model 50, since the case, keyboard, and video options are almost identical. The only way to tell the machines apart is by the model number inscribed on the IBM nameplate. Internally, the machines are quite different. In addition to the 80386 microprocessor, the Model 70 motherboard contains two 32-bit expansion slots, which are not available in the Model 50. The Model 70 also contains 64K of memory cache and its controller, which are designed to improve system performance by providing faster access to frequently used data.

Table 1.14. *IBM PS/2 Model 60 Hardware Summary*

DEVICE	SPECS	DESCRIPTION
Processor	80286	10-MHz Intel microprocessor with 16 Mbytes address space and one wait state
NDP	80287	Optional Intel math coprocessor
Memory	ROM RAM	128K BIOS; includes BASIC 1 Mbyte, expandable to 16 Mbytes
Power	207 W 225 W	Protected, autosensing, in Model 60-041 Protected, autosensing, in Model 60-071
Display	VGA 8514/A	Monochrome and color alphanumeric and 640 by 480 pixels, 16-color APA graphics Monitors: Monochrome display, Model 8503 Color displays, Models 8512, 8513, and 8514 Optional high-resolution graphic system; 1026 by 768 pixels, 256-color APA graphics
I/O ports	Serial Parallel Mouse	Built-in RS-232C serial port Built-in bidirectional parallel port Built-in pointing-device port
Storage	Microdisk Hard disk	1.4-Mbyte 3½-in drive 44-, 70-, 88-, or 120-Mbyte
Keyboard	101 keys	PS/2 standard keyboard with programmable delay and typematic rate

Table 1.15. *IBM PS/2 Model 70 Hardware Summary*

DEVICE	SPECS	DESCRIPTION
Processor	80386 80486	Intel microprocessor with 4 gigabytes address space; 16-, 20-, or 25-MHz with zero to two wait states Model 70-A21 optional upgrade
NDP	80287 or 80387	Optional Intel math coprocessors
Memory	ROM RAM	128K BIOS, includes BASIC 1-Mbyte, expandable to 16 Mbytes
Power	132 W	Protected, autosensing
Display	VGA 8514/A	Monochrome and color alphanumeric 640 by 480 pixels, 16-color APA graphics. Monitors: Monochrome display, Model 8503 Color displays, Models 8512, 8513, and 8514 Optional high-resolution graphic system; 1026 by 768 pixels, 256-color APA graphics.
I/O ports	Serial Parallel Mouse	Built-in RS-232C serial port Built-in bidirectional parallel port Built-in pointing-device port
Storage	Microdisk Hard disk	1.4-Mbyte 3½-in drive 60- or 120-Mbyte
Keyboard	101 keys	PS/2 standard keyboard with programmable delay and typematic rate

In the Model 70-A21, the 80386 CPU is mounted on a removable card, together with the Intel 82385 cache controller chip and 64K of cache RAM. The optional 80387 math coprocessor, if installed, is also located on this card. This removable card can be replaced with one containing the Intel 80486, thus upgrading the system to this technology.

The Model 70 hard disk drives are also different from the Model 50's; in addition to being faster, the hard disk controller in the Model 70 is integrated with the drive, while in the Model 50 the controller takes up one of four expansion slots. This feature allowed the elimination of one expansion slot in the Model 70. Table 1.15 lists the principal features of the Model 70.

1.2.6 The PS/2 Model 80

The floor-standing Model 80 is the largest and most expensive member of the PS/2 family. This model was introduced in April 1987, along with Models 30, 50, and 60. Like the Model 60, the Model 80 was conceived as the hub of a small network; it contains enough options and expansion space to assure this role.

The Model 80 is equipped with the Intel 80386 microprocessor operating at 16 or 20 MHz. The machine has the largest storage capacity of the PS/2 line, including one or two 1.44-Mbyte micro disk drives and hard disk options with up to 314 Mbytes of space. The Model 80 has four 32-bit and three 16-bit expansion slots, which is a record for PS/2 computers. With regard to input/output facilities, display options, and keyboard, it is identical to Models 50, 60, and 70. Table 1.16 lists the principal features of the Model 80.

Table 1.16. *IBM PS/2 Model 80 Hardware Summary*

DEVICE	SPECS	DESCRIPTION
Processor	80386	Intel microprocessor with 4 gigabytes address space; 16- or 20-MHz with zero to two wait states
NDP	80287 or 80387	Optional Intel math coprocessors
Memory	ROM RAM	128K BIOS; includes BASIC 1 or 2 Mbytes, expandable to 16 Mbytes
Power	225 W	Protected, autosensing and autoswitching
Display	VGA 8514/A	Monochrome and color alphanumeric and 640 by 480 pixels, 16-color APA graphics Monitors: Monochrome display, Model 8503 Color displays, Models 8512, 8513, and 8514 Optional high-resolution graphic system; 1026 by 768 pixels, 256-color APA graphics
I/O ports	Serial Parallel Mouse	Built-in RS-232C serial port Built-in bidirectional parallel port Built-in pointing-device port
Storage	Microdisk Hard disk	1 or 2 drives; 1.4-Mbytes 3½-in 44-, 70-, 115-, or 314-Mbyte
Keyboard	101 keys	PS/2 standard keyboard with programmable delay and typematic rate

1.3 IBM System Identification

Quite frequently a program must determine the characteristics of the system on which it executes. The IBM BIOS contains a machine identification byte, stored at address F000:FFFEH (Table 1.17). The code fragment following Table 1.17 allows inspection of the machine ID byte.

Table 1.17. *IBM System Identification*

BYTE AT F000:FFFEH	MACHINE	BIOS DATE	SUBMODEL
FFH	IBM PC	04-24-81	—
		10-19-81	—
		10-27-82	—
FEH	IBM PC XT	11-08-82	—
FBH	IBM PC XT	01-10-86	00
		05-09-86	00
FDH	IBM PCjr	06-01-83	—
FCH	IBM PC AT	01-10-84	—
		06-10-85	00
		11-15-85	01
	IBM XT 286	04-21-86	02
F9H	IBM Convertible	09-13-85	—
FAH	PS/2 Model 25	06-27-87	—
	PS/2 Model 30	09-02-86	—
FCH	PS/2 Model 50	02-13-87	04
	PS/2 Model 60	02-13-87	05
F8H	PS/2 Model 70 (1)	04-11-88	09
	PS/2 Model 70 (2)		04
	PS/2 Model 70 (3)		0D
	PS/2 Model 80	10-07-87	01

```
;****************
;
;       obtain
;     machine ID
;****************
;
; The byte at address F000:FFFEH is encoded as follows:
; PC systems
;          FFH              Personal Computer
;          FEH              PC XT
;          FDH              PCjr
;          FCH              PC AT
;          F9H              PC Convertible
; PS/2 systems
;          FAH              Model 25/30
;          FCH              Model 50/60
;          F8H              Model 70/80
```

```
; Get machine ID
        MOV     AX,0F000H              ; Base
        MOV     ES,AX                  ; To extra segment
        MOV     AL,ES:[0FFFEH]         ; Machine ID byte to AL
; AL now holds the machine identification code
```

1.3.1 System Configuration Information

The data offered by the machine ID byte is sometimes insufficient. For example, the machine ID byte F8H corresponds to both Model 70 and Model 80 machines. In order to determine which of these two possibilities is correct, the program will have to examine the submodel byte (see Table 1.16). In this case, a submodel byte value of 09 indicates a Model 70. The submodel byte, as well as other system configuration information, can be obtained by using service number 192 of INT 15H. This service is available for AT BIOS dated 06-10-85 and later, for the PC XT BIOS dated 01-10-86 and later, for the XT 286, for the PC Convertible, and for all models of the PS/2 line. The following code sample can be used to obtain the model and submodel, if this data is available.

```
;******************
;    obtain system
;    configuration
;******************
; Obtain system configuration using service number 192 of
; INT 15H
        MOV     AH,192         ; Service request number
        INT     15H
; On return:
; AH = 128 if system is a PC or PCjr
; AH = 134 if system is PC XT with BIOS dated 11/08/82 or AT
;          BIOS dated 01/10/84
; AH = 0 if ES:BX is a valid pointer to the system descriptor
;          table in ROM
; Test for valid pointer
        CMP     AH,0           ; Valid?
        JNZ     EXIT_TEST      ; Go if invalid
; ES:BX points to the configuration table. Byte at offset + 2
; holds the equipment code stored at F000:FFFEH. Byte at offset
; +3 holds the submodel
        INC     BX
        INC     BX             ; Bump pointer to code byte
        MOV     DL,ES:[BX]     ; Equipment code to DL
        INC     BX             ; Bump pointer to submodel
        MOV     DH,ES:[BX]     ; Submodel to DH
EXIT_TEST:
; Code can determine equipment configuration from values in AH,
; DH, and DL
```

Table 1.18 lists the information provided by service number 192 of interrupt 15H.

Table 1.18. *INT 15H, Service Number 192, System Descriptor*

OFFSET	DATA SIZE	CONTENTS
0	Word	Feature information byte (see Figure 1.1)
2	Byte	Model byte (see Table 1.17)
3	Byte	Submodel byte (see Table 1.17)
4	Byte	BIOS revision level: 01 = PC XT 01-10-86 PC AT 06-10-85 02 = PC XT 05-09-86
5	Byte	Feature information byte (see Figure 1.1)

Note: If AH=0, ES:BX -- > system descriptor vector in ROM.

1.3.2 The System Descriptor Area

The system descriptor area in ROM contains other data in addition to the machine model and submodel described in Section 1.3.1 (see Table 1.18). The byte at offset 5 of the system descriptor area is called the *feature information byte*. Figure 1.1 is a bit map of the feature information byte.

The following code fragment determines the presence of a real-time clock by testing bit number 5 of the feature information byte. Other tests for hardware elements encoded in the feature information byte can be derived from this example by modifying the mask used by the TEST instruction.

```
;*******************
; test for real-time
;      clock
;*******************
; Obtain system configuration using service number 192 of
; INT 15H
        MOV    AH,192          ; Service request number
        INT    15H
; Code assumes a valid system descriptor table
; ES:BX points to the configuration table base. Feature
; information is the byte at offset + 5
;
;*******************
; get feature info
;*******************
        ADD    BX,5            ; Bump pointer to feature info
```

```
                              ; byte
      MOV    DL,ES:[BX]       ; Feature info byte to DL
      TEST   DL,00010000B     ; Is bit 5 set?
                              : Note: This mask can be modified
                              ; to test for other hardware
                              ; elements in the info byte
      JNZ    RT_CLOCK         ; Jump if real-time clock
                              ; in system
; Execution drops if no real-time clock detected
      .
      .
      .

; Processing for real-time clock in system
RT_CLOCK:
      .
      .
      .
```

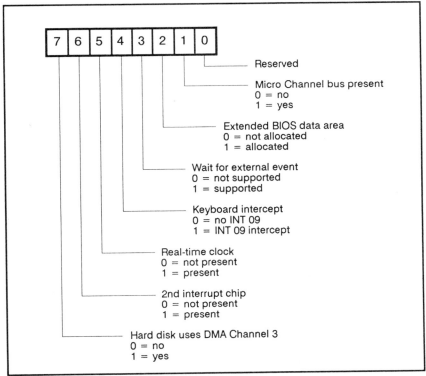

Figure 1.1. *Feature Information Byte in System Descriptor Area*

1.4   The IBM-Compatible Microcomputers

Soon after the introduction of the IBM Personal Computer in August 1981, other hardware manufacturers started producing components that could be used by the PC, mostly in the form of video boards and monitors. Two independent factors made possible the proliferation of third-party products for the Personal Computer: the machine's open architecture and IBM's policy of providing detailed technical information regarding the hardware and software elements. These same factors, together with the PC's market success, also permitted the appearance of complete systems that were technically similar to the Personal Computer.

These machines, usually called *IBM-compatible*, accept IBM-type expansions and adapters and are capable of running software designed and coded for the IBM microcomputers. But this compatibility is seldom absolute. Depending on the hardware and software used in imitating the PC, some machines approximate the goal of total compatibility more than others. The following general classification can be used to describe degrees of IBM compatibility:

1. *DOS-compatible machines*. These microcomputers use the same operating system as the corresponding IBM model and, consequently, are able to run programs that execute their functions exclusively through DOS services. The Hewlett-Packard microcomputers fall in this category.

2. *BIOS-compatible machines*. These microcomputers, in addition to MS DOS, also use a set of BIOS services similar to IBM BIOS. One such software product, called the Phoenix BIOS, has been commercially available since 1983.

3. *Hardware-compatible machines*. These machines use hardware components that are identical to those in the corresponding IBM model or that operate similarly. Ideally, this type of compatible machine will run all software designed for the IBM.

1.4.1 The Compaq Microcomputers

The original Compaq was the first IBM-compatible computer marketed in the United States. The machine, unveiled in January 1983, was designed as a portable microcomputer. The keyboard could be secured to the main case by two latches, forming a closed cabinet. The carrying handle was built into the case. In addition to portability, the Compaq offered other interesting features; for instance:

1. The Compaq came equipped with 320K, double-sided drives, while at the time IBM's single-sided drives provided only 180K of storage.

2. The Compaq consolidated monochrome and color display in a single adapter, which could be configured to operate either like an IBM CGA or like an MDA card.

3. The Compaq came equipped with 128K of RAM, expandable to 256K, while in 1982 the PC still came with 16K.

These and other technological improvements, together with a sales price substantially below that of the PC, made the Compaq computer an immediate success. Compaq later increased its product line to include several laptop and desktop models. Table 1.19 lists the principal features of the Compaq Deskpro 386S.

Table 1.19. *Compaq Deskpro 386S Hardware Summary*

DEVICE	SPECS	DESCRIPTION
Processor	80386S	Intel microprocessor with 4 gigabytes address space; at 16 MHz with zero wait states
NDP	80387	Optional Intel math coprocessor
Memory	ROM RAM	Compaq BIOS 1 Mbyte, expandable to 13 Mbytes
Power	140 W	Protected
Display	VGA board	Monochrome and color alphanumeric and 640 by 480 pixels, 16-color APA graphics
I/O ports	Serial Parallel Mouse	Built-in RS-232C serial port Built-in bidirectional parallel port Built-in (IBM PS/2-compatible)
Storage	Floppy Microdisk Hard disk	Standard 1.2-Mbyte 5¼-in drive Optional 1.4-Mbyte 3½-in drive 20-, 40-, or 110-Mbyte
Keyboard	101 keys	PS/2-compatible

1.4.2 The Tandy IBM-Compatible Microcomputers

Radio Shack, a division of Tandy Corporation, was an early participant in the microcomputer revolution. The TRS-80 Model I was available in 1977, when the only other desktop microcomputers were the Apple and the Commodore Pet. In 1985, Tandy introduced their first IBM-compatible models, which soon became the hub of their product line. Table 1.20 lists the more popular models of the Tandy microcomputer product line. Table 1.21 lists the principal features of the Tandy Model 5000 MC.

1.4.3 The Hewlett-Packard IBM-Compatible Microcomputers

Hewlett-Packard Corporation made its reputation in the fields of laboratory equipment and mainframe computers. More recently this company has been very successful in the field of laser printers. In their microcomputer product line, Hewlett-Packard includes innovative desktop models like the HP 150, which has a touch-sensitive screen. But the only IBM-compatible model manufactured by this company is the Hewlett-Packard Vectra personal computer. The Vectra was conceived as a high-end version of the IBM PC AT. It uses an 8-MHz 80286, which is approximately 30 percent faster than the 6-MHz version of the chip used in the original PC AT. A newer version of the Vectra, designated the Vectra ES/12, uses a 12-MHz 80286 chip.

Table 1.20. *Microcomputers by Tandy Corporation (Radio Shack)*

MODEL	PROCESSOR	OPERATING SYSTEM	IBM-COMPATIBLE
TRS-80 Model I	Z-80	TRSDOS	No
TRS-80 Model II	Z-80	TRSDOS	No
TRS-80 Model III	Z-80	TRSDOS	No
TRS-80 Model 4	Z-80A	TRSDOS	No
TRS-80 Model 4P	Z-80A	TRSDOS	No
Color Computer (2-3)	6809	OS-9	No
Tandy 102	80C85	Laptop	No
Tandy 200	80C85	Laptop	No
Tandy 1000 (EX-HX-SX)	8088	MS DOS	Yes
Tandy 1000 TX	80286	MS DOS	Yes
Tandy 1400 LT	NEC V-20	MS DOS	Yes
Tandy 2000	80186	MS DOS	Yes
Tandy 3000 (HL)	80286	MS DOS	Yes
Tandy 4000	80386	MS DOS	Yes
Tandy 6000	68000	XENIX	No

Table 1.21. *Tandy 5000 MC Hardware Summary*

DEVICE	SPECS	DESCRIPTION
Processor	80386	Intel microprocessor with 4 gigabytes address space, at 20 MHz. Intel 82385 memory cache controller with 32K static RAM
NDP	80387	Optional Intel math coprocessor
Memory	RAM	2 Mbytes, expandable to 16 Mbytes
Power	192 W	Protected
Display	VGA	Monochrome and color alphanumeric and 640 by 480 pixels, 16-color APA graphics
I/O ports	Serial Parallel Mouse	Built-in RS-232C serial port Built-in parallel port Built-in
Storage	Microdisk Hard disk	1.4-Mbyte 3½-in drive 40- or 80-Mbyte
Keyboard	101 keys	PS/2-compatible

Note: The Tandy 5000 MC uses IBM Micro Channel technology.

2

The Microprocessors

2.0 The Intel iAPX Family

A microcomputer is a system of miniature electronic devices, coupled to provide computer functions on a small scale. The fundamental elements of a microcomputer system are:

1. A central processing unit (microprocessor)
2. A primary storage facility (memory)
3. World interface devices (input and output facilities)

Figure 2.1 shows the fundamental elements of a microcomputer system.

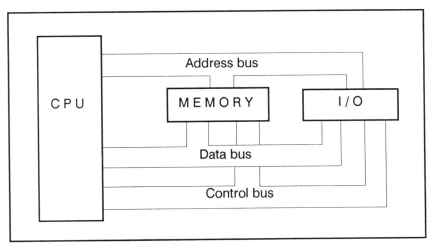

Figure 2.1. *Elements of a Microcomputer System*

Table 2.1. Architecture of the 8-, 16-, and 32- Bit Intel Microprocessors

FEATURES	8080	8086	8088	80186	80188	80286	80386	80386SX	486*
Address bus (in bits)	8	16	8	16	8	16	32	16	32
Internal data path (in bits)	8	16	16	16	16	16	32	32	32
Clock speed (in MHz)	2, 2.6, 6.3	5, 8, 10	5, 8	8, 10 12.5	8, 10, 12.5	6, 8, 10, 12.5, 20	16, 20, 25, 33	16	25
Register to register (μs/data word)	1.3	0.3	0.38	0.2	0.3	0.125	0.125	0.125	0.04
Interrupt response time (μs)	7.3	6.1	8.6	3.36	6.2	2.52	3.5	2.52	3.5
Memory address range	64K	1 Mbyte	1 Mbyte	1 Mbyte	1 Mbyte	16 Mbytes	4 giga-bytes	4 giga-bytes	4 giga-bytes
Addressing modes	5	24	24	24	24	24	28	28	28
Coprocessor	NO	8087	8087	8087	8087	80287	80287/ 80387	80287/ 80387	On chip
Number of general-purpose registers	6	8	8	8	8	8	8	8	8
Number of segment registers	0	4	4	4	4	4	6	6	6
Interrupt controller chip	8259-A	8259-A	8259-A	On chip	On chip	8259-A	8259-A	82335	μPLD
Timer-counter chip	8253	8253/54	8253/54	On chip	On chip	8253/54	8253/54	8253/54	On chip

* The 486 contains integral cache controller and 8K of static RAM

All IBM microcomputers of the PC and PS/2 lines are characterized by their use of Intel microprocessors of the iAPX family. This is also true of the IBM-compatible systems made by other manufacturers. Although Intel has manufactured 8-bit microprocessors since 1971, it is the 8080 that can be considered the immediate predecessor of the iAPX family. The 8080 was introduced in April 1974 as a general-purpose 8-bit microprocessor. The chip executes approximately 290,000 operations per second and addresses a memory area of 64K. An operational microcomputer using the 8080 could be built with only six additional chips. Table 2.1 lists the fundamental characteristics of some Intel microprocessors. Table 2.2 shows the use of Intel chips in IBM microcomputers.

Table 2.2. *IBM Microcomputers and the Intel 80x86 Family*

INTEL PROCESSOR	PC LINE			PS/2 LINE			
	PC PC XT	PCjr	PC AT XT 286	MODEL 25 MODEL 30	MODEL 50 MODEL 60	MODEL 70 MODEL 80	MODEL 70 A21
8088	X	X					
8086				X			
80286			X		X		
80386						X	X*
80486							X*

* Optional in the Model 70-A21 removable processor card.

2.1 The 8086/8088 Microprocessors

In June 1978, Intel unveiled the 8086 as their first 16-bit microprocessor. In spite of its many technological advances, the 8086 was not an immediate success. Building a microcomputer requires not only a microprocessor, but also operating systems and other software and hardware components. Many of these were not available at the time. A year after the introduction of the 8086, Intel released a more practical version of the chip that was designated the 8088. This CPU had an internal architecture identical to that of the 8086, but it used a more economical 8-bit bus. Table 2.3 shows the fundamental characteristics of the Intel 8088 CPU.

In 1980, IBM formed a design team for the Personal Computer. This group, based in Boca Raton, Florida, was called the Entry Systems Division. One of the team's first decisions was the selection of the Intel 8088 as the CPU for the new machines. The Intel 8086, the Motorola 68000, and the Zilog Z8000 were the other options considered by the designers. One of the factors that influenced their decision in favor of the 8088 was the economical advantages offered by the CPU's 8-bit bus. The original Intel 8086 was not used in an IBM microcomputer until the PS/2 Model 25 and Model 30, introduced in 1987.

Table 2.3. *Intel 8088 Microprocessor Hardware Summary*

CHARACTERISTIC	SPECIFICATIONS
Mathematical coprocessor	8087
Bus interface	8 bits
Internal data path	16 bits
Available clock frequencies	5, 8, and 10 MHz
Memory addressability	1 Mbyte
Virtual memory	No
Memory management and protection	No
I/O addressability	65,535 ports
Registers	Arithmetic: 8 Index: 4 Segment: 4 General purpose: 8
Intel support chips	Clock: 8284-A Controller: 8288 Interrupts: 8259-A DMA: 8237/82258 Timer: 8253/54 DRAM: 8207/8208
Number of pins	40
Power requirements	5 V

2.1.1 Internal Architecture

A microprocessor is an electronic semiconductor device capable of performing data operations according to an internal set of instructions. An individual instruction is recognized by its predefined code, called the *opcode*. Before a microprocessor can execute an instruction, it must first obtain the operation codes from their memory residence. This part of the process is called the *fetch cycle*. Once the instruction's codes have been fetched and decoded, then the CPU's internal circuitry can proceed to *execute* the opcode. Figure 2.2 is a diagram of the CPU's internal architecture.

This *fetch-execute* sequence can force some elements in a conventional CPU to wait until an instruction is obtained and decoded before its execution can begin. In order to prevent this wasted time, the designers of the 8086 chip divided the CPU into two separate units. The bus interface unit, or BIU, fetches the instruction opcodes from memory and places them in an instruction queue. The execution unit, or EU, decodes and executes the opcodes in the queue. Since the units operate independently, the BIU can be fetching a new instruction while the EU is executing the previous one. When the EU is ready for a new task, it will usually find the next opcode waiting in the instruction queue, which can hold up to 4 bytes.

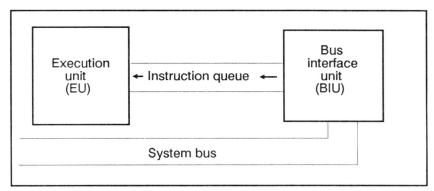

Figure 2.2. *80x86 CPU Internal Architecture*

When the next instruction to be executed does not reside in a sequential address, then the parallel operation of the BIU and the EU is disrupted. In this case, the execution unit informs the bus interface unit of the new address and must then wait for the instruction queue to be refilled.

2.1.2 Registers

The 8086/8088 CPU contains 14 internal registers. These registers can be classified as follows:
1. Data registers
2. Index and pointer registers
3. Segment registers
4. Status and control registers

Figure 2.3 is a diagram of the internal registers in the 8086/8088 CPU.

2.1.2.1 The Data Registers. Each of the four data registers can hold 16 bits of information. The upper and lower half of each data register can be addressed independently. These 8-bit half-registers of AX, BX, CX, and DX are designated AH and AL, BH and BL, CH and CL, and DH and DL.

The data registers are used in arithmetic and logical operations and in performing data transfers. Usually the programmer can designate which data register will be used in an instruction, but there are cases in which the instruction set specifically designates a data register for a certain operation. This implicit use of the 8086/8088 registers can be seen in Table 2.4.

2.1.2.2 The Index and Pointer Registers. The 16-bit registers called stack pointer (SP), base pointer (BP), source index (SI), and destination index (DI) usually contain offset values for addressing elements within a segment. They can also be used in arithmetic and logic operations. The two pointer registers, SP and BP, provide easy access to items located in the current stack segment. The

index registers, SI and DI, are used in accessing items located in the data and
extra segments. If no special provisions are contained in the instruction, the
pointer registers refer to the current stack segment, and the index registers refer
to the current data segment. SI and DI are used implicitly by 8086/8088 string
operations.

Data   Registers

AH	AL	AX
BH	BL	BX
CH	CL	CX
DH	DL	DX

Index   and   Pointer   Registers

Stack pointer	SP
Base pointer	BP
Source index	SI
Destination index	DI

Segment   Registers

Code segment	CS
Data segment	DS
Stack segment	CS
Extra segment	ES

Status   and   Control   Registers

Instruction pointer	IP
Flags	

Figure 2.3. *8086/8088 Registers*

Table 2.4. *Implicit Use of 8086/8088 Data Registers*

REGISTER	USED IMPLICITLY IN
AX	MUL, IMUL (word-size source operand) DIV, IDIV (word-size source operand) IN (word input) OUT (word output) CWD String operations
AL	MUL, IMUL (byte-size source operand) DIV, IDIV (byte-size source operand) IN (byte input) OUT (byte output) XLAT AAA, AAD, AAM, AAS (ASCII operations) CBW (convert to word) DAA, DAS (decimal arithmetic) String operations
AH	MUL, IMUL (byte-size source operand) DIV, IDIV (byte-size source operand) CBW (convert to word)
BX	XLAT
CX	LOOP, LOOPE, LOOPNE String operations with REP prefix
CL	RCR, RCL, ROR, ROL (rotates with byte count) SHR, SAR, SAL (shifts with byte count)
DX	MUL, IMUL (word-size source operand) DIV, IDIV (word-size source operand) String operations addressing ports

2.1.2.3 The Segment Registers.   The segment registers are the 16-bit registers named code (CS), data (DS), stack (SS), and extra (ES) segments. These registers are used in addressing the 1-Mbyte 8086 memory space by dividing it into 16 segments of 64K each. (See Chapter 3 for information related to the 8086 memory space.)

All instructions must reside in the current code segment, addressed through the CS register. The offset of the instruction is determined by the IP register (see Section 2.1.2.4). Program data is usually located in the data segment, addressed through the DS register. The stack is addressed through the SS register. The extra segment register, as the name implies, can be used to address operands, data, memory, and other items outside the current data and stack segments. Many IBM programs use the ES segment register as a pointer into video display memory.

2.1.2.4 The Control and Status Registers.   The instruction pointer register (IP) is similar to the program counter register of previous generations of microprocessors. This control register is managed by the bus interface unit of the CPU so that it holds the offset from the beginning of the code segment to the next instruction to be executed. The IP register cannot be manipulated directly by the programmer.

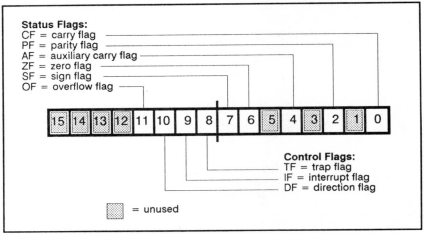

Status Flags:
CF = carry flag
PF = parity flag
AF = auxiliary carry flag
ZF = zero flag
SF = sign flag
OF = overflow flag

| 15 | 14 | 13 | 12 | 11 | 10 | 9 | 8 | 7 | 6 | 5 | 4 | 3 | 2 | 1 | 0 |

Control Flags:
TF = trap flag
IF = interrupt flag
DF = direction flag

▨ = unused

Figure 2.4. *The 8086/8088 Flag Registers*

Table 2.5. *8086/8088 Flags*

BIT	FLAG NAME	CODE	FUNCTION
11	Overflow	OF	Set to show arithmetic overflow
10	Direction	DF	Used to determine direction of string moves
9	Interrupt enable	IF	Used to enable and disable maskable interrupts
8	Trap	TF	Places the CPU in the single-step mode (used mainly by debugger programs)
7	Sign	SF	Used in signed arithmetic to show whether the result is positive (SF = 0) or negative (SF = 1)
6	Zero	ZF	Set if the result of the previous operation is zero
4	Auxiliary carry	AF	Used in decimal arithmetic to show a carry out of the low nibble or a borrow from the high nibble
2	Parity	PF	Set if the result of the previous operation has an even number of 1 bits (used mainly to check for data transmission errors)
0	Carry	CF	Set if there is a carry or a borrow to the high-order bit of the result. Also used by rotate instructions

The 16-bit status word or flag register holds 3 control and 6 status bits, called the *flags*. The unused bits in the status register cannot be accessed directly in the 8086/8088 CPU.

Figure 2.4 shows the 8086/8088 flag register. The functions of these flags can be seen in Table 2.5.

2.1.3 System RESET

The designers of a microcomputer chip must make provision for ways to start or restart the system. This means that the processor must begin execution in an identical manner every time power is applied to the corresponding lines. The 8086/8088 chip responds to POWER-ON or RESET by executing the instruction located at FFFF:0000H. The contents of the CPU registers at this time can be seen in Table 2.6.

Table 2.6. *8086/8088 CPU State on Power-up and RESET*

CPU ELEMENT	STATE
Flags	All clear
Instruction pointer	0000H
CS register	FFFFH
DS register	0000H
SS register	0000H
ES register	0000H
First opcode at	FFFF:0000H

In the IBM microcomputers, logical address FFFF:0000H contains a jump to the first instruction in a BIOS routine, called the power-on self-test (or POST), which tests and initializes the system hardware.

2.1.4 The 8086/8088 Operation Codes

At the machine level, the 8086/8088 CPU has about 300 possible operations in its instruction set. Each instruction can range in length from 1 to 6 bytes. For example, a move instruction (MOV) can be from 2 to 6 bytes long and can be encoded in 28 different forms. Table 2.7 shows the first byte of the 8086/8088 machine codes.

Bits 2 to 7 of the first byte of the operation code form the *opcode field*. This 6-bit field is always associated with each encoding (see Figure 2.5). The other 2 bits of the first byte can be part of the opcode or not. Of these 2 bits, bit 1 is called the sign or direction bit and bit 0 the word/byte bit. The second byte of the instruction, if present, contains the mode (MOD), the register (REG), and the register/memory (R/M) fields. This byte is sometimes referred to as the Modrm byte; the MOD field occupies bits 7 and 6 of the Modrm byte. The REG field follows the MOD field and occupies bits 5, 4, and 3; and the R/M field takes up bits 2, 1, and 0. The use of these fields is shown in Figure 2.5.

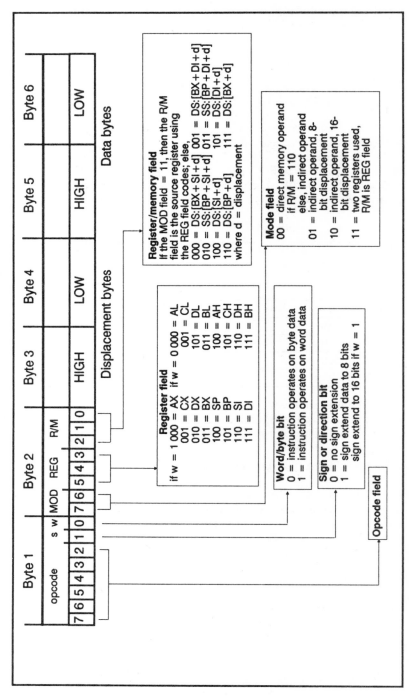

Figure 2.5. 8086/8088 Machine Code Format

2.1.5 The 8086/8088 Instruction Set

At the assembler level, the 8086/8088 instruction set appears to have about 100 instructions. This simplification is possible by considering several machine operations as a single function; for example, the assembly language MOV mnemonic includes all 28 possible variants of the machine move operation. The assembler programs available for the IBM microcomputers translate these mnemonic operation codes and operands into the corresponding machine codes that can be executed by the CPU. Table 2.8 lists the 8086/8088 assembler instructions.

Table 2.7. *First Byte of 8086/8088 Machine Codes*

	LOW ⟶							
HI	0	1	2	3	4	5	6	7
0	ADD	ADD	ADD	ADD	ADD	ADD	PUSH	POP
1	ADC	ADC	ADC	ADC	ADC	ADC	PUSH	POP
2	AND	AND	AND	AND	AND	AND	SEG	DAA
3	XOR	XOR	XOR	XOR	XOR	XOR	SEG	AAA
4	INC	INC	INC	INC	INC	INC	INC	INC
5	PUSH	PUSH	PUSH	PUSH	PUSH	PUSH	PUSH	PUSH
6								
7	JO	JNO	JB	JNB	JE	JNE	JBE	JNBE
8	*	*	*	*	TEST	TEST	XCHG	XCHG
9	NOP	XCHG	XCHG	XCHG	XCHG	XCHG	XCHG	XCHG
A	MOV	MOV	MOV	MOV	MOVS	MOVS	CMPS	CMPS
B	MOV	MOV	MOV	MOV	MOV	MOV	MOV	MOV
C	**	**	RET	RET	LES	LDS	MOV	MOV
D	**	**	**	**	AAM	AAD		XLAT
E	LOOPNE	LOOPZ	LOOP	JCXZ	IN	IN	OUT	OUT
F	LOCK		REP	REP	HLT	CMC	TEST NOT NEG MUL	IMUL DIV IDIV

* = ADD, OR, ADC, SBB, AND, SUB, XOR, CMP
** = ROL, ROR, RCL, RCR, SHL, SHR, SAR

(continued)

Table 2.7. *First Byte of 8086/8088 Machine Codes (Continued)*

HI	LOW → 8	9	A	B	C	D	E	F
0	OR	OR	OR	OR	OR	OR	PUSH	
1	SBB	SBB	SBB	SBB	SBB	SBB	PUSH	POP
2	SUB	SUB	SUB	SUB	SUB	SUB	SEG	DAS
3	CMP	CMP	CMP	CMP	CMP	CMP	SEG	AAS
4	DEC	DEC	DEC	DEC	DEC	DEC	DEC	DEC
5	POP	POP	POP	POP	POP	POP	POP	POP
6	PUSH	IMUL	PUSH	IMUL				
7	JS	JNS	JP	JNP	JL	JNL	JLE	JNLE
8	MOV	MOV	MOV	MOV	MOV	LEA	MOV	POP
9	CBW	CWD	CALL	WAIT	PUSHF	POPF	SAHF	LAHF
A	TEST	TEST	STOS	STOS	LODS	LODS	SCAS	SCAS
B	MOV	MOV	MOV	MOV	MOV	MOV	MOV	MOV
C			RET	RET	INT	INT	INTO	IRET
D	ESC	ESC	ESC	ESC	ESC	ESC	ESC	ESC
E	CALL	JMP	JMP	JMP	IN	IN	OUT	OUT
F	CLC	STC	CLI	STI	CLD	STD	INC DEC CALL	JMP PUSH

Table 2.8. 8086/8088 Assembler Instructions

	FLAG ACTION O D I T S Z A P C	DESCRIPTION
AAA	? - - - ? ? M ? M	**ASCII ADJUST FOR ADDITION** Changes the contents of AL into an unpacked decimal number, zeroing the high-order nibble. Valid unpacked decimals are in the range 0H to 09H.
AAD	? - - - M M ? M ?	**ASCII ADJUST FOR DIVISION** Prepares the AL register for dividing two unpacked decimal numbers so that the quotient will be a valid unpacked decimal. In dividing unpacked decimals, AH must be zero. The quotient is returned in AL and the remainder in AH. Both high-order nibbles are zeroed. Unpacked decimals are in the range 0H to 9H.
AAM	? - - - ? ? M ? M	**ASCII ADJUST AFTER MULTIPLICATION** Corrects the result of a multiplication of two unpacked decimals. Two BCD digits are returned to AH (MSD) and AL (LSD). The instruction divides the binary product in AL by 10. The quotient is left in AH as the MSD and the remainder in AL as the LSD.
AAS	? - - - ? ? M ? M	**ASCII ADJUST FOR SUBTRACTION** Corrects the result of a subtraction of two unpacked decimals which had the destination operand in AL. The content of AL is converted into an unpacked decimal number, in the range 0 to 9.
ADC	M - - - M M M M M	**ADD WITH CARRY** Performs the sum of byte- or word-size operands and adds 1 if the carry flag is set. Both operands must be signed or unsigned binary numbers. Since ADC sets the carry flag, it can be used in routines to add numbers larger than word size.
ADD	M - - - M M M M M	**ADDITION** Performs the sum of two byte or word operands. Both operands must be signed or unsigned binary digits. The sum is found in the destination operand.
AND	M - - - M M ? M M	**LOGICAL AND** Performs a logical AND operation of two byte- or word-size operands. A bit in the result is set if both operands are set; otherwise the bit is cleared.
CALL	- - - - - - - - -	**CALL A PROCEDURE** A CALL instruction can refer to a procedure in the same code segment or in a different code segment. Procedures in the same segment are designated NEAR, those in another segment as FAR.

(continued)

Table 2.8. *8086/8088 Assembler Instructions (Continued)*

	FLAG ACTION O D I T S Z A P C	DESCRIPTION
CBW	- - - - - - - - -	**CONVERT BYTE TO WORD** Extends the sign of the contents of register AL throughout register AH. It is commonly used to produce a word-size dividend from a byte-size operand prior to byte division.
CLC	- - - - - - - - 0	**CLEAR CARRY FLAG** Zeros the carry flag.
CLD	- 0 - - - - - - -	**CLEAR DIRECTION FLAG** Zeros the direction flag, causing string instructions to automatically increment the D and (or) the DI registers.
CLI	- - 0 - - - - - -	**CLEAR INTERRUPT FLAG** Zeros the interrupt enable flag so that the 8086/8088 will not recognize an interrupt request on the INTR line. All maskable interrupts are disabled. Nonmaskable interrupts on the NMI line will be honored.
CMC	- - - - - - - - M	**COMPLEMENT CARRY FLAG** Toggles the state of the carry flag.
CMP	M - - - M M M M M	**COMPARE** Subtracts the right operand from the left operand but returns the result only in the flag register. The action can be visualized by substituting a minus sign for the comma that separates the operands. Compare operations are usually followed by a conditional jump.
CMPS	M - - - M M M M M	**COMPARE STRINGS** **CMPSB = COMPARE BYTES** **CMPSW = COMPARE WORDS** Compare the string elements pointed by DS:SI and ES:DI. The simulated subtract takes the form [SI] minus [DI]. CMPS is used to find matching or differing strings. If CMPS is prefixed by REPE, the operation continues if CX is not zero and the strings equal (Z flag = 1). With the prefix REPNE; the operation continues if CX is not zero and the strings are not equal.
CWD	- - - - - - - - -	**CONVERT WORD TO DOUBLEWORD** Extends the sign of the word in the AX register through the DX register. This instruction is used to produce a doubleword dividend prior to word division.

(continued)

Table 2.8. *8086/8088 Assembler Instructions (Continued)*

	FLAG ACTION O D I T S Z A P C	DESCRIPTION
DAA	? - - - M M M M M	**DECIMAL ADJUST FOR ADDITION** Changes the contents of AL to two packed decimal digits. It is normally used to correct the result of adding two packed decimals with the destination operand in AL. A packed decimal is an unsigned value representing a decimal digit in each nibble. The valid range for each nibble is 0H to 9H. For a byte, the valid range is 0H to 99H.
DAS	? - - - M M M M M	**DECIMAL ADJUST FOR SUBTRACTION** Changes the contents of AL to two packed decimal digits. Normally used to correct the result of subtracting two packed decimals with the destination operand in AL. A packed decimal is an unsigned value representing a decimal digit in each nibble. The valid range for each nibble is 0H to 9H.
DEC	M - - - M M M M M	**DECREMENT BY 1** Decrements a byte or word operand by 1.
DIV	? - - - ? ? ? ? ?	**DIVIDE** Divides AX or AX:DX by a byte or word operand. The operation can take two forms: (1) byte source AX/source = AL (remainder in AH); (2) word source AX:DX/source = AX (remainder in DX).
ESC	- - - - - - - - -	**ESCAPE** Provides a way for other processors to receive instructions from the 8086/8088 stream and make use of the 8086 addressing modes. The main processor fetches the memory operand and places it on the bus. The instruction includes a 6-bit parameter that can be read by a coprocessor. The source operand can be a register or memory.
HLT	- - - - - - - - -	**HALT** Activates the processor's halt state, which ends with a NMI or RESET.
IDIV	? - - - ? ? ? ? ?	**INTEGER DIVIDE** Performs a signed division of AX or AX:DX by a byte or word operand. For byte integer division, the quotient must be in the range +127 to -127. For word integer division, the quotient must be in the range +32,767 to -32,767. If the quotient exceeds these limits, a type 0 interrupt is generated.

(continued)

Table 2.8. *8086/8088 Assembler Instructions (Continued)*

	FLAG ACTION O D I T S Z A P C	D E S C R I P T I O N
IMUL	M - - - ? ? ? ? M	**INTEGER MULTIPLY** Signed multiplication of the source and the accumulator. The instruction can take two forms: (1) byte operands to word result: AL * byte operand = product in AX; (2) word operands to doubleword result: AX * word operand = product in DX:AX. If the C and O flags are set, AH or DX contains significant digits.
IN	- - - - - - - - -	**INPUT** (byte or word) Receives a byte or word from the designated port into the AL or AX registers. The port number can be specified as an operand or entered in DX. The latter form allows access to port numbers up to 65,535.
INC	M - - - M M M M -	**INCREMENT BY 1** The byte or word operand is incremented by 1. The operand is treated as an unsigned binary number. If the operand is at the maximum value for the storage unit, the INC instruction will make it wrap around to zero; for example, if AL = FFH, after INC AL, AL = 00H.
INT	- - 0 0 - - - - -	**SOFTWARE INTERRUPT** Transfers control to a service routine vector located at the interrupt type times 4. The vector table is located in RAM at 000H to 3FCH and contains 256 entries. The vector stores the destination address in the form OFFSET:SEGMENT.
INTO	- - 0 0 - - - - -	**INTERRUPT ON OVERFLOW** Generates a type 4 software interrupt if the overflow flag is set. The interrupt vector for a type 4 interrupt is located at absolute address 0000:0010H.
IRET	M M M M M M M M M	**INTERRUPT RETURN** Transfers control to the instruction following the INT xxH instruction. IRET pops IP, CS, and the flags from the stack. All flags are affected, since they are restored to the values at the time of the interrupt. IRET is normally the last instruction in an interrupt handler.
JA JNBE	- - - - - - - - -	**JUMP ON ABOVE** Transfers control to the target operand if CF and ZF = 0.
JAE JNB JNC	- - - - - - - - -	**JUMP ON ABOVE OR EQUAL** Transfers control to the target operand if CF = 0.
JB JNAE JC	- - - - - - - - -	**JUMP IF BELOW** Transfers control to the target operand if CF = 1.

(continued)

Table 2.8. 8086/8088 Assembler Instructions (Continued)

	FLAG ACTION O D I T S Z A P C	DESCRIPTION
JBE JNA	- - - - - - - - -	**JUMP IF BELOW OR EQUAL** Transfers control to the target operand if CF or ZF = 1.
JC JB JNAE	- - - - - - - - -	**JUMP ON CARRY** Transfers control to the target operand if CF = 1.
JCXZ	- - - - - - - - -	**JUMP IF CX = ZERO** Transfers control to the target operand if the CX register = 00H. This instruction is useful when two terminations must be handled differently, for example, in a REPE SCASB sequence.
JE JZ	- - - - - - - - -	**JUMP ON EQUAL** Transfers control to the target operand if ZF = 1.
JG JNLE	- - - - - - - - -	**JUMP IF GREATER** Transfers control to the target operand if ((SF XOR OF) OR ZF) = 0.
JGE JNL	- - - - - - - - -	**JUMP IF GREATER OR EQUAL** Transfers control to the target operand if (SF XOR OF) = 0.
JL	- - - - - - - - -	**JUMP IF LESS** Transfers control to the target operand if (SF XOR OF) = 1.
JLE JNG	- - - - - - - - -	**JUMP IF LESS OR EQUAL** Transfers control to the target operand if ((SF XOR OF) OR ZF) = 1.
JMP	- - - - - - - - -	**JUMP (UNCONDITIONAL)** Transfers control to the target label unconditionally. An intrasegment jump adds the relative displacement of the target to the IP register. Jumps to within +/- 127 bytes are SHORT. Intrasegment jumps to within +/- 32K are NEAR jumps. Intersegment jumps also change the contents of CS.
JNC JAE JNB	- - - - - - - - -	**JUMP IF NO CARRY** Transfers control to the target operand if CF = 0.
JNE	- - - - - - - - -	**JUMP IF NOT EQUAL** Transfers control to the target operand if ZF = 0.
JNO	- - - - - - - - -	**JUMP IF NO OVERFLOW** Transfers control to the target operand if OF = 0.
JNP JPO	- - - - - - - - -	**JUMP IF NO PARITY** Transfers control to the target operand if PF = 0.

(continued)

Table 2.8. *8086/8088 Assembler Instructions (Continued)*

	FLAG ACTION O D I T S Z A P C	D E S C R I P T I O N
JNS	- - - - - - - - -	**JUMP IF NO SIGN** Transfers control to the target operand if SF = 0. The sign flag indicates whether the signed result of a previous operation is positive (high bit cleared) or negative (high bit set). The SF flag can be ignored in unsigned arithmetic.
JO	- - - - - - - - -	**JUMP IF OVERFLOW** Transfers control to the target operand if OF = 1. The overflow flag is set if the signed result of an arithmetic operation exceeds the capacity of the destination operand. The OF can be ignored in unsigned arithmetic.
JP JPE	- - - - - - - - -	**JUMP IF PARITY** Transfers control to the target operand if PF = 1. The parity flag indicates whether the number of 1 bits in the result is odd (PF = 0) or even (PF = 1). This flag can be used in checking data integrity. It has no use in normal arithmetic or logic operations.
JS	- - - - - - - - -	**JUMP IF SIGN** Transfers control to the target operand if SF = 1. The sign flag indicates whether the signed result of a previous operation is positive (high bit cleared) or negative (high bit set). The SF may be ignored when performing unsigned arithmetic.
LAHF	- - - - - - - - -	**LOAD AH FROM FLAGS** Loads the AH registers from the flag register as follows: AH Bits: 7 6 5 4 3 2 1 0 — CF — PF — AF — ZF — SF
LDS	- - - - - - - - -	**LOAD POINTER AND DS** Assume a doubleword in memory holding an offset and segment address. The offset is loaded into the operand register and the segment into DS.
LEA	- - - - - - - - -	**LOAD EFFECTIVE ADDRESS** Transfers the offset of a memory operand to the destination operand, which must be a 16-bit general register.
LES	- - - - - - - - -	**LOAD POINTER AND ES** Assumes a doubleword in memory holding an offset and segment address. The offset is loaded into the operand register and the segment into ES.

(continued)

Table 2.8. *8086/8088 Assembler Instructions (Continued)*

	FLAG ACTION O D I T S Z A P C	DESCRIPTION
LODS	- - - - - - - - -	**LOAD STRING** Transfers the byte or word addressed by DS:SI to the AL or AX register and updates SI to point to the next string element.
LOOP	- - - - - - - - -	**LOOP** Decrements the CX register and transfers control to the target if CX is not 0. If CX = 0, execution drops to the next instruction.
LOOPE LOOPZ	- - - - - - - - -	**LOOP WHILE EQUAL** Decrements CX by 1 and transfers control to the target operand if CX is not 0 and if ZF is set.
LOOPNE LOOPNZ	- - - - - - - - -	**LOOP WHILE NOT EQUAL** Decrements CX by 1 and transfers control to the target operand if CX is not 0 and if ZF is clear.
MOV	- - - - - - - - -	**MOV** (byte or word) Transfers a byte or word from the source to the destination operand.
MOVS MOVSB MOVSW	- - - - - - - - -	**MOVE STRING ELEMENT** Transfers a byte or word element from the source string (addressed by DS:SI) to the destination string (addressed by ES:DI) and bumps SI and DI to the next string elements. Can be used, in conjunction with CX and the REP prefix, to move memory blocks with a single instruction. The setting of the direction flag determines whether the pointers (SI and DI) are incremented or decremented.
MUL	M - - - ? ? ? ? M	**MULTIPLY** Unsigned multiplication of the source operand and the accumulator. The operation can take the forms: AL * byte source = product in AX AX * word source = product in DX:AX When CF and OF are set, AH or DX contains significant digits.
NEG	M - - - M M M M *	**NEGATE** Subtracts the operand from zero. Forms the 2's complement of the number, reversing the sign of an integer. CF = 1 except when the operand is zero, then CF = 0.
NOP	- - - - - - - - -	**NO OPERATION** Causes the CPU to do nothing. NOP can be used as a filler instruction or as a time delay. The only register changed is IP.
NOT	- - - - - - - - -	**LOGICAL NOT** Performs a logical NOT operation of two byte- or word-size operands. The NOT operation forms the 1's complement of a number by inverting all bits.

(continued)

Table 2.8. *8086/8088 Assembler Instructions (Continued)*

	FLAG ACTION O D I T S Z A P C	D E S C R I P T I O N
OR	0 - - - M M ? M 0	**LOGICAL OR** Inclusive OR of a byte or word operand. A bit in the result is set if either or both operand bits are set. Otherwise the bit is cleared.
OUT	- - - - - - - - -	**OUTPUT** (byte or word) Transfers a byte or word from the AL or AX register to a designated output port. The port number can be specified as an operand or entered in the DX register. The latter form allows access to port numbers up to 65,535.
POP	- - - - - - - - -	**POP STACK** Transfers the word at the top of the stack to a memory, register, or segment register operand and increments the SP by 2 to point to a new stack top. POP CS is not allowed.
POPF	M M M M M M M M M	**POP FLAGS** Transfers the word at the top of the stack into the flag register. SP is then incremented by 2, to point to a new stack top. The PUSHF and POPF sequence can be used to preserve the caller's flags.
PUSH	- - - - - - - - -	**PUSH** The stack top pointer is decremented by 2 and the word operand is transferred to the location pointed to by SP. The PUSH and POP sequence is used to store data on the stack and for passing parameters to a procedure.
PUSHF	- - - - - - - - -	**PUSH FLAGS** Decrements the stack pointer by 2 and transfers the flag register to the next stack top. PUSHF and POPF are used to preserve the caller's flags. The only way to change the trap flag is to execute PUSHF, alter bit 8 of the stack top word, then POPF.
RCL	M - - - - - - - M	**ROTATE LEFT THROUGH CARRY** The byte or word operand is rotated left through the carry flag. The count must be 1 or a value in CL. 80286 and 80386 systems allow immediate values larger than 1.
RCR	M - - - - - - - M	**ROTATE RIGHT THROUGH CARRY** The byte or word operand is rotated right through the carry flag. The count must be 1 or a value in CL. 80286 and 80386 systems allow immediate values larger than 1.

(continued)

Table 2.8. *8086/8088 Assembler Instructions (Continued)*

	FLAG ACTION O D I T S Z A P C	DESCRIPTION
REP REPE REPZ	- - - - - - - - -	**REPEAT** (string operation prefix) Used in conjunction with the string instructions MOVS and STOS, causes CX to be decremented and execution of the string operation to continue until CX = 0. When used with SCAS or CMPS instruction, the operation will continue as long as CX is not zero and ZF = 1 (strings equal).
REPNE	- - - - - - - - -	**REPEAT WHILE NOT EQUAL** (string operation prefix) Used in conjunction with the string instructions MOVS and STOS, causes CX to be decremented and execution of the string operation to continue until CX = 0. When used with SCAS or CMPS instruction, the operation continues as long as CX is not zero and ZF = 1 (strings equal).
RET	- - - - - - - - -	**RETURN FROM PROCEDURE** Transfers control to the instruction following the CALL. If the procedure was defined as FAR, the RET instruction retrieves CS and IP from the stack. If the procedure was defined as NEAR, only the IP is changed. An optional digit can be added to the stack pointer after the return. This is used to discard parameters that were pushed on the stack before the CALL.
ROL	M - - - - - - - M	**ROTATE LEFT** Rotates left the byte or word operand in memory or a register. In 8086/8088 systems, the rotation count must be 1 or the value stored in CL.
ROR	M - - - - - - - M	**ROTATE RIGHT** Rotates right the byte or word operand in memory or a register. In 8086/8088 systems, the rotation count must be 1or the value stored in CL.

SAHF	- - - - M M M M M	**STORE AH IN FLAGS**
		The contents of the AH register are transferred to the flag register in the following pattern:
		AH Bits: 7 6 5 4 3 2 1 0
		                                          └── CF
		                                    ── PF
		                              ── AF
		                    ── ZF
		              ── SF

SAL SHL	M - - - M M ? M M	**SHIFT ARITHMETIC LEFT** All bits in the byte or word operand are shifted left. In 8086/8088 systems, the shift count must be 1 or the value stored in CL. 80286/80386 systems allow integer values other than 1 for the shift count.

(continued)

Table 2.8. *8086/8088 Assembler Instructions (Continued)*

	FLAG ACTION O D I T S Z A P C	D E S C R I P T I O N
SAR	M - - - M M ? M M	**SHIFT ARITHMETIC RIGHT** Bits in the byte or word operand are shifted right. In 8086/8088 systems, the shift count must be 1 or the value stored in CL. 80286 and 80386 systems allow integer values other than 1 for the shift count. The bits shifted in on the left are equal to the original high-order bit.
SBB	M - - - M M M M M	**SUBTRACT WITH BORROW** Subtracts the source operand from the destination. If the carry flag is set, one more is subtracted. The operands may be bytes or words and signed or unsigned binary numbers. Since SBB incorporates the borrow of a previous operation, it can be used in routines that subtract numbers longer than one word.
SCAS	M - - - M M M M M	**SCAN STRING** (byte or word) Compares the byte or word elements in a string addressed by ES:DI with the contents of AL or AX. Updates DI to the next string element.
SHR	M - - - M M ? M M	**SHIFT LOGICAL RIGHT** The bits in the operand are shifted right while a 0 is shifted into bit 7. In 8086/8088 systems the shift count must be 1 or the value in CL. 80286 and 80386 systems, allow larger values for the shift count.
STC	- - - - - - - - 1	**SET CARRY FLAG** Set the carry flag (CF = 1). This instruction can be used to pass a return code to an error handler.
STD	- 1 - - - - - - -	**SET DIRECTION FLAG** Sets the direction flag, causing string instructions to automatically decrement the pointer register SI or DI.
STI	- - 1 - - - - - -	**SET INTERRUPT FLAG** Sets the interrupt enable flag, making the processor recognize maskable interrupt requests on the INTR line. A pending interrupt will not be honored until the instruction following STI has executed.
STOS	- - - - - - - - -	**STORE STRING** (byte or word) Stores the contents of the AX or AL register in the memory address pointed at by ES:DI and bumps DI to the next string element. The STOS instruction can be used to fill a memory area with a constant.
SUB	M - - - M M M M M	**SUBTRACT** Subtracts the source operand from the destination. The operands may be bytes or words and signed or unsigned binary numbers.

(continued)

Table 2.8. *8086/8088 Assembler Instructions (continued)*

	FLAG ACTION O D I T S Z A P C	DESCRIPTION
TEST	0 - - - M M ? M M	**TEST** Updates the flags as if a logical AND operation of the two operands had been performed. If the TEST operation is followed by a JNZ instruction, the jump will be taken if there are corresponding 1 bits in both operands.
WAIT	- - - - - - - - -	**WAIT** Causes the CPU to enter the wait state. The wait state ends when the TEST line becomes active.
XCHG	- - - - - - - - -	**EXCHANGE** Exchanges the contents of the byte or word operands, which may be general registers or memory. Segment registers cannot be exchanged.
XLAT	- - - - - - - - -	**TRANSLATE** Table look-up instruction. The base address of the table must be loaded in BX and the offset (byte to be translated) in AL. XLAT then loads AL with the byte at [BX + AL].
XOR	0 - - - M M ? M 0	**EXCLUSIVE OR** Performs the EXCLUSIVE OR of a byte or word operand and returns the result to the destination operand. A bit in the result is set if the corresponding bits in both operands contain opposite values.

Flag codes:
M = modified by the instruction
? = unpredictable
- = not affected
0 or 1 = set or reset by the instruction

2.2 The Intel 80286

This chip, introduced in 1982, is a descendant of the 8086/8088 microprocessor. The 286, as it is frequently called, provides on-chip memory management, which makes possible the simultaneous execution of several tasks. Multitasking systems are aimed at the high end of the market, specifically for business applications and for office and industrial automation. The PC AT microcomputer was the first IBM machine equipped with the 80286 microprocessor. The chip is used in the XT 286 and the PS/2 Model 50 and Model 60, the Compaq 286, the Tandy Model 1000-TX and Model 3000-HL, the Hewlett-Packard Vectra, and others.

The following are the most important features of the Intel 80286:

1. Sixteen Mbytes of physical address space

2. One gigabyte of virtual address space

3. A *real address* operating mode in which the 286 emulates and is compatible with the 8086/8088 CPU

4. A *protected virtual address* operating mode which implements the advanced features of the 286

5. On-chip memory management

6. A protection mechanism based on four privilege levels

7. Multitasking support by providing a separate logical address space for each task

Table 2.9 lists the fundamental characteristics of the Intel 80286 CPU.

Table 2.9. *Intel 80286 Microprocessor Hardware Summary*

CHARACTERISTIC	SPECIFICATIONS
Mathematical coprocessor	80287
Bus interface	16 bits
Internal data path	16 bits
Available clock frequencies	6, 8, 10, 12.5, and 20 MHz
Memory addressability	16 Mbytes
Virtual memory	Yes, 1 gigabyte/task
Memory management and protection	Yes
I/O addressability	65,535 ports
Registers	Arithmetic: 8 Index: 4 Segment: 4 General purpose: 8
Intel support chips	Clock: 82284 Controller: 82288 Interrupts: 8259-A DMA: 82258 Timer: 8253/54 DRAM: 8207/8208
Number of pins	68
Power requirements	5 V

2.2.1 The 80286 Internal Architecture

The 286 CPU is formed by four processing units which operate independently and in parallel. This design is called a *pipeline architecture*. The bus unit (BU) prefetches instructions from memory in a manner similar to that of the bus interface unit of the 8086/8088 processors (see Section 2.1.1). In operation, the BU assumes that the instructions are located sequentially in memory. If execution continues at a nonsequential location, the instruction queue is cleared and prefetching must be reinitiated. The bus unit handles all memory and port access operations for the CPU.

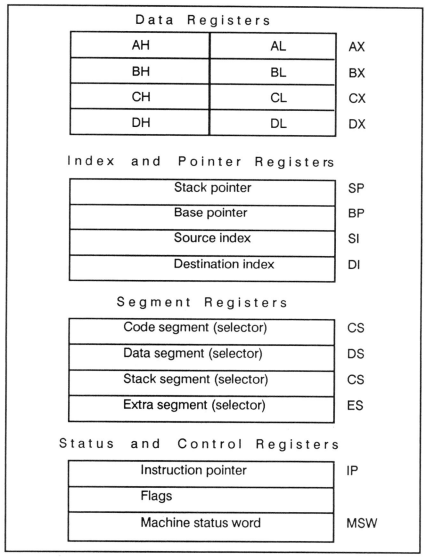

Figure 2.6. *80286 Registers*

The instruction unit (IU) reads the operation codes in the queue created by the bus unit, decodes the instructions, and places them, three deep, in a decoded instruction queue. The execution unit (EU) obtains the opcodes from this queue and performs the arithmetic and logical operations of each instruction. Finally, the address unit (AU) provides the memory management and protection functions of the 286 and converts protected-mode virtual addresses into physical addresses.

2.2.2 The 80286 Internal Registers

The 80286 CPU contains 15 internal registers, classified as follows:

1. Data registers
2. Index and pointer registers
3. Segment registers
4. Status and control registers

Figure 2.6 shows the 80286 internal registers. The data, index, and segment registers of the 80286 are identical to those of the 8086/8088 CPU, described in Section 2.1.2 and the following sub-sections.

2.2.2.1 The 80286 Control and Status Registers. One difference between the 80286 and its predecessors, the 8086 and 8088 CPUs, is in regard to the status and control registers. The 286 flag register has two additional fields, designated as NT and IOPL, for use in protected-mode execution. In addition, the CPU is equipped with a new control register, also for protected-mode operation, called the machine status word register, or MSW (see Section 2.2.1.2). The 80286 status and control registers (flags) can be seen in Figure 2.7. The functions of these flags are listed in Table 2.10.

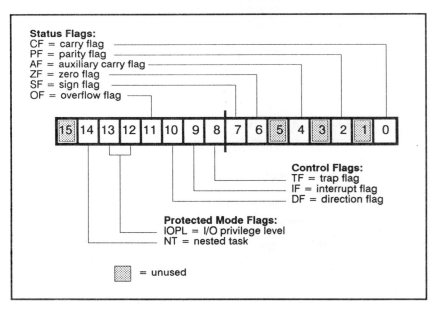

Figure 2.7. *The 80286 Flag Register*

Table 2.10. *80286 Flags*

BIT	FLAG NAME	CODE	FUNCTION
14	Nested task	NT	Indicates a nested task condition during task switch operations
12–13	I/O privilege	IOPL	Controls access to input/output devices and designates the lowest task level with I/O privilege
11	Overflow	OF	Set to show arithmetic overflow
10	Direction	DF	Used to determine direction of string moves
9	Interrupt enable	IF	Used to enable and disable maskable interrupts
8	Trap	TF	Places the CPU in the single-step mode (used mainly by debugger programs)
7	Sign	SF	Used in signed arithmetic to show whether the result is positive (SF = 0) or negative (SF = 1)
6	Zero	ZF	Set if the result of the previous operation is zero
4	Auxiliary carry	AF	Used in decimal arithmetic to show a carry out of the low nibble or a borrow from the high nibble
2	Parity	PF	Set if the result of the previous operation has an even number of 1 bits (used mainly to check for data transmission errors)
0	Carry	CF	Set if there is a carry or a borrow to the high-order bit of the result. Also used by rotate instructions.

2.2.2.2 The 80286 Machine Status Word Register.   The 80286 MSW register has no counterpart in 8086 or 8088 systems. Its purpose is to show the configuration and status of the 80286 special functions that are not available in the 8086/8088 CPU. The register is 16 bits wide, but only the lower 4 bits are meaningful in the 286. Since the 80386 uses the higher bits in this register, 286 software, in order to ensure compatibility, should not modify bits 4 to 15. The 80286 machine status word register is shown in Figure 2.8.

The MSW register bits can be considered as supplementary flags, whose functions are as follows:

1. PE (*protected-mode enable*). The PE flag places the 286 in protected mode. Since this bit cannot be cleared, real mode can be reactivated only by a system RESET.

2. MP (*math coprocessor present*). The MP flag indicates that the 80287 chip is installed in the system.

3. EM (*emulator mode*). The emulator flag indicates that no 80287 is available in the system. If the 286 encounters an ESC instruction with EM = 1 and MP = 0, the processor will automatically execute interrupt 07H. A handler located at this vector can emulate the 80287 in software.

4. TS (*task switch*). The task switch flag is set with the first use of the math coprocessor within a task. This allows software protection of the coprocessor context.

The machine status word flags are modified with the LMSW (load machine status word) instruction. If the PE flag is set when LMSW executes, the 80286 enters protected mode. This instruction can be used only by operating-system software. Application programs can read the MSW flags using the SMSW (store machine status word) instruction.

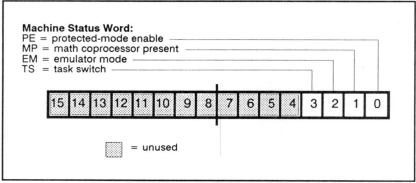

Figure 2.8. *The 80286 Machine Status Word (MSW) Register*

2.2.3 The 80286 Real Mode

The 80286 processor starts up in the real address mode. This mode is activated also upon a system RESET. In the real mode, the 286 CPU performs identically to the 8086 and the 8088. In general, the 80286 will execute RAM and ROM resident programs written for the 8086 or the 8088 CPU.

The 80286 CPU differs from its predecessors, the 8086 and the 8088, in having several new interrupt vector assignments, a higher clock speed, and minor differences in the operation of some 8086 instructions.

2.2.3.1 The 80286 Extended Instruction Set. The 80286 CPU is provided with seven new instructions that are not available in the 8086/8088. In addition, the PUSH and IMUL instructions can be used with immediate operands in the 286. This extended instruction set is also available in the 80186 and 80188 microprocessors. The 80286 real-mode instructions that are not available in the 8086/8088 CPU are described in Table 2.11.

Table 2.11. *80286 Real-Mode Instructions*

	FLAG ACTION O D I T S Z A P C	D E S C R I P T I O N
BOUND	- - - - - - - - -	**DETECT VALUE OUT OF RANGE** Check whether the value in a general register is within the bounds contained in two successive memory locations. Note: This instruction generates an INT 05H, which is in conflict with the IBM Print Screen function.
ENTER	- - - - - - - - -	**ENTER HIGH-LEVEL PROCEDURE** Creates a stack frame for entering a high-level language procedure. The first operand contains the number of bytes to be allocated. The second operand determines the number of frame pointers copied onto the new stack.
IMUL	M ? - - ? ? ? - M	**INTEGER MULTIPLY WITH IMMEDIATE OPERAND** (byte or word) Allows multiplication by an immediate value. This mode of IMUL requires three arguments: a register in which to store the product, a second operand (which can be the same register, another register, or a location in memory), and an immediate value.
INS	- - - - - - - - -	**INPUT STRING** (byte or word) Transfers a data byte or word from a port (port number in DX) to the memory location pointed at by ES:DI. DI is automatically bumped to the next memory location. If the REP prefix is used, then CX is the repetition counter.
LEAVE	- - - - - - - - -	**EXIT HIGH-LEVEL PROCEDURE** Reverses the action of the ENTER instruction and executes a procedure return. Releases the stack space and restores the caller's frame.
OUTS	- - - - - - - - -	**OUTPUT STRING** (byte or word) Transfers a data byte or word from a memory location pointed at by DS:SI to the output port numbered by DX. SI is automatically bumped to the next memory location. With the REP prefix, CX is the repetition counter.
POPA	- - - - - - - - -	**POP ALL REGISTERS** Pops all eight general registers from the stack reversing a previous PUSHA instruction.
PUSH	- - - - - - - - -	**PUSH IMMEDIATE OPERAND** (byte or word) Allows immediate data to be pushed onto the stack. Byte data is extended to word size before it is pushed.
PUSHA	- - - - - - - - -	**PUSH ALL REGISTERS** Pushes all eight general registers onto the stack, in the order AX, CX, DX, BX, SP, BP, SI, and DI.
ROL	M - - - - - - - M	**ROTATE LEFT IMMEDIATE OPERAND** Left rotate destination byte or word by the immediate operand.

(continued)

Table 2.11. *80286 Real-Mode Instructions (Continued)*

	FLAG ACTION O D I T S Z A P C	D E S C R I P T I O N
ROR	M - - - - - - - M	**ROTATE RIGHT IMMEDIATE OPERAND** Right rotate destination byte or word by the immediate operand.
SAL SHL	M - - - M M ? M M	**SHIFT LEFT IMMEDIATE OPERAND** Shift left, logical or arithmetic, by the immediate operand.
SAR	M - - - M M ? M M	**SHIFT RIGHT IMMEDIATE OPERAND** Shift right arithmetically by the immediate operand.

Flag codes:
M = modified by the instruction
? = unpredictable
- = not affected
0 or 1 = set or reset by the instruction

2.2.4 The 80286 Protected Mode

The 286 protected address mode is initiated by loading the machine status word (LMSW instruction) with the protection enable (PE) flag set (see Section 2.2.1.2). Once the protected mode is attained, the system must be reset in order to return to real address mode execution. The 80286 protected mode provides the following features:

1. On-chip memory management of a virtual address space of up to 1 gigabyte

2. A hierarchy of up to four privilege levels to improve system reliability and to separate multiple users

3. Support for multiple tasks with separate address spaces and task switching

The 80286 protected-mode instructions are described in Table 2.12.

2.2.4.1 Memory Management. The architecture of the 80286 chip increases the 1-Mbyte physical memory address space of 8086/8088 systems to 16 Mbytes. The total memory space visible to a protected-mode program, called the *virtual address space*, is 1 gigabyte.

Application programs executing in 80286 protected mode do not have access to physical memory. In protected mode, the four segment registers, CS, SS, DS, and ES, do not reference a physical memory address. Instead, they load an index value into a special table (descriptor table) that is managed by the operating system. In this manner, the segment base element in the physical address remains invisible to the application. Therefore, programs have no access to physical memory and cannot intentionally or accidentally obliterate code or data that does not belong to them. The virtual memory structure is shown in Figure 2.9.

Table 2.12. *80286 Protected-Mode Instructions*

	FLAG ACTION O D I T S Z A P C	D E S C R I P T I O N
ARPL	- - - - - M - - -	**ADJUST RPL FIELD OF SELECTOR** Adjust requested protection level (RPL) of first operand to not less than that of second operand. Used by operating-system software to ensure that the calling routine does not obtain a higher privilege than it is entitled to.
CLTS	- - - - - - - - - TS = 0	**CLEAR TASK SWITCH FLAG** Clears the TS flag in the machine status word. This flag is used to manage the numeric data processor.
LAR	- - - - - M - - -	**LOAD ACCESS RIGHTS BYTE** The second operand (a selector) is loaded into the high byte of the first operand, and the low byte is set to zero. The ZF is set if DPL≥ CPL and if DPL ≥ selector RPL, that is, if selector index is within the table limit. The ZF is cleared otherwise.
LGDT	- - - - - - - - -	**LOAD GLOBAL DESCRIPTOR TABLE REGISTER** The GDTR is loaded from the 6-byte memory operand.
LIDT	- - - - - - - - -	**LOAD INTERRUPT DESCRIPTOR TABLE REGISTER** The IDTR is loaded from the 6-byte memory operand.
LLDT	- - - - - - - - -	**LOAD SELECTOR INTO LOCAL DESCRIPTOR TABLE REGISTER** The word operand (register or memory) contains a selector to the GTD. The LDTR is loaded.
LMSW	- - - - - - - - -	**LOAD MACHINE STATUS WORD** The MSW register is loaded from the word-size operand. This instruction is used to enable protected mode.
LSL	- - - - - M - - -	**LOAD SEGMENT LIMIT FIELD** Load the left operand with the value in the limit field of the descriptor addressed by the right operand. The ZF is set if the loading was performed, and cleared otherwise.
LTR	- - - - - - - - -	**LOAD TASK REGISTER** The task register is loaded from the source register or memory operand. The TSS is labeled busy.
SGDT	- - - - - - - - -	**STORE GLOBAL DESCRIPTOR TABLE REGISTER** Copies the 6-byte descriptor table register into the memory location addressed in the operand.

(continued)

Table 2.12. *80286 Protected-Mode Instructions (Continued)*

	FLAG ACTION O D I T S Z A P C	D E S C R I P T I O N
SIDT	- - - - - - - - -	**STORE INTERRUPT DESCRIPTOR TABLE REGISTER** Copies the 6-byte descriptor table register into the memory location addressed in the operand.
SLDT	- - - - - - - - -	**STORE SELECTOR OF LOCAL DESCRIPTOR TABLE REGISTER** The selector portion of the LDTR is copied into the 2-byte register or memory operand.
SMSW	- - - - - - - - -	**STORE MACHINE STATUS WORD** The machine status word register is stored in the 2-byte register or memory operand.
STR	- - - - - - - - -	**STORE TASK REGISTER** The task register is stored in the 2-byte register or memory operand.
VERR VERW	- - - - - M - - -	**VERIFY SEGMENT FOR READ/WRITE** Verify that a segment can be read or written from the current privilege level. The operand (register or memory) contains a selector that points to a descriptor. If the segment is accessible, the ZF is set.

Flag codes:
M = modified by the instruction
? = unpredictable
- = not affected
0 or 1 = set or reset by the instruction

In protected mode, the segment registers are designated as the segment selectors CS, SS, DS, and ES. Each selector contains a 13-bit field (index field) which represents the sequential order of one of 8192 possible segments (2^{13}) in each descriptor table. The TI (table indicator) field selects one of two possible descriptor tables, labeled global and local descriptor tables. This increases the number of possible segments to 16,384 (2^{14}). Since each segment can be as large as 64K (2^{16}), the total virtual address space in 80286 protected mode is

$$2^{14} * 2^{16} = 1 \text{ gigabyte}$$

The selector also has a table indicator field (TI bit) that marks either a local or a global address space. The global address space is used for system-level data and services that are shared with applications. The local address space is private to each particular task. Figure 2.10 shows the 80286 segment selectors.

All memory access in 80286 systems is based on three descriptor tables named the global descriptor table (GDT), the interrupt descriptor table (IDT), and the local descriptor table (LDT). The address and length of these tables are stored in the system address registers. Each address register is named for its corresponding table; the global descriptor table register (GDTR), the interrupt descriptor table register (IDTR), and the local descriptor table register

(LDTR). The address registers contain a 24-bit field (named the base) which holds the physical address for the beginning of the table, and a 16-bit field (called the limit) which specifies the offset of the last valid entry. The LDTR also contains a *selector* portion that is visible to the application. This area is formatted exactly like a segment selector (see Figure 2.10). The 80286 system address registers can be seen in Figure 2.11.

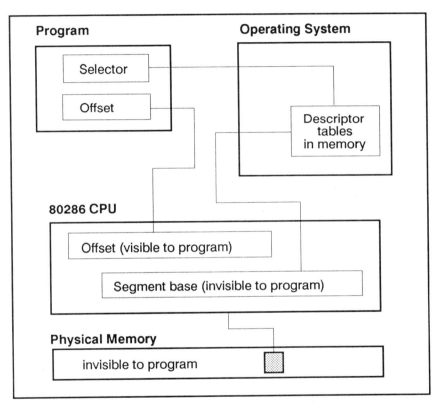

Figure 2.9. *80286 Virtual Memory*

In 80286 protected mode, the value stored in the index field of the segment selectors (registers CS, DS, ES, and SS) serves as an index into the descriptor tables (see Figure 2.10). The 13-bit index field allows from 1 to 8192 possible entries in each table. Table entries are formatted in 8-byte areas, as shown in Figure 2.12. The offset of a particular entry from the start of the descriptor table is calculated by multiplying the value in the index field by the 8 bytes in each entry.

Byte 5 of the segment descriptor table entry is known as the *access rights byte*. The format of the access rights byte for code and data segment descriptors is different from that for system and special segment descriptors. This format can be seen in Figure 2.13.

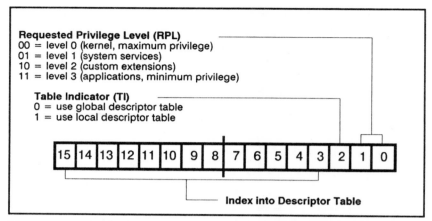

Figure 2.10. *80286 Segment Selectors (Registers CS, DS, ES, and SS)*

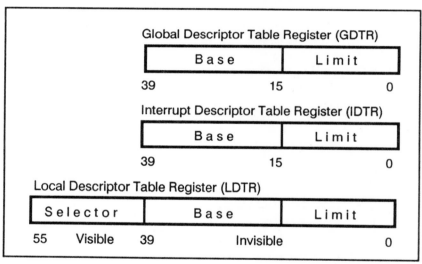

Figure 2.11. *80286 System Address Registers*

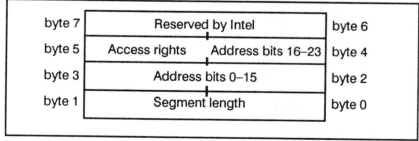

Figure 2.12. *Format of 80286 Descriptor Table Entries*

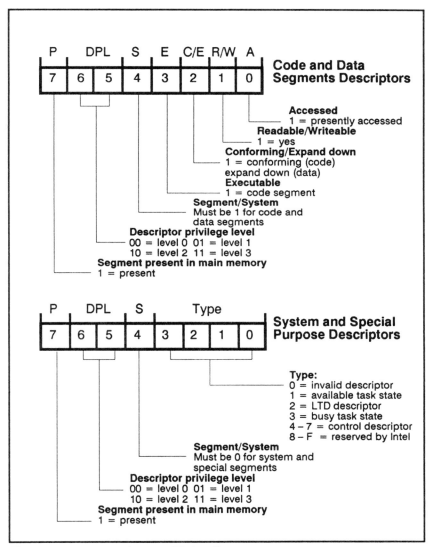

Figure 2.13. *80286 Access Rights Byte*

2.2.4.2 Protection Mechanisms. The hardware protection mechanisms in the 80286 serve to achieve the following functions:

1. System software is isolated from application programs.
2. Tasks execute independently of one another.
3. Segments are used according to their data types.

Protection is implemented by establishing limitations on the use of memory and by restricting the instruction set available to applications. The degree of limitation is determined by a hierarchy of four privilege levels supported by the 80286, as can be seen in Figure 2.14. Nevertheless, system programs do not have to enable all privilege levels; for example, the OS/2 operating system for the IBM microcomputers uses only three of the four privilege levels available in the chip.

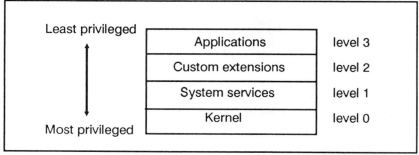

Figure 2.14. *80286 Privilege Levels*

The privilege level is controlled through three privilege-level indicators:

1. **DPL** (*descriptor privilege level*). The DPL is stored in bits 5 and 6 of the access rights byte of each descriptor (see Figure 2.13). Its value indicates the privilege level of the entire segment.
2. **CPL** (*current privilege level*). The CPL is stored in bits 0 and 1 of the current *code segment* selector (see Figure 2.10). It indicates the privilege level of the task currently executing.
3. **RPL** (*requested privilege level*). The RPL is stored in bits 0 and 1 of a segment selector. The RPL differs from the CPL in that the CPL refers to the code segment selector, while the RPL can refer to any segment.

The 80286 CPU follows specific rules for granting access to data and code segments. For instance, data access is granted if DPL ≥ CPL — in other words, if the privilege level of the data segment is lower than or equal to the privilege level of the current code segment. Note that the higher the privilege level, the lower the numerical value of DPL, CPL, and RPL. Regarding other code segments, access is granted if CPL = DPL, but more privileged code segments can be accessed via special descriptors called *call gates*.

2.2.4.3 Tasks. The unit of execution for the 80286 CPU is called a *task*. The term *thread of execution* is sometimes used in a similar context. The microprocessor can execute only one task at a time. The CPU switches tasks as a result of an interrupt or a JMP, CALL, or IRET instruction. The 80286 hardware provides complete isolation between tasks. This isolation is based on each task having its own independent address space, and on the protection mechanisms described in Section 2.2.4.2.

The currently executing task is defined by the contents of the processor registers. This is known as the *task* or *processor state*. The task register, which is part of the 80286 CPU, contains a selector to the descriptor of the current task. The task segment descriptor has the same 8-byte structure and format as the other 80286 segment descriptors, see Figure 2.12. The access rights byte of the task segment descriptor is shown in Figure 2.15.

Bytes 2, 3, and 4 of the task segment descriptor (see Figure 2.12) contain the physical address of the task state segment (TSS). Each task has a unique TSS, which stores the task's address space and present state. The TSS is structured as shown in Figure 2.16.

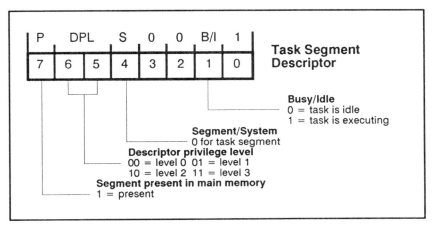

Figure 2.15. *80286 Task Segment Access Rights Byte*

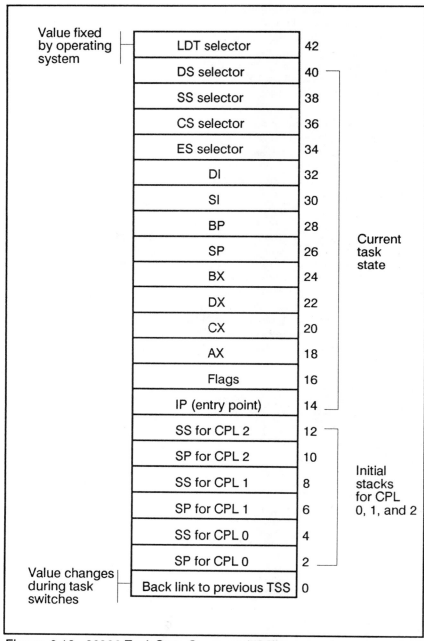

Figure 2.16. *80286 Task State Segment (TSS)*

2.3 The Intel 80386

The 80386, introduced in 1985, is a 32-bit Intel microprocessor of the Intel iAPX family. The chip is used in the IBM PS/2 Model 70 and Model 80, the Compaq 386, the Tandy Model 4000 and Model 5000, and others. The architecture of the 386 is based on a 32-bit bus, internal data path, and registers. This means that the processor can address 4 gigabytes (4294 million bytes) of physical memory. Its virtual address space is extended to 64 terabytes. The 80386 is compatible with its predecessors in the Intel iAPX family (the 8086, 8088, 80186, 80188, and 80286). MS DOS programs for the 8086/8088 will run in the 80386. Furthermore, the 80386 is capable of multitasking programs developed for the DOS environment. The 80286 protected mode is emulated by the 80386, with very few variations. Therefore, applications and system programs developed for the 80286 protected mode will execute unmodified in the 386.

Like its predecessor, the 80286, the 386 chip provides memory management and protection and supports multitasking. The 386 architecture permits the simultaneous use of several operating systems. The fundamental characteristics of the 80386 CPU can be seen in Table 2.13.

Table 2.13. *Intel 80386 Microprocessor Hardware Summary*

CHARACTERISTIC	SPECIFICATIONS
Mathematical coprocessor	80287 or 80387
Bus interface	32 bits
Internal data path	32 bits
Available clock frequencies	12.5, 16, 25, and 33 MHz
Memory addressability	4 gigabytes
Virtual memory	64 terabytes/task
Memory management and protection	Yes, with paging
I/O addressability	65,535 ports
Registers	Arithmetic: 8 Index: 8 Segment: 6 General purpose: 8
Intel support chips	Clock: 82384 Controller: TTL or PAL Interrupts: 8259-A DMA: 82258 Timer: 8253/54 DRAM: PAL
Number of pins	132
Power requirements	5 V

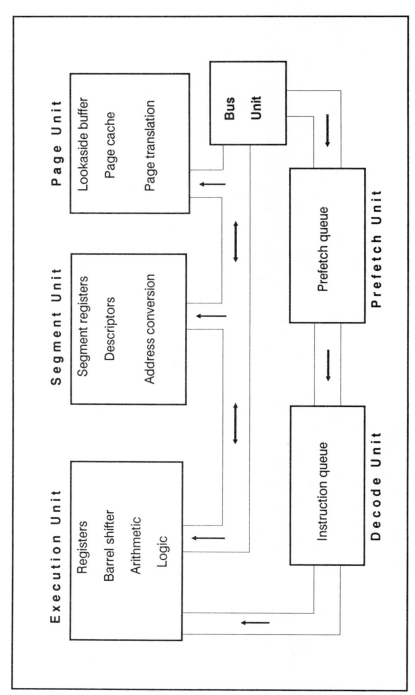

Figure 2.17. *80386 Pipeline Architecture*

Internally, the 386 chip is divided into six independent units that can execute in parallel with one another. This design, sometimes called a *pipeline architecture*, makes possible the execution of over 3 million instructions per second. This architecture can be seen in **Figure 2.17**.

The independent execution units of the 80386 microprocessor operate as follows:

1. The *bus unit* is the interface of the 80386 with the outside world. The unit handles the processor's interaction with coprocessor chips.

2. The *execution unit* contains all the general-purpose and control registers. Input into the execution unit comes from the decoder and from the bus unit. The arithmetic logic unit (ALU) is part of the execution unit. The execution unit is the only element of the CPU that can be directly controlled by the programmer.

3. The *segment unit* contains the 80386 segment registers. This unit receives read-write addresses from the execution unit in the form of a displacement and a scaled index. The segmentation unit performs the virtual-to-physical conversion, which yields a linear address.

4. The *page unit* takes part in virtual-to-physical address conversions when paging is enabled. When paging is disabled, the address obtained by the segment unit becomes the physical address used to access memory. Together, the segment and page units form the microprocessor's memory management unit, or MMU.

5. The *prefetch unit* takes advantage of idle bus cycles to read the next 4 bytes of instructions from memory into the 16-byte prefetch queue. Its operation is similar to the prefetch function of the 80286 bus unit, as described in Section 2.2.1.

6. The *decode unit* converts the instructions into an internal format that expedites their execution. These individual operations are called *microinstructions*.

2.3.1 Processing Modes

The 80386 can operate in three different processing modes:

1. Real address mode

2. Protected mode

3. Virtual 8086 mode

The 80386 powers up in the *real address mode*, or real mode. This mode is very similar to the 80286 real mode, described in Section 2.2.3. In the real mode the 80386 appears as a fast and enhanced 8086 CPU.

The *protected mode* is the 80386 native environment. In this mode, all the features of the CPU and of its 32-bit architecture are available.

The *virtual 8086 mode,* or V86 mode, is in reality a submode of the 80386 protected mode. This mode, characteristic of the 386, allows the execution of one or more 8086/8088 programs in a protected mode environment. This means that programs designed and coded for the single-task 8086/8088 environment can be multitasked in the 80386 virtual 8086 mode.

The V86 mode is based on the concept of a *virtual machine,* in which the program can execute as if it were in its native 8086 environment. To the 8086/8088 program, the 80386 (in V86 mode) appears as an 8086 machine. But the microprocessor alone cannot create this environment. On IBM microcomputers, 8086 emulation requires software that will handle interrupts, exceptions, and input/output operations in a manner consistent with the 80386 protected mode. OS/2, up to version 1.1, does not provide support for V86 mode. Nevertheless, the following programs do provide V86-mode execution of 8086/8088 software:

1. Concurrent DOS 386 (Digital Research)

2. DESQview/386 (Quarterdeck Office Systems)

3. PC-MOS/386 (The Software Link)

4. Windows/386 (Microsoft Corporation)

2.3.1.1 The 80386 Extended Instruction Set. The 80286 brought few changes to the basic 8086/8088 instruction set. Most of the new instructions were either variations of 8086 operations, such as IMUL, INS, and POPA, or of little practical use, like BOUND, ENTER, and LEAVE (see Table 2.13). However, it should be noted that the 80286 does include a substantial set of new opcodes for protected-mode operation (see Table 2.13).

The 80386 does contain some additions to the 8086/8088 instruction set, in addition to the expanded addressing modes that result from the 32-bit register size and data paths. The new real-mode instructions refer to bit manipulations and to preserving a current flag state condition for later use. Also, they include the introduction of doubleword modes for several existing opcodes. These instructions can be seen in Table 2.14.

Table 2.14. *80386 Real-Mode Instructions*

	FLAG ACTION O D I T S Z A P C	D E S C R I P T I O N
BSF	- - - - - M - - -	**BIT SCAN FORWARD** Find the first 1 bit in the second operand, starting at the low bit. The bit position (offset) of the bit is stored in the second operand.
BSR	- - - - - M - - -	**BIT SCAN REVERSE** Find the first 1 bit in the second operand, starting at the high bit. The bit position (offset) of the bit is stored in the second operand.
BT	- - - - - - - - M	**BIT TEST** Saves the bit (number in second operand) of a register or memory variable (first operand) in the carry flag.

(continued)

Table 2.14. *80386 Real-Mode Instructions (Continued)*

	FLAG ACTION O D I T S Z A P C	DESCRIPTION
BTC	- - - - - - - - M	**BIT TEST AND COMPLEMENT** Saves the bit (number in second operand) of a register or memory variable (first operand) in the carry flag, then complements (inverts) the bit tested.
BTR	- - - - - - - - M	**BIT TEST AND RESET** Saves the bit (number in second operand) of a register or memory variable (first operand) in the carry flag, then clears the bit tested.
BTS	- - - - - - - - M	**BIT TEST AND SET** Saves the bit (number in second operand) of a register or memory variable (first operand) in the carry flag, then sets the bit tested.
CWDE	- - - - - - - - -	**CONVERT WORD TO DOUBLEWORD** Converts a word in the AX register into a doubleword in EAX by extending the high bit of AX into EAX.
CDQ	- - - - - - - - -	**CONVERT DOUBLEWORD TO QUADWORD** Converts a doubleword in EAX into a quadword in EDX:EAX by extending the most significant bit of EAX into all the bits of EDX.
SETcc	- - - - - - - - -	**SET BYTE ON CONDITION** Stores the state of one or more flag bits in the destination operand if the condition is met. OPCODE: CONDITION: SETA/NBE CF and ZF = 0 SETAE/NB/NC CF = 0 SETB/C/NAE CF = 1 SETBE CF = 1 or ZF = 1 SETE/Z ZF = 1 SETG/NLE ZF = 0 and SF = 0F SETGE/NL SF = 0F SETL/NGE SF ≠ 0F SETLE/NG ZF = 1 or SF ≠ 0F SETNA CF = 1 or ZF = 1 SETNE/NZ ZF = 0 SETNO OF = 0 SETNP/PO PF = 0 SETNS SF = 0 SETO OF = 1 SETP/PE PF = 1 SETS SF = 1
SHLD	? - - - M M ? M M	**DOUBLE PRECISION SHIFT LEFT** Shifts left the bits in the first operand the number of bits (count) in the second operand. The count can be an immediate value or the contents of the CL register.
SHRD	? - - - M M ? M M	**DOUBLE PRECISION SHIFT RIGHT** Shifts right the bits in the first operand the number of bits (count) in the second operand. The count can be an immediate value or the contents of the CL register.

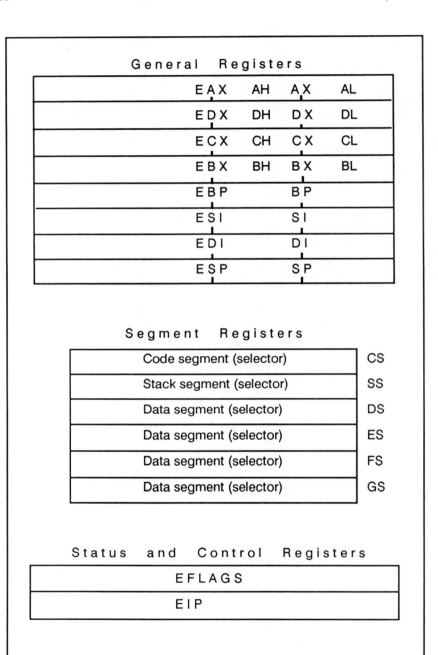

Figure 2.18. *80386 General Registers*

2.3.2 The 80386 Memory Organization and Registers

The 32-bit registers and data paths of the 80386 allow 4 gigabytes of physical address space (2^{32} = 4,294,967,296 bytes). This is four times the virtual memory space of a 286 system (see Section 2.2.4.1). The virtual address space of the 386 protected mode consists of 16,383 linear spaces of 4 gigabytes each. The 4-gigabyte linear memory representation is called a *flat memory model*. The 64-terabyte logical address space representation of virtual memory is called the *segmented memory model*.

The unit for a contiguous address space retains the name of *segment*, but each 386 segment may be as large as 4 gigabytes, in contrast with 8086/8088 and 80286 segments, which cannot exceed 64K. A single 80386 register (32 bits wide) can serve as a pointer into this 4-gigabyte address space. The register structure of the 80386 CPU is shown in Figure 2.18. The 386 contains the same number of data and pointer registers as its predecessors, the 8086, the 8088, and the 80286. However, in the 386 these eight registers are 32 bits wide. The four general registers, EAX, EDX, ECX, and EBX, can also be addressed as 16-bit or 8-bit registers by using either the 8086/8088 register names: AX (AH and AL), DX (DH and DL), CX (CH and CL), and BX (BH and BL). The 32-bit registers EBP, ESI, EDI, and ESP can also be addressed by their 16-bit names BP, SI, DI, and SP. This 80386 feature ensures downward compatibility with the 8086/8088 and 80286 microprocessors.

The 80386 contains a total of six segment registers, two more than the 8086, 8088, and 80286. The segment register classification is slightly different, since the designation of ES as an extra segment is no longer used. Instead, the segment registers DS, ES, FS, and GS are all labeled data segments. The segment registers are still 16 bits wide, and operate similarly to the segment registers in the 80286. Note that the increased address space of the 80386 is the result of the expansion of the offset component of the logical address from 16 to 32 bits, while the segment base component continues to be a 16-bit register. The instruction pointer register (EIP) holds the offset of the currently executing instruction.

2.3.2.1 The 386 Eflags Register. The 80386 flag register, named *eflags*, contains two significant bits that are not present in the 80286. These are the VM (virtual-mode) flag, used in enabling the 80386 virtual 8086 mode, and the RF (resume flag) bit, used in debugging with the breakpoint registers. The 80386 flag register is shown in Figure 2.19.

2.3.2.2 The 386 Auxiliary Registers. The 80386 contains several registers that are not normally visible to the applications programmer. Some of these auxiliary (sometimes called ancillary) registers have counterparts in the 286 CPU. For example, the global descriptor table register (GDTR), the interrupt descriptor table register (IDTR), the local descriptor table register (LDTR), and the task register (TR) have equivalent structures in the 80286 (see Figure 2.11). The 80386 auxiliary registers can be seen in Figure 2.20.

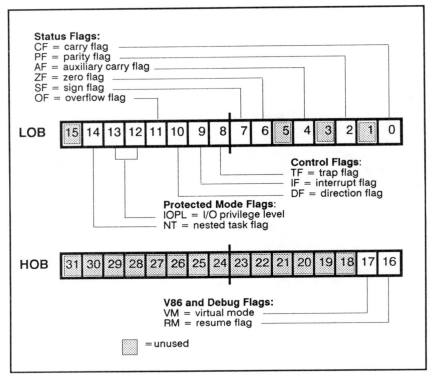

Figure 2.19. *The 80386 Flags Register*

Other 80386 auxiliary registers originated with this CPU and serve to support its unique features. For instance, the 386 contains support hardware to implement instruction and data breakpoints during debugging. This is accomplished through four debug address registers, a debug control register, and a debug status register. Other registers are used to support the memory paging feature of the 386; these are the page fault address register (CR2) and the page directory base register (CR3). Finally, for converting linear addresses to physical addresses, the 386 uses a special cache which is named the translation lookaside buffer, or TLB. The CPU contains two registers used in testing the TLB during system initialization. These test registers are designated TR6 and TR7.

The 80386 stores the machine status word in control register CR0. There are 2 bits in the 386 status word which do not exist in the 286 (see Figure 2.8). One of them, the extension type bit, records whether the mathematical coprocessor is an 80287 or an 80387. This is necessary, since the 386 can use either coprocessor chip. The PG bit is used to enable the paging feature. Figure 2.21 shows the 80386 machine status word register.

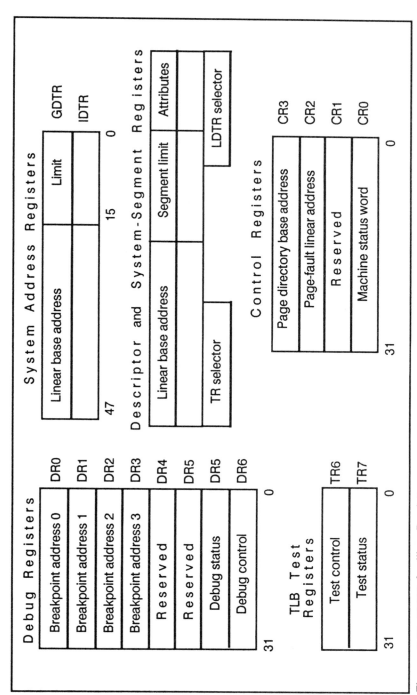

Figure 2.20. 80386 Auxiliary Registers

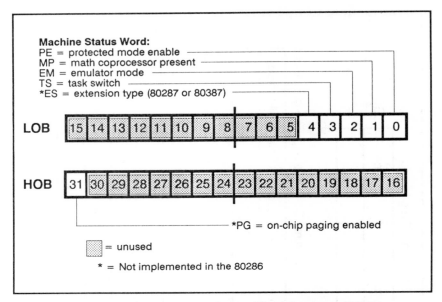

Figure 2.21. *The 80386 Machine Status Word Register (CR0)*

2.4 The Intel 486

The 486 microprocessor, of the Intel iAPX family, was introduced in 1989. The chip, which uses 32-bit architecture, includes on-chip memory management, a floating-point processor, a cache controller, and 8K of static RAM. The implementation of all these features in a single package require over 1.2 million transistors, which make the 486 one of the most complex and powerful microprocessors presently available.

To the programmer, the 486 appears similar to an 80386/80387 system with cache memory. The following list contains the differences in the programming models of the 80386 and 486 processors.

1. The AC flag (alignment check) has been added to the 80386 flag register (see Figure 2.22). This flag is used in conjunction with a new AM bit in CR0.

2. Five new bits are implemented in the CR0 register. These bits, labeled CD, NW, AM, WP, and NE, can be seen in Figure 2.23. The function of these bits is related to the cache memory controller and to the on-chip floating-point processor.

3. Two new bits are implemented in the CR3 register. These bits are designated PCD and PWT. The PCD bit performs a page-level cache disable function. The PWT bit controls page-level cache write-through in an external cache, on a cycle-by-cycle basis.

4. Six new opcodes have been added to the instruction set. The new 486 instructions are described in Table 2.15.

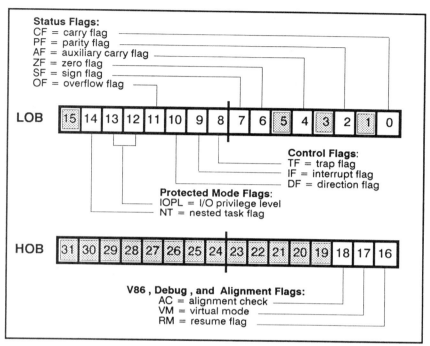

Figure 2.22. *The 486 Flag Register*

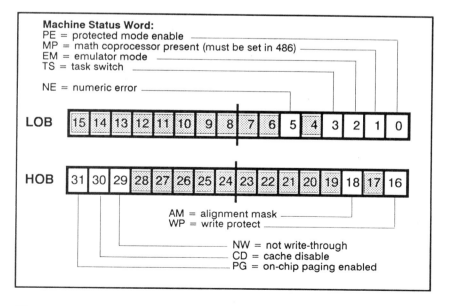

Figure 2.23. *The 486 Machine Status Word Register (CR0)*

The IBM microcomputer model 70-A21 can be equipped with the Intel 486 processor. The upgrade is achieved by installing a special board, named the 486/25 Power Platform.

Table 2.15. *486 Proprietary Instructions*

	FLAG ACTION O D I T S Z A P C	DESCRIPTION
BSWAP	- - - - - - - -	**BYTE SWAP** Reverse the byte order of a 32-bit register from the little-big endian to big-little endian format.
CMPXCHG	M - - - M M M M	**COMPARE AND EXCHANGE** Compare accumulator register with destination and load source into destination if values are equal. If not, load destination into accumulator.
INVD	- - - - - - - -	**INVALIDATE CACHE** Flush internal cache and discard data in write-back external cache. A special bus cycle is issued to indicate that external caches should also be flushed at this time.
INVLPG	- - - - - - - -	**INVALIDATE TLB ENTRY** Invalidate a single entry in the cache used for page table entries.
WBINVD	- - - - - - - -	**WRITE-BACK AND INVALIDATE CACHE** Flush internal cache. A special bus cycle is issued to indicate that external cache should write-back to main memory. Another special bus cycle directs the external cache to flush itself.
XADD	M - - - M M M M	**EXCHANGE AND ADD** Load destination into source and add destination and original value of source into destination.

3

Programmable
System Board Components

3.0 The IBM Microcomputer System Boards

The *system board,* also called the *motherboard*, is the machine's main circuit board. It fits in the system unit case and contains the primary electronic components of the microcomputer. These can be classified as follows:

1. Microprocessor
2. Memory
   a. Read-only memory (ROM)
   b. Random-access memory (RAM)
3. System support elements
   a. Direct memory access
   b. Interrupt system
   c. System clock
   d. Programmable timers
   e. Coprocessors
   f. Speakers and audio systems
   g. Other system-specific elements
4. Peripheral connectors and controllers
   a. Magnetic and optical storage
      (1) Diskette drives
      (2) Hard disk drives
      (3) Magnetic tape drives
      (4) Other storage devices
   b. Keyboard
   c. Video display
   d. Communications ports
      (1) Serial ports

(2) Parallel ports

(3) Auxiliary device ports (mouse)

5. Input/output channel connectors (slots)

6. Address, data, and control busses

7. Power supply

Although all IBM and IBM-compatible microcomputers contain elements from each principal classification in the preceding list, not all of these elements are present in every configuration or model. For example, the IBM PCjr does not support direct memory access, coprocessors, or hard disk drives. In fact, some of these elements, like the math coprocessors, are optional components in all systems, while others, like the hard disk drives, are standard in some systems and optional in others. The *hardware summary* tables that appear in Chapter 1 list the optional and standard components of many IBM and IBM-compatible machines.

Note that group 4, above, refers to connectors and auxiliary controllers for the peripheral devices. The devices themselves are not considered part of the system board and are discussed in other chapters. Some elements of the system board, because of their complexity, are also discussed separately, for example, the microprocessor (in Chapter 2) and the coprocessors (in Chapter 5). Non-programmable devices, like connectors, power supplies, and busses, are described in Chapter 1, "Microcomputer Systems," or with the devices of which they are part.

3.1 Main Memory

Computer systems require means for storing programs and data for future use. Computer terminology equates memory with storage. In this sense it is correct to speak of disk or diskette memory. However, the more common use of the term (adopted in this book) limits the word *memory* to nonmechanical storage of digital information. Magnetic, optical, or other mechanical storage devices are therefore excluded. The terms *main* and *auxiliary* memory are also used in this context.

Main memory on IBM microcomputers is provided in semiconductor devices. A typical component consists of an array of cells contained in a silicon wafer and housed in a rectangular, integrated-circuit package. In operation, the memory chips can be classified as read-only memory (ROM) or read-and-write memory, RAM. The unit of data storage is called a *memory cell*. Each cell is a transistor flip-flop circuit capable of storing 1 bit of information.

3.1.1 Memory Organization

Memory cells are arranged in groups of 8 bits, called *bytes*. The byte is the smallest addressable storage element in IBM microcomputers. This means that the CPU and other devices must read from and write to memory in groups of 8 bits. Table 3.1 shows other units of storage used in IBM microcomputers.

Table 3.1. *Units of Memory*

UNIT	EQUALS TO	NUMERICAL RANGE
Bit		2
Nibble	4 bits	16
Byte	8 bits 2 nibbles	256
Word	16 bits 2 bytes	65,535
Doubleword	32 bits 4 bytes 2 words	4,294,967,295
Quadword	64 bits 8 bytes 4 words	1.844670406 E19
Paragraph	128 bits 16 bytes 8 words	3.402823665 E38
Page	2048 bits 256 bytes 128 words 16 paragraphs	
Kilobyte	1024 bytes	
Megabyte	1,048,576 bytes 1024 kilobytes	
Gigabyte	1,073,741,824 bytes 1,048,576 kilobytes 1024 megabytes	
Terabyte	1,048,576 megabytes 1024 gigabytes	

Memory is organized linearly; the sequential number assigned to each unit is called the *memory address*. The maximum number of memory units that can be addressed directly in a certain system depends on the internal architecture of the microprocessor. Table 3.2 shows the amount of physical memory that can be addressed by various Intel microprocessors used in IBM microcomputers. Figure 3.1 shows the size of some common memory units.

Table 3.2. *IBM Microprocessors and Physical Memory*

INTEL iAPX CPU	INTERNAL REGISTERS AND DATA PATHS	DIRECTLY ADDRESSABLE MEMORY
8088 8086 80286	16 bits	2^{16} = 65,536 bytes
80386 80486	32 bits	2^{32} = 4,294,967,295 bytes

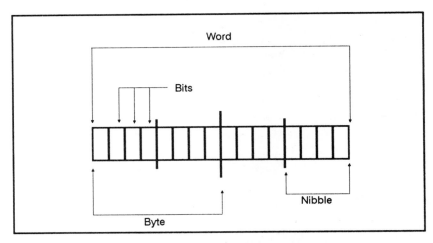

Figure 3.1. *Bit, Byte, Nibble, and Word*

3.1.2 Memory Addressing

In order to expand the amount of usable memory, Intel microprocessors of the iAPX family use an addressing scheme known as *segmented memory*. In this scheme, memory is divided into segments, each segment corresponding to a linear space of 64K. Four segment registers are provided in the 8086/8088 and 80286, and six in the 80386. The memory address is obtained from two CPU registers; one of them (the segment register) designates the 16-bit base, and the second specifies the offset from the start of this base. The 20-bit address in physical memory is obtained by combining the two registers as shown in Figure 3.2. This form of addressing allows access to 2^{20} bytes of memory (1 Mbyte).

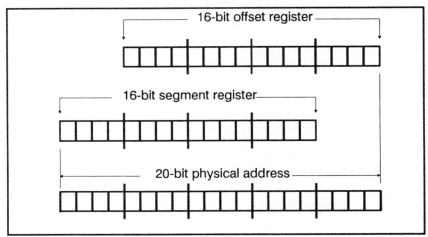

Figure 3.2. *iAPX Segmented Memory Addressing*

Because the low-order 4 bits of the physical address are always derived from the offset element, segment bases must start at paragraph boundaries (16 bytes). For example, the first segment in memory starts as physical address 00000H (segment register = 0000H), so the next consecutive segment must begin at 00010H (segment register = 0001H). For the same reason, segments can overlap by multiples of 16 bytes. This means that a memory address can be reached using several segment-offset combinations. For example, the byte at physical address 00020H can be accessed using the following two sets of segment-offset values:

Set number	1	2
Segment	0000H	0001H
Offset	0020H	0010H
Physical address	00020H	00020H

The system may simultaneously address as many segments as there are segment registers in the CPU.

A memory address, expressed in terms of its segment base and offset component, is often referred to as the *logical address*. Logical addresses are conventionally written in the form segment:offset, for example, physical address AC214H can be expressed as logical address AC21:0004H or as logical address AC00:0214H.

3.1.3 Data in Memory

Byte units of information are stored consecutively in memory. Units larger than a byte (words, doublewords, and quadwords) are conventionally stored by Intel iAPX microprocessors with the lower-order component in the lower-numbered memory address. This storage form is sometimes called the *little-endian* format. The storage of numerical data is described in Chapter 5, in relation to the mathematical coprocessors. Figure 3.3 illustrates the residence in memory of word and doubleword values.

3.1.4 CPU Access to Memory

The byte (8 bits) is the unit of memory storage in IBM microcomputers. Therefore, in order to determine the state (set or cleared) of a particular memory bit, the CPU must use one of the bit TEST instructions in conjunction with a corresponding mask. Bit masking is also required to write a specific memory bit without affecting the other bits in the byte.

```
; Sample code to determine whether bit 2 of the memory location
; named MEM_BYTE is set or cleared
        TEST   MEM_BYTE,00000100B ; Testing bit number 2
        JNZ    BIT2_SET                ; Jump if bit is set
; Execution drops if bit 2 is not set (bit = 0)
        .
        .
        .
```

```
; Jump is taken if bit 2 is set (bit = 1)
BIT2_SET:
        .
        .
        .

; Sample code to set bit 3 of the memory location named
; MEM_BYTE
        OR      MEM_BYTE,00001000B ; OR mask with bit 3 set
        .
        .
        .
; Sample code to clear bit 2 of the memory location named
; MEM_BYTE
        AND     MEM_BYTE,00000100B ; AND mask with bit 2
                                   ; clear
```

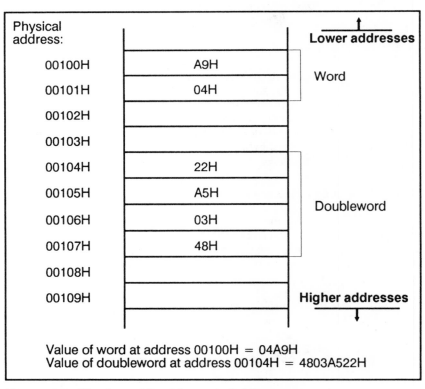

Figure 3.3. *Words and Doublewords in Memory*

The microprocessors of the Intel iAPX family (80x86 or 8088 designation) implement addressing modes that permit direct access to memory. In the cases allowed, the CPU grants memory variables the same status as microprocessor registers. For example, if a memory byte is designated in the source with the variable name MEM_BYTE, it is possible to code in assembly language:

MOV	AL,MEM_BYTE	; Register loaded from ; variable

or

MOV	MEM_BYTE,CL	; Variable loaded from ; register

Since register and variable addressing imply that the instruction refers to *the contents* of the register or variable, the form MOV AL,[MEM_BYTE] is redundant and not legal in Intel iAPX assembly language.

3.1.5 Memory Use

The use of memory resources by the IBM microcomputers can be classified as follows:

1. Storing nonvolatile programs and data (ROM)
2. System and user memory (RAM)
3. Video display memory

Figure 3.4 is a map of memory assignments under DOS.

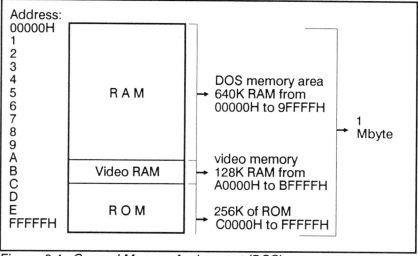

Figure 3.4. *General Memory Assignment (DOS)*

3.1.5.1 ROM Systems. The contents of ROM are fixed at the time the chips are manufactured. In IBM microcomputers, ROM is used to store the system initialization and testing routines, as well as a collection of input and output services. This program is called the basic input/output system, or BIOS. Some systems also store a version of the BASIC program in ROM.

IBM publishes the source code of the BIOS programs up to the PS/2 line. These listings can be found in the IBM Technical Reference Manual for each system. Non-IBM machines that claim compatibility with the IBM microcomputers use versions of the BIOS developed by the hardware manufacturers or by independent software companies. The Phoenix BIOS, by Phoenix Technologies, is one of these products.

3.1.5.2 RAM Systems. Although the letters RAM stand for the words "random-access memory," it is often considered that this type of memory would be better represented as read-and-write memory. In contrast with read-only memory (see Section 3.1.5.1), the principal characteristic of RAM is that it allows both storage and retrieval of data.

In IBM microcomputers, RAM is used for storing system data, operating systems, and applications programs, as well as user and application data. Video memory (see Section 3.1.5.3) is also RAM. On power-up, all RAM is blank or contains irrelevant data, called *garbage*. Programs and data are loaded into RAM from ROM or from permanent storage devices, like floppy and hard disk drives.

Two areas of RAM are reserved for system use in all IBM microcomputers: the interrupt vector table, from 0 to 400H, and the BIOS data area, from 400 to 4FFH. Specific systems may also have other reserved areas.

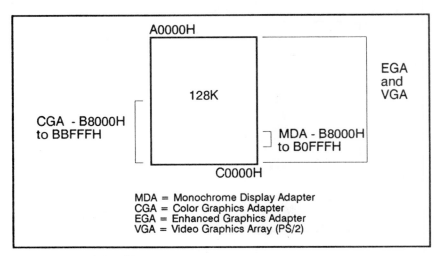

Figure 3.5. *Video Memory*

3.1.5.3 Video Memory. IBM microcomputer video systems are memory-mapped. This means that the video image is stored in a dedicated area in RAM. This area is known by the names of *video buffer, video memory, display buffer,* or *regen* (regenerative) *buffer.* Details of video memory operation are found in Chapter 4. Figure 3.5 shows the areas of memory used by various IBM video systems.

3.1.6 Memory Management in DOS

MS DOS can manage up to 1 Mbyte of RAM, but only the first 640K of this area are actually available for operating-system code and for user programs and data (see Figure 3.4). This area (from 00000H to 9FFFFH) is sometimes called the *DOS memory area* or *conventional memory.*

DOS memory can be divided into an operating-system area and a transient program area, or TPA. The portion located in lower memory is always the operating-system part, but exact boundaries depend on the DOS version, on the installed device drivers, on memory-resident utilities, on the number of disk buffers reserved, and on other factors. Figure 3.6 shows the map for the first 640K of memory under DOS.

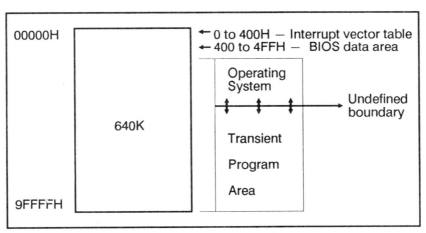

Figure 3.6. *RAM Memory in DOS Systems*

At load time, the transient program area is dynamically allocated to applications by DOS. There are also DOS services to request memory, to release allocated memory, and to modify existing allocations. In theory, programs should make use of these services to manage their own execution space and should not make use of memory resources without notifying DOS. In practice, most DOS applications behave as if they owned all the transient program area.

3.1.6.1 Expanded Memory (LIM). Several techniques have been developed for expanding the memory resources in machines with a limited memory space. One of these techniques, called *bank switching*, assigns several blocks of memory to the same physical address space. A bank selection register determines which bank is active at the time of a memory access. By changing the value in the selection register, an application can address more memory than is visible to the CPU. Memory expansion methods based on bank switching require both hardware and software resources and must pay a considerable performance penalty.

In 1985, Lotus Development Corporation and Intel Corporation jointly announced a bank-switched memory expansion standard for the IBM microcomputers called expanded memory specification, or EMS. Shortly afterward Microsoft Corporation joined in the project, which was then designated as LIM EMS (Lotus, Intel, Microsoft expanded memory specification).

Expanded memory allows applications to access up to 8 Mbytes of RAM in expanded memory boards through a software support product called the expanded memory manager, or EMM. This program is installed by the CONFIG.SYS file and, thereafter, becomes part of MS DOS. Expanded memory is available in blocks of 16K, called logical pages. Four logical pages reside in a 64K area called the *page frame*. The user can locate the page frame anywhere above the 640K block used by DOS (see Figure 3.4).

```
;****************************************************************
;                          EMMTEST.ASM
;****************************************************************
; Assembly language program to test for LIM expanded memory
; in a DOS system
;
; *********************** stack ***************************
STACK SEGMENT stack
;
        DB      0100H DUP ('?')
;
STACK ENDS
;
; *********************** data ***************************
DATA   SEGMENT
;
DEVICE_NAME          DB      'EMMXXXX0',0
DUMMY_BUFF           DW      0      ; Dummy buffer for IOCTL
;
; Message strings formatted for DOS service number 9
YES_EMM_MSG          DB      'EMM present in system',0DH,0AH,'$'
NO_EMM_MSG           DB      'No EMM in system',0DH,0AH,'$'
;
DATA   ENDS
;
; *********************** code ***************************
```

```
;
; CODE          SEGMENT
;
          ASSUME          CS:CODE
;
;
;
START:
;
;
; Establish data and extra segment addressability
          MOV     AX,DATA
          MOV     DS,AX
          ASSUME          DS:DATA
          MOV     ES,AX
          ASSUME          ES:DATA
;
; Use MS DOS IOCTL function to test for EMM
;*****************
; open EMM device
;*****************
          MOV     AH,61         ; DOS service to open file
          MOV     AL,0          ; Read-only mode
          LEA     DX,DEVICE_NAME     ; Standard name of driver
          INT     21H           ; DOS service request
          JC      NO_EMM        ; Open failed, no EMM
; The open call will also be successful if there is a DOS file
; with the name EMMXXXX0
; Use IOCTL to exclude this possibility
;*****************
;   test for file
;   using IOCTL
;*****************
; Device handle is returned in AX
          MOV     BX,AX         ; Handle to BX
          MOV     AH,68         ; DOS service for IOCTL
          MOV     AL,7          ; Subservice for output status
          MOV     CX,0          ; No bytes to read. This is a
                                ; dummy call
          LEA     DX,DUMMY_BUFF      ; Dummy buffer
          INT     21H           ; DOS service request
; If AL = 0, then the device opened was a file, not a driver
          CMP     AL,0          ; Test for not ready
          JE      NO_EMM        ; Device was a DOS file
;*****************
;   EMM present
;*****************
          LEA     DX,YES_EMM_MSG     ; Message pointer
          JMP     EXIT
;*****************
;
```

```
;      no EMM
;*****************
;
NO_EMM:
        LEA     DX,NO_EMM_MSG        ; Message pointer
;*****************
;
; display message
;    and EXIT
;*****************
;
EXIT:
        MOV     AH,9                 ; DOS service request number
                                     ; to display string
        INT     21H
; Exit to DOS
        MOV     AH,76                ; DOS service request number
                                     ; to exit
        MOV     AL,0                 ; No error code returned
        INT     21H                  ; To DOS
;
CODE    ENDS
        END     START
```

Applications communicate with the expanded memory manager using the services of interrupt 67H. This process is quite similar to the DOS services of interrupt 21H; the service request number is loaded in the AH register and INT 67H is executed. Some services also require other registers to pass specific information.

Note that, for expanded memory to be useful, applications must be designed to take advantage of this resource. Programs that are not equipped to manage expanded memory do not benefit by its presence.

MS DOS versions 4.x include a driver program to support expanded memory. The driver, named XMA2EMS.SYS, is loaded by the CONFIG.SYS file. Once this driver is installed, applications can make use of expanded memory using the LIM specification. In addition, 80386 systems running DOS 4.x have access to a driver named XMAEM.SYS, which allows memory beyond the 1-Mbyte DOS limit to be configured so as to emulate expanded memory.

3.1.7 Memory Management in OS/2

OS/2 memory management is based on the facilities provided by the 80286 CPU (see Section 2.2.4.1). The manipulations are based on the 80286 protected-mode memory model and on the concept of segmented virtual memory (see Figure 2.9). The idea of *virtual* memory stems from the fact that, in protected mode, the segment registers contain a logical handle into a table (descriptor table).

In the real mode, the segment registers, which are directly accessible to the program, contain the base element of a physical address, while in protected mode, the memory data structures are managed by OS/2 and applications have limited access to them. If an application attempts to change the contents of a segment register directly, or to access memory in any illegal way, the CPU automatically generates an exception (protection fault) that serves to notify OS/2 of an impending violation.

Protected-mode segments are accessed through selectors. These selectors, which are held in the segment registers CS, DS, SS, and ES, are an index into a descriptor table where the physical addresses are stored. The location of this table can be obtained only at the operating-system level. The segment descriptors stored in the descriptor table contain a 24-bit physical address for the segment base (see Figure 2.12). This 24-bit value allows OS/2 access to 16 Mbytes of linear memory, in contrast with the 1 Mbyte that can be accessed by DOS. Protected-mode selectors are also used in implementing virtual memory by swapping physical memory areas to disk files or other secondary storage devices. Figure 3.7 shows a map for 16 Mbytes of memory in OS/2.

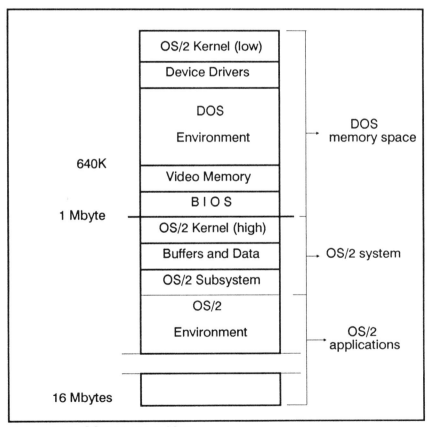

Figure 3.7. *OS/2 Memory Map*

In OS/2 each executing task has its own memory space, which is isolated from that of other tasks and from system memory. OS/2 manages all memory resources on behalf of applications, which have limited access to code and data that they do not own. One exception is the operating-system service routines (application programming interface), which can be accessed by any task.

DOS programs can execute in a special OS/2 environment called the *DOS compatibility session*. In this mode the CPU is switched to the real mode and DOS programs execute normally, being able to manipulate the segment registers directly. However, the OS/2 user can disable the DOS compatibility session completely or reduce the size of the DOS environment. To disable the DOS session, the CONFIG.SYS file must contain the command PROTECTONLY = YES. The RMSIZE command is used to reduce the size of the DOS environment. For example, to reduce the DOS environment to 320K, the CONFIG.SYS file will contain the statement RMSIZE = 320.

3.2 System Support Elements

In addition to the CPU, memory, and the optional coprocessor, the IBM system boards contain several electronic circuits that support system functions. These circuits are implemented in one or more electronic microdevices and auxiliary components. Some of these elements have undergone little change in the several models of the IBM PC, PS/2, and compatible microcomputers, while others have suffered several substantial modifications.

3.2.1 Direct Memory Access (DMA)

The CPU has many chores to perform in a microcomputer system. Some of these chores can be temporarily delayed while the processor handles another task, but others require instant attention. For example, honoring an interrupt request that originated in the system timer, removing data read by a disk controller, and refreshing a memory cell about to lose its contents are operations that cannot be postponed without consequence. One way of preventing this possibility of conflict (by no means the only one) is to have an alternative mechanism for the direct control of memory access (DMA). An added advantage of this scheme is a substantial improvement in the system's memory read-write performance.

All IBM microcomputers, except the PCjr, use direct memory access hardware. The computers of the PC line and those of the PS/2 line that do not have Micro Channel architecture (the Model 25 and Model 30) use the Intel 8237A-5 DMA controller chip (see Section 3.2.1.1). The computers of the PS/2 line with Micro Channel (Model 50, 60, 70, and 80) use a proprietary IBM VLSI component for direct memory access. This IBM chip is compatible with the 8237 but has additional capabilities that are not available in the Intel DMA component.

The DMA controllers used in IBM microcomputers are programmable and managed by the CPU. Usually, the processor loads the DMA chip with a start address where the transfer is to take place and a count for the number of bytes to be transferred. A command to start the transfer is then issued, and the DMA device takes over the system's address and data busses. At this point the processor is free to perform other operations while the transfer of data between the input/output device and memory is handled by the DMA component.

3.2.1.1 The Intel 8237 DMA Controller. This chip is used in all the IBM microcomputers of the PC line except the PCjr, and in Model 25 and Model 30 of the PS/2 line. PS/2 computers with Micro Channel architecture use a proprietary IBM DMA controller, described in Section 3.2.1.4.

The IBM Personal Computer uses the Intel 8238-2 DMA controller, the XT uses the 8237A-5, and the AT and the PS/2 Model 25 and Model 30 use two 8237A-5 chips. From a programming viewpoint, these versions of the Intel integrated circuit can be considered identical; for this reason we will refer generically to the 8237 DMA controller in the following discussion.

The Intel 8237 is a dedicated microprocessor designed for transferring data from memory to memory or between memory and input/output devices. However, note that memory-to-memory transfers are not possible in the PC and XT because of the use of the DMA channels. The maximum data transfer rate is 1.6 Mbytes/s, but in 8088 systems the 8237 is programmed to allow the CPU access to the bus after each transfer. This reduces the transfer rate to 422K/s. Table 3.3 shows the priorities and use of the several channels of the 8237 DMA controller in the IBM PC and XT.

Table 3.3. *8237 DMA Controller Transfer Channels (PC and XT)*

CHANNEL NUMBER	PRIORITY	USE IN PC AND PC XT
0	1 (highest)	Memory refresh
1	2	Not assigned
2	3	Diskette drive
3	4 (lowest)	Hard disk (if installed)

To the programmer, the 8237, as configured in the IBM PC and XT, appears as four independent channels. Channel assignments and priorities are shown in Table 3.3. Channel 0, the highest priority, is assigned to memory refresh operations. Memory refresh consists of performing a dummy read-write cycle for each memory cell so that the RAM chips do not lose the information they store. The pulse for the memory refresh is provided by timer channel 1 (see Section 3.2.4.1). In the PC and XT, this pulse occurs every 15 μs. To use either DMA channel 0 or timer channel 1 for other purposes risks the integrity of RAM.

Memory-to-memory transfers are not possible in PC and XT systems because the 8237 requires channel 0 for this operation. However, the AT does not use the DMA controllers for memory refresh operations, which are handled through independent circuitry.

3.2.1.2 The 8237 Programmable Registers. Programming the 8237 takes place through eight internal registers accessible through ports 0 to 15. Some 8237 registers admit both read and write operations, while others are write-only or read-only. The DMA port assignments in IBM systems that use the 8237 are listed in Table 3.4.

Table 3.4. *8237 DMA Controller Port Assignments*

PORT NUMBER	OPERATION	FUNCTIONS
0	Read Write	Channel 0 current address Channel 0 base and current address
1	Read Write	Channel 0 current byte count Channel 0 base and current byte count
2	Read Write	Channel 1 current address Channel 1 base and current address
3	Read Write	Channel 1 current byte count Channel 1 base and current byte count
4	Read Write	Channel 2 current address Channel 2 base and current address
5	Read Write	Channel 2 current byte count Channel 2 base and current byte count
6	Read Write	Channel 3 current address Channel 3 base and current address
7	Read Write	Channel 3 current byte count Channel 3 base and current byte count
8	Read Write	To status register To command register
9	Write	To request register (not used in PC)
10	Write	Single mask register bit
11	Write	To mode register
12	Write	Clear byte pointer flip-flop
13	Read Write	Temporary register (not used in PC) Clear all
14	Write	Clear mask register
15	Write	All mask register bits

For each DMA channel there are two *address* and two *byte count registers*. In write operations, the address and byte count registers consist of a *base* and a *current* component for each channel. The base element of the address or the byte count retains the initial values primed into the registers at the start of the transfer. These values are used for automatically reinitializing the current registers at the end of a transfer cycle, but only if bit 4 of the mode register (see Figure 3.11) is set. The current register holds the present value and address of the count in that channel.

The 8237 address registers are 16 bits wide, because the chip was designed for systems with a 64K address space. For this same reason, an additional register, called the *page register*, is required in order to access the 1-Mbyte space of the PC and XT. The system board contains four such page registers, one for each channel. Table 3.5 shows the page register assignments in the PC and XT. Channel 0, used only in memory refresh, is mapped to the same port as channel 1. In the PC and XT the page register is a 74LS670 IC.

Table 3.5. *Page Register Assignments for PC and XT*

PORT NUMBER	CHANNEL NUMBER	USE
83H	0	Memory refresh
83H	1	Unassigned
81H	2	Diskette
82H	3	Hard disk

The page register holds the 4 most significant bits of the 20-bit physical address, while the remaining 16 bits are stored in the address register. The physical address is obtained from the corresponding 8086/8088 segment and pointer registers, as listed in Figure 3.8. If the data transfer crosses a page boundary (64K pages), the page and address registers must be reinitialized. To the programmer, this means that a data transfer may require one or two DMA operations. A sample of the required coding is shown in the code fragment given later in this section.

Another complication arises from the fact that the 8237 registers must be primed 8 bits at a time. Therefore, to output a 16-bit value to the address register requires two OUT operations to the corresponding port, one to enter the low-order byte of the address and one for the high-order byte. An internal flip-flop, which selects the low-order or the high-order input, is toggled by every read and write operation. Writing to port number 12 sets the initial state of the flip-flop to the low-order component. The coding is shown in the sample later in this section.

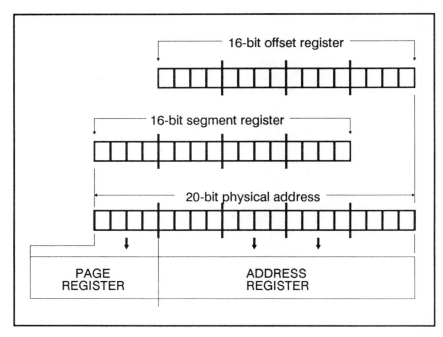

Figure 3.8. *Memory Addressing in DMA Operations*

The 8237 *command register*, located at port 8, is a write-only register that is preset, in IBM microcomputers, to the chip's operating mode. The command register should not be changed by the programmer. The BIOS initialization routine outputs a value of 4 to the command register to disable DMA operation and a value of 0 to enable DMA.

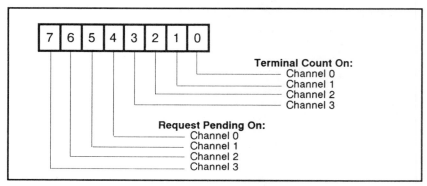

Figure 3.9. *8237 Status Register Bit Map*

The *status register*, a read-only register also located at port 8, serves to determine which channels have terminated the count and which are still pending. Figure 3.9 shows the bit map of the 8237 status register. The sample code later in this section contains a loop for polling the status register to determine whether the DMA transfer is complete. Reading the status register resets the bits that indicate a terminated count. This is necessary since there is no write operation available that can clear the status register.

The *mask register* is a write-only register located at ports 10, 14, and 15. Any output to port 14 will clear all masks in the register. Port 15 is used to set or clear all 4 bits in the mask register. Port 10 is used to enable or disable specific channels. Since there is no way to read the mask register, the program must keep track of the state of each individual channel. For instance, software for the PC line must always unmask channel 0 so as not to disable memory refresh. Figure 3.10 shows the bit map of the 8237 mask register.

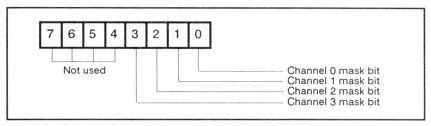

Figure 3.10. *8237 Mask Register Bit Map*

The 8237 *mode register* is a write-only register accessible through port 11. Bits 6 and 7 must be set, as shown in Figure 3.11, in order to select the single-byte transfer mode required in the IBM PC. Figure 3.11 also shows the function of the remaining bits of the mode register.

```
; Code fragment to illustrate DMA
; The routine programs the 8237 to transfer 16K of data
; from an imaginary input device into a buffer in the data
; segment. If a page boundary is crossed, the transfer is
; performed in two steps
;
DATA   SEGMENT
;
DMA_BUF      DB      65536 DUP (00H)      ; 64K null bytes
;
DATA   ENDS
;
CODE   SEGMENT

          .
          .
          .

; Program and device initialization not shown
; The code assumes the DS register pointing to a data
```

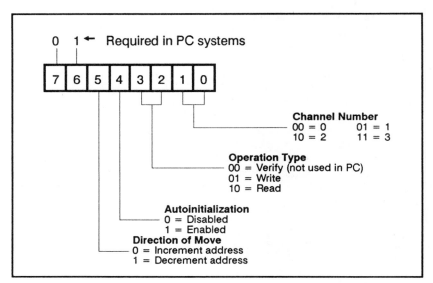

Figure 3.11. *8237 Mode Register Bit Map*

```
; segment that contains a 64K buffer named DMA_BUF and
; an input device connected to the system bus and ready for DMA
;********************
;   obtain value for
;      page register
;********************
        MOV     AX,DS        ; Segment base of buffer
        MOV     BX,0         ; Clear BX
        MOV     CX,4         ; Set up bit counter for shift
ROT_4_BITS:
        SAL     AX,1         ; Carry set if bit shifted out
        RCL     BX,1         ; Rotate carry bit into BX
        LOOP    ROT_4_BITS   ; Repeat 4 times
;********************
;   obtain value for
;   address register
;********************
; The 20-bit segment address is now in BX:AX
; Add in the buffer offset
        ADD     AX,OFFSET DMA_BUF
; This addition can produce a carry. Add in the carry to BX
        ADC     BX,0                 ; Adding 0 and the carry equals
                                     ; adding the carry
; BX now holds the 4 bits that go into the page register
; AX has the value that goes into the 8237 address register
```

```
;********************
;   check boundary
;        crossing
;********************
         PUSH  BX              ; Save page register element
         PUSH  AX              ; and address register element
         ADD   AX,16383        ; Add 16K - 1 to offset
         JNC   NOT_CROSSED;    64K boundary not crossed if no
                               ; carry from adding 16K
;********************
;   2-step transfer
;********************
         POP   AX              ; Restore offset
; Get number of bytes to transfer in first step
         MOV   CX,0FFFFH       ; Maximum for address register
         SUB   CX,AX           ; Minus actual value is count for
                               ; first transfer
         PUSH  CX              ; Save count
         CALL  DMA             ; Procedure to perform DMA
         POP   AX              ; Byte count recovered
         MOV   CX,16382        ; 16K - 2
         SUB   CX,AX           ; CX = second byte count
         POP   BX              ; Restore page register value
         INC   BX              ; Bump value to next page
         MOV   AX,0            ; AX = address register value
         CALL  DMA             ; Second step of transfer
         JMP   END_OF_DMA
;********************
;   1-step transfer
;********************
NOT_CROSSED:
         POP   AX              ; Restore address value
         POP   BX              ; and page value
         MOV   CX,16383        ; 16K - 1 bytes to transfer
         CALL  DMA
;
;******************
;       exit
;******************
END_OF_DMA:
              .

              .

              .
;*****************************
;   procedure for DMA transfer
;*****************************
DMA   PROC  NEAR
; On entry:
```

```
;                      CX = number of bytes to transfer
;                      BX = value to load into the page register
;                      AX = value to load into the address register
; Code assumes transfer using channel 1

;******************
;  set up address
;     registers
;******************
; First set internal flip-flop to low-order element of address
              OUT    12,AL          ; Output any value to port 12
; Output address to channel 1 address register at port 2
              OUT    2,AL           ; Low-order byte of address
              MOV    AL,AH          ; High-order byte to AL
              OUT    2,AL           ; To address register
; Output count to channel 1 count register at port 3
              MOV    AX,CX          ; Count to AX
              OUT    3,AL           ; Low-order byte of count
              MOV    AL,AH          ; High-order byte to AL
              OUT    3,AL           ; To count register
; Load page register
              MOV    AX,BX          ; Page value to AX
              OUT    83H,AL         ; To channel 1 page register
;******************
;   set up mode
;     register
;******************
              MOV    AL,01000101B   ; 0 1 0 0 0 1 0 1
                                    ;
                                    ;      ┬ ┬ ┬   ┬ ┬
                                    ;      │ │ │   │ └____ Channel 1
                                    ;      │ │ │   └_____ Write
                                    ;      │ │ └_____ No auto
                                    ;      │ │                 init
                                    ;      │ └_____ Increment
                                    ;      │                  address
                                    ;
              OUT    11,AL          ; To mode register
;******************
; unmask channel 1
;******************
              MOV    AL,00001100B   ; Channel 0 (refresh) also
                                    ; unmasked
              OUT    10,AL          ; To mask register
; DMA now executes
;******************
;   read status
;     register
;******************
GET_STATUS:
```

```
        IN     AL,8           ; Status register to AL
        TEST   AL,00000010B   ; Test channel 1 terminal count
        JZ     GET_STATUS     ; Loop if bit not set
; Execution drops if transfer has concluded
;******************
;
;   mask channel 1
;******************
;
        MOV    AL,00001110B   ; Mask channel 1. Channel 0
                              ; remains unmasked for refresh
        OUT    10,AL
        RET
DMA     ENDP
```

3.2.1.3 DMA Hardware in the PC AT. The Personal Computer AT uses the Intel 8237A-5 DMA controller, which is almost identical to the one in the PC and the XT. However, there are substantial differences in how the DMA operations are performed. In the first place, the AT uses a separate integrated circuit for memory refresh. This frees DMA channel 0 for other operations. A second difference is the use of two 8237 chips with four channels each. Table 3.6 lists the 8237 transfer channels in the PC AT.

Table 3.6. *8237 DMA Controller Transfer Channels (PC AT)*

CONTROLLER NUMBER	CHANNEL NUMBER	USE
1	0	Not assigned
	1	Synchronous data link control (SDLC)
	2	Diskette drive
	3	Not assigned
2	4	Cascade for controller 1
	5	Not assigned
	6	Not assigned
	7	Not assigned

The presence of three additional channels (channel 4 is used to cascade the first four channels) requires additional page registers. Table 3.7 shows the page register addresses for the AT.

Channels 0, 1, 2, and 3 of the Personal Computer AT, associated with DMA controller number 1, are compatible with the 8237 DMA controller used in the PC and PC XT, described in Sections 3.2.1.1 and 3.2.1.2. AT channels 5, 6, and 7, associated with DMA controller number 2, support 16-bit data transfers throughout the 16-Mbyte address space of the AT. In channels 5, 6, and 7, DMA takes place in blocks of 128K. For this reason, the base count is a word, instead of a byte. The port assignments for the 8237-5 DMA controller in the AT and PS/2 Micro Channel systems can be seen in Table 3.8.

Table 3.7. *Page Register Assignments for the Personal Computer AT*

PORT NUMBER	CHANNEL NUMBER	USE
87H	0	Unassigned
83H	1	Unassigned
81H	2	Diskette
82H	3	Hard disk
8BH	5	Unassigned
89H	6	Unassigned
8AH	7	Unassigned
8FH	NA	Memory refresh

Table 3.8. *8237A-5 DMA Controller Number 2 Port Assignments for the PC AT and PS/2 Micro Channel*

PORT NUMBER	OPERATION	FUNCTIONS
C0H	Read Write	Channel 4 current address Channel 4 base and current address
C2H	Read Write	Channel 4 current word count Channel 4 base and current word count
C4H	Read Write	Channel 5 current address Channel 5 base and current address
C6H	Read Write	Channel 5 current word count Channel 5 base and current word count
C8H	Read Write	Channel 6 current address Channel 6 base and current address
CAH	Read Write	Channel 6 current word count Channel 6 base and current word count
CCH	Read Write	Channel 7 current address Channel 7 base and current address
CEH	Read Write	Channel 7 current word count Channel 7 base and current word count
D0H	Read Write	To status register To command register
D2H	Write	To request register (not used in PC AT)
D4H	Write	Single mask register bit
D6H	Write	To mode register
D8H	Write	Clear byte pointer flip-flop
DAH	Read Write	Temporary register (not used in PC AT) Clear all
DCH	Write	Clear mask register
DEH	Write	All mask register bits

DMA controller number 2 page registers, in the Personal Computer AT, divide the 16-Mbyte address space into 128K pages. The physical address is a 23-bit value, with its high-order 7 bits placed in bits 1 to 7 of the page register and its low-order 16 bits placed in the corresponding address register. Bit 0 of the page register is not used.

When programming the DMA controller in the AT, it is necessary to consider that back-to-back port access commands will not allow the chips enough recovery time. The problem can be solved by inserting a short jump after every IN or OUT instruction, as follows:

```
IN      0D0H,AL      ; Read status port
JMP     SHORT $ + 2 ; The $ symbol indicates the
                     ; present value in the program
                     ; counter. The 2-byte jump
                     ; goes to the next instruction
AND     AL,00000111B ; Execution can now continue
OUT     0D0H,AL      ; with an OUT to the same port
```

It is a good programming practice to always insert an input/output delay instruction to ensure portability of the code.

3.2.1.4 DMA Hardware in Micro Channel Systems. The PS/2 microcomputers with Micro Channel architecture, Models 50, 60, 70, P70, and 80, use a proprietary IBM VLSI component for DMA operations. The IBM chip is register- and program-compatible with the Intel 8237A-5, as configured in the Personal Computer AT. Therefore, it is compatible with software written for the DMA controller in the Personal Computer and the PC XT. In addition, the Micro Channel DMA controller has additional capabilities that are not available in the Intel DMA component.

One difference between the 8237 and the Micro Channel DMA IC is that the latter makes all eight channels available, while the AT configuration uses channel 4 of controller number 2 for cascading controller number 1. In the IBM DMA chip, the page register for channel 4 is accessed at port 8FH. Micro Channel DMA hardware also contains an ARBUS (arbitration bus) register, used for selecting the arbitration level in virtual DMA operations.

The Micro Channel DMA hardware supports operations that are not available in the 8237 DMA controller. These extended operations are available through an *address decode* and a *function register*, and through the *extended-mode register*. The following steps are required for accessing the Micro Channel DMA internal registers:

1. The function register (see Figure 3.12) is accessed through port 18H. The program will set up the bit pattern for the required channel and execute an OUT instruction to this port. This will select the desired command and channel for the subsequent instruction, except for those commands that execute directly (marked * in Figure 3.12).

2. Commands are executed by performing IN or OUT instructions to port 1AH. Those that require multiple bytes (marked **#** in **Figure** 3.12) consist of two or more successive operations. The number of bytes can be determined from the bits field in Figure 3.12. The I/O sequence proceeds from low- to high-order elements.

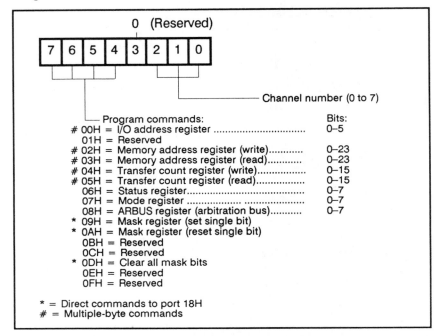

Figure 3.12. *Micro Channel DMA Function Register Bit Map*

The Micro Channel contains an extended-mode register for each DMA channel (see Figure 3.13). Note that all registers are read-write during extended-mode operations. This allows reading of the contents of the mode and mask registers, which are write-only in systems using the 8237 DMA controller. The following code fragment demonstrates writing and reading to the mode register using extended DMA operations in PS/2 Micro Channel computers.

```
; Write and read the mode register for channel 1 using extended
; DMA operations
      MOV   AL,01110001B  ; 0 1 1 1 0 0 0 1
                          ;   _____   ____
                          ;     |          |__ Channel 1
                          ;     |
                          ;     |___ 07H = mode register
      OUT   18H,AL        ; Select mode register
      JMP   SHORT $ + 2   ; I/O delay
```

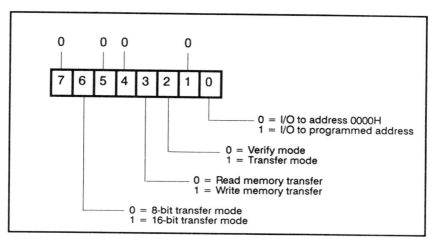

Figure 3.13. *Micro Channel DMA Extended-Mode Register Bit Map*

```
;
; Enter value into channel 1 mode register
      MOV    AL,00001101B  ; 0 0 0 0 1 1 0 1
                           ;            | |  |_ Programmed I/O
                           ;            | |____ Transfer mode
                           ;            |_____ Write memory
      OUT    1AH,AL        ; Output to mode register
      JMP    SHORT $ + 2   ; I/O delay
;
; Read contents of channel 1 mode register
      MOV    AL,01110001B  ; Select mode register for
                           ; channel 1
      OUT    18H,AL        ; Enter selection
      JMP    SHORT $ + 2   ; I/O delay
      IN     AL,1AH        ; Read mode register for
                           ; channel 1
; AL now holds mode register contents for channel 1
```

3.2.2 The Interrupt System

Computer systems contain external devices that require the occasional attention of the central processor, such as, keyboards, disk and diskette drives, and printers. One method of servicing external devices is to test them frequently to determine which, if any, require attention. This method, usually called *polling*, wastes considerable time in checking devices that do not need service. A more efficient method is to allow each device to *interrupt* the CPU whenever it wants. Compared with polling, the interrupt method substantially increases system performance.

The interrupt system in IBM microcomputers can be described as a mechanism that allows the central processing unit to respond to unpredictable events. When an interrupt signal is received, the CPU immediately diverts its attention from the task currently executing, but in a manner that will allow the future resumption of this task. The processor then executes a routine that is specific to each particular interrupt. In the microprocessors of the Intel iAPX family, as used in IBM microcomputers, interrupts may be classified as follows:

1. *Internal interrupts* are those that originate inside the CPU, for example, the divide by zero or the single-step interrupt.

2. *External interrupts* are those initiated by external hardware. External interrupts are signaled to the CPU on the interrupt request line (INTR) or the nonmaskable interrupt line (NMI). On all IBM microcomputers the INTR line is driven by an Intel 8259A programmable interrupt controller.

3. *Software interrupts* are those initiated by an INT or INTO instruction.

Interrupt sources in IBM microcomputers are shown in Figure 3.14. The interrupt encoding is shown in Table 3.9.

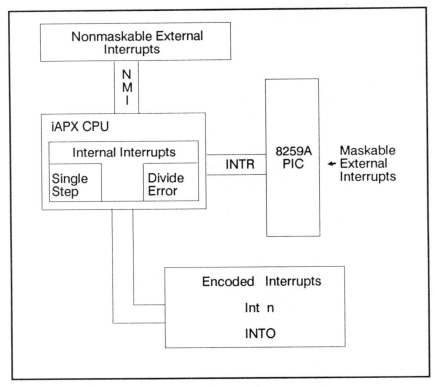

Figure 3.14. *Interrupt Sources*

Table 3.9. *Interrupt Encoding on Intel iAPX Systems*

OPCODE	BYTES IN OPCODE	INTERRUPT TYPE
CCH	1	Type 3 interrupt (breakpoint)
CEH	1	Type 4 interrupt (INTO instruction)
CDH	2	Type 0 to 256 (interrupt type is encoded in the second byte)

Most internal, external, or software interrupts present to the CPU a specific signature, which is encoded in a byte that follows the interrupt opcode. This signature, sometimes called the *interrupt type*, serves to identify each interrupt to the CPU. However, interrupts generated by a breakpoint or by the INTO (interrupt on overflow) instruction do not contain a signature byte.

The breakpoint interrupt, typically used in debuggers, is planted at the location where execution is to be detained. The breakpoint handler is usually a routine to display registers and memory areas or perform other debugger functions. The breakpoint interrupt had to be designed as a 1-byte instruction so that it could be planted in the memory space occupied by even the shortest opcode in the instruction set.

The INTO instruction (interrupt on overflow) is triggered by the microprocessor's overflow flag (OF). The INTO instruction is used after an arithmetic or logical operation to detect if the signed result cannot be contained in the space of the destination operand. Because of its special nature, it does not require a signature byte.

Interrupt processing first tests whether the interrupt was triggered by a breakpoint or by an interrupt on overflow instruction (1-byte opcodes in Table 3.9). If it was triggered by a breakpoint, the CPU executes interrupt type 3, and it executes type 4 if the interrupt was triggered by an interrupt on overflow instruction. If the interrupt was triggered by neither a breakpoint nor an overflow condition, then the CPU uses the signature byte to calculate the address of the corresponding interrupt handler. The special memory area that holds address pointers to each handler is called the *interrupt vector table*. The interrupt mechanism requires that the following conditions exist in the system:

1. The vector table in RAM, at segment 0000H, offset 0000H to 03FFH (1K), must have been initialized with the address of a service routine for each interrupt active in the system. The maximum number of entries is 256.

2. Each 4-byte entry stores a doubleword address in the standard segment:offset form.

3. Interrupt types that do not have a service routine located at offset = type *4 must not be generated by the processor, by the hardware, or by an INT instruction.

Table 3.10 shows the interrupts implemented in the original version of the IBM Personal Computer. Most of these vectors have been maintained by IBM up to the PS/2 line.

Table 3.10. *Interrupt Types and Vectors*

ADDRESS	TYPE	INTERRUPT GROUP AND DESCRIPTION	
		NMI, Single-step, Breakpoint, Etc.	
0000H	0H	Divide by zero	
0004H	1H	Single-step	
0008H	2H	Nonmaskable interrupt (NMI)	
000CH	3H	Breakpoint	
0010H	4H	Interrupt on overflow (INTO)	
		Print Screen and Reserved	
0014H	5H	Print screen	
0018H	6H	Reserved by IBM	
001DH	7H	Reserved by IBM	
		Maskable External (8259 PIC)	
0020H	8H	System timer	IRQ0
0024H	9H	Keyboard handler	IRQ1
0028H	0AH	Reserved	IRQ2
002CH	0BH	Communications COM2	IRQ3
0030H	0CH	Communications COM1.....	IRQ4
0034H	0DH	Disk	IRQ5
0038H	0EH	Diskette	IRQ6
003CH	0FH	Printer	IRQ7
		Bios Services and Data Areas	
0040H	10H	Video functions	
0044H	11H	Equipment check	
0048H	12H	Memory size	
004CH	13H	Diskette and disk	
0050H	14H	Communications	
0054H	15H	Cassette (AT extended services)	
0058H	16H	Keyboard	
005CH	17H	Printer	
0060H	18H	Resident BASIC language	
0064H	19H	Bootstrap	
0068H	1AH	Time-of-day	
006CH	1BH	Keyboard break	
0070H	1CH	User timer tick	
0074H	1DH	Video parameters ....Area	
0078H	1EH	Diskette parameters ....Area	
007CH	1FH	Graphic characters ....Area	

(continued)

Note that some vectors do not store pointers to service routines. For instance, address 0074H stores a pointer to a data area reserved for video parameters. The two addresses that follow also store pointers to data areas (see Table 3.10). Interrupts whose vectors do not contain pointers to service routines cannot be executed. Interrupt priorities are shown in Table 3.11.

The INT n instruction generates an interrupt to the vector contained in the operand, independent of the nature of the original interrupt. For example, INT 00H generates a divide by zero interrupt as if this condition had actually occurred in the microprocessor.

Table 3.10. *IInterrupt Types and Vectors (Continued)*

ADDRESS	TYPE	INTERRUPT GROUP AND DESCRIPTION
		DOS Services
0080H	20H	DOS program terminate
0084H	21H	DOS general service call
0088H	22H	DOS terminate address
008CH	23H	DOS control break exit address
0090H	24H	DOS fatal error exit
0094H	25H	DOS absolute disk read
0098H	26H	DOS absolute disk write
009CH	27H	DOS terminate and stay resident
		DOS, BASIC and User Software
00A0H	28H	Reserved for DOS
0100H	40H	Diskette BIOS revector
0104H	41H	Hard disk parameters
0108H	42H	Reserved by IBM
0118H	46H	Hard disk parameters
011CH	47H	Reserved by IBM
0128H	4AH	User alarm
012CH	4BH	Reserved by IBM
0180H	60H	Reserved for user software
01A0H	68H	Not used
01C0H	70H	Real-time clock
01C4H	71H	Reserved by IBM
01D4H	75H	Math coprocessor
01D8H	76H	Hard disk controller
01D8H	77H	Reserved by IBM
0200H	80H	Reserved or used by BASIC
03C4H	F1H	Reserved for user software

3.2.2.1 The 8259A Interrupt Controller. The Intel 8259A programmable interrupt controller (PIC) is an integrated circuit designed to manage the external interrupts in a microcomputer system. The 8259A is used in all IBM microcomputers of the PC and PS/2 lines, although it is not always configured in the same manner. For example, the IBM Personal Computer, the PC XT, the PCjr, and Models 25 and 30 of the PS/2 line use a single 8259A chip, while the PC AT and the Micro Channel models of the PS/2 line use two 8259A controllers. Furthermore, the 8259A controllers used in non-Micro Channel and in Micro Channel systems are initialized to be triggered differently.

In operation, the 8259A can be described as consisting of four internal registers, as shown in Figure 3.15.

Table 3.11. *Interrupt Priorities*

INTERRUPT	PRIORIY
Divide overflow	Highest
INT n instruction	
INTO (interrupt on overflow)	
NMI (nonmaskable interrupt)	
External interrupt on INTR line	
Single-step	Lowest

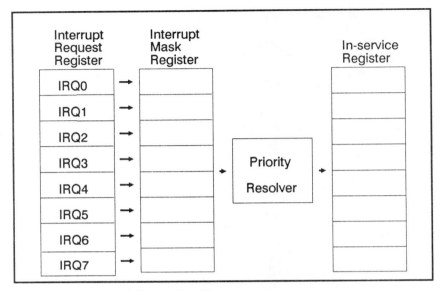

Figure 3.15. *8259A Operation Diagram*

1. The *interrupt request register* (IRR) contains 1 bit for each interrupt channel (IRQ0 to IRQ7). The individual bits reflect which channels are requesting service. The IRR register can be read by the CPU.

2. The *interrupt mask register* (IMR) is an 8-bit register, one for each interrupt level. A bit set prevents the corresponding channel from generating an interrupt (masked).

3. The *priority resolver register* (PR) determines whether the interrupt's priority is sufficient to interrupt an executing interrupt service routine, according to the programmed priority scheme.

4. The *in-service register* (ISR) contains a bit for each interrupt level. This bit is set to indicate that the corresponding interrupt channel is being serviced. The ISR can be read by the CPU.

Intel microprocessors of the iAPX line have two physical lines to signal interrupts, designated as INTR and NMI. The INTR line (interrupt request) is driven by an Intel 8259A interrupt controller. All interrupt-driven external devices must be connected to the 8259A. The original purpose of an NMI line was to warn the microprocessor of an impending catastrophic event, like an imminent power failure, or of a parity error in memory. But some IBM systems use this line for other purposes, for instance, in the IBM PCjr, the NMI line is attached to the keyboard circuit, and in systems with an 8087 or 80287 math coprocessor, the NMI line is used to report an error exception.

The 8259A handles interrupts that originate in up to eight external devices by assigning a unique code to each interrupt source. This code, called the *interrupt type code*, is used by the CPU in locating, in the vector table, the address of the corresponding service routine. Interrupts that originate in the 8259A are maskable; that is, they can be individually enabled and disabled by programming the controller's interrupt mask register (see Figure 3.15). In addition, all external interrupts can be temporarily disabled by clearing the processor's interrupt flag (IF) with a CLI instruction. The STI instruction resets IF, thus reenabling external interrupts. The term *nonmaskable interrupt* is used to designate all interrupts that do not originate in the 8259A interrupt controller and are not affected by the processor's interrupt flag.

In IBM systems that use a single 8259A chip (such as the Personal Computer, the PC XT, the PCjr, and Models 25 and 30 of the PS/2 line), all external interrupts are mapped to eight lines, designated as IRQ0 to IRQ7 (see Figure 3.15). The PC AT and the Micro Channel models of the PS/2 line use two 8259A chips, designated as interrupt controllers 1 and 2. In this case there is a total of 16 interrupt lines, IRQ0 to IRQ15. Since IRQ2 is used to cascade the interrupts from controller number 2, it is not assigned to any specific interrupt. Interrupt mapping for one-controller systems can be seen in Table 3.12. The mapping in two-controller systems is shown in Table 3.13.

Table 3.12. *8259A Interrupt Mapping in One-Controller Systems (PC, PC XT, PCjr, PS/2 Model 25, and PS/2 Model 30)*

LINE	TYPE	ADDRESS	EXTERNAL DEVICE
IRQ0	08H	0020H	Timer channel 0
IRQ1	09H	0024H	Keyboard (unused in PCjr)
IRQ2	0AH	0028H	Color Graphics Adapter (unused in PCjr)
IRQ3	0BH	002CH	Serial port 2 (built-in serial port in PCjr)
IRQ4	0CH	0030H	Serial port 1 (internal modem in PCjr)
IRQ5	0DH	0034H	Fixed disk in PC and XT (vertical retrace in PCjr)
IRQ6	0EH	0038H	Diskette
IRQ7	0FH	003CH	Parallel port 1

3.2.2.2 Programming the 8259A. Programming the 8259A consists of initializing the chip to a certain operation mode and controlling its functions during interrupt processing. Both initialization and control take place through commands sent by the CPU to the 8259A. In IBM microcomputers, each 8259A is addressed through two ports, as shown in Table 3.14. These ports are used for the chip's initialization and control commands.

Table 3.13. *8259A Interrupt Mapping in Two-Controller Systems (PC AT and PS/2 Micro Channel Models)*

Controller Number 1

LINE	TYPE	ADDRESS	EXTERNAL DEVICE
IRQ0	08H	0020H	Timer channel 0
IRQ1	09H	0024H	Keyboard
IRQ2	0AH	0028H	Cascade for controller 2
IRQ3	0BH	002CH	Serial port 2
IRQ4	0CH	0030H	Serial port 1
IRQ5	0DH	0034H	Parallel port 2 in AT Reserved in PS/2 systems
IRQ6	0EH	0038H	Diskette
IRQ7	0FH	003CH	Parallel port 1

Controller Number 2

LINE	TYPE	ADDRESS	EXTERNAL DEVICE
IRQ8	70H	01C0H	Real-time clock
IRQ9	71H	01C4H	Redirected to IRQ2
IRQ10	72H	01C8H	Reserved
IRQ11	73H	01CCH	Reserved
IRQ12	74H	01D0H	Reserved in AT Auxiliary device interrupt in PS/2 systems
IRQ13	75H	01D4H	Math coprocessor
IRQ14	76H	01D8H	Hard disk controller
IRQ15	77H	01DCH	Reserved

There are four initialization commands (designated ICW1 to ICW4) and three operation commands (OCW1 to OCW3). Initialization and operation commands are output to the two access ports for each 8259A (see Table 3.14). The 8259A can differentiate between an initialization sequence and an operation command because an initialization sequence begins with an OUT instruction to the first control port (even-numbered port), in which bit 4 of the

Table 3.14. *8259A Access Ports in IBM Systems*

CONTROLLER	ADDRESS	DESIGNATION
Controller number 1	20H 21H	First access port Second access port
Controller number 2	A0H A1H	First access port Second access port

command byte is set, while operation commands to the first control port must have bit 4 clear.

Figure 3.16 shows the initialization options for the 8259A interrupt controller in IBM systems. Figure 3.17 is a flowchart of the 8259A logic during initialization.

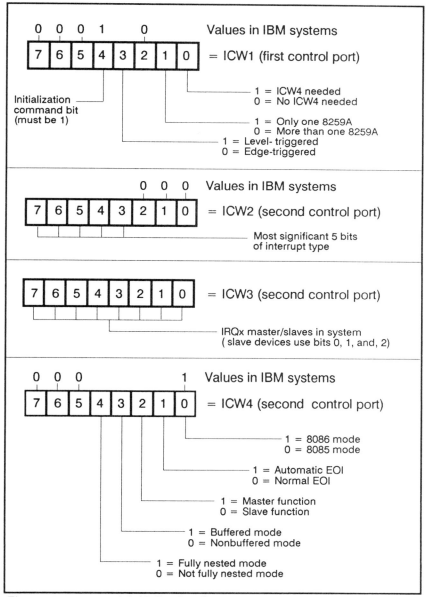

Figure 3.16. *8259A Initialization Command Words*

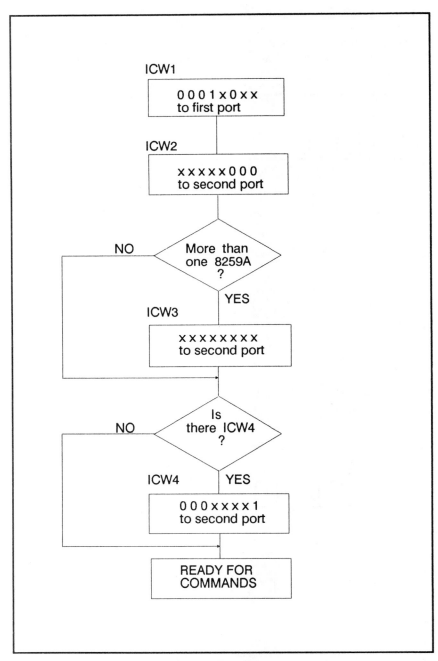

Figure 3.17. *8259A Initialization Flowchart*

The following code fragments correspond with the initialization routines in the IBM Personal Computer and the PC AT BIOS.

```
; Code for initializing the 8259A configured as a single controller
; (PC, PC XT, PCjr, PS/2 Model 25, PS/2 Model 30, and
; compatible systems)
;*********************
;       ICW1
;*********************
        MOV   AL,13H      ; 0 0 0 1 0 0 1 1  = 13H
        ;                        | |   | |_ ICW4 needed
        ;                        | |   |__ Only one
        ;                        | |_____ Edge-triggered
        ;                        |_____ Init mode
        OUT   20H,AL      ; To first control port
;*********************
;       ICW2
;*********************
        MOV   AL,8H       ; Interrupt type 8H to 0FH
        OUT   21H,AL      ; To second control port
; ICW3 not required since there is only one 8259A
;*********************
;       ICW4
;*********************
        MOV   AL,09H      ; 0 0 0 0 1 0 0 1  = 09H
        ;                          | | | |_ 8086 mode
        ;                          | | |___ Normal EOI
        ;                          | |_____ As slave
        ;                          |_____ Buffered mode
        ;                          |_____ Not nested
        OUT   21H,AL      ; To second control port
        .
        .
; Code for initializing the two 8259A controllers configured
; in cascade (PC AT)
;*********************************
;    initialize controller number 1
;*********************************
;*********************
;       ICW1
;*********************
        MOV   AL,11H      ; 0 0 0 1 0 0 0 1  = 11H
        ;                        | |   | |_ ICW4 needed
        ;                        | |   |___ Two 8259As
        ;                        | |_____ Edge-triggered
        ;                        |_____ Init mode
; Note: PS/2 systems use level-triggered interrupts
        OUT   20H,AL      ; To controller number 1 first port
```

```
          JMP    SHORT $ + 2 ; I/O wait
;********************
;     ICW2
;********************
          MOV    AL,8H          ; Interrupt type 8H to 0FH
          OUT    21H,AL         ; To controller number 1 second port
          JMP    SHORT $ + 2 ; I/O wait
;********************
;     ICW3
;********************
          MOV    AL,4H          ; 0 0 0 0 0 1 0 0    = 4H
                                :                |_____ Cascade using
                                :                          IRQ2
          OUT    21H,AL         ; To controller number 1 second port
          JMP    SHORT $ + 2 ; I/O wait
;********************
;     ICW4
;********************
          MOV    AL,01H         ; 0 0 0 0 0 0 0 1 = 09H
                                :               | | | | |_ 8086 mode
                                :               | | | |__ Normal EOI
                                :               | | |_____ Not significant
                                :               | |          in nonbuffered
                                :               | |          mode
                                :               | |        Nonbuffered
                                :               | |_____ 
                                :               |_____ Not nested
          OUT    21H,AL         ; To controller number 1 second port
          JMP    SHORT $ + 2 ; I/O wait
;********************************
;   initialize controller number 2
;********************************
;********************
;     ICW1
;********************
          MOV    AL,11H         ; 0 0 0 1 0 0 0 1 = 11H
                                :         | |     | |_ ICW4 needed
                                :         | |     |__ Two 8259As
                                :         | |_____ Edge-triggered
                                :         |_____ Init mode
; Note: PS/2 systems use level-triggered interrupts
          OUT    0A0H,AL        ; To controller number 2 first port
          JMP    SHORT $ + 2 ; I/O wait
;********************
;     ICW2
;********************
          MOV    AL,70H         ; Interrupt type 70H to 7FH
          OUT    0A1H,AL        ; To controller number 2 second port
          JMP    SHORT $ + 2 ; I/O wait
```

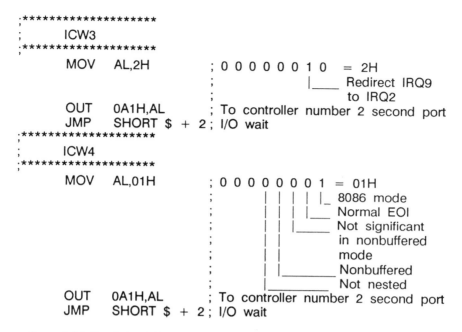

```
;********************
;         ICW3
;********************
        MOV     AL,2H           ; 0 0 0 0 0 0 1 0   = 2H
                                ;               |____ Redirect IRQ9
                                ;                     to IRQ2
        OUT     0A1H,AL         ; To controller number 2 second port
        JMP     SHORT $ + 2     ; I/O wait
;********************
;         ICW4
;********************
        MOV     AL,01H          ; 0 0 0 0 0 0 0 1 = 01H
                                ;         | | | | |_ 8086 mode
                                ;         | | | |___ Normal EOI
                                ;         | | |_____ Not significant
                                ;         | |           in nonbuffered
                                ;         | |           mode
                                ;         | |_____ Nonbuffered
                                ;         |_____ Not nested
        OUT     0A1H,AL         ; To controller number 2 second port
        JMP     SHORT $ + 2     ; I/O wait
```

Once initialized (and if the processor's interrupt flag is set), the 8259A is ready to accept interrupt requests on its eight lines. The interrupt mask register of the 8259A (see Figure 3.15) permits enabling and disabling of the individual interrupt lines. The *first operation command* (OCW1) is used to read or write to the interrupt mask register. This command is output through the second control port, which is mapped to port 21H in one-controller systems and to port A1H in two-controller systems. Figure 3.18 shows the bit map for one-controller and two-controller systems.

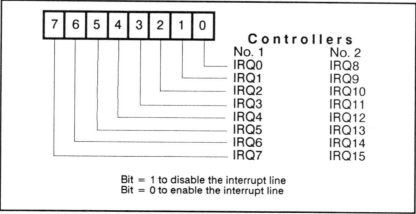

Figure 3.18. *8259A Interrupt Mask Register Bit Map*

It is frequently necessary to enable or disable a specific interrupt line without affecting the remaining lines in the interrupt system. The following code fragment illustrates the processing.

```
; Sample code to enable the 8259A line for printer interrupt
; IRQ7 without affecting setting of the remaining lines
; in controller number 1
        IN      AL,21H          ; Read interrupt mask
        AND     AL,01111111B    ; Clear bit 7
        OUT     21H,AL          ; Replace mask
```

As the 8259A sends an interrupt signal to the processor through the INTR line, it automatically suspends all other interrupts. This explains why the interrupt service routine must signal the 8259A that processing of the interrupt has concluded, so that other interrupts can be allowed. The end of interrupt signal constitutes the *second operation command* (OCW2). This command is output through the first control port, which is mapped to port 20H in one-controller systems and to port A0H in two-controller systems. In IBM microcomputers, the command code is the value 20H. The following code fragment demonstrates the end-of-interrupt command to the 8259A.

```
; Signal end-of-interrupt to controller number 1
        MOV     AL,20H          ; "End of interrupt" code
        OUT     20H,AL          ; To first control port
```

The *third operation command* (OCW3) allows reading of the interrupt request register (IRR) and the in-service register (ISR) in the 8259A. It also contains a polling control bit used in operating additional 8259A controllers that access the CPU through the input/output channel. The bit map for OCW3 can be seen in Figure 3.19.

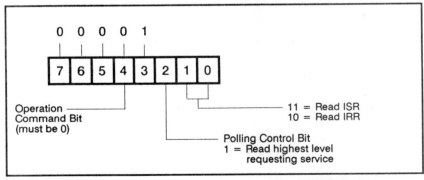

Figure 3.19. *8259A Third Operation Command (OCW3) Bit Map*

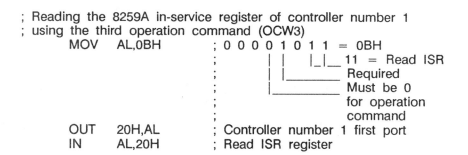

```
; Reading the 8259A in-service register of controller number 1
; using the third operation command (OCW3)
        MOV    AL,0BH      ; 0 0 0 0 1 0 1 1  =  0BH
                           ;          |_|__ 11  =  Read ISR
                           ;         | |_____  Required
                           ;         |_____  Must be 0
                           ;                     for operation
                           ;                     command
        OUT    20H,AL      ; Controller number 1 first port
        IN     AL,20H      ; Read ISR register
```

3.2.3 System Clocks

Every computer system must contain a means of producing the pulse that runs the digital circuits. This clock signal serves also to synchronize the different electronic components in the system so that they will maintain correct time and phase relations with one another. In IBM microcomputers the system clock is external to the microprocessor and its type and speed are determined by the system's CPU. Nevertheless, some Intel microprocessors used in IBM-compatible microcomputers use an on-chip clock generator. The various clock generators can be seen in Table 3.15.

Table 3.15. *Clock Generators for Intel Microprocessors*

	8086	8088	80186	80188	80286	80386
Clock	8284A	8284A	On-chip	On-chip	82284	82384
Speed, MHz	4, 7, 8, 10	4, 7, 8	8, 10, 12.5	8, 10	6, 8, 10 12.5	12.5, 16, 25

3.2.4 Programmable Timers

Many computer operations require some form of synchronization. All IBM microcomputers contain a dedicated IC (or equivalent circuits in a larger electronic device) that provides various timing services. For instance, the IBM Personal Computer, the PC XT, the PCjr, and the PS/2 Model 25 and Model 30 use the Intel 8253 programmable interval timer, while the PC AT employs a similar component designated as the Intel 8254-2. The Micro Channel computers of the PS/2 line are equipped with proprietary IBM circuits. However, these circuits are software-compatible with the 8253 and 8254-2 chips.

3.2.4.1 The Intel 8253/8254 Programmable Interval Timer. The Intel 8253 timer is used in IBM microcomputers that use the 8086 or the 8088 microprocessor (see Section 3.2.4). Microcomputers that use the 80286 or 80386 CPU are equipped with the Intel 8254-2 or with proprietary circuits that are compatible with the 8254. Figure 3.20 is a diagram of the 8253 timer chip.

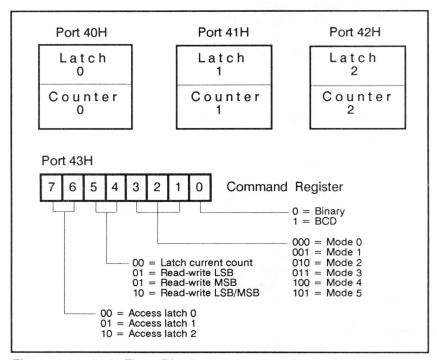

Figure 3.20. *8253 Timer Diagram*

The 8253 timer is driven by the system clock, but the hardware divides the clock beat so as to generate a square wave with a frequency of 1.19318 MHz (1,193,180 times per second). The 8253/8254 timer has three internal and independent counters known as channels 0, 1, and 2 (see Figure 3.20). Each channel has a 16-bit latch register and a 16-bit counter. In operation, each tick of the internal timer (1,193,180 times per second) decrements the value in the counter register for that channel. When the count reaches zero, the channel generates a signal on its output line. Channels 0, 1, and 2 are initialized so that at the end of each counting cycle, the counter register is automatically reloaded with the value stored in the latch.

In addition to the latches and counter registers, the 8253 has a 1-byte command register that is used for programming the chip's operation. The command register is shown in the lower part of Figure 3.20. Bits 6 and 7 of the command register serve to select which access latch is active. Bits 4 and 5 determine how the latching will take place. Note that the latch registers hold one word of data (16 bits), while port input/output operations take place 1 byte at a time. Setting bits 4 and 5 of the command register to the read-write LSB then MSB option allows reading or writing to the latch registers by issuing two consecutive IN or OUT instructions. This is the latching mode enabled during the BIOS initialization of the 8253.

Bits 1, 2, and 3 of the command register serve to select one of six modes in which each channel can operate. Mode 2 is used by the BIOS for timer channel 1, which is dedicated to memory refresh operations in non-Micro Channel systems. Mode 3, which generates a symmetrical wave, is used by the BIOS for timer channels 0 and 2.

The 8253 timer has several preassigned functions in IBM systems:

1. *Timer channel 0* is connected to the IRQ0 interrupt line (see Table 3.12). Each pulse of this channel generates an interrupt type 08H, which is vectored to the BIOS time-of-day clock. This channel is also used in timing diskette motor operations. The pulse rate is approximately 18.2 times per second.

2. *Timer channel 1* is linked to the memory refresh mechanism (DMA controller) on IBM microcomputers that do not use Micro Channel architecture. This channel is undocumented in Micro Channel systems. In PS/2 Models 25 and 30, it is used in system diagnostics. Channel 1 is used in keyboard timing in the PCjr.

3. *Timer channel 2* is routed to the internal speaker and used in generating sounds.

4. *Timer channel 3* is a watchdog timer that can be used to determine if IRQ0 is not being serviced and also in counting operations. This channel exists only in PS/2 Micro Channel systems.

Table 3.16 shows the timer-related interrupts.

Table 3.16. *Timer-Related Interrupts*

TYPE CODE	NAME	OPERATIONS
08H	System timer	Driven by timer channel 0 at a rate of 18.2 times per second. Maintains a count used to determine time of day. Decrements a counter used to turn off the diskette motor. Calls a user routine at interrupt 1CH, on every timer tick.
1AH	Time of day	BIOS service to read and set the internal counters maintained by the system timer.
1CH	User timer	Allows a user-written routine which is called by INT 08H 18.2 times per second.

3.2.4.2 Programming the 8253 Timer. Programming of the 8253/8254 timer takes place in two operations. The first one consists of selecting the channel to be accessed, the latching method, the mode, and the binary or BCD numerical base. The selection is performed by sending the corresponding bit pattern to the command register (see Figure 3.20). The second operation involves storing a divisor word in the corresponding latch register.

The pulse rate for each timer channel is determined by the internal clock rate of 1,193,180 beats per second and by the value stored in the latch register. For example, if the latch register of timer channel 0 is initialized with a value of 4, the 1,193,180 times per second pulse is converted to one-fourth of this value (297,500 times per second). Since the largest number that can be stored in a 16-bit latch register is 65,536, the slowest possible pulse of a timer channel can be calculated by dividing the pulse rate by this maximum:

$$\frac{1,193,180}{65,536} = 18.2 \text{ cycles per second}$$

The actual divisor primed by the BIOS routines into timer channel 0 is 65,636. The output of channel 0 is connected to the IRQ0 interrupt line. For this reason, interrupt 08H, which is the timekeeping routine in the IBM BIOS, receives control 18.2 times per second.

The following code fragment corresponds to the BIOS initialization of the 8253 timer in the IBM Personal Computer.

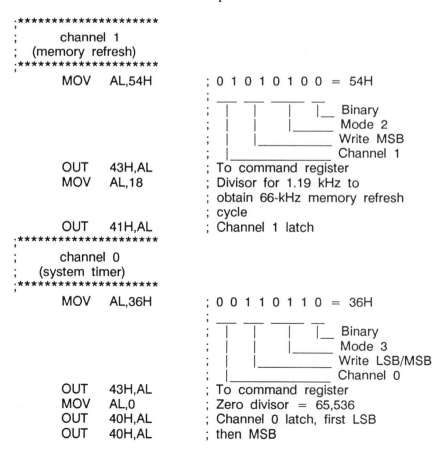

```
;*********************
;        channel 1
;    (memory refresh)
;*********************
        MOV   AL,54H      ; 0 1 0 1 0 1 0 0 = 54H
                          ;
                          ; __ __ __ __ __ __
                          ;  |   |   |   |   |__ Binary
                          ;  |   |   |   |_____ Mode 2
                          ;  |   |   |_____ Write MSB
                          ;  |   |_____ Channel 1
        OUT   43H,AL      ; To command register
        MOV   AL,18       ; Divisor for 1.19 kHz to
                          ; obtain 66-kHz memory refresh
                          ; cycle
        OUT   41H,AL      ; Channel 1 latch
;*********************
;        channel 0
;    (system timer)
;*********************
        MOV   AL,36H      ; 0 0 1 1 0 1 1 0 = 36H
                          ;
                          ; __ __ __ __ __ __
                          ;  |   |   |   |   |__ Binary
                          ;  |   |   |   |_____ Mode 3
                          ;  |   |   |_____ Write LSB/MSB
                          ;  |   |_____ Channel 0
        OUT   43H,AL      ; To command register
        MOV   AL,0        ; Zero divisor = 65,536
        OUT   40H,AL      ; Channel 0 latch, first LSB
        OUT   40H,AL      ; then MSB
```

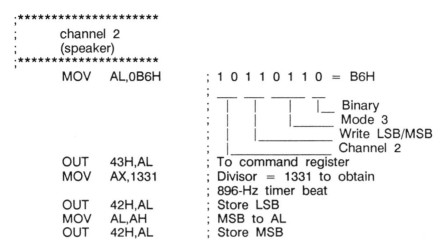

```
;*********************
;      channel 2
;      (speaker)
;*********************
        MOV    AL,0B6H      ; 1 0 1 1 0 1 1 0 = B6H
                            ;  ̄  ̄  ̄  ̄   ̄  ̄  ̄  ̄
                            ;  |  |     |   |_ Binary
                            ;  |  |     |_____ Mode 3
                            ;  |  |_____ Write LSB/MSB
                            ;  |_____ Channel 2
        OUT    43H,AL       ; To command register
        MOV    AX,1331      ; Divisor = 1331 to obtain
                            ; 896-Hz timer beat
        OUT    42H,AL       ; Store LSB
        MOV    AL,AH        ; MSB to AL
        OUT    42H,AL       ; Store MSB
```

The BIOS initialization routines set timer channel 0 to approximately 18.2 cycles per second. However, the programmer can increment this frequency by entering another divisor word for this channel. Because the value 65,536 is the largest number that can be represented in 16 bits, timer channel 0 cannot be made to operate at a slower rate than 18.2 cycles per second. Nevertheless, a program can effectively reduce this frequency by skipping one or more beats.

Many mechanical and digital devices operate at rates faster than 18.2 cycles per second. For instance, dot-matrix printers can output more than 100 characters per second and normal transmission speeds in serial communications exceed 1000 bits per second. To accommodate fast devices, it is possible to accelerate the rate of any timer channel to a maximum of more than one million pulses per second by adjusting the value held in the channel's latch register.

Since timer channel 1 is used in memory refresh, it should not be modified or used for any other purpose. Timer channel 2, normally routed to the speaker, can be modified at will and used for other functions. However, since channel 2 is not linked to a hardware interrupt line, the program will have to poll the channel's counter register.

Because channel 0 is linked to the interrupt system, every time the counter register is decremented to zero, an INT 08H is automatically executed. A program can set a specific time cycle by modifying the value in the latch register, then installing an intercept routine of INT 08H in order to receive control at every beat of the new cycle. However, the programmer using timer channel 0 should consider that its beat is also used by the interrupt 08H service routine to keep the system time-of-day clock and for timing diskette motor operations. If the frequency of timer channel 0 is changed, the diskette's motor shutoff time is altered, with unpredictable results, and the time-of-day counters become useless. These consequences can be avoided by designing an interrupt service routine that maintains 18.2 cycles per second to the original handler, although the interrupt may be taking place at a different rate.

The following formula calculates the divisor required for obtaining a certain frequency on a timer channel.

$$\frac{1,193,180}{\text{Desired frequency}} = \text{new divisor}$$

For example, to change the frequency of timer channel 0 from the installed 18.2 cycles per second to 100 cycles per second,

$$\frac{1,193,180}{100} = 11,932 \text{ (approximately)}$$

The calculations can also be based on the frequency produced by the maximum divisor value (65,536). The following code fragment shows the encoding for changing the frequency of timer channel 0 from 18.2 cycles per second to 182 cycles per second.

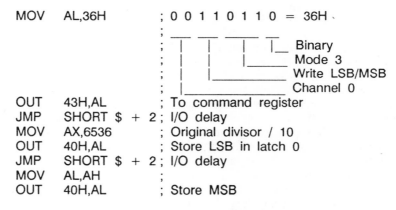

```
MOV    AL,36H         ; 0 0 1 1 0 1 1 0  =  36H
                      ;   ___ ___ ___ ___
                      ;    |   |    |   |__ Binary
                      ;    |   |    |_____ Mode 3
                      ;    |   |_____ Write LSB/MSB
                      ;    |_____ Channel 0
OUT    43H,AL         ; To command register
JMP    SHORT $ + 2    ; I/O delay
MOV    AX,6536        ; Original divisor / 10
OUT    40H,AL         ; Store LSB in latch 0
JMP    SHORT $ + 2    ; I/O delay
MOV    AL,AH          ;
OUT    40H,AL         ; Store MSB
```

To adjust the system to the increased speed of timer channel 0, it is necessary to find a way to maintain a rate of 18.2 cycles per second to the BIOS original interrupt 8 handler. This can be accomplished by establishing a secondary counter, which is primed with the factor of the frequency increase. The new intercept routine will decrement this secondary counter on every cycle. When the counter reaches zero, execution is transferred to the original BIOS routine. Note that interrupt 1CH is called by INT 08H on exit from this service. For this reason it cannot be used as an intercept.

3.2.4.3 Programming the PS/2 Timer.   The PS/2 Micro Channel timer is compatible with the Intel 8253/8254 programmable interval timers used in non-Micro Channel systems. Software written for the 8253 and 8254 chips is generally compatible with the Micro Channel hardware. However, as happens with the PC AT, back-to-back IN or OUT commands may not permit enough recovery. This problem can be solved by inserting a short jump between instructions, as shown in Section 3.2.1.3. The same problem is found with IN and OUT instructions followed by STI. The following additional differences between the two systems can be noted:

1. The Micro Channel timer does not document channel 1, which is used for memory refresh in non-Micro Channel systems.

2. The Micro Channel timer contains channel 3, which has no equivalent in non-Micro Channel systems.

Channel 3 in the Micro Channel timer contains its own command register, accessible through port 47H, as shown in Figure 3.21. The commands available for channel 3 are a subset of the commands for channels 0 and 2. The following differences can be noted in the commands active for channels 0 and 2 and for channel 3:

1. The binary/BCD select bit is not active for channel 3, which always operates in the binary mode.

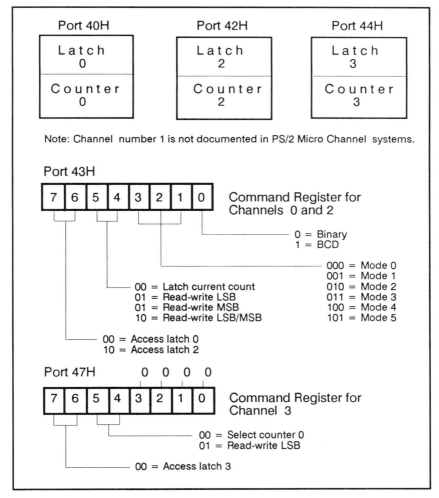

Figure 3.21. *PS/2 Micro Channel Timer Diagram*

2. The mode select bits (1, 2, and 3) are not active for channel 3, which operates in a mode equivalent to mode 0 of the 8253 component.

3. The channel 3 latch and counter registers are 8 bits wide. This determines that the functions of command bits 4 and 5, related to the most significant byte (MSB), are not active in the channel 3 commands.

4. Bits 6 and 7 must be zero in the channel 3 command byte, since no other register can be selected through this command port in its present implementation.

Note that mode 0 is not used in the IBM implementations of the 8253 and 8254 timers. While modes 2 and 3 (used in channels 0 and 2) provide periodic signals (the counter register reloads automatically at the end of each counting cycle), mode 0 continues to decrement below zero.

In the default state, channel 3 is initialized as a watchdog timer for channel 0. This function may be used to detect if the IRQ0 interrupt line is not being serviced. BIOS service number 195 (C3H) of INT 15H allows enabling and disabling the watchdog function. When the watchdog function is disabled, channel 3 can be used as an 8-bit downcounter for program delays and for other functions.

3.2.5 Sound Systems

All IBM microcomputers are capable of generating sound through an on-board speaker. Although the individual hardware components vary in different systems, IBM has maintained software compatibility in sound generation from the original Personal Computer to the PS/2 line. One exception is the IBM PCjr, which, in addition to the standard sound hardware, is equipped with a secondary sound system which includes an analog multiplexer and a Texas Instruments sound generation chip (76496N). This custom audio system of the PCjr has three programmable frequencies that can be used to mix simultaneous musical notes, with independently adjustable volume, as well as a noise source for creating special effects. The sound generation capabilities of the PCjr are unequalled in any other model of the PC or PS/2 line.

The sound generation hardware can be combined to produce sound by two different methods, as can be seen in Figure 3.22. In *method number 1*, the CPU programs timer channel 2 to generate a square wave, which is gated to the speaker through bits 0 and 1 of port 61H. The tone is determined by the frequency to which timer channel 2 is set (see Section 3.2.4.1). In *method number 2*, the CPU generates a wave by toggling bit 1 of port 61H on and off. A software delay loop for the on and off cycles determines the frequency of the waves, and consequently the tone produced by the speaker. When method number 2 is used, the speaker is disconnected from timer channel 2 by clearing bit 0 in port 61H.

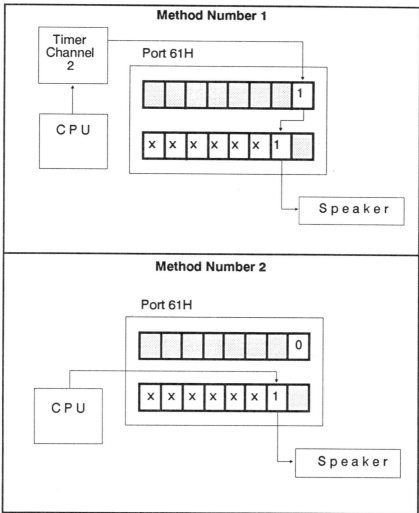

Figure 3.22. *Sound Generation Diagrams for IBM Systems*

```
;****************************************************************
;            sound  generation  using  method  number  1
;****************************************************************
;
;****************
;    equates
;****************
;
;
; Formula  for  calculating  divisor  word:
;                1,193,180
;            – – – – – – – – –  =  divisor  word
;            Desired  frequency
;
LOW_TONE      EQU    14914          ; Divisor for 80-Hz wave
MED_TONE      EQU    1989           ; Divisor for 600-Hz wave
HIGH_TONE     EQU    397            ; Divisor for 3000-Hz wave
;
; Note: The  human  audible  range  is  approximately  20  to  20,000 Hz
              .
              .
              .
; Call  sound  procedures  to  generate  low,  medium,  and  high  tones
        MOV    BX,LOW_TONE
        CALL   SPKR_ON
        CALL   SPKR_OFF
;
        MOV    BX,MED_TONE
        CALL   SPKR_ON
        CALL   SPKR_OFF
;
        MOV    BX,HIGH_TONE
        CALL   SPKR_ON
        CALL   SPKR_OFF
              .
              .
              .
;**************************************
;     sound  generation  procedures
;          using  timer  channel  2
;**************************************
;*****************
;    speaker  on
;*****************
SPKR_ON                PROC  NEAR
; On  entry, BX  holds  divisor  for  desired  frequency
;            CX  holds  counter  for  tone  duration
;
; Set  bits  0  and  1  in  port  61H
        IN     AL,61H          ; Read current port status
```

```
        OR      AL,03          ; xxxx xx11 bit pattern
        JMP     SHORT $ + 2 ; I/O delay
        OUT     61H,AL         ; To port
; Program timer channel 2
        MOV     AL,0B6H        ; 1 0 1 1 0 1 1 0
                               ;
                               ;  __ __ __   __ __
                               ;  |  |  |    |  |__ Binary
                               ;  |  |  |    |_____ Mode 3
                               ;  |  |  |_____ LSB then MSB
                               ;  |  |_____ Channel 2
        JMP     SHORT $ + 2
        OUT     43H,AL         ; To 8253 command register
; Enter divisor
        MOV     AL,BL          ; LSB
        JMP     SHORT $ + 2
        OUT     42H,AL         ; To timer channel 2
        MOV     AL,BH          ; MSB
        JMP     SHORT $ + 2
        OUT     42H,AL
; Use TIME_DELAY procedure to wait 1 s (18 timer beats)
        MOV     BX,18          ; Parameter passed to counter
        CALL    TIME_DELAY
        RET
SPKR_ON     ENDP
;****************
;    speaker off
;****************
;
SPKR_OFF    PROC  NEAR
;
; Turn off speaker and wait
; Reset bits 0 and 1 of port 61H to turn off the speaker
        IN      AL,61H
        AND     AL,0FCH        ; xxxx xx00 bit pattern
        JMP     SHORT $ + 2
        OUT     61H,AL
; Use TIME_DELAY procedure to wait 2 s (36 timer beats)
        MOV     BX,36          ; Parameter passed to counter
        CALL    TIME_DELAY
        RET
SPKR_OFF    ENDP
;****************
;    time delay
;****************
;
TIME_DELAY  PROC  NEAR
; Time delay using system time-of-day clock at INT 1AH
; On entry:
;           BX = timer counts to skip in 1/18 s
;                minimum delay is 1/18 s
```

```
;
        MOV     AH,0            ; Read timer counter service
                                ; request
        INT     1AH
; DX  =  low-order byte of timer counter
        ADD     BX,DX           ; BX = counts to skip plus
                                ; present count
DELAY_LOOP:
        INT     1AH             ; Call service again
        CMP     BX,DX           ; Compare to end count
        JNZ     DELAY_LOOP      ; Repeat if not at end
        RET
TIME_DELAY     ENDP
```

Although method number 2 of sound generation (see Figure 3.22) is more flexible than method number 1, it has some important drawbacks. In the first place, in method number 2, the processor takes a direct part in the sound generation process and cannot attend to other matters.

In the second place, method number 2 uses the CPU as a timing device for generating the sound wave. Since different processors operate at different speeds, the frequency and duration of the tone change in different systems. For instance, the instructions which generate a high tone of 1 s duration in an IBM Model 70 (80386 CPU) will create a much lower tone of approximately 3 s duration in an IBM Personal Computer or PC XT (8088 CPU). Compensating for these differences requires elaborate programming.

Finally, in method number 2, interrupts must be disabled while the sound is being produced. If they are not, the system timer interrupt, which takes place 18.2 times per second, creates considerable interference with the generated sound. Disabling interrupts can affect the system clock count and its dependent functions.

```
;*************************************************************
;          sound generation using method number 2
;*************************************************************
        MOV     DX,2000         ; Duration of the tone
        IN      AL,61H          ; Read port 61H
        AND     AL,11111110B    ; Clear timer bit to disconnect
                                ; speaker from timer channel 2
        JMP     SHORT $ + 2     ; I/O delay
        OUT     61H,AL
        CLI                     ; Interrupts off to avoid interference
ON_OFF_CYCLE:
;*******************
;     speaker on
;*******************
        OR      AL,00000010B    ; Turn on speaker
        OUT     61H,AL          ; At port 61H
        JMP     SHORT $ + 2     ; I/O delay
```

```
        MOV    CX,300              ; Frequency of tone
SPEAKER_ON:
        LOOP   SPEAKER_ON   ; Delay while speaker on
;*******************
;   speaker off
;*******************
        AND    AL,11111101B  ; Turn off speaker
        OUT    61H,AL
        JMP    SHORT $ + 2 ; I/O delay
        MOV    CX,300              ; Frequency of tone
SPEAKER_OFF:
        LOOP   SPEAKER_OFF ; Delay while speaker off
; Repeat on-off cycle while DX not zero
        DEC    DX                  ; Decrement tone time count
        JNZ    ON_OFF_CYCLE
        STI                        ; Interrupts back on
```

Chapter

4

Video Components

4.0 IBM Microcomputer Video Systems

The video display hardware in IBM microcomputers has undergone many
changes with the different models of the PC and PS/2 lines. Some systems have
video display options that can be selected by the buyer. Other systems come
equipped with a basic video hardware, and the user's options are limited to
certain refinements. Finally, a few systems are made up of standard video
elements over which the user has little or no control.

In the Personal Computer, the PC XT, and the PC AT, the buyer configures
the video system according to need. The original options included an alphanumeric monochrome display and a color graphics display. Several high-resolution graphics alternatives for these systems have been marketed by IBM and by
other companies.

The PCjr, the Portable PC, and all the models of the PS/2 line come equipped
with a video system that is part of the motherboard. However, in the PS/2 models
the user has certain configuration and upgrade options beyond the off-the-shelf
hardware.

Most video displays used in the PC and PS/2 lines are memory-mapped. The
exception is the 8514/A display adapter while operating in the advanced function mode. In memory-mapped video displays, a part of the system's memory
space is dedicated to video functions. This area can be reached both by the
8086/8088 microprocessor and by the electronic components that handle the
actual screen display operations. For this reason it has been called a dual-ported
system. Because of their relatively slow response, memory-mapped displays are
not well suited for animated graphics applications.

Table 4.1. BIOS Video Modes in the IBM Microcomputers

MODE	TYPE	DEFINITION	MONO OR COLOR	BUFFER ADDRESS	BUFFER SIZE	CHARACTER BOX SIZE	MDA	CGA	EGA	PCjr	VGA	MCGA
								PC LINE			PS/2 LINE	
0	Text	40 x 25	B & W	B8000H	2K	8 x 8		X	X	X	X	X
1	Text	40 x 25	Color	B8000H	2K	8 x 8		X	X	X	X	X
2	Text	80 x 25	B & W	B8000H	2K	8 x 8		X	X	X	X	X
3	Text	80 x 25	Color	B8000H	4K	8 x 8		X	X	X	X	X
4	APA	320 x 200	Color	B8000H	8K	8 x 8		X	X	X	X	X
5	APA	320 x 200	B & W	B8000H	8K	8 x 8		X	X	X	X	X
6	APA	640 x 200	B & W	B8000H	16K	8 x 8		X	X	X	X	X
7	Text	80 x 25	B & W	B0000H	4K	9 x 14	X		X		X	
8	APA	160 x 200	Color	B8000H	16K	8 x 8				X		
9	APA	320 x 200	Color	B8000H	32K	8 x 8				X		
10	APA	640 x 200	Color	B8000H	32K	8 x 8				X		
13	APA	320 x 200	Color	A0000H	8K	8 x 8			X		X	
14	APA	640 x 200	Color	A0000H	16K	8 x 8			X		X	
15	APA	640 x 350	B & W	A0000H	28K	8 x 14			X		X	
16	APA	640 x 350	Color	A0000H	28K	8 x 14			X		X	
17	APA	640 x 480	Color	A0000H	38K	8 x 16					X	X
18	APA	640 x 480	Color	A0000H	38K	8 x 16					X	
19	APA	640 x 480	Color	A0000H	38K	8 x 8					X	X

Abbreviations: MDA = Monochrome Display Adapter CGA = Color Graphics Adapter MCGA = PS/2 Multicolor Graphics Array
EGA = Enhanced Graphics Adapter VGA = PS/2 Video Graphics Array

4.0.1 Video Modes

The original version of the IBM BIOS classified the possible settings of the video hardware into display modes, which are numbered consecutively starting with mode 0. The modes are classified as alphanumeric or graphics. The alphanumeric modes, also called text or alpha modes, are capable of displaying the individual, predesigned characters of the IBM character set (see Figure 4.3). The graphics modes, also known as all-points addressable or APA modes, allow control of the individual screen dots that constitute the display surface.

The definition of the text modes is usually expressed in terms of the number of characters per screen row and the total number of rows displayed. In the APA modes, the definition is the number of screen dots (called pixels) in each row by the number of pixel rows on each screen. Some video modes are in color, while others can display only monochrome images. Monochrome modes are also called black-and-white. Table 4.1 lists the fundamental characteristics of each video mode.

In an effort to provide greater flexibility, Operating System/2 does not use the BIOS number codes for the video display modes. Under OS/2, display modes are identified by the following characteristics:

1. Mode type
2. Number of colors
3. Number of text columns
4. Number of text rows
5. Number of pixels per row
6. Number of pixel rows

Table 4.2 shows the display modes supported by OS/2. Table 4.3 refers to the high-resolution graphics modes.

4.1 Video Systems of the PC Line

Most computers of the PC line, namely the PC, PC XT, and PC AT, require plug-in adapters for the video functions. The following are among the better known video adapter cards used in the PC line:

1. *The Monochrome Display Adapter by IBM (MDA)*. The MDA is a black-and-white card that can be installed in all computers of the PC line, except the PCjr.
2. *The Color Graphics Adapter by IBM (CGA)*. This was the first color and graphics card offered for the PC line.
3. *The Enhanced Graphics Adapter by IBM (EGA)*. This is a color graphics card designed to improve the graphics quality and overcome the problems of its predecessor, the Color Graphics Adapter.
4. *The Professional Graphics Controller by IBM*. This is a high-quality graphics card intended mainly for technical applications that require graphics with higher definition than those that can be obtained with the CGA and the EGA.

Table 4.2. *OS/2 VIO Display Modes*

					TEXT ELEMENTS		
BIOS MODE	TYPE	MONO/ COLOR	NUMBER OF COLORS	RESOLUTION	COLUMNS	ROWS	CELL
0	Text	B&W	16	320 x 200	40	25	8 x 8
	Text	B&W	16	320 x 350	40	43	8 x 14
	Text	B&W	16	360 x 400	40	50	9 x 16
1	Text	Color	16	320 x 200	40	25	8 x 8
	Text	Color	16	320 x 350	40	43	8 x 14
	Text	Color	16	360 x 400	40	50	9 x 16
2	Text	B&W	16	640 x 200	80	25	8 x 8
	Text	B&W	16	640 x 350	80	43	8 x 14
	Text	B&W	16	720 x 400	80	50	9 x 16
3	Text	Color	16	640 x 200	80	25	8 x 8
	Text	Color	16	640 x 350	80	43	8 x 14
	Text	Color	16	720 x 400	80	50	9 x 16
4	APA	Color	4	320 x 200			
5	APA	Color	2	320 x 200			
6	APA	Color	2	640 x 200			
7	Text	B&W		720 x 350	80	25	9 x 14
	Text	B&W		720 x 400	80	25	9 x 16
13	APA	Color	16	320 x 200			
14	APA	Color	4	640 x 200			
15	APA	Color	2	640 x 350			
16	APA	Color	16	640 x 350			
17	APA	Color	2	640 x 480			
18	APA	Color	16	640 x 480			
19	APA	Color	256	320 x 200			

5. *The Hercules Graphics Card by Hercules Computer Technology*. This card makes possible high-resolution graphics on the IBM monochrome display.

6. *The VGA cards*. These cards, manufactured by IBM and by other manufacturers, allow certain models of the PC line to be upgraded to the VGA graphics standard of the PS/2 line.

7. *The 8514/A Display Adapter by IBM*. This adapter can be considered the PS/2 version of the Professional Graphics Controller. When equipped with the optional memory expansion, the 8514/A can address 1024 X 768 pixels in 256 colors.

Table 4.3. *IBM High-Resolution APA Graphic Modes*

MODE	NUMBER OF COLORS	ALPHA BOX SIZE	TEXT LINES	BUFFER ADDRESS	PAGES	DEFINITION
EGA and VGA modes						
13	16	8 x 8	40 x 25	A0000H	8	320 by 200
14	16	8 x 8	80 x 25	A0000H	4	640 by 200
15	—	8 x 14	80 x 25	A0000H	2	640 by 350
16	16	8 x 14	80 x 25	A0000H	2	640 by 350
MCGA and VGA mode						
17	2	8 x 16	80 x 30	A0000H	1	640 by 480
VGA-only modes						
18	16	8 x 16	80 x 30	A0000H	1	640 by 480
19	256	8 x 8	40 x 25	A0000H	1	320 by 200

A few models of the PC line have video systems that are furnished as standard hardware. These are the PCjr, the PC Convertible, and the Portable PC. On the other hand, all models of the PS/2 line come equipped with integrated display support that includes color and graphics capabilities. On both lines, PC and PS/2, there is some flexibility in the selection of display monitors.

4.1.1 The Monochrome Display Adapter

The Monochrome Display Adapter was the original text display card distributed by IBM. This card, sold as a monochrome display and printer adapter, can display the entire range of alphanumeric and graphic characters in the IBM character set (see Figure 4.3). However, the IBM MDA card cannot control the individual screen pixels, whereas the Hercules Graphics Card performs all the monochrome operations of the MDA and, in addition, can operate the display in a bit-mapped graphics mode. The Hercules card includes a parallel printer port, as does the MDA. Both cards are compatible with the IBM PC, PC XT, and PC AT.

The Monochrome Display Adapter is used with a monochrome monitor of long-persistence P39 phosphor. The adapter uses the Motorola 6845 CRT controller to provide the timing and control signals for the display. The MDA contains 4K of memory, starting at absolute address B0000H. This value is shifted right 4 bits when used as a base in a segment register, thus becoming B000H. Video display memory contains 2000 character bytes and 2000 attribute bytes. The adapter can address 4000 of its 4096 bytes (4K). The remaining 96 bytes, although not display memory, can be accessed by the CPU. Figure 4.1 is a memory map of the video buffer in the Monochrome Display Adapter.

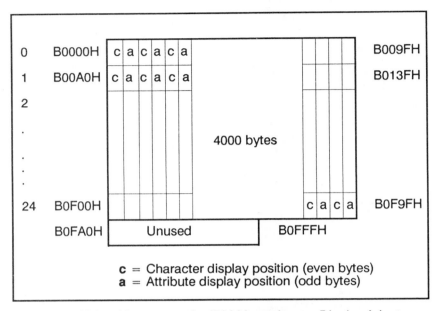

Figure 4.1 *Video Memory on the IBM Monochrome Display Adapter*

The Monochrome Display Adapter is classified as an alphanumeric display. A character table in ROM contains the bit map for each ASCII or graphic character that can be displayed (see Figure 4.3). The MDA character set cannot be changed, except by installing a new ROM chip. Special video circuitry operated by the 6845 CRT controller outputs these bit patterns to the screen. Figure 4.2 shows the bit patterns for the letter A in both the Monochrome Display Adapter and the Color Graphics Adapter. The hexadecimal codes listed to the right of each character correspond to those in the ROM bit maps.

The graphic characters in the range B0H to DFH were designed for constructing screen boxes and for shading screen areas. Although the character generator does not include bit maps for the entire rectangle of dots in these graphic characters, the hardware fills in the empty spaces so that uninterrupted shades and lines are shown on the screen. All the illustrations in this book were composed using the IBM character set and printed on a Hewlett-Packard LaserJet Series II printer. All the alphanumeric and graphic characters in the ROM set can be seen in Figure 4.3.

The symbols in the IBM character set can be classified as follows:

1. The ASCII characters. These include the letters of the alphabet, the Arabic numerals, and conventional symbols (20H to 7FH).
2. Four playing card suits (03H to 06H).
3. Two genetic symbols (0BH and 0CH).
4. Two musical notes (0DH and 0EH).
5. Two proofreader's marks (14H and 15H).

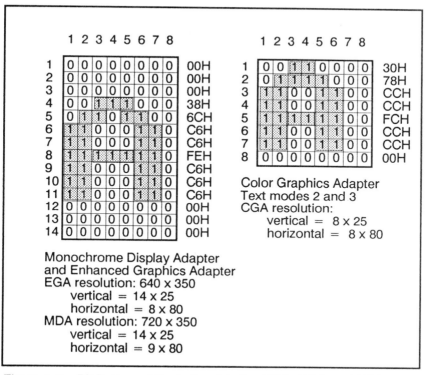

Figure 4.2. *Bit Pattern of the Letter A in the MDA, CGA, and EGA*

6. An assortment of drawing symbols, including circles, arrows, and faces.

7. Letters and symbols for the Spanish, French, and German alphabets.

8. Special characters for drawing boxes and lines (B3H to DFH).

9. Shading symbols (B0H to B2H).

10. Mathematical and engineering symbols (F0H to FDH).

11. An assortment of Greek letters (E1H to EDH).

12. Symbols for yen, pounds, cents, fractions, and others.

The hardware in the Monochrome Display Adapter appears to the programmer as four input and output ports, as shown in Figure 4.4.

Figure 4.1 shows that each character is encoded in two video buffer bytes. The first buffer byte (marked with the letter c) holds the encoding (according to Figure 4.3) for the character in the top left screen position. The following buffer byte (marked with the letter a) holds a code that determines how the character will be displayed. This code is usually called the *attribute*. Each succeeding even byte in the video buffer contains the character code for the corresponding screen position, and each odd byte contains the attribute for the preceding character. The bit map for the attribute byte in the Monochrome Display Adapter can be seen in Figure 4.5.

	Characters ØH to 7FH						
Hex	**Ø**	**1**	**2**	**3**	**4**	**5**	**6**	**7**
Ø		►		Ø	@	P	`	p
1	☺	◄	!	1	A	Q	a	q
2	●	↕	"	2	B	R	b	r
3	♥	‼	#	3	C	S	c	s
4	♦	¶	$	4	D	T	d	t
5	♣	§	%	5	E	U	e	u
6	♠	▬	&	6	F	V	f	v
7	•	↨	'	7	G	W	g	w
8	◘	↑	(	8	H	X	h	x
9	○	↓	)	9	I	Y	i	y
A	◙	→	*	:	J	Z	j	z
B	♂	←	+	;	K	[	k	{
C	♀	∟	,	<	L	\	l	¦
D	♪	↔	-	=	M	]	m	}
E	♫	▲	.	>	N	^	n	~
F	☼	▼	/	?	O	_	o	Δ

Figure 4.3. *IBM Character Set*

Characters 8ØH to FFH								
Hex	8	9	A	B	C	D	E	F
Ø	Ç	É	á	░	└	╨	α	≡
1	ü	æ	í	▒	┴	╤	β	±
2	é	Æ	ó	▓	┬	╥	Γ	≥
3	â	ô	ú	│	├	╙	π	≤
4	ä	ö	ñ	┤	─	╘	Σ	⌠
5	à	ò	Ñ	╡	┼	╒	σ	⌡
6	å	û	ª	╢	╞	╓	μ	÷
7	ç	ù	º	╖	╟	╫	τ	≈
8	ê	ÿ	¿	╕	╚	╪	Φ	○
9	ë	Ö	⌐	╣	╔	┘	Θ	∙
A	è	Ü	¬	║	╩	┌	Ω	·
B	ï	¢	½	╗	╦	█	δ	√
C	î	£	¼	╝	╠	▄	∞	ⁿ
D	ì	¥	¡	╜	═	█	φ	²
E	Ä	₧	«	╛	╬	█	∈	■
F	Å	ƒ	»	┐	╧	▀	∩	

Figure 4.3. *IBM Character Set* (*continued*)

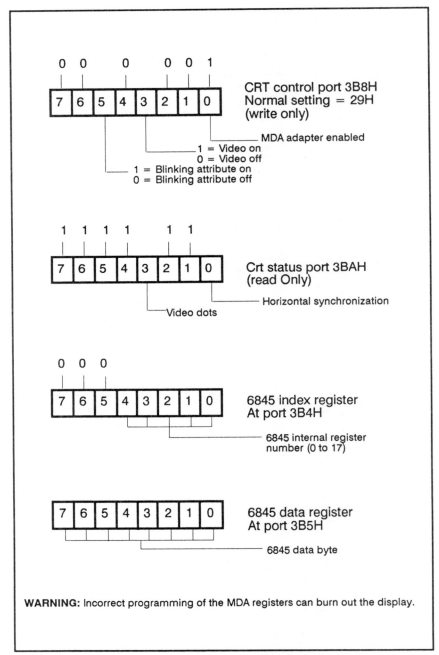

Figure 4.4. *Monochrome Display Adapter Programmable Registers*

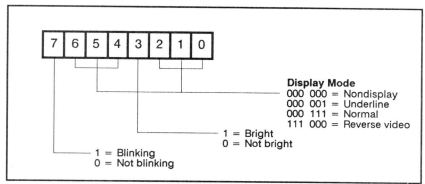

Figure 4.5. *MDA Attribute Byte Bit Codes*

4.1.2 The Color Graphics Adapter

The CGA was the first color and graphics card developed and distributed by IBM for the Personal Computer. The card displays in the following modes:

1. *Mode 0.* 40 by 25 black-and-white alphanumeric mode. The text characters are displayed in 16 shades of grey. Characters are double width, and only 40 can be fitted on a screen line. This mode is not compatible with the Monochrome Display Adapter.

2. *Mode 1.* 40 by 25 color alphanumeric mode. Double-width characters in the same format as mode 0, but in color. This mode is not compatible with the Monochrome Display Adapter.

3. *Mode 2.* 80 by 25 black-and-white alphanumeric mode. The text characters are displayed in 16 shades of grey. 80 characters are displayed per screen line. The screen structure in this mode is compatible with that of the Monochrome Display Adapter.

4. *Mode 3.* 80 by 25 color alphanumeric mode. The text characters are displayed with 16 possible foreground colors and 8 possible background colors. The screen structure in this mode is compatible with that of the Monochrome Display Adapter.

5. *Modes 4, 5, and 6.* These are the graphics modes. In these modes the programmer can control the state of each individual screen dot, also called a picture element or pixel. Mode 4 is in color, and modes 5 and 6 are in monochrome.

Although the CGA can be used with a standard television set, it performs best when used with an RGB color monitor. Timing and control signals are provided by a Motorola 6845 CRT controller identical to the one used in the Monochrome Display Adapter. The Motorola 6845 CRT controller is discussed in Section 4.4.1. Figure 4.6 shows the mapping of video memory in the Color Graphics Adapter.

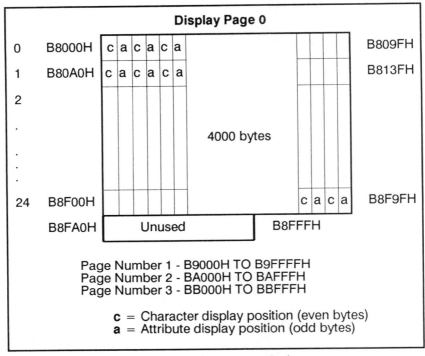

Figure 4.6. *CGA Video Memory (80 x 25 modes)*

The CGA contains 16K of memory, which is four times the memory in the Monochrome Display Adapter. Since only 4K are needed to fill the video screen in an alphanumeric mode, the adapter can simultaneously hold enough data for four full screens (see Figure 4.6). These individual memory areas are called *display pages*. The programmer can select which of the four pages is displayed at a given time. The absolute address of the video buffer in the CGA is B8000H. The segment base corresponding to this physical address is B800H. Programs that access screen memory directly must take into account the different locations of video memory in the MDA and the CGA.

Video memory in the CGA is structured in consecutive character and attribute bytes, as described in Section 4.1.1 for the Monochrome Display Adapter. In the monochrome modes, the only difference in the bit patterns of the CGA and the MDA is that the underline attribute is not available in the CGA. In the color modes, bits 0 to 6 of the CGA attribute byte are used to control the 16 foreground and 8 background colors of the character cell. The bit map for the attribute byte in the CGA and EGA alphanumeric modes can be seen in Figure 4.7.

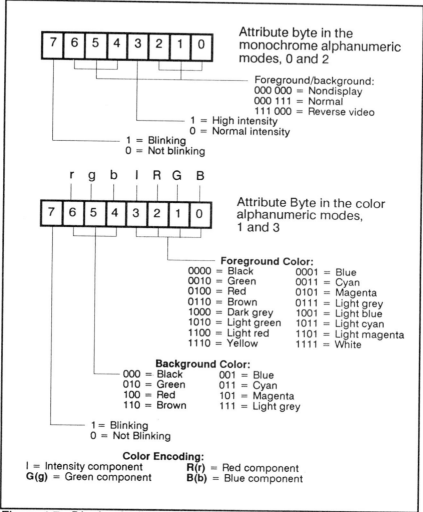

Figure 4.7. *Display Attributes in CGA and EGA Alphanumeric Modes*

Figure 4.2 shows the bit maps for the letter A in the Monochrome Display Adapter and the Color Graphics Adapter. It is evident from the number of picture elements used to display the letters that the definition of the CGA is considerably lower than that of the monochrome equivalent. This lower resolution is the cause of a certain graininess in the display which has often been found objectionable for applications that require prolonged screen observation.

4.1.2.1 Other CGA Registers. To the programmer, the CGA appears as three programmable ports, two registers that serve as the light pen latch, a Motorola 6845 CRT controller, and 16K of on-board video memory. Figure 4.8 shows the bit structure of the mode and the color select registers. Figure 4.9 shows the CGA status and 6845 access registers.

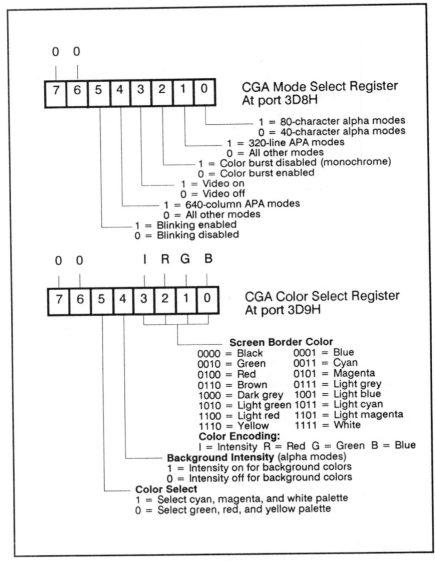

Figure 4.8. *CGA Mode and Color Select Registers*

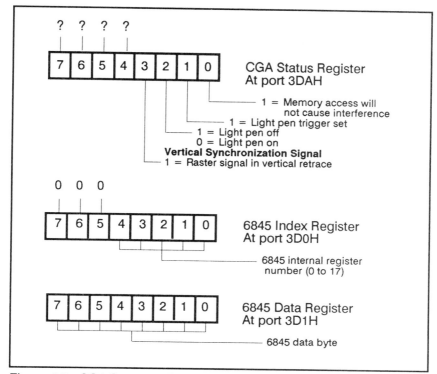

Figure 4.9. *CGA Status and 6845 Access Registers*

4.1.2.2 Preventing CGA Snow.

Alphanumeric programs that directly address the video memory of the Color Graphics Adapter must deal with an interference problem that results when the CPU and the video controller attempt to gain access to the buffer simultaneously. The visible effect of this interference, sometimes called *snow*, consists of dots that appear to move across the screen.

One solution to this interference problem is to require that microprocessor access to the screen buffer area be timed with the retrace phase of the CRT refresh cycle. Note that this problem does not affect the Monochrome Display Adapter, the Enhanced Graphics Adapter, the PCjr, or video systems of the PS/2 line. Neither does it affect the Color Graphics Adapter in the graphic modes.

Synchronization of buffer access and the refresh cycle must take place on a character-by-character basis. This timing requirement brings about much slower execution of the display functions. The resulting "sluggishness" is not apparent in routines that display individual characters, or even short messages, but it becomes quite evident during screen operations that involve moving a large number of characters, such as screen scrolling.

Confronted with the dilemma of interference versus slowness, the designers of the IBM BIOS opted for turning off the display during buffer update. But the CRT blinks every time the display is turned off, and this effect is perhaps more disturbing than the original problem.

To turn off the video display, the code must access the CGA internal registers. The following code fragment turns off the video function during the retrace cycle. This code does not operate satisfactorily in hardware different from the CGA.

Note that the techniques illustrated in the following code fragments were coded for maximum speed of execution. The register addresses of the CRT controller are loaded directly into the DX register. This is permissible because we can safely assume that only the Color Graphics Adapter is subject to access synchronization problems.

```
; The base address of the 6845 CRT controller in CGA systems
; is port 3D4H. The CRT status port is at 3DAH
        MOV    DX,3DAH        ; CGA status port
WAIT:
        IN     AL,DX          ; Get status byte
        TEST   AL,00001000B   ; Bit 3 is vertical retrace bit
        JZ     WAIT           ; Bit not on, keep waiting
; CRT is in the vertical retrace cycle
        SUB    DX,2           ; 6845 mode select register is
                              ; 3D8H
        MOV    AL,00100101B   ; Bits 0, 2, and 5 on and video
                              ; disable bit (number 3) off
        OUT    DX,AL          ; Video display off
; CRT is OFF. Video buffer access can now take place
;
;
; After access to buffer has finished, the CRT must be turned on
; The value used by the BIOS for setting the mode select register
; is stored in the BIOS table at offset 0065H
        PUSH   ES             ; Save segment base
        MOV    AX,0040H       ; BIOS table segment to AX
        MOV    ES,AX          ; And to ES
        MOV    AL,ES:[0065H]  ; Get byte from table
        POP    ES             ; Restore segment address
        MOV    DX,3D8H        ; CGA mode select register
        OUT    DX,AL          ; Video back on
;
```

Another way of avoiding CGA snow is to time each character moved into the buffer with the retrace phase of the CRT refresh cycle. In this case, the program must test the low bit of the status register to determine when it is safe for the CPU to access the buffer (see Figure 4.9). Because of the brevity of the retrace cycle, only one character can be output during each iteration. This explains why the option of turning off the CRT is sometimes preferred in time-critical applications.

```
; Timing of CPU access to the video buffer with the horizontal
; retrace cycle of the 6845 CRT controller in the CGA card
; The code assumes that the character to be displayed is in
; the AL register and that ES:DI holds the segment base and
; the offset into the video buffer
        PUSH    AX              ; Save character
        MOV     DX,03DAH        ; 6845 status register
; If the retrace cycle has started, the routine must wait for it
; to end, since there might not be enough time left in the cycle
; to permit access to the buffer without causing interference
WAIT_4_LOW:
        IN      AL,DX           ; Get status byte
        TEST    AL,1            ; Retrace in progress?
        JNZ     WAIT_4_LOW      ; Yes, wait until end of cycle
        CLI                     ; Interrupts off during access
WAIT_4_HIGH:
        IN      AL,DX           ; Get status again
        TEST    AL,1            ; Retrace starting?
        JZ      WAIT_4_HIGH     ; Wait until retrace is high
; Output byte
        POP     AX
        STOSB
        STI
```

If these routines are used in programs that can run in non-CGA systems, additional processing should be provided so that the timing operation is effective only if the CGA card is detected.

4.1.2.3 The CGA Graphics Modes. CGA modes 4, 5, and 6 (see Table 4.1) are all-points-addressable or graphics modes. In these modes the code controls each individual screen pixel by setting or clearing one or more bits in the adapter's video memory area. This form of video display control requires familiarity with the mapping of the screen pixels to the memory buffer for each mode. Video memory mapping in the CGA high-resolution graphics mode can be seen in Figure 4.10.

In APA mode 6 (see Figure 4.10), the video buffer is divided into two banks. The first bank, starting at address B8000H, stores the data corresponding to the even-numbered pixel rows. The second bank, starting at address BA000H, stores the pixels in the odd-numbered rows. The individual bits in each buffer byte are mapped to the video display, as shown in the lower part of Figure 4.10. Assuming that a pixel is defined by its row and column numbers (x and y coordinates), the code can proceed as follows:

1. Divide the row number (x coordinate) by 2 to determine the pixel's offset in the corresponding bank. If the pixel is located in an even row, the memory byte will be in the first bank; if odd, it will be in the second bank.

2. Multiply the result obtained in step 1 by 80 (80 bytes per row) to obtain the pixel's offset from the start of the bank.

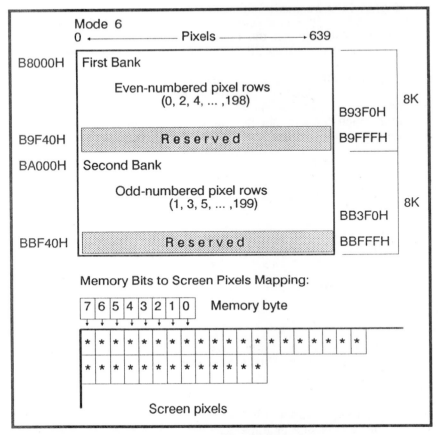

Figure 4.10. *CGA High-Resolution Graphics Mode*

3. Divide the column number (*y* coordinate) by 8 to obtain the byte offset in the row and add this value to the offset obtained in step 2.

4. Use the remainder from step 3 to calculate a mask for setting the desired pixel.

The following code fragment shows the processing for setting a pixel located at row number 90, column number 310, in CGA graphics mode 6.

```
;********************
; preliminary steps
;********************
; Set ES to start of video memory in mode 6
        MOV    AX,0B800H      ; Segment base for B8000H
        MOV    ES,AX          ; To ES
; Set mode 6
        MOV    AL,6           ; Mode
```

```
        MOV    AH,0            ; BIOS service request
        INT    10H
; Clear 16K of adapter RAM starting at B8000H
        MOV    CX,4000H        ; 16K
        MOV    AL,0            ; All 0 bits to blank display
        MOV    DI,0            ; Point to video buffer start
        CLD                    ; Forward
        REP    STOSB           ; Store AL in ES:DI, repeat 16K times
;*******************
;  pixel calculations
;*******************
; Set pixel at row 90, column 310
; Pixel row to BX, pixel column to CX
        MOV    BX,90           ; x coordinate of pixel
        MOV    CX,310          ; y coordinate of pixel
;*******************
;  determine bank
;*******************
; Low-order bit will be set in all odd-numbered rows
        ROR    BX,1            ; Low bit to carry flag
                               ; also divides by 2
        PUSHF                  ; Save carry flag in stack
        MOV    AL,80           ; Number of bytes per row
        MUL    BX              ; AX = offset of row in bank
        MOV    BX,AX           ; Save value in BX
        POPF                   ; Restore carry flag
        JNC    EVEN_ROW
        ADD    BX,2000H        ; Add offset of second bank if odd
;*******************
;   add offset
;*******************
;        BX = byte offset of pixel row in video memory
;        CX = y coordinate of pixel
EVEN_ROW:
        MOV    AX,CX           ; Pixel offset to AX
; Prepare for division
        MOV    CL,8            ; Divisor
        DIV    CL              ; AX/CL = quotient in AL and
                               ; remainder in AH
        MOV    CL,AH           ; Save remainder in CL
; Subtract remainder from pixel offset in row
        MOV    AH,0            ; Clear high byte
        ADD    BX,AX           ; Byte offset of pixel to BX
;*******************
;  determine mask
;*******************
; Compute bit mask from remainder
        MOV    AH,10000000B ; Unit mask for 0 remainder
```

```
        SHR    AH,CL              ; Shift right CL times
; At this point:
;       BX  =  byte offset of pixel into buffer
;       AH  =  bit mask for writing pixel
;       ES  =  segment address of video memory
;*******************
;     set pixel
;*******************
        MOV    ES:[BX],AH
```

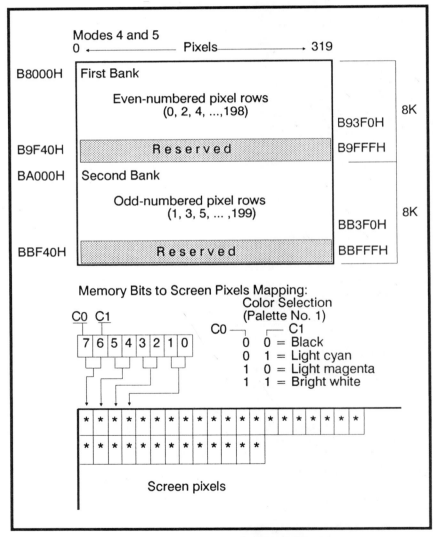

Figure 4.11. *CGA Medium-Resolution Graphics Mode*

Figure 4.11 shows the memory mapping in the CGA medium-resolution graphics mode.

In the medium-resolution color graphics modes (4 and 5), CGA video memory mapping is based on 2 memory bits per pixel, as shown in the lower part of Figure 4.11. These bits, usually designated as C0 and C1, allow encoding four colors for each pixel. The buffer is divided into two banks, as in graphics mode 6, previously described. Because each pixel requires 2 memory bits, the 16K of video memory in the adapter's RAM support only 320 pixels per row. The calculations for addressing video memory must take this structure into account.

4.1.3 The Hercules Graphics Card

Hercules Computer Technologies manufactures several display cards for IBM microcomputers. One of their best known products is the Hercules Graphics Card, introduced in 1982. In its default mode, the HGC emulates the IBM Monochrome Display Adapter. Like the MDA, the HGC includes a parallel printer port. But, in addition to an alphanumeric mode compatible with the IBM Monochrome Display Adapter, the HGC has a bit-mapped graphics mode with 720 by 348 dots definition. The Hercules Graphics Card will drive a standard IBM monochrome monitor.

The graphics mode is activated by setting bit 1 of the display control register, as shown in Figure 4.12. The adapter comes with 64K of video memory. Since 720 by 348 dots require approximately 30K, the HGC contains two graphics pages. Bit 7 of the display control register (see Figure 4.12) is used to select the active video page. Figure 4.13 shows the text-mode bit map of the attribute in the Hercules Graphics Card.

An interesting feature of the Hercules Graphics Card is the 2732 EPROM used as a character generator. Since this chip can be erased and reprogrammed, the on-board character set can be modified or new characters can be added to those furnished with the adapter.

Video memory in the HGC is structured in a unique manner that is related to the way in which the display is scanned by the video hardware. Each scan line contains 720 pixels, which require 90 bytes of storage. The graphics screen consists of 348 scan lines, as can be seen in Figure 4.14. The adapter contains 64K of RAM divided into two 32K display pages. The screen pixels are mapped to each display page in four frames of 8K each. The first frame holds the data for scan rows 0, 4, 8, and all other successive scan lines, by increments of 4, up to scan line 344. The second, third, and fourth frames are structured in a similar manner (see Figure 4.14).

In 1986, Hercules introduced a new version of the graphics card named the Hercules Graphics Card Plus. This adapter is compatible with the IBM MDA card and the Hercules Graphics Card, but also offers the possibility of displaying 3072 different characters. This company has also developed color cards that are compatible with the IBM CGA, EGA, and VGA standards.

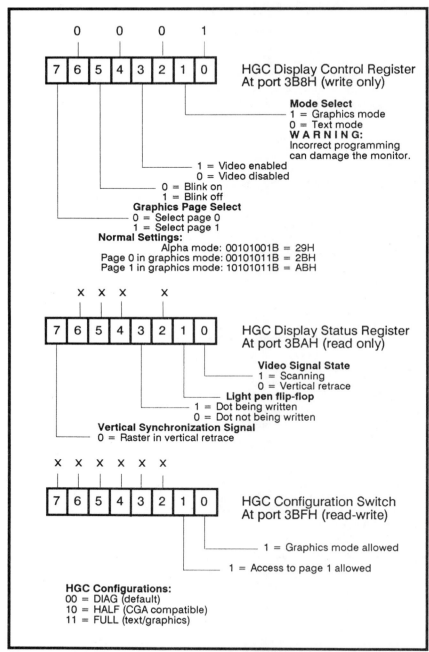

Figure 4.12. *Hercules Graphics Card Programmable Registers*

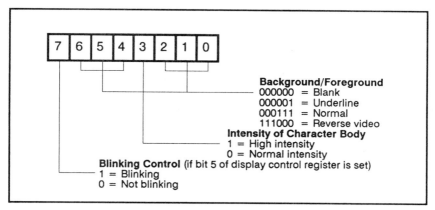

Figure 4.13. *Hercules Graphics Card Attribute Byte (Text Modes)*

4.1.4 The Enhanced Graphics Adapter

The Enhanced Graphics Adapter is a later-version color card for the IBM PC line. The hardware was released in January 1985, at the same time as the Personal Computer AT. The card can emulate most of the functions of either the Color Graphics Adapter or the Monochrome Display Adapter. The EGA has greater character definition in the alphanumeric modes and is not plagued with the video interference problems and timing requirements of the CGA.

The EGA has four display modes that are not available in previous graphics cards. These are called the enhanced graphics modes and provide high-resolution APA graphics. The enhanced graphics modes are numbered 13 through 16. Modes 8 through 12 are not implemented in either the CGA or the EGA (see Table 4.1).

Although the chips installed in the EGA emulate those of the CGA, the programmer must be aware of certain basic differences. In the first place, the EGA video controller custom chip has port and register assignments that differ from those of the Motorola 6845 controller used in the Color Graphics Adapter. Programs that access the 6845 video controller directly, like those that set the different modes or control the system cursor, do not operate satisfactorily on the Enhanced Graphics Adapter.

The segment address of video memory in the Enhanced Graphics Adapter can be referenced off three different bases:

1. B000H when the system has been set to BIOS display mode 7, compatible with the Monochrome Display Adapter

2. B800H when the system has been set to BIOS display modes 0 through 6, compatible with the Color Graphics Adapter

3. A000H when the system has been set to the EGA enhanced graphics modes 13 through 16, not compatible with either the Color Graphics or the Monochrome Display Adapter.

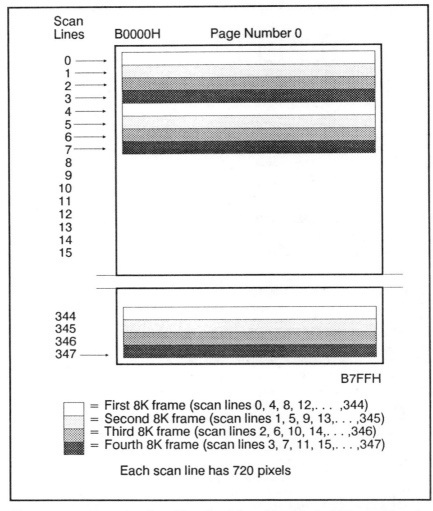

Figure 4.14. *Hercules Graphics Card Graphics Mode Memory Mapping*

For direct access to the video buffer, the segment base corresponding to the active video mode must be selected by the program.

The EGA is furnished with on-board RAM in blocks of 64K. The standard EGA card has a 64K video buffer, while the maximum available RAM is 256K. The actual amount of installed memory can be determined using service number 18 of INT 10H.

4.1.4.1 EGA/VGA Compatibility.

The video systems used in the IBM Video Graphics Array of the PS/2 line and the EGA card of the PC line are quite similar and generally compatible. The characteristics of these high-resolution modes are listed in Table 4.3.

The most important difference is that graphics modes 17, 18, and 19 are available in the PS/2 systems and not in the EGA. Also, the EGA does not support read operations to many of its internal registers, making it practically impossible for software to detect and preserve the state of the EGA registers. This explains why the EGA is unsuitable for memory-resident applications or for coexisting in a multitasking or multiprogramming environment in which the memory image displayed must be saved and restored.

The programmable components of the VGA system, namely the CRT controller, the sequencer, the graphics controller, and the attribute controller, are quite similar to those used in the VGA. The memory-to-screen mapping and the programming techniques for pixel read and write operations also are similar. For these reasons, EGA and VGA hardware and programming are described jointly, starting at Section 4.5.

4.1.5 PCjr Video Hardware

In contrast to that of other members of the PC family, the PCjr's video display hardware is not provided in a video card, but as part of the main system board. The hardware includes the Motorola 6845 CRT controller and a custom LSI chip called the video gate array (LSI5220). The PCjr video/color graphics subsystem includes circuitry and components designed to improve performance in comparison with the Color Graphics Adapter and also minimize manufacturing costs.

The designers of the PCjr made special efforts to maintain compatibility with programs intended for the Color Graphics Adapter, even with those that address screen memory directly. Although there is no physical memory at address B8000H in the PCjr, a CRT processor page register and associated circuitry allow the programmer to address the video buffer *as if it were located at address B8000H*. The compatibility between the PCjr and the Color Graphics Adapter does not extend to all the programmable components and registers. However, most applications do not need to program these components directly, since this can usually be done using the services provided in the BIOS.

The PCjr's video subsystem includes extended graphics modes 8, 9, and 10, which are not available in the Color Graphics Adapter, the Enhanced Graphics Adapter, or the VGA (see Table 4.1).

The PCjr base system includes 64K of dedicated video memory. With the use of an optional 64K memory and display expansion card, video RAM can be expanded to 128K.

4.2 Video Systems of the PS/2 Line

The PS/2 microcomputers, unveiled in 1987, introduced two new video standards, named the Multicolor Graphics Array, or MCGA, and the Video Graphics Array, or VGA. The PS/2 line also brought a change from digital to analog technology for display driver operation. This explains why the monitors of the PC line are incompatible with the MCGA and VGA standards and vice versa. Analog monitors can produce a much larger array of colors. Regarding other graphic improvements, both PS/2 video standards, the MCGA and the VGA, provide 640 by 480 pixel APA modes (see Section 4.7).

4.2.1 The PS/2 MCGA System

The Multicolor Graphics Array video system was introduced with the IBM Model 30 of the PS/2 line. The MCGA standard is also used in the PS/2 Model 25. Note that the PS/2 line includes the video display hardware as part of the system board. But the PS/2 Model 25 and Model 30 are also compatible with the video cards used in the PC line. In fact, the MCGA models are the only computers in the PS/2 line that accept the MDA, CGA, and EGA cards and monitors.

The MCGA video subsystem emulates the Color Graphics Adapter and maintains compatibility with all the CGA modes. In addition, the MCGA has two high-resolution graphics modes, MCGA mode 17, with a definition of 640 by 480 pixels in 2 colors, and mode 19, with 320 by 200 pixels in 256 colors. The effective resolution of the text modes is 640 by 400, which corresponds to an 8 by 16 character box. The MCGA systems can be upgraded to the VGA standard by means of a PS/2 display adapter.

4.2.2 The PS/2 VGA System

The IBM PS/2 computers with Micro Channel (Models 50, 60, 70, and 80) are equipped with a video system named the Video Graphics Array. The VGA comes with 256K of video memory divided into four 64K video maps, or bit planes. The system supports all the display modes of the MDA, the CGA, and the EGA. The VGA also provides graphics mode 18, with 640 by 480 pixels resolution in 16 colors, which is exclusive of this standard (see Section 4.7).

The effective resolution of the text modes is 720 by 400. Three text fonts with different box sizes can be selected in order to display text in the graphics modes. The Video Graphics Array circuitry operates in conjunction with a digital-to-analog converter. VGA hardware and programming are discussed starting in Section 4.5.

4.2.3 PS/2 Monitors

The PS/2 microcomputers are equipped with a 15-pin D-shell connector for the monitor cable. This connector is not compatible with the 9-pin connectors used with the monitors of the PC line. Furthermore, the video systems of the PS/2 line use an analog monitor interface, instead of the digital interface of the PC line. Table 4.4 lists the different monitors used in the PS/2 line.

Table 4.4. *IBM Monitors of the PS/2 Line*

MODEL	TYPE	IMAGE DIMENSIONS (IN)			ASPECT RATIO	SYSTEMS
		DIAGONAL	LENGTH	WIDTH		
8503	Monochrome	10	8	6	4:3	MCGA/VGA
8513	Color	10	8	6	4:3	MCGA/VGA
8512	Color	12	9.6	7.2	4:3	MCGA/VGA
8514	Color	14	11.2	8.4	4:3	8514/A

The horizontal scan rate of the VGA and MCGA systems has a sweep frequency of 31.5 kH, and the vertical scan rate is between 50 and 70 Hz. The video bandwidth is 28 MHz. Horizontal and vertical definitions have a maximum of 720 pixels and 480 pixels per line, except in the 8514/A display adapter, which has a maximum definition of 1024 pixels per line horizontally and 768 pixels per line vertically.

4.3 Very High Resolution Graphics

Some computer applications, like computer assisted design (CAD) and professional desktop publishing programs, require even higher resolution than can be obtained from the standard graphics systems and boards. Microcomputer manufacturers and designers, including IBM, have created very high resolution graphics options to compete with the dedicated systems in CAD and other fields.

For the PC line, IBM offers a Professional Graphics System (PGS) that includes a high resolution board and monitor capable of 640 by 480 pixels graphics. For the PS/2 group the very high resolution alternative is the 8514/A display adapter. The system includes a display card for Micro Channel, a memory expansion kit, and a monitor. The 8514/A is compatible with the PS/2 Micro Channel models. The graphics modes available in the 8514/A are listed in Table 4.5.

Table 4.5. *8514/A Display Adapter Video Modes*

MODE	RESOLUTION	COLORS	PALETTE
20	640 x 480	256	262,144
21	1024 x 768	256	262,144

4.4 Programmable Video Components of the PC Line

The most important integrated circuit chips used in the PC line are the Motorola 6845 CRT controller and the video gate array. The 6845 is common to several PC video systems. The video gate array is a custom chip used exclusively in the PCjr. The Enhanced Graphics Adapter uses neither of these chips and is more related to the video systems of the PS/2 line.

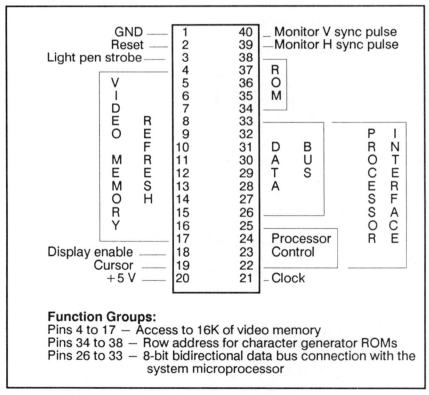

Figure 4.15. *MC6845 Pin Assignments (by Function)*

4.4.1 The Motorola 6845 CRT Controller

The following display adapters and systems of the IBM PC line use the Motorola 6845 CRT controller (CRTC) chip:

1. The Monochrome Display and Printer Adapter
2. The Color Graphics Adapter
3. The IBM PCjr
4. The Hercules Graphics Card

The Enhanced Graphics Adapter and PS/2 video systems use chips that are similar to the Motorola 6845 CRTC.

The 6845 CRTC is a special-purpose integrated circuit that serves as a link between the microprocessor and the CRT display. It also allows interfacing with a character ROM generator chip. Figure 4.15 shows the pin assignment on the MC6845.

4.4.1.1 The 6845 Programmable Registers. The Motorola 6845 CRTC has 18 programmable registers that are accessible through two locations on the system's memory space. Table 4.6 shows the 6845 CRTC registers.

Table 4.6. *MC6845 CRT Controller Registers*

BASE ADDRESS	REGISTER NAME	NUMBER	FUNCTION
3x4H	Address register		Select active register
3x5H	Horizontal format	0–3	Determine the horizontal display parameters
	Vertical format	4–8	Determine the vertical display parameters
	Interlace mode	9	Select normal sync, interlace sync, or interlace sync and video
	Cursor start	10	Determine the scan line for the start of the cursor and blink/no blink operation
	Cursor end	11	Determine the scan line for the end of the cursor
	Start address (high and low)	12–13	Determine the start address of display memory
	Cursor address (high and low)	14–15	Determine the display position for the cursor

The horizontal and vertical format registers are initialized by the BIOS start-up routines and normally require no other manipulation. The address of the 6845 CRT controller has a variable element, sometimes represented by the letter "x." The physical address of the 6845 in different IBM systems is shown in Table 4.7.

Table 4.7. *Address of the 6845 CRT Controller Registers*

DISPLAY CARD OR SYSTEM	ADDRESS	REGISTERS
PCjr	3D4H 3D5H	Address register Registers 0 to 15
CGA	3D4H 3D5H	Address register Registers 0 to 15
MDA	3B4H 3B5H	Address register Registers 0 to 15
Hercules Graphics Card	3B4H 3B5H	Address register Registers 0 to 15

One of the functions of the 6845 CRT controller is the display and control of the system cursor. Three 6845 registers are directly related to cursor management. These are shown in Figure 4.16.

The actual size of the cursor varies according to the vertical definition of the display hardware. In the Color Graphics Adapter and the PCjr, which have 200 scan lines of vertical definition and 25 screen text lines, the cursor size is 8 scan lines (200/25 = 8). In the Monochrome Display Adapter, with 350 scan lines of vertical definition, the cursor size is 14 scan lines (350/25 = 14). Figure 4.17 shows the default cursor in several IBM video systems.

The cursor can be modified by reprogramming the scan lines for the cursor start and end on the 6845 CRT controller. These are registers 10 and 11 in Table 4.6. The following code fragment illustrates changing the MDA default cursor from scan lines 12 and 13 to scan lines 1 to 7.

```
MOV   DX,3B4H      ; 6845 address register in the MDA
MOV   AL,0AH       ; Cursor start register number
OUT   DX,AL        ; Select this register
MOV   DX,3B5H      ; 6845 programmable registers
MOV   AL,1         ; Start scan line for new cursor
OUT   DX,AL        ; Set in 6845 register
MOV   DX,3B4H      ; Address register again
MOV   AL,0BH       ; Cursor end register number
OUT   DX,AL        ; Select this register
MOV   DX,3B5H      ; 6845 programmable registers
MOV   AL,7         ; End scan line for new cursor
OUT   DX,AL        ; Set in 6845 register
```

By setting the contents of the cursor address registers on the 6845 CRT controller, the cursor can be positioned anywhere on the video display. The cursor address registers are numbered 14 and 15, respectively. Register 15 (offset 0FH) holds the low byte of a 14-bit address that extends to the full 16K RAM addressed by the 6845. Register 14 (offset 0EH) holds the 6 significant bits of the high-order byte. The bit map for the cursor address registers is shown in Figure 4.16.

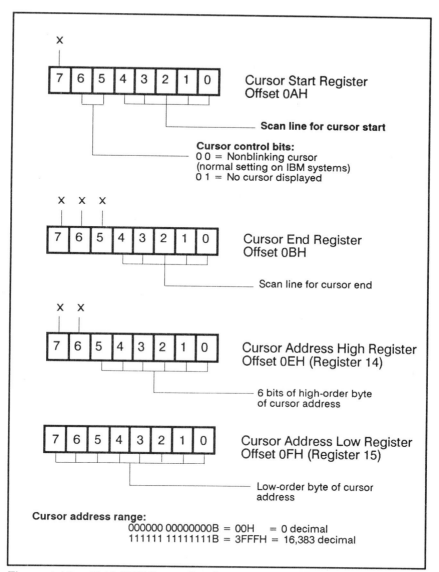

Figure 4.16. *6845 CRT Controller Cursor Registers*

The following code fragment will position the cursor at the start of the third screen row. The code assumes an 80 by 25 alphanumeric mode in the Monochrome Display Adapter. The offset of the second row is calculated as 80 by 2 = 160 bytes from the start of the adapter RAM. Consequently, the cursor address high register must be zeroed and the cursor address low register set to 160.

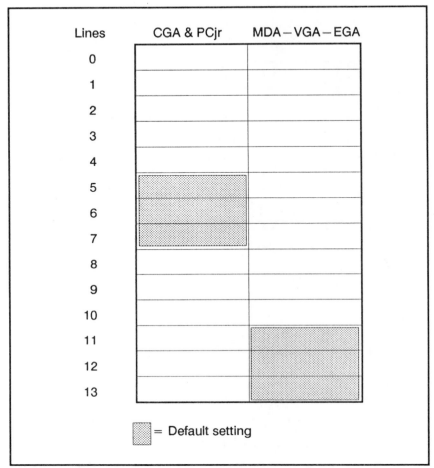

Figure 4.17. *Cursor Scan Lines in IBM Systems*

```
MOV   DX,3B4H       ; 6845 address register
                    ; in the MDA
MOV   AL,0EH        ; Cursor high address register
OUT   DX,AL         ; Select this register
MOV   DX,3B5H       ; 6845 programmable registers
MOV   AL,0          ; Zero high bit of address
OUT   DX,AL         ; Set in 6845 register
MOV   DX,3B4H       ; Address register again
MOV   AL,0AH        ; Cursor low address register
OUT   DX,AL         ; Select this register
MOV   DX,3B5H       ; 6845 programmable registers
```

```
     MOV   AL,160        ; 160 bytes from adapter start
     OUT   DX,AL         ; Set in 6845 register
; Cursor now set at the start of the third screen row
```

The display memory address registers of the 6845 CRT controller can address up to 16K of memory space, as shown in Figure 4.18. Since the 80 by 25 alphanumeric modes require less than 2K of memory per screen, up to eight pages of text can be stored in the adapter. In practice, the number of display pages is limited to the memory assignment in the system's video buffer.

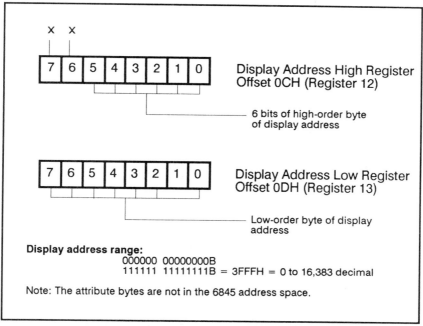

Figure 4.18. *6845 CRT Controller Display Start Address Registers*

The 6845 CRT controller can be programmed to start the screen display from any address in the video buffer. Since the attribute bytes are not represented in the 6845 address space, the offset in 6845 will be one-half of the buffer offset. For example, in the CGA 80 by 25 alphanumeric mode, the first byte of display page 3 is located at offset 2000H (8194 decimal) in the video buffer and offset 1000H (4096 decimal) in the 6845. The 6845 display memory start address registers are programmed in a similar manner to the cursor address registers previously described. This feature of the 6845 allows hardware scrolling operations by character, by line, or by page.

4.4.2 The Video Gate Array (PCjr)

The video gate array is a programmable IC used in the PCjr video subsystem. It should not be confused with the Video Graphics Array (VGA) used in the Micro Channel computers of the PS/2 line. Register mapping of the PCjr video gate array can be seen in Table 4.8.

Table 4.8. *PCjr Video Gate Array Registers at Port 3DAH*

OFFSET	REGISTER NAME
00H	Mode control 1
01H	Palette mask
02H	Border color
03H	Mode control 2
04H	Reset
10H to 1FH	Palette registers

Programming any one of the video gate array internal registers is a three-step process. The first step consists of a read operation to port 3DAH. This sets the video gate array to the register select state. The second step consists of selecting one of the video gate array's internal registers by performing an OUT instruction to the same port, 3DAH, with the register's offset as an operand. The third step is to send the desired value to the selected register. The following code fragment illustrates the process.

```
;*******************
;
;         step  1
;*******************
;
          MOV    DX,03DAH     ; Video gate array I/O address
          IN     AL,DX        ; Read operation
; Now the video gate array is in the register select mode
; The status of the video gate array is in AL
;*******************
;
;         step  2
;*******************
;
; Select register
          MOV    AL,02H       ; Register at offset 02H
          OUT    DX,AL        ; Border color register selected
;*******************
;
;         step  3
;*******************
;
; Write to selected register
          MOV    AL,01H       ; Value to write to the register
          OUT    DX,AL        ; Write it
```

Selecting a PCjr video mode requires programming the two video gate array mode control registers at offsets 00H and 03H. Normally, it is preferable to use BIOS service number 0, INT 10H, to set the video modes than to program the video system's registers directly. Figures 4.19 and 4.20 show the PCjr programmable registers.

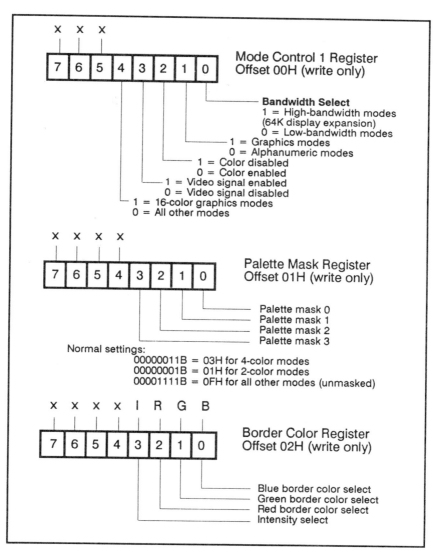

Figure 4.19. *PCjr Mode Control 1, Palette Mask, and Border Color Registers*

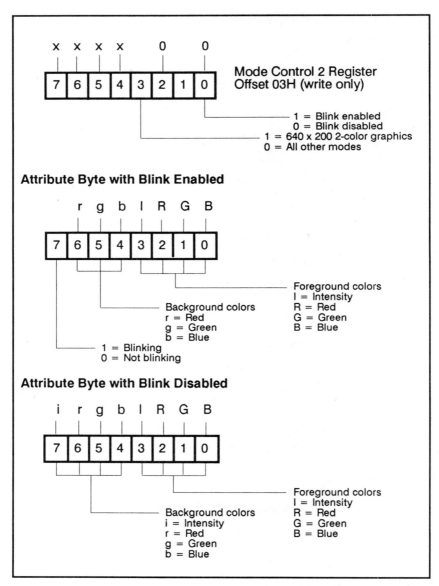

Figure 4.20. *PCjr Attribute Byte and Mode Control Register 2*

The border color register (at offset 02H of the video gate array) can be programmed to display any one of 16 colors on a screen frame area that is several pixels wide. The setting of the significant bits can be determined from Table 4.9. The default color of the screen border is black.

The blink control bit of the video gate array mode control register 2 (see Figure 4.20) also defines two different interpretations of the attribute byte in the alphanumeric modes. If the blink control bit of mode control register 2 is set, then the high bit of the attribute byte can be used to set the character to blinking or not blinking. This setting limits character background to eight possible colors. On the other hand, if the blink control bit in mode control register 2 is cleared, then bit 7 of the attribute byte controls the intensity of the background colors, which expands the number of possible background colors to 16 (see Figure 4.20). In the graphics modes, the blink control bit can be used to switch between two color sets at the blink rate. The colors are determined by the upper and lower halves of the palette register, as shown in Figure 4.21.

The video gate array reset register (see Figure 4.21) is programmed by the BIOS during the video system initialization. This register should not be altered during system operation.

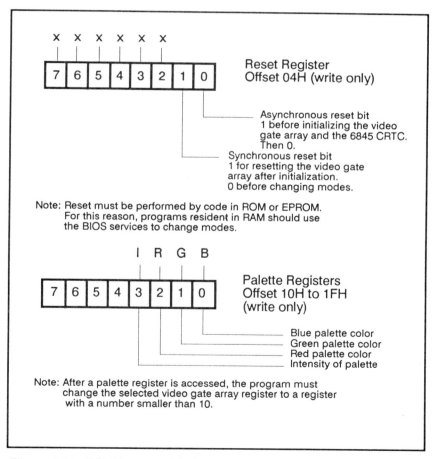

Figure 4.21. *PCjr Reset and Palette Registers*

Table 4.9. *PCjr Palette Register Addresses and Color Encodings*

PALETTE REGISTER OFFSET	ATTRIBUTE (IN HEX)	PALETTE I R G B	COLOR
10H	00H	0 0 0 0	Black
11H	01H	0 0 0 1	Blue
12H	02H	0 0 1 0	Green
13H	03H	0 0 1 1	Cyan
14H	04H	0 1 0 0	Red
15H	05H	0 1 0 1	Magenta
16H	06H	0 1 1 0	Brown
17H	07H	0 1 1 1	White
18H	08H	1 0 0 0	Grey
19H	09H	1 0 0 1	Light blue
1AH	0AH	1 0 1 0	Light green
1BH	0BH	1 0 1 1	Light cyan
1CH	0CH	1 1 0 0	Light red
1DH	0DH	1 1 0 1	Light magenta
1EH	0EH	1 1 1 0	Yellow
1FH	0FH	1 1 1 1	Bright white

There are 16 palette registers, located at offsets 10H to 1FH in the video gate array. These registers can be seen in Table 4.9.

By changing the default setting of any one of the palette registers, the programmer can alter the interpretation of the color codes by the attribute byte. For example, to display a character in red, the attribute byte must be 04H. At the same time, the palette register at offset 14H in the video gate array (see Table 4.9) holds the default IRGB code for red, 0100B. In order to have red characters displayed as brown characters, the contents of the red palette register at offset 14H must be changed from the default setting of 0100B to the corresponding IRGB code for brown, 0110B.

The following code fragment illustrates the processing steps required to change the contents of a video gate array palette register. The status register (see Figure 4.22) is used to synchronize the change with the vertical retrace cycle of the CRT controller, thus avoiding any visible interference.

```
        MOV    DX,03DAH       ; Video gate array port
; Synchronize palette change with the start of a vertical
; retrace cycle
RETRACE_HIGH:
        IN     AL,DX          ; Read status register
```

```
          TEST   AL,00001000B  ; Is vertical retrace on?
          JNZ    RETRACE_HIGH       ; Yes, wait for end of cycle
RETRACE_LOW:
          IN     AL,DX         ; Read status register again
          TEST   AL,00001000B  ; Is vertical retrace on?
          JNZ    RETRACE_LOW;  Wait for cycle start
; Vertical retrace cycle has just started
          IN     AL,DX         ; Set the video gate array in
                               ; register select mode
          MOV    AL,14H        ; Offset for red palette register
          OUT    DX,AL         ; Select register
          MOV    AL,00000110B  ; IRGB code for brown
          OUT    DX,AL         ; Store this code in register 14H
; Palette register for red attribute now changed to brown
; Video gate array must now be set to an active register
; less than 10 to reenable video
          IN     AL,DX         ; Register select mode
          MOV    AL,5          ; Any register less than 10
          OUT    DX,AL         ; Select
```

In addition to the vertical retrace bit, the video gate array status register has bits for the state of the light pen trigger and switch, for the video state, and for testing purposes. The PCjr status and page select registers can be seen in Figure 4.22.

The CRT/processor page register (see Figure 4.22) is used to select the area of system memory that is mapped to the video display. This register is independent of the video gate array and of the 6845 CRT controller. Bits 0, 1, and 2 of the CRT/processor page register select which of the eight possible video pages is actually displayed. If no expansion RAM is available in the system, the number of display pages is reduced to four. Bits 3, 4, and 5 select which video page is mapped to address B8000H. The 2 high bits of the CRT/processor page register are set according to the selected video mode.

4.4.3 PCjr Graphics Mode Memory Mapping

The PCjr graphics modes (see Table 4.10) allow three screen resolutions. The low-resolution mode, number 8, is 160 by 200 pixels. Medium-resolution modes, numbers 4, 5, and 9, are 320 by 200 pixels. High-resolution modes, numbers 6 and 10, are 640 by 200 pixels. Note that the vertical resolution remains at 200 pixel rows for all modes. The characteristics of the PCjr graphics modes can be seen in Table 4.10.

Pixel mapping in the PCjr is different for each graphics mode. In modes 4, 5, 6, and 8 (16K of video memory), storage is organized into two 8K banks. In modes 9 and 10 (32K of video memory), storage is organized into four 8K banks, as seen in Figure 4.23. Pixel-to-memory mapping in the different modes can be seen in Figure 4.24.

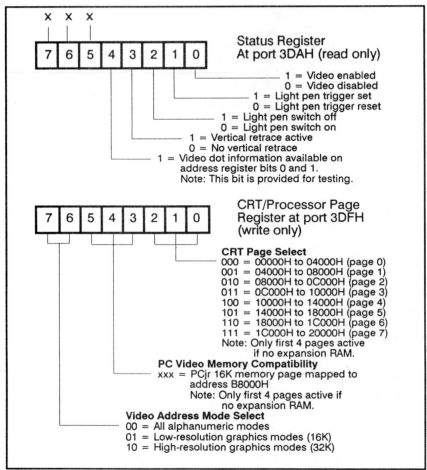

Figure 4.22. *PCjr Status and CRT/Processor Page Registers*

Table 4.10. *PCjr Graphics Modes*

MODE	128K RAM EXPANSION	MEMORY	NO. OF PAGES	MONO / COLOR	NO. OF COLORS	DEFINITION
4	No	16K	1	Color	4	320 x 200
5	No	16K	1	B&W	4	320 x 200
6	No	16K	1	Color	2	640 x 200
8	No	16K	1	Color	16	160 x 200
9	Yes	32K	1	Color	16	320 x 200
10	Yes	32K	1	Color	4	640 x 200

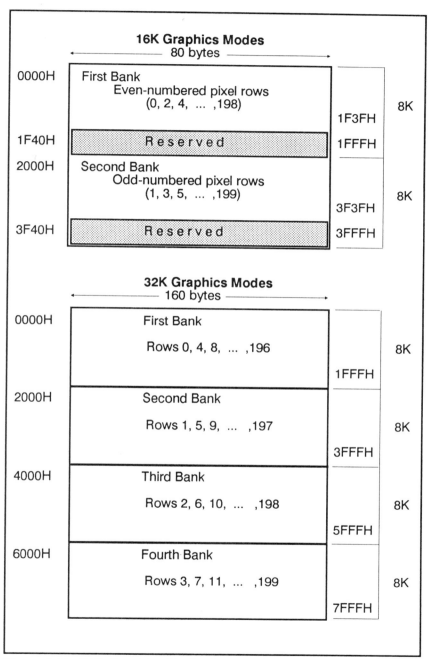

Figure 4.23. *PCjr Graphics Modes Storage Structure*

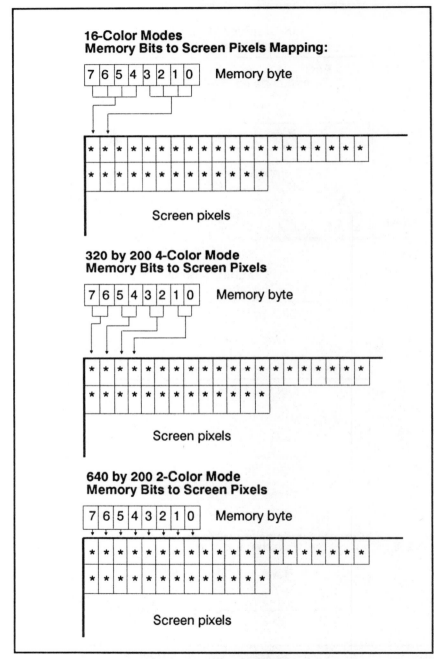

Figure 4.24. *PCjr Graphics Modes Pixel Mapping*

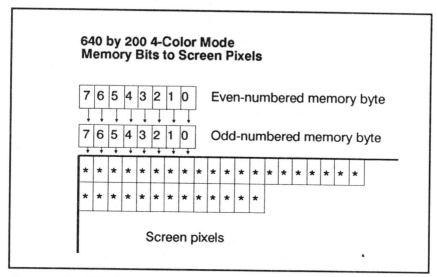

Figure 4.24. *PCjr Graphics Modes Pixel Mapping (continued)*

4.5 EGA and VGA Graphics Display Components

From a programmer's perspective, the Enhanced Graphics Adapter of the PC line and the Video Graphics Array of the PS/2 line are similar devices. Both use the same programmable registers, located at the same addresses, use similar bit mapping of the color planes, and can be programmed using the same BIOS services. This similarity is even more noticeable if the EGA system is furnished with the maximum 256K of on-board RAM. Table 4.11 shows the VGA registers and ports. Table 4.12 shows the corresponding elements in the EGA.

Note that there are some features of the VGA that are not present in the Enhanced Graphics Adapter. For example, the maximum resolution in the EGA card is 640 by 350 pixels, while the VGA is capable of 640 by 480 pixels (see Section 4.7). Table 4.1 shows the characteristics of the display modes available in the VGA and EGA systems. Note that VGA graphics modes 17, 18, and 19 are not implemented in the EGA. Additionally, some hardware and software problems of the EGA have been corrected in the VGA, and most of the programmable registers have been made read-write.

The VGA is designed to emulate all the alphanumeric and graphics modes of the Monochrome Display Adapter, the Color Graphics Adapter, and the Enhanced Graphics Adapter. The standard VGA configuration includes 256K of video RAM.

Table 4.11. *PS/2 VGA Registers and Ports*

REGISTER	READ/ WRITE	MDA	CGA	EITHER
			EMULATING	
A. General Registers				
1. Miscellaneous output	Write Read			03C2H 03CCH
2. Input status 0	Read			03C2H
3. Input status 1	Read	03BAH	03DAH	
4. Feature control	Write Read	03BAH	03DAH	03CAH
5. Video subsystem enable	R/W			03C3H
6. DAC state	Read			03C7H
B. Attribute Registers				
1. Address	R/W			03C0H
2. Other	Write Read			03C0H 03C1H
C. CRT Controller Registers				
1. Index	R/W	03B4H	03D4H	
2. Other CRT controller	R/W	03B5H	03D5H	
D. Sequencer Registers				
1. Address	R/W			03C4H
2. Other	R/W			03C5H
E. Graphics Registers				
1. Address	R/W			03CEH
2. Other	R/W			03CFH

Table 4.12. *EGA Registers and Ports*

REGISTER	READ/ WRITE	EMULATING		
		MDA	CGA	EITHER
A. General Registers				
1. Miscellaneous output	Write			03C2H
2. Input status 0	Read			03C2H
3. Input status 1	Read	03BAH	03DAH	
4. Feature control	Write	03BAH	03DAH	
B. Attribute Registers				
1. Address	Write			03C0H
2. Other	Write			03C0H
C. CRT Controller Registers				
1. Index	Write	03B4H	03D4H	
2. Light pen	Read	03B5H	03D5H	
3. Other	Write	03B5H	03D5H	
D. Sequencer Registers				
1. Address	Write			03C4H
2. Other	Write			03C5H
E. Graphics Registers				
1. Graphics 1 position				03CCH
2. Graphics 2 position				03CAH
3. Address	R/W			03CEH
4. Other	R/W			03CFH

4.5.1 The General Registers

The general registers have often been called the external registers in EGA systems. They are used primarily in initialization of the video system and in mode setting. There are some general registers in the VGA system that have no counterpart in the EGA. To ensure portability, it is normally preferable to let the system handle the initialization of the video components. Figures 4.25 and 4.26 show the programmable components in the VGA and EGA general registers.

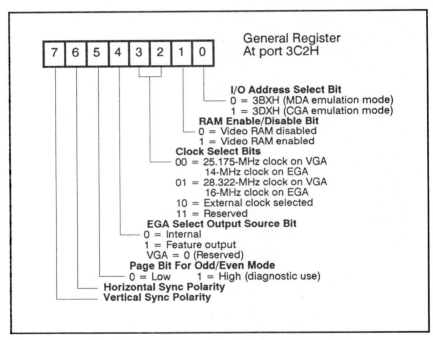

Figure 4.25. *The VGA/EGA Miscellaneous Output Register*

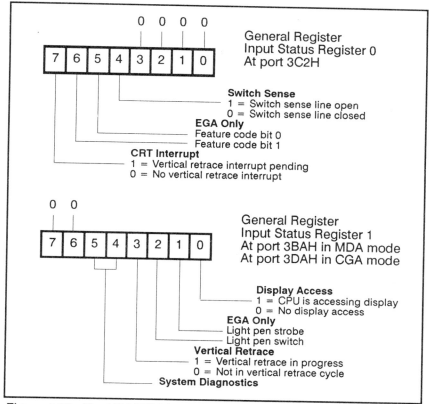

Figure 4.26. *The VGA/EGA Input Status Registers 0 and 1*

4.5.2 The CRT Controller

The CRT controller is the EGA/VGA equivalent of the Motorola 6845 CRT controller in the PC line. When the EGA or VGA is emulating the MDA, the address register of the CRT controller is located at 03B4H. When the EGA or VGA emulates the CGA, then the address register is located at 03D4H. These values correspond to those used by the MDA and CGA cards (see Table 4.7). The CRT controller registers are shown in Table 4.13. Figures 4.27, 4.28, and 4.29 show several programmable registers in the CRT controller used in VGA and EGA systems.

Table 4.13. *VGA/EGA CRT Controller Register*

PORT	OFFSET	DESCRIPTION
03x4H		Address register
03x5H	00H	Total horizontal characters minus 2 (EGA)
		Total horizontal characters minus 5 (VGA)
	01H	Horizontal display end characters minus 1
	02H	Start horizontal blanking
	03H	End horizontal blanking
	04H	Start horizontal retrace pulse
	05H	End horizontal retrace pulse
	06H	Total vertical scan lines
	07H	CRTC overflow
	08H	Preset row scan
	09H	Maximum scan line
	*0AH	Scan line for cursor start
	*0BH	Scan line for cursor end
	*0CH	Video buffer start address, high byte
	*0DH	Video buffer start address, low byte
	*0EH	Cursor location, high byte
	*0FH	Cursor location, low byte
	10H	Vertical retrace start
	11H	Vertical retrace end
	12H	Last scan line of vertical display
	13H	Additional word offset to next logical line
	14H	Scan line for underline character
	15H	Scan line to start vertical blanking
	16H	Scan line to end vertical blanking
	17H	CRTC mode control
	18H	Line compare register

Notes: Registers signaled with (*) are detailed in separate figures.
3x4H/3x5H = 3B4H/3B5H when emulating the MDA
3x4H/3x5H = 3D4H/3D5H when emulating the CGA

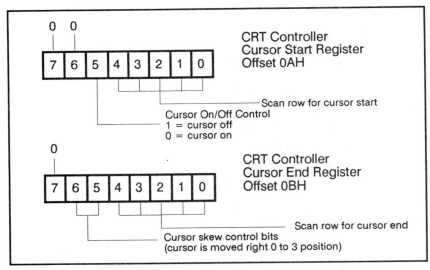

Figure 4.27. *VGA/EGA Cursor Size Registers*

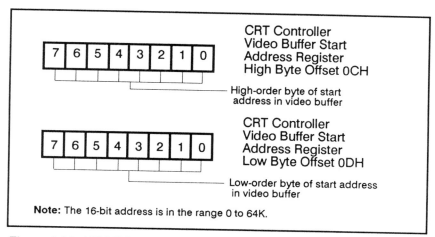

Figure 4.28. VGA/EGA Video Buffer Start Address Registers

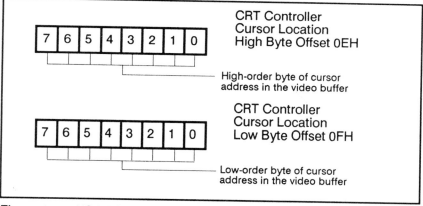

Figure 4.29. *VGA/EGA Cursor Location Registers*

4.5.3 The Sequencer

The EGA and VGA sequencer register uses the character clock for controlling memory fetch operations and also provides the timing for the dynamic RAMs. This allows the microprocessor to access video memory in cycles inserted between the display memory cycles. To the programmer, the most interesting registers in the sequencer are the map mask and character map select registers. The map mask registers allow the protection of any specific memory map by masking it from the microprocessor and from the character map select register. Table 4.14 lists the VGA/EGA sequencer registers. Figures 4.30, 4.31, and 4.32 show three programmable registers in the VGA/EGA sequencer.

Table 4.14. *The VGA/EGA Sequencer Registers*

PORT	OFFSET	DESCRIPTION
03C4H		Address register
03C5H	00H 01H *02H *03H *04H	Synchronous or asynchronous reset Clocking mode Map mask Character map select Memory mode

Note: Registers signaled with an (*) are detailed in separate figures.

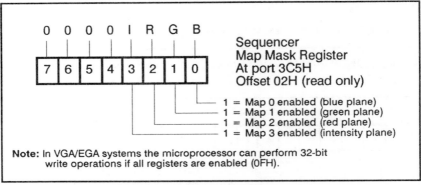

Figure 4.30. *The VGA/EGA Map Mask Register*

In the color graphics modes, the map mask can be used to select the color in which one or more pixels are displayed. The color is encoded in the IRGB format (see Figure 4.30). The address register, at port 3C4H, must first be loaded with the offset of the map mask register (02H). After the pixel or pixels have been set, the map mask should be reset to its default value of 0FH. The following code fragment illustrates setting eight pixels to a bright red color. The code is compatible with EGA and VGA systems.

```
; Setting eight pixels to bright red in a EGA or VGA
; color graphics mode
        MOV   DX,3C4H        ; Address register of sequencer
        MOV   AL,02H         ; Offset of the map mask
        OUT   DX,AL          ; Map mask selected
        MOV   DX,3C5H        ; Data to map mask
        MOV   AL,00001100B   ; Intensity and red bits set
                             ; in IRGB code
        OUT   DX,AL          ; Map mask = 0000 IR00
; Setting the pixels consists of writing a 1 bit in the
; corresponding buffer address.
```
The following code assumes that ES is set to the video segment

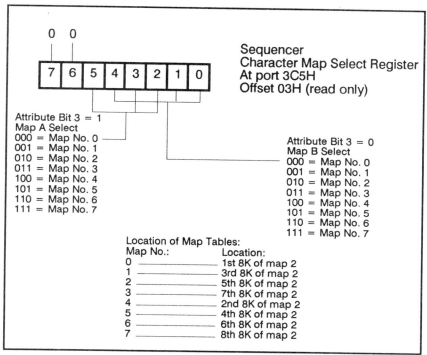

Figure 4.31. *The VGA/EGA Character Map Select Register*

```
; base  and  BX  to  the  offset  of  the  first  pixel  to  set
        MOV    AL,ES:[BX]      ; Dummy read operation
        MOV    AL,11111111B    ; Set all bits
        MOV    ES:[BX],AL
; Reset  the  Map  Mask  to  the  default  state
        MOV    DX,3C4H         ; Address register of sequencer
        MOV    AL,02H          ; Offset of the map mask
        OUT    DX,AL           ; Map mask selected
        MOV    DX,3C5H         ; Data to map mask
        MOV    AL,00001111B    ; Default IRGB code for map mask
        OUT    DX,AL           ; Map mask = 0000 IRGB
          .
          .
          .
```

In the alphanumeric modes, bit 3 of the attribute byte normally serves to control the foreground intensity. But if memory mode bit 1 of the sequencer is set and the values of the map A select and map B select bits are different, then bit 3 of the attribute byte serves as a switch between character sets (see Figure 4.32).

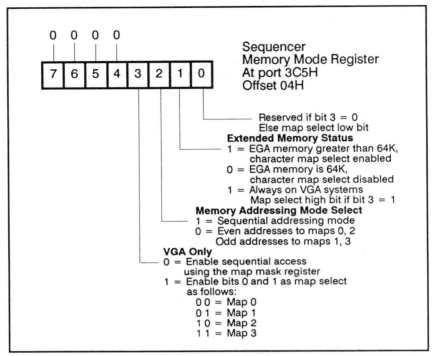

Figure 4.32. *The VGA/EGA Memory Mode Register*

4.5.4 The Graphics Controller

In a graphics mode, the graphics controller serves to interface video memory with the attribute controller and with the system microprocessor. In the APA modes the graphics controller is bypassed. Table 4.15 lists the VGA/EGA graphics controller registers.

Table 4.15. *The VGA/EGA Graphics Controller Registers*

PORT	OFFSET	DESCRIPTION
03CEH		Address register
03CFH	00H	Set/reset
	01H	Enable set/reset
	02H	Color compare for read mode 1 operation
	03H	Logical operation select and data rotate
	04H	Select map for read operations
	05H	Select graphics mode
	06H	Miscellaneous operations
	07H	Read mode 1 color don't care
	08H	Bit mask

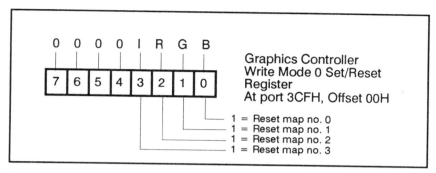

Figure 4.33. *VGA/EGA Write Mode 0 Set/Reset Register*

The set/reset register of the graphics controller may be used to permanently set or clear a specific bit plane. This register is shown in Figure 4.33. The set/reset register affects only write mode 0 operations. The use of the set/reset register requires the use of the enable set/reset register, shown in Figure 4.34.

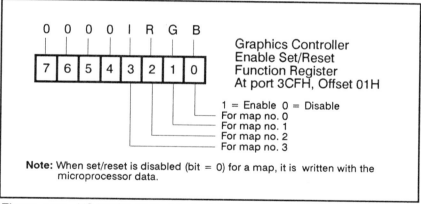

Figure 4.34. *VGA/EGA Write Mode 0 Enable Set/Reset Function Register*

The graphics controller color compare register, shown in Figure 4.35, is used during read mode 1 operations to test for the presence of memory bits corresponding to one or more color maps. For example, a program can check for bright red screen pixels if bit 2 (red) and bit 3 (intensity) of the color compare register are set. Thereafter, each memory read will reflect as set the pixels whose intensity and red maps are 1. All other combinations will be reported with 0 bits. One or more bit planes can be excluded from the compare by setting the corresponding bit in the color don't care register, shown in Figure 4.36.

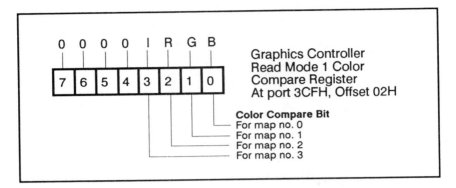

Figure 4.35. *VGA/EGA Read Mode 1 Color Compare Register*

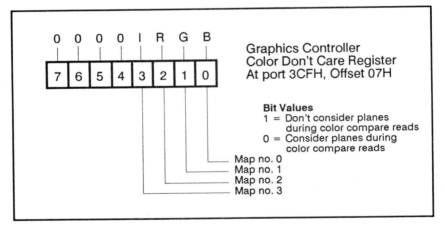

Figure 4.36. *VGA/EGA Color Don't Care Register*

One function of the logical operation select and data rotate register of the graphics controller is to determine how data is combined with data latched in the system microprocessor registers. The possible logical operations are AND, OR, and XOR. If bits 3 and 4 are reset, data is unmodified. A second function of this register is to right-rotate data from 0 to 7 places. This function is controlled by bits 0 to 2. The logical operation select and data rotate register is shown in Figure 4.37.

VGA/EGA video memory structure in the graphics modes (see Section 4.6.2 and Figure 4.50) is based on encoding the color of a single pixel into several memory maps. The read operation map select register, in Figure 4.38, is used to determine which map is read by the system microprocessor.

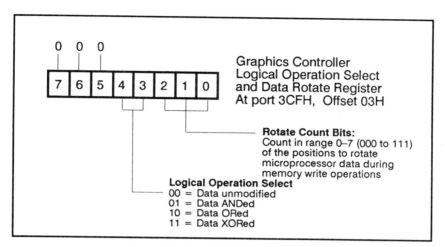

Figure 4.37. *VGA/EGA Logical Operation Select and Data Rotate Register*

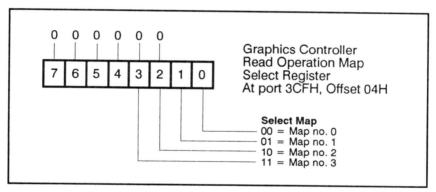

Figure 4.38. *VGA/EGA Read Operation Map Select Register*

The following code fragment shows the use of the read operation map select register.

```
; Code to read the contents of the four color maps in VGA mode 18
; Code assumes that read mode 0 has been previously set
; On entry:
;                       ES = A000H or equivalent OS/2 selector
;                       BX = byte offset into video map
; On exit:
;                       CL = byte stored in intensity map
;                       CH = byte stored in red map
;                       DL = byte stored in green map
;                       DH = byte stored in blue map
```

```
; Set counter and map selector
        MOV     CX,4            ; Counter for four maps to read
        MOV     DI,0            ; Map selector code
READ_IRGB:
; Select map from which to read
        MOV     DX,3CEH         ; Graphic controller address
                                ; register
        MOV     AL,4            ; Read operation map select
        OUT     DX,AL           ; register
;
        INC     DX              ; Graphic controller at 3CFH
        MOV     AX,DI           ; AL = map selector code DI
        OUT     DX,AL           ; IRGB color map selected
; Read 8 bits from selected map
        MOV     AL,ES:[BX]      ; Get byte from bit plane
        PUSH    AX              ; Store it in the stack
        INC     DI              ; Bump selector to next map
        LOOP    READ_IRGB       ; Execute loop 4 times
; Four maps are stored in stack
; Retrieve maps into exit registers
        POP     AX              ; B map byte in AL
        MOV     DH,AL           ; Move B map byte to DH
        POP     AX              ; G map byte in AL
        MOV     DL,AL           ; Move G map byte to DL
        POP     AX              ; R map byte in AL
        MOV     CH,AL           ; Move R map byte to CH
        POP     AX              ; I map byte in AL
        MOV     CL,AL           ; Move I map byte to CL
        .
        .
        .
```

In order to understand the VGA/EGA select graphics mode register of the graphics controller, familiarity with the various write and read modes is necessary. The select graphics mode register is shown in Figure 4.39.

There are three write modes in EGA systems and four in VGA systems. The purpose and use of each write mode is as follows:

1. Write mode 0 is the default write mode. In this write mode, the map mask register of the sequencer, the bit mask register of the graphics controller, and the CPU are used to set any screen pixel to a desired color.

2. In write mode 1, the contents of the latch registers are first loaded by performing a read operation, then copied directly onto the color maps by performing a write operation. This mode is often used in moving areas of memory.

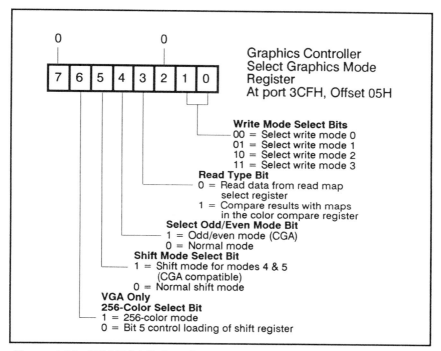

Figure 4.39. *VGA/EGA Select Graphics Mode Register*

3. Write mode 2, a simplified version of write mode 0, also allows an individual pixel to be set to any desired color. However, in write mode 2, the color code is contained in the CPU byte.

4. In write mode 3 (available in VGA systems only), the byte in the CPU is ANDed with the contents of the bit mask register of the graphic controller. This value is used as a bit mask during the write operation.

The write mode is selected by setting bits 0 and 1 of the graphic controller's graphics mode register. When modifying this register, it would be a sound practice to preserve the remaining bit fields (see Figure 4.39). This is possible in VGA systems, where the program can read the contents of the graphics mode register, alter the write mode bits, and then reset the register without changing the remaining bits. But in EGA systems, the graphics controller is a write-only register. In this case, the program must evaluate the setting of these bits according to their function. The following code fragment sets write mode 2 in EGA and VGA systems. All other bits in the select graphics mode register are cleared.

```
; Set the graphics controller's select graphics mode register
; to write mode 2
        MOV    DX,3CEH         ; Graphics controller address
                               ; register
```

```
        MOV    AL,5            ; Offset of the mode register
        OUT    DX,AL           ; Select this register
        INC    DX              ; Point to data register
        MOV    AL,2            ; Write mode 2
        OUT    DX,AL           ; Selected
```

Once the write mode is selected, the program can access memory to write screen pixels, as in the following code fragment:

```
; Write mode 2 pixel-setting routine
; On entry:
;                     ES = A000H (or equivalent selector in OS/2)
;                     BX = byte offset into the video buffer
;                     AL = pixel color in IRGB format
;                     AH = bit pattern to set (mask)
;
; Note: This procedure does not reset the default read or write
; modes or the contents of the bit mask register
; The code assumes that write mode 2 has been set previously
        PUSH   AX              ; Color byte
        PUSH   AX              ; Twice
;*****************
;   set bit mask
;*****************
; Set bit mask register according to mask in AH
        MOV    DX,3CEH         ; Graphics controller address
        MOV    AL,8            ; Offset = 8
        OUT    DX,AL           ; Select bit mask register
;
        INC    DX              ; To 3CFH
        POP    AX              ; Color code once from stack
        MOV    AL,AH           ; Bit pattern
        OUT    DX,AL           ; Load bit mask
;*****************
;   write color
;*****************
        MOV    AL,ES:[BX]      ; Dummy read to load latch
                              ; registers
        POP    AX              ; Restore color code
        MOV    ES:[BX],AL      ; Write the pixel with the
                              ; color code in AL
```

The EGA and the VGA also provide two read modes. In read mode 0, which is the default, the CPU is loaded with the contents of one of the color maps. In read mode 1, the contents of the maps are compared with a predetermined value before being loaded into the CPU. The active read mode depends on the setting of bit 3 of the select graphics mode register in the graphics controller (see Figure 4.39).

The miscellaneous register of the graphics controller, shown in Figure 4.40, is used in conjunction with the select graphics mode register to enable certain graphics functions. Bits 2 and 3 of this register control the mapping of the video buffer in the system's memory space. The normal mapping of each mode can be seen in Table 4.1.

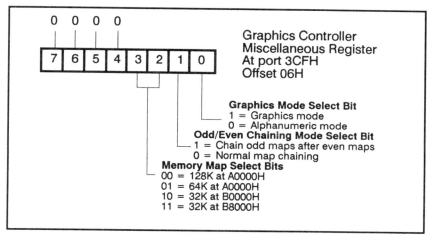

Figure 4.40. *VGA/EGA Miscellaneous Register*

All read and write operations performed by the VGA and EGA video controller take place at a byte level. Therefore, bit masking is required to determine the state of an individual screen pixel (read) or to set an individual pixel (write) to a certain color. The 8086/8088 TEST instruction, with a mask operand, can be used to determine the state of an individual pixel following a read operation. The bit mask register of the graphics controller, shown in Figure 4.41, permits setting individual pixels while in write modes 0 and 2. The preceding code fragment shows the use of the bit mask register.

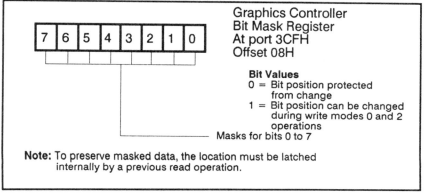

Figure 4.41. *VGA/EGA Bit Mask Register*

The bit mask for setting an individual screen pixel can be found from a look-up table or by right-shifting a unit bit pattern (10000000B). The following code fragment calculates the offset into the video buffer and the bit mask required for writing an individual pixel using VGA write mode 0 or 2.

```
; Mask and offset computation from x and y pixel coordinates
; Code is for VGA mode 18 (640 by 480 pixels)
; On entry:
;                 CX = x coordinate of pixel (range 0 to 639)
;                 DX = y coordinate of pixel (range 0 to 479)
; On exit:
;                 BX = byte offset into video buffer
;                 AH = bit mask for the write operation using
;                      write mode 0 or 2
;******************
; compute address
;******************
          PUSH   AX          ; Save accumulator
          PUSH   CX          ; Save x coordinate
          MOV    AX,DX       ; y coordinate to AX
          MOV    CX,80       ; Multiplier (80 bytes per row)
          MUL    CX          ; AX = y * 80
          MOV    BX,AX       ; Free AX and hold in BX
          POP    AX          ; x coordinate from stack
; Prepare for division
          MOV    CL,8        ; Load divisor
          DIV    CL          ; AX/CL = quotient in AL and
                             ; remainder in AH
; Add in quotient
          MOV    CL,AH       ; Save remainder in CL
          MOV    AH,0        ; Clear high byte
          ADD    BX,AX       ; Offset into buffer to BX
          POP    AX          ; Restore AX
; Compute bit mask from remainder
          MOV    AH,10000000B ; Unit mask for 0 remainder
          SHR    AH,CL       ; Shift right CL times
; The byte offset (in BX) and the pixel mask (in AH) can now
; be used to set the individual screen pixel
```

4.5.5 The Attribute Controller

The attribute controller receives data from the graphics controller and formats it for the video display hardware. Input is always converted into the required 8-bit digital color value. Blinking, underlining, and cursor display logic are controlled by this register. In VGA systems, the output of the attribute controller goes directly to the video DAC and the CRT. Table 4.16 shows the registers in the VGA/EGA attribute controller.

Table 4.16. *The VGA/EGA Attribute Controller Registers*

PORT	OFFSET	DESCRIPTION
03C0H		Attribute address and palette address register
03C1H		Read operations (VGA systems only)
03C0H	00H–0FH	Palette registers
	10H	Attribute mode control
	11H	Screen border color control (overscan)
	12H	Color plane enable
	13H	Horizontal pixel panning
	14H	Color select (VGA systems only)

Internal addressing of the registers in the attribute controller is performed differently than with the other EGA and VGA registers, since the attribute controller does not have a dedicated bit to control the selection of its internal address and data registers. In the attribute controller, an internal flip-flop toggles the address and data functions. Figure 4.42 shows the attribute and palette address registers in the VGA/EGA attribute controller.

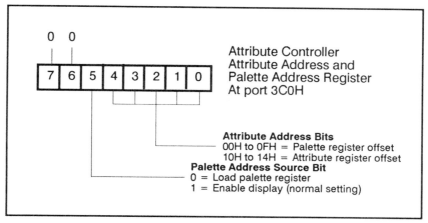

Figure 4.42. *EGA/VGA Attribute Address and Palette Address Register*

The sequence of operations for writing data is as follows:

1. An IN operation is performed to address 3BAH for MDA emulation modes and to address 3DAH for CGA emulation modes. This clears the flip-flop and selects the address function of the attribute controller.

2. Interrupts are disabled.

3. Using an OUT instruction, the address register at port 03C0H is loaded with the value of the data register desired. This selects the desired data register of the attribute controller.

4. Another OUT instruction is now used to load the selected data register with the desired value.

5. Interrupts are enabled.

The setting of the 16 palette colors (offset 00H to 0FH) determines how the IRGB values are displayed, as shown in Table 4.17. These registers are programmed via the palette register of the attribute controller, seen in Figure 4.43.

Table 4.17. *Default Setting of VGA/EGA Palette Registers*

REGISTER OFFSET	HEX	BITS 0–5 r g b R G B	COLOR
00H	00H	0 0 0 0 0 0	Black
01H	01H	0 0 0 0 0 1	Blue
02H	02H	0 0 0 0 1 0	Green
03H	03H	0 0 0 0 1 1	Cyan
04H	04H	0 0 0 1 0 0	Red
05H	05H	0 0 0 1 0 1	Magenta
06H	14H	0 1 0 1 0 0	Brown
07H	07H	0 0 0 1 1 1	White
08H	38H	1 1 1 0 0 0	Dark grey
09H	39H	1 1 1 0 0 1	Light blue
0AH	3AH	1 1 1 0 1 0	Light green
0BH	3BH	1 1 1 0 1 1	Light cyan
0CH	3CH	1 1 1 1 0 0	Light red
0DH	3DH	1 1 1 1 0 1	Light magenta
0EH	3EH	1 1 1 1 1 0	Yellow
0FH	3FH	1 1 1 1 1 1	Intensified white

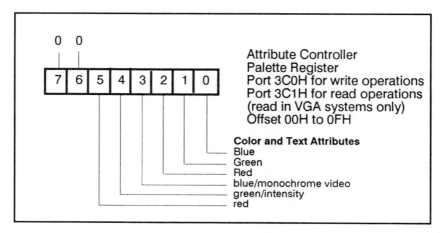

Figure 4.43. *The EGA/VGA Palette Register*

For example, normal monochrome text on a VGA/EGA system is displayed as white characters (palette number 07H) on a black background (palette number 00H). If the palette register at offset 07H (value 07H) is changed to the bit pattern for yellow (value 3EH), normal text characters will be displayed as yellow on a black background. BIOS service number 16 of INT 10H can be used to set the palette register.

The attribute mode control register of the attribute controller serves to select the mode characteristics, as shown in Figure 4.44. When alphanumeric characters in the range C0H to DFH are used (see Figure 4.3), bit 2 generates unbroken horizontal lines. This feature refers to the MDA emulation mode, since other character fonts do not require the ninth dot. The BIOS sets this bit automatically in the modes that require it. The function of the other bit fields of the attribute mode control register can be seen in Figure 4.44.

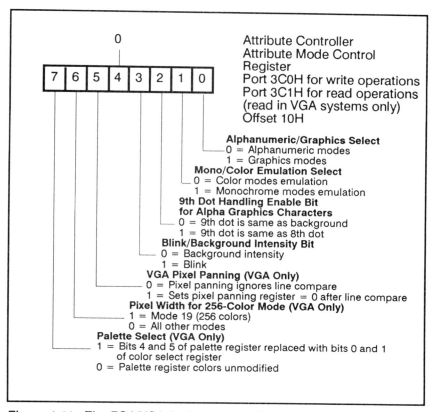

Figure 4.44. *The EGA/VGA Attribute Mode Control Register*

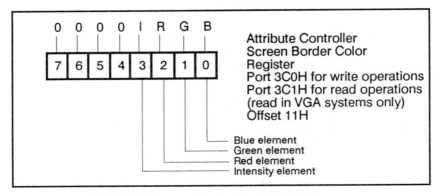

Figure 4.45. *VGA/EGA Screen Border Color Register*

The border color register, also called the overscan register, determines the color of a band around the display area. This register is shown in Figure 4.45. Normally the screen border is not noticeable, due to the fact that the default border color is black. The width of the color band is one column in the 80-column mode. The border color is not available in the 40-column alphanumeric modes or in the graphics modes with 320 pixel rows, except for VGA graphics mode 19.

Bits 0 to 3 of the color plane enable register of the attribute controller are used to limit the bit planes accessed during read or write operations. This register is shown in Figure 4.46. Thus, compatibility with more limited hardware is ensured, such as an EGA card equipped with less than 256K. Bits 4 and 5 are used in system diagnostics.

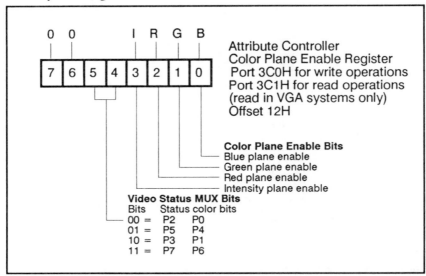

Figure 4.46. *VGA/EGA Color Plane Enable Register*

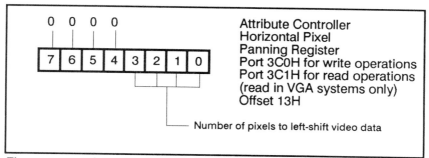

Figure 4.47. *VGA/EGA Horizontal Pixel Panning Register*

The horizontal pixel panning register of the attribute controller is used to shift video data horizontally to the left. This register is shown in Figure 4.47. This feature is available in the alphanumeric and graphics modes. The number of pixels that can be shifted is determined by the display mode. In the VGA 256-color graphics mode, three is the maximum number of allowed pixels. In alphanumeric modes 0, 1, 2, 3, and 7, the maximum is eight pixels. In all other modes, the maximum is seven pixels.

The color select register of the attribute controller exists only in VGA systems. This register is shown in Figure 4.48. The color select register can be used to rapidly switch between sets of displayed colors. When bit 7 of the attribute mode control register is clear, the 8-bit color value (256 colors) is formed by the 6 bits from the palette register and bits 2 and 3 of the color select register (see Figure 4.44). If bit 7 of the attribute mode control register is set, then the 6-bit color value is formed by the lower 4 bits of the palette register and the 2 bits of the color select register. Since these bits affect all palette registers simultaneously, the program can rapidly change all colors displayed by changing the value in the color select register. The color select register is not used in the 256-color graphics mode number 19.

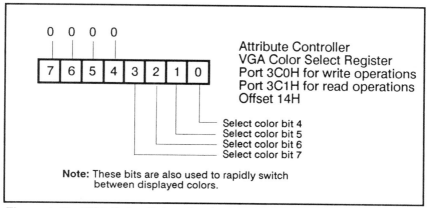

Figure 4.48. *VGA Color Select Register*

4.5.6 The Digital-to-Analog Converter (DAC)

The digital-to-analog converter, or DAC, is a programmable device used only in VGA systems. It provides a color look-up table as well as three drivers for an analog display. The color look-up table permits the display of 256 color combinations from a total of 262,166 possible colors. Table 4.18 shows the addresses used in the DAC.

Table 4.18. *VGA Video Digital-to-Analog Converter Addresses*

REGISTER	OPERATIONS	ADDRESS
Pixel address (write operations)	Read-Write	03C8H
Pixel address (read operations)	Write only	03C7H
DAC state register	Read only	03C7H
Pixel data register	Read-Write	03C9H
Pixel mask register	Read-Write	03C6H

Note: Applications must not write to the pixel mask register or the color look-up table could be destroyed.

The DAC pixel address register holds the address of a location in the color look-up table. A write operation to this address forces three bumps of the address pointer to successive memory locations. This operation allows rapid access to three locations within the color look-up table. The write sequence to address 03C8H consists of three successive writes to the pixel data register at address 03C9H. Because each entry in the color look-up table is 18 bits wide, the write operation is performed using the least significant 6 bits of each byte. The recommended order of operations for the WRITE function is as follows:

1. Select the starting address with a write operation to the pixel address register at 03C8H.

2. Disable interrupts.

3. Write the 18-bit color code that selects the desired color out of 256K possible combinations. Notice that with 18 bits, it is possible to generate any number in the range 0 to 256K. The write operation is performed by using the 6 low-order bits in the 3 consecutive bytes output to the pixel data register.

4. The DAC transfers the contents of the pixel data register to the location contained in the pixel address register.

5. The pixel address register increments automatically to point to the subsequent memory location.

6. If more than one color is to be changed, the sequence of operations can be repeated from step number 3.

7. Re-enable interrupts.

Read or write operations to the video DAC must be spaced 240 ns. Assembly language code can meet this timing requirement if a short JMP instruction is inserted between successive IN or OUT opcodes.

4.6 EGA and VGA Video Memory Architecture

In EGA systems, the display buffer consists of a 64K RAM chip installed in the card itself. Up to three more 64K blocks of video memory can be optionally added on the piggyback memory expansion card. The maximum memory supported is 256K, divided into four 64K blocks. VGA systems always contain the maximum 256K video memory as part of the system board. As in the EGA, this memory is logically divided into four 64K blocks that form video maps 0 to 3. These maps are sometimes referred to as bit planes 0 to 3.

4.6.1 VGA/EGA Memory Structure in the Alphanumeric Modes

The alphanumeric or text modes are listed in Table 4.1. Their numbers are 0, 1, 2, 3, and 7. Of these, modes 0, 2, and 7 are in monochrome, and modes 1 and 3 are in color.

When an alphanumeric mode is active, the video buffer is structured to hold the character codes at the even addresses and the attribute byte at the odd addresses. Figures 4-1 and 4-6 show the pattern of character codes and attributes as they are stored at consecutive locations in the buffer. The possible functions of the attribute byte can be seen in Figure 4.49.

Bit 3 of the mode control register in the attribute controller selects the background intensity or blink select function of bit 7 of the attribute byte (see Figure 4.44). Bit 3 of the attribute byte is the character set select function. This function is active if bit 1 of the memory mode register of the sequencer is set (see Figure 4.32) and if the value of character map select A does not equal that of character map select B of the character map select register (see Figure 4.31).

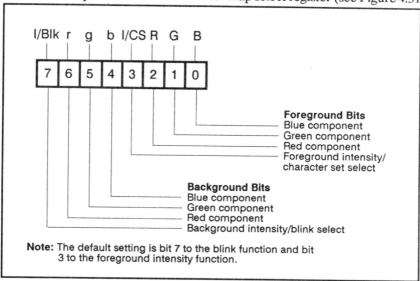

Figure 4.49. *Functions of the Attribute Byte*

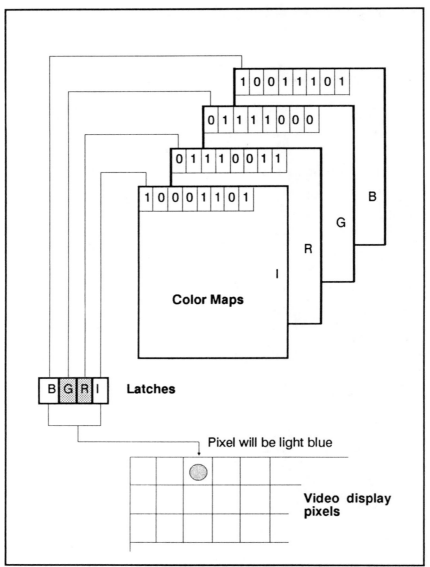

Figure 4.50. *Structure of Video Memory in VGA Mode 18*

4.6.2 VGA/EGA Memory Structure in the Graphics Modes

In order to compress the extensive graphic image data into the limited memory space of IBM microcomputers under MS DOS, the designers of the EGA and VGA standards have resorted to a special technique. It consists of a folded color memory implemented through latch registers, which results in several color maps located at the same physical address. Each memory map is imaged consecutively through a latching mechanism.

Figure 4.50 represents the map and pixel structure in VGA graphic mode 18. The illustration is designed to help visualize an image structure that is divided into several maps, all located at the same physical address.

In Figure 4.50 the color codes for the first eight screen pixels are stored in four maps, labeled I, R, G, and B (intensity, red, green, and blue). All four maps are located at address A0000H in VGA/EGA systems. In Figure 4.50, the first screen pixel has the intensity and blue bits set, therefore it appears light blue. For the same reason, the pixel at offset 1, which has the red and green bits set, will be displayed as yellow.

4.7 Video Resolution Symmetry

The resolution of a video display system can be expressed in terms of the total number of separately addressable elements per unit area, or, more concretely, in pixels per inch. For example, a VGA system, with 8-in screen rows containing a total of 640 pixels, has a horizontal resolution of 80 pixels per inch (640/8 = 80). This same VGA system (graphics mode 18) has 6-in-tall screen columns containing a total of 480 pixels. Therefore the vertical resolution is also 80 pixels per inch (480/6 = 80).

When the vertical and horizontal resolutions are equal, as in VGA graphics mode 18, the pixel structure forms a symmetrical grid. On the other hand, if the vertical and horizontal resolutions are different, the pixel grid is asymmetrical. Symmetrical pixel grids facilitate plotting on the screen surface, since it can be treated by the software as if it were quadrille graphing paper. An asymmetrical grid of horizontal and vertical pixels deforms geometrical screen forms. Figure 4.51 shows this effect of screen resolution symmetry in several graphics modes.

These deformations affect all geometrical figures; a circle appears as an ellipse when plotted on an asymmetrical grid, and all other geometrical pixel patterns are also displayed in a deformed manner. The correction of these aberrations requires software compensations that complicate graphics programming.

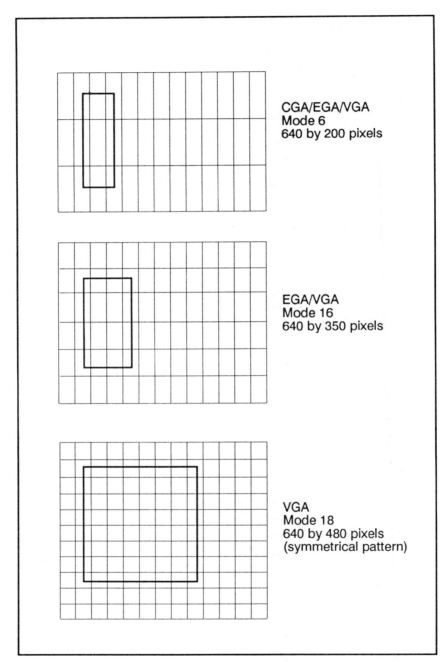

Figure 4.51. *Resolution Symmetry in Different Graphics Modes*

5

The Mathematical

Coprocessors

5.0 Microcomputer Mathematics on IBM Systems

The central processing unit of all IBM and IBM-compatible microcomputers manufactured to date is an Intel microprocessor of the iAPX family (see Chapter 2). These processors were conceived and designed as general-purpose devices; their mathematical instructions are limited to the fundamental arithmetic operations on signed and unsigned binary numbers and on unsigned decimals, specifically addition, subtraction, multiplication, division, and numerical conversions between binary and binary-coded decimal numbers. The more advanced processors in the iAPX family (80286 and 80386) have an expanded numerical range, but no new functions have been added.

However, numerical calculations are often an important part of a computing task. Furthermore, in many technical and financial applications, the fundamental task of the computer system is to obtain one or more numerical results. In this type of service, the system's effectiveness is measured by the accuracy of the results and the speed with which these results are obtained. In this respect, the iAPX family of central processing units has very limited possibilities.

Because of these limitations of the central processors, designers of integrated circuits conceived the idea of developing coprocessor chips to assist the central processor in some specialized tasks. These include coprocessors for graphics, text, data, communications, and mathematical calculations. Some Intel coprocessors are the 8089 input/output channel processor for data operations, the 82586 coprocessor for communications, the 82730 text processor, and the 80x87 family of mathematical coprocessors. Of these, the mathematical coprocessors are the only ones that have obtained meaningful application in IBM microcomputers.

5.1 The Intel Numeric Data Processors

In 1980, Intel introduced the 8087 mathematical coprocessor for the 8086 central processing unit. The original design work was performed by John Palmer and Bruce Ravenel. The 8087 chip is also known by the names numeric data processor (NDP), numeric data coprocessor, math coprocessor, and numeric processor extension (NPX). Numeric coprocessors are available for all iAPX central processors, as shown in Table 5.1. However, the 80486 chip includes the floating-point operations of the NDP in its own instruction set. For this reason, it does not require a numerical processor extension. The designation 80x87 is sometimes used to refer generically to any member of the Intel family of mathematical coprocessors.

The numerical data processor is not standard equipment in IBM microcom-

Table 5.1. *80x87 Coprocessors for the iAPX Processing Units*

iAPX CPU	80x87 COPROCESSOR
8086	8087
8088/80C88	8087
80186/80188	8087
80286	80287
80386	80287 or 80387
486	No NDP required

puters, although most IBM systems include an empty, wired socket for its installation. Two exceptions are the IBM PCjr and the PC Convertible, in which this socket is not available. Installation of the coprocessor in an IBM microcomputer consists of pushing the 8087, 80287, or 80387 chip into the appropriate socket. Some earlier hardware also requires changing the position of a mechanical switch. Other systems require the running of a software initialization routine to log the newly installed coprocessor.

The 80x87 component can be imitated in software by a program called an 80x87 emulator. This software allows the programmer to do all the mathematical calculations using 80x87 instructions, even if the target system is not equipped with the physical coprocessor. If the emulator has been adequately designed and coded, the only difference between using the 80x87 chip and using its software version would be that execution takes longer with the emulator than with the coprocessor. 80x87 emulators are available from Intel Corporation and from other software houses.

According to Intel, the 8087 component improves execution speeds of mathematical calculations by a factor of 10 to 100, compared with equivalent processing performed by 80x86 software. The 8087 extends the functions of the iAPX CPU by adding an instruction set of approximately 70 instructions and eight specialized registers for numerical operands.

5.1.1 Applications and Limitations

The mathematical coprocessor processes and stores numerical data encoded in seven different formats, but all internal calculations are performed in an 80-bit format that allows representation of 19 significant decimal digits. The maximum precision available to the user is in the long real format, which encodes 15 to 16 significant decimal digits. The processing capability includes the following operations:

1. Data transfers, from memory into the processor's registers and vice versa, of all data formats; conversion from ASCII into the processor's floating-point formats and vice versa must be executed in external software.

2. Arithmetic of integers and floating-point numbers.

3. Square roots, scaling, absolute value, remainder, sign change, and extraction of the integer and fractional parts of a number.

4. Direct loading of the constants 0, 1, π, and several logarithms.

5. Comparison and testing of internal processor operands.

6. Partial tangent and arc tangent (from which other trigonometric functions can be calculated), and several exponential and transcendental bases.

7. Control instruction to initialize the processor, to set internal operational modes, to store and restore the processor's registers and status, and to perform other housekeeping and auxiliary functions.

One limitation in programming the numerical data processor is that this chip must operate on encoded binary numbers in floating-point format. This means that the user's ASCII input must be converted into one of the machine's internal binary forms before calculation can take place. For the same reason, the results of the calculations must be converted from the internal formats into ASCII representations that can be interpreted by the user. These conversions require elaborate external software routines (see Section 5.6.2 and Appendix A).

Another limitation is in relation to the calculation of trigonometric and logarithmic functions in 8087 and 80287 systems. In the trigonometric functions, for example, only the tangent can be obtained, and only for an angle in the range 0 to $\pi/4$ radian. Sine and cosine functions must be calculated from the tangent, and the user's input must be previously scaled (see Section 5.6.4).

5.1.2 CPU and Coprocessor Interface

The iAPX central processor and the 80x87 numeric data processor form a unit that has the combined instruction set and processing capabilities of both chips. To the programmer, the combination appears as a single device. The CPU and the mathematical coprocessor use the same clock generator, system bus, and interface components.

Instructions for the central processor and the math coprocessor are intermixed in memory in the instruction stream. The first 5 bits of the opcode identify a coprocessor escape sequence (bit code 11011xxx). This bit pattern identifies the 80x86 ESC (escape) operation code. All instructions that match these first 5 bits are executed by the coprocessor. However, the iAPX CPU distinguishes between escape instructions that reference memory and those that do not. If the instruction contains a memory operand, the CPU performs the address calculations on behalf of the coprocessor. On the other hand, if the escape instruction does not contain a memory operand, then the iAPX CPU ignores it and proceeds to execute the next instruction in line.

5.1.3 Synchronization

The coprocessor mechanism in microprocessor systems was pioneered by Intel with the 8087 NDP. The fundamental design allows a central processor and a coprocessor to execute simultaneously. The hardware elements that make possible coprocessor operation are a BUSY pin in NDP, connected to a TEST pin in the CPU. The NDP's BUSY pin sends a signal whenever the coprocessor is executing. The CPU's TEST pin, upon receiving a WAIT (or FWAIT) instruction, forces the central processor to detain execution until the coprocessor has finished.

Understanding processor and coprocessor synchronization is complicated by the fact that it is implemented differently in the 8087 than in the 80287 and 80387 hardware.

Configurations that use the 8087 must not present a new instruction to the NDP while it is still executing the previous one. This condition can be prevented by inserting a 80x86 WAIT instruction either before or after every coprocessor ESC opcode. If the WAIT follows the ESC, then the central processor does nothing while the NDP is executing. In order to allow concurrent processing by the CPU and the NDP, most assembler programs insert the WAIT instruction before the coprocessor ESC opcode. In this case, the CPU can continue executing its own code until it finds the next ESC in the instruction stream.

However, when the WAIT precedes the ESC, it becomes possible for the CPU to access a memory operand before the coprocessor has finished acting on it. If this possibility exists, the programmer must detect it and insert an additional FWAIT. The alternative mnemonic FWAIT is usually preferred in this case, since some emulator libraries do not recognize the WAIT opcode. The following code fragment shows a typical circumstance that requires the insertion of an FWAIT instruction.

```
FSTCW CTRL_WORD    ; Store control word in memory
FWAIT              ; Force the CPU to wait for NDP
                   ; to finish before
MOV    AX,CTRL_WORD        ; recovering the control word
                   ; into the AX register
```

Synchronization requirements are different in 80286/80287 and 80386/80387 systems. The 80286 and 80386 CPUs automatically check that the NDP has finished executing the previous instruction before sending it the next one. Unlike the 8087, the 80287 and 80387 do not require the WAIT instruction for synchronization. However, the possibility of both processors accessing the same memory operand simultaneously also exists in 80287/80387 systems and must be prevented as previously described for the 8087 (see preceding code fragment).

Programs that are intended for 8087 systems must follow 8087 synchronization requirements. However, some 80287 assemblers (such as Intel's ASM286) omit the FWAIT opcode. Other assemblers (such as Microsoft's MASM version 5.0 and later) have options that allow the FWAIT instructions to be automatically inserted or not inserted. In either case, code in which the ESC instructions are not accompanied by a CPU FWAIT will not execute correctly in 8087 systems. If the assembler program used to generate the machine code does not automatically insert the FWAIT instruction preceding each coprocessor escape, then, if the program is to run in 8087 systems, the programmer will have to manually insert the FWAIT opcode in the source file.

Some NDP processor control instructions have an alternative mnemonic that instructs the assembler not to prefix the instruction with a CPU FWAIT. This mnemonic form is characterized by the letters FN, signifying NO WAIT, for example, FINIT/FNINIT and FENI/FNENI. The no-wait form should be used only if CPU interrupts are disabled and the NDP is set up so that it cannot generate an interrupt that would precipitate an endless wait. In all other cases, the normal version of the instruction should be used.

5.1.4 Versions of the NDP

Three versions of the mathematical coprocessor have been released by Intel. The original chip, intended for use with the 8086/8088 and also compatible with the 80186 and 80188, is designated the 8087. The 80287 is the version designed to function with the 80286 CPU, and the 80387 is the version designed to function with the 80386 central processor (see Table 5.1).

5.1.4.1 The 8087 NDP.
8087 is Intel's designation for the original mathematical coprocessor chip. The chip was first offered to the public in 1980. It was developed simultaneously with the IEEE proposed standard for binary floating-point arithmetic, whose original version was published in 1979. For this reason, there are some minor differences between the 8087 chip and the standard; in most cases the difference consists of the 8087 exceeding the standard's requirements. The pertinent IEEE standard is number 754.

5.1.4.2 The 80287 NDP.
The 80287, introduced in 1983, is the version of the Intel mathematical coprocessor designed for the 80286 CPU. The 80287 extends numerical coprocessing to the protected-mode, multitasking environment of the 80286 CPU. When multiple tasks execute in the 80287, they receive the memory management and protection features of the central processor. According to Intel, the performance of the 80287 chip is 41 to 266 times that of equivalent software routines. The 80287 is also compatible with the 80386 central processor.

The internal architecture and instruction set of the 80287 are almost identical to those of its predecessor, the 8087. Most programs for the 8087 will execute unmodified in the 80287 protected mode, except for the handling of numeric exceptions. The following are the major differences between the 80287 and the 8087:

1. The 80286 uses a dedicated line to signal processing errors to the CPU. This signal does not pass through the system's interrupt controller.

2. The 8087 instructions for enabling and disabling interrupts, FENI/FNENI and FDISI/FNDISI, serve no purpose and are not implemented in the 80287. The opcodes are ignored by the processor.

3. The 80287 instruction opcodes are not saved when executing in protected mode, but exception handlers can retrieve these opcodes from memory.

4. While the address of the ESC instruction saved by the 8087 does not include leading prefixes (such as segment overrides), the 80287 does include them.

5. The FSETPM instruction, used to enable 80287 protected-mode operation, has no equivalent in the 8087.

6. The FSTSW and FNSTSW instructions in the 80287 allow the AX register as a destination operand. Writing the status word to a processor register optimizes conditional branching.

8087 instructions must be preceded by an FWAIT instruction to synchronize processor and coprocessor. This opcode is automatically generated by most assemblers. The FWAIT instruction is not required for the 80287, which has an asynchronous interface with the main processor. For this reason, reassembling programs intended for the 80287 exclusively may result in a more compact code that executes slightly faster (see Section 5.1.3). On the other hand, this code will not execute on 8087 systems.

5.1.4.3 The 80387 NDP. The Intel 80387 is a mathematical coprocessor intended for the 80386 central processing unit. The 80387 supports all 8087 and 80287 operations and instructions. Programs developed for the 8087 or the 80287 will generally execute unmodified on the 80387.

The 80387 conforms with the final version of the IEEE 754 standard for binary floating-point arithmetic, approved in 1985. This has made necessary the following changes in coprocessor behavior:

1. Automatic normalization of denormalized operands.

2. Affine interpretation of infinity. Note that the 8087 and 80287 support both affine and projective infinities.

3. Unordered compare instructions which will not generate an invalid operation exception if one operand is a NAN.

4. A partial remainder instruction that will behave as expected in the IEEE 754 standard. The 80387 version of the FPREM instruction is named FPREM1.

The 80387 instructions FUCOM, FUCOMP, and FUCOMPP differ from the previous FCOM, FCOMP, and FCOMPP instructions in that they do not generate an invalid operation exception if one of the operands is tagged as not-a-number (NAN). The 80387 instruction set has been expanded with the opcodes FSIN, to calculate sines, FCOS, to calculate cosines, and FSINCOS, to calculate both sine and cosine functions simultaneously. This last instruction can be followed by a division operation to directly obtain tangents and cotangents.

The operand range of the instructions FPTAN, FPATAN, F2XM1, and FSCALE has been expanded, as shown in Table 5.2. This expansion simplifies the calculation of some trigonometric and transcendental functions.

5.2 Coprocessor Architecture

The mathematical coprocessors of the 80x87 family have many common elements in their architecture. Internally, the NDP is divided into a control unit (CU) and a numeric execution unit (NEU). But the processor's internal structure is generally transparent to the programmer, who perceives the NDP as consisting of the following data areas:

1. A stack of eight operational registers
2. A control register
3. A status register
4. A tag word, consisting of 2 tag bits for each stack register
5. An instruction pointer
6. A data pointer

Table 5.2. *Expanded Operands in 80387 Instructions*

OPERATION	OPCODE	80387 OPERAND RANGE	80287/8087 OPERAND RANGE
Partial tangent	FPTAN	$|st(0)| < 2.0\ E63$	$|st(0)| < \pi/4$
Arctangent	FPATAN	Unrestricted	$|st(0)| < |st(1)|$
$2^x - 1$	F2XM1	$-1 \le st(0) \le 1$	$0 \le st(0) \le 0.5$
Scale	FSCALE	Unrestricted	Undefined in the range $0 < st(1) < 1$

5.2.1 The Register Stack

The numeric execution unit of the NDP contains eight internal registers for operational data. Many instructions allow these registers to be addressed explicitly, that is, according to their designation in the ST(i) form. Figure 5.1 is a representation of the NDP register stack.

In Figure 5.1, the explicit designation appears to the left of each register. Most assemblers allow the designations ST and ST(0) for the register at the stack top. For example, the instruction

FADD   ST,ST(2)

adds the third stack register (ST(2)) to the stack top register (ST). The sum replaces the previous value of ST.

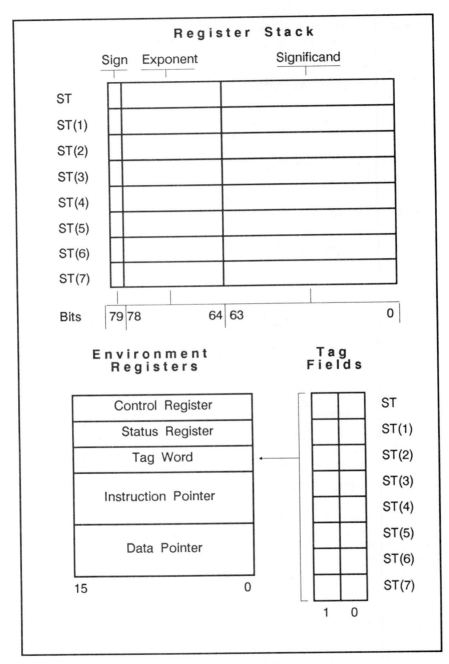

Figure 5.1. *NDP Registers*

Other NDP instructions operate implicitly on the register at the stack top. For example, the instruction FSQRT replaces the contents of the ST register with its square root.

Each of the stack registers is 80 bits wide. The data storage format corresponds to the NDP temporary real numeric format (see Section 5.3). This data format is used internally by the NDP in all its calculations. The left column in Figure 5.1 shows the designation of each register in the ST(i) form.

5.2.2 The Control Register

The NDP operates in several modes. The programmer selects the mode of operation by loading a memory word into the control register.

A program can inspect or change the contents of the control register using the instructions FLDCW (load control word) or FSTCW (store control word). Figure 5.2 is a bit map of the control register.

These NDP operational modes can be classified as computational and exception response modes. The exception response mode is determined by the settings of bits 0 to 5, and, in 8087 systems, also by bit 7 of the control register (see Figure 5.2). Bits 0 to 5 (exception masks) define the error conditions that can generate an interrupt. If the exception mask for the condition is set (mask = 1), a default handling of the error condition automatically takes place inside the NDP. These on-chip responses to computational errors are usually adequate for most applications.

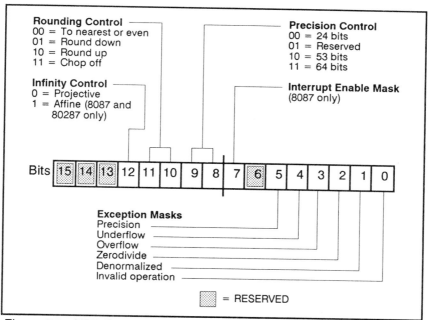

Figure 5.2. *NDP Control Register*

However, if the exception flag for the condition is clear (mask = 0), an interrupt is immediately generated. An error handler routine can intercept this interrupt. In 8087 systems, bit 7 of the control register (the interrupt enable mask bit) must also be clear (bit = 0) for the interrupt to take place. This bit field is not implemented in 80287 and 80387 systems.

The error conditions determined by the exception mask bits are the following:

1. *Invalid operation*. This error is usually a product of programming errors, for example, loading a nonempty register or popping an empty register, and also by stack overflow and underflow. Undefined operations can also generate an invalid operation error, for example, a division of zero by zero or the square root of a negative number. The invalid operation exception is frequently the only one that requires independent processing by means of an interrupt handler.

2. *Overflow*. Overflow occurs when a number exceeds the range of the destination data format.

3. *Underflow*. Underflow occurs when a number is too small for the destination data format.

4. *Zerodivide*. This error consists of a division by zero of a nonzero operand.

5. *Denormalized*. This error occurs if an operation is attempted when one or both operands are denormals.

6. *Precision*. This error indicates loss of numeric precision during the last operation. The most frequent cause of a loss of precision is internal rounding by the NDP.

The remaining fields of the control register determine the computational modes of operation.

7. *Precision control*. The NDP is designed to round the results of all floating-point operations before storing them in one of the stack registers (see Figure 5.2). The setting of the precision control bits determines the format (temporary real, long real, or short real) to which the rounding will take place. The temporary real precision control mode (rounding to 64 bits) is the one best suited for most purposes. The other settings were added to provide compatibility with earlier processors and to meet a requirement of the IEEE 754 standard.

8. *Rounding control*. The rounding control field determines how the rounding takes place. Rounding to the nearest even number is the most common setting, since it is the least biased mode and is suitable for most applications (see Figure 5.2). By changing the value in the rounding control field, a routine can be designed to execute the calculations twice, once rounding up and another time rounding down. Afterward, the two results can be compared and the upper and lower bounds of the exact result can be determined. This technique allows certifying that the result is correct within a certain interval.

9. *Infinity control.* The most common treatment of infinity recognizes the existence of infinitely large and infinitely small numbers. The IEEE standard supports only this treatment of infinity, known as *affine closure*, and so does the 80387. Nevertheless, the 8087 and 80287 also allow a treatment of infinity known as the *projective method of closure.* In this method, there is no relation between infinity and ordinary signed numbers. The infinity control bit in the 8087 and 80287 control register permits the selection of either model of infinity. In the 80387, the infinity control bit is not active.

5.2.3 The Status Register

The status register reflects the state of the NDP at the instant that it is accessed. The instruction FSTSW can be used to store the status register in a memory variable, where the program can inspect it. By coding FSTSW AX, 80287 and 80387 systems also allow transferring the contents of the status register into the AX register. Figure 5.3 is a map of the status register.

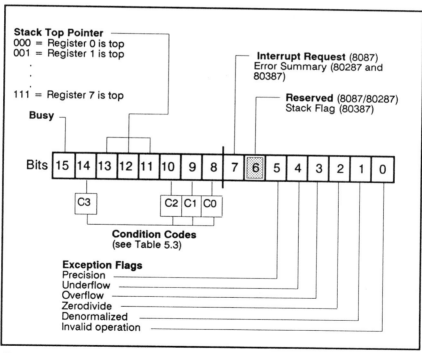

Figure 5.3. *NDP Status Register*

Status register bits 0 to 5 reflect the error conditions of precision, underflow, overflow, division by zero, denormalized operand, and invalid operation described in Section 5.2.2. If one of these conditions has occurred, the corresponding bit in the status register will be set. This action is independent of the setting of the exception masks of the control register. Once an error has occurred, the corresponding error flag remains set until it is explicitly reset with a FCLEX (clear exceptions) instruction or until the coprocessor is reinitialized.

In 8087 systems, bit 7 of the status register is called the interrupt request bit. Intel literature on the 80287 refers to this bit as the error summary bit. In both cases, this bit is set if an unmasked exception bit is set in the status register. Therefore, bit 7 of the status register can be used to test whether an interrupt condition is pending.

The NDP condition code bits can be compared to the flag bits in the CPU. Their state is determined by NDP computational operations, and their setting reflects the outcome of these operations. The condition code bits can be tested by loading the status word into a CPU register. The test can be used in conditional branching. Table 5.3 summarizes the various interpretations of the condition code bits after executing the corresponding test instructions. The condition code bits are also used to report the last 3 significant bits of the quotient generated by the partial remainder instruction, FPREM.

Table 5.3. *NDP Condition Codes*

INSTRUCTION	CONDITION CODE BITS				INTERPRETATION
	C3	C2	C1	C0	
FCOM, FCOMP, FCOMPP, FICOM, FICOMP	0	0	?	0	ST > source
	0	0	?	1	ST < source
	1	0	?	0	ST = source
	1	1	?	1	ST or source undefined
FTST	0	0	?	0	ST is positive and nonzero
	0	0	?	1	ST is negative and nonzero
	1	0	?	0	ST is zero (+ or -)
	1	1	?	1	ST is not comparable
FXAM	0	0	0	0	+Unnormal
	0	0	1	0	− Unnormal
	0	1	0	0	+Normal
	0	1	1	0	− Normal
	1	0	0	0	+0
	1	0	1	0	− 0
	1	1	0	0	+Denormal
	1	1	1	0	− Denormal
	0	0	0	1	+ NAN
	0	0	1	1	− NAN
	0	1	0	1	+Infinity
	0	1	1	1	− Infinity
	1	?	?	1	Empty
FUCOM, FUCOMP, FUCOMPP	0	0	?	0	ST > source
	0	0	?	1	ST < source
	1	0	?	0	ST = source
	1	1	?	1	Unordered

The field composed of bits 11, 12, and 13 encodes the number of the NDP register which is currently the stack top (see Figure 5.3). After initialization, the value of this bit field is 000B. When a value is loaded onto the NDP stack, the stack top pointer field changes to 111B (7 decimal). Each successive operation that loads the NDP stack decrements the stack top pointer field, and each store increments it. One of the few practical uses of this bit field is in interpreting the tag register (see Section 5.2.4).

The busy bit (bit number 15 in Figure 5.3) indicates whether the NDP is idle or executing an instruction. This bit is of little practical use to applications.

5.2.4 The 8087 Tag Register

Each 2-bit field of the tag register (see Figure 5.1) is associated with a stack register. The tag code defines the contents of each one of the eight stack registers. The tag word register is shown in Figure 5.4.

The tag code is used internally by the processor in optimizing performance. The tag codes are accessible to the program and can be used to determine the stack contents. It is necessary to inspect the stack top pointer field of the status register to determine which tag corresponds to which stack register. Stack register contents can usually be determined more precisely using the FXAM or FTST instructions and interpreting the resulting condition code bits (see Table 5.3).

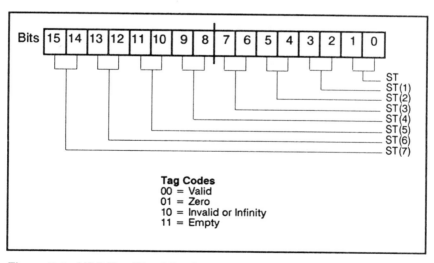

Figure 5.4. *NDP Tag Word Register*

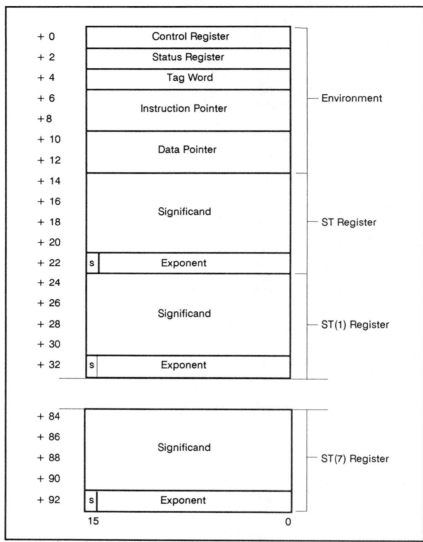

Figure 5.5. *NDP State Memory Map*

5.2.5 The Instruction and Data Pointers

These NDP registers (see Figure 5.1) have also been called the *exception pointers*. After a computational instruction executes, the NDP automatically saves the instruction's operation code, its address, and, if included in the instruction, the operand address in the instruction and data pointer registers. This information can be examined by storing the processor's environment in memory through an FSTENV instruction (see Figure 5.1) or by storing the entire processor's state (environment and stack registers) by means of the FSAVE instruction (see Figure 5.5). An exception handler can use this information to identify the instruction that generated an error. Figure 5.5 is a memory map of the NDP state register.

In 80287 and 80387 systems, the storage format for the instruction and data pointers depends on the operating mode. In the real mode, the value stored is in the form of a 20-bit physical address and an 11-bit 8087 opcode. In protected mode, the value stored is the 32-bit virtual address of the last coprocessor instruction.

5.3 Numeric Data Types

The NDP operates on three different data types and a total of seven numeric formats (see Table 5.5). All numeric formats are stored in memory following the rule that the lowest significant element is located at the lowest-numbered memory address. Figure 5.6 shows the NDP data formats.

The data types are classified as follows:

1. *Binary integers*. This data type corresponds with the word, doubleword, and quadword units of data storage. The sign bit is located at the highest numbered memory location; 1 = negative and 0 = positive. Negative numbers are represented in 2s complement form. The binary integer formats (see Table 5.4) are named *word integer, short integer*, and *long integer*.

2. *Decimal integers*. This data type corresponds with the *packed decimal* format shown in Table 5.4. The sign bit is located at the highest-numbered memory location; 1 = negative and 0 = positive. Two decimal digits are packed into each byte in binary-coded decimal form.

3. *Real numbers*. The NDP real-number formats are named *short real, long real*, and *temporary real* (see Figure 5.6). As in the other formats, the sign bit is located at the highest memory address; 1 = negative and 0 = positive. In all real formats the number's digits are stored in the significand field. The logarithmic terms *mantissa* and *characteristic* are sometimes used to refer to the significand and exponent fields.

The exponent in the real formats is stored in bias form; bias 7FH for the short real format, bias 3FFH for the long real format, and bias 3FFFH for the temporary real format. The significand is stored in normalized form, that is, as a binary representation of a decimal number greater than 1 and less than 2. This form of normalization eliminates leading zeros when representing small values and maximizes the number of significant digits. The number of bits in the binary fraction is 23 in the short real, 52 in the long real, and 63 in the temporary real. The integer bit is implicit in the short and long real formats and explicit in the temporary real format. The implied binary decimal point follows the first digit of the significand. Table 5.4 lists the numerical range of the various data formats.

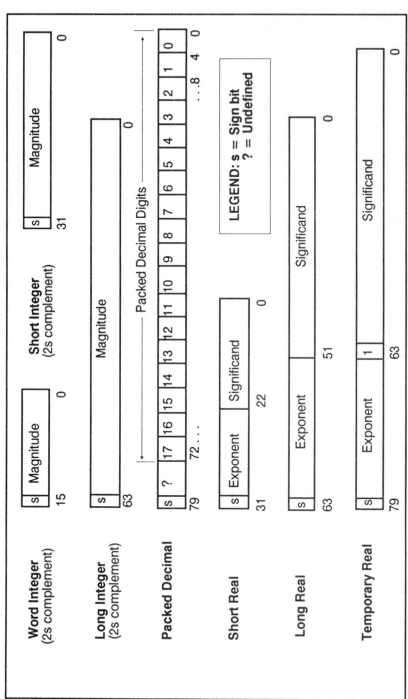

Figure 5.6. *NDP Data Formats*

Table 5.4. *Numerical Range of NDP Data Types*

DESIGNATION	BITS	SIGNIFICANT DIGITS	APPROXIMATE RANGE
Word integer	16	4–5	$-32{,}768$ to $32{,}767$
Short integer	32	9	$-2\text{x}10^9$ to $2\text{x}10^9$
Long integer	64	18	$-9\text{x}10^{18}$ to $9\text{x}10^{18}$
Packed decimal	80	18	18 decimal digits
Short real	32	6–7	$8.43\text{x}10^{-37}$ to $3.37\text{x}10^{38}$
Long real	64	14–15	$4.19\text{x}10^{-307}$ to $3.37\text{x}10^{308}$
Temporary real	80	18–19	$3.4\text{x}10^{-4932}$ to $1.2\text{x}10^{4932}$

Except for the temporary reals, all NDP numeric formats exist only in memory. When a number is loaded into an NDP stack register, it is automatically converted into a temporary real. All internal computations are carried out in temporary real numbers. The extended precision of this format provides a safety net for the computational errors that result from rounding, overflow, and underflow. This temporary real format can also be used for the storage of constants and intermediate results. However, it is better to refrain from using this format to increase the accuracy of computations, since this would compromise the safety features mentioned above.

5.4 NDP Emulator Software

Intel and other firms make available software products called 8087, 80287, or 80387 emulators. These programs are designed to offer a software alternative to the mathematical coprocessor hardware. Ideally, an emulator will make systems without the NDP chip execute all 80x87 instructions exactly as if there were a coprocessor installed. The vendors of software emulators often claim that the only difference between a system equipped with the coprocessor hardware and an emulated one is the slower execution of NDP instructions in the emulated version. In reality, emulator designers must make concessions, for the sake of performance, that determine small variations in emulator behavior in relation to the hardware counterpart. This is particularly true in regard to computational precision and rounding.

A limitation of the Intel emulator for 80x86/8087 systems is that the decision to use the software or the real component must be made at link time. Consequently, once a program has been linked with the emulator, it will not use the hardware component even if one is available in the host system.

The 80286 and 80386 central processors (see Chapter 2) allow configuring of the numerics environment during system initialization. The MP (math present) and EM (emulate) bits in the processor's machine status word indicate whether an NDP is available in the system or not. If the MP bit is set (math coprocessor present), execution of the ESC instruction transfers control to the NDP in the normal manner. On the contrary, if the EM bit is set, an INT 7 is generated. Systems programmers can install the NDP emulator at this interrupt vector, thus making emulation transparent to applications. Note that the LMSW instruction, to change the machine status word, must be executed at the highest privilege level.

5.4.1 Detecting the NDP

The first step in configuring the numeric environment is to test for the presence of the physical numeric data processor. The following code fragment shows a simple way to detect the 8087, 80287, or 80387 chip. The test is based on the effect on the NDP status word of the initialization instruction FNINIT.

```
; Program to detect the presence of the NDP in an IBM system
;
; ************************* stack ****************************
;
STACK  SEGMENT stack
;
       DB     0100H DUP ('?')
;
STACK  ENDS
;
; ************************* data *****************************
;
DATA   SEGMENT
;
CTRL_87        DW     00H     ; NDP control word storage
                              ; Initialized to zeros
;
MSG_YES87      DB     '80x87 installed',0AH,0DH,'$'
MSG_NO87       DB     'No 80x87 installed',0AH,0DH,'$'
;
DATA   ENDS
;
; ************************* code *****************************
;
;
CODE   SEGMENT
```

```
        ASSUME      CS:CODE
START:
;
; Establish data and extra segment addressability
        MOV    AX,DATA
        MOV    DS,AX
        ASSUME      DS:DATA

;*********************
;    initialize NDP
;*********************
        FNINIT                 ; Initialize NDP, no wait
        FNSTCW      CTRL_87    ; Store control word in memory
        MOV    AX,CTRL_87      ; Control word to AX
        CMP    AH,03H          ; High byte will be 03H if
                               ; a coprocessor installed
        JNE    NO_87           ; No coprocessor in system
;*********************
;    NDP in system
;*********************
        MOV    AH,09H          ; DOS service request number
        LEA    DX,MSG_YES87;   Message
        INT    21H             ; DOS service
        JMP    DOS_EXIT        ; Exit

;*********************
;  No NDP in system
;*********************
NO_87:
        MOV    AH,09H          ; DOS service request number
        LEA    DX,MSG_NO87 ;   Message
        INT    21H             ; DOS service

;*********************
;   exit to DOS
;*********************
DOS_EXIT:
        MOV    AH,4CH          ; DOS service request code
        MOV    AL,0            ; No error code returned
        INT    21H             ; To DOS
;
CODE  ENDS
        END    START
```

5.5 Encodings in the Temporary Real Format

The temporary real format is the internal data format used by the NDP for all values stored in the stack registers. All other data formats exist only in memory (see Section 5-3). Table 5.5 shows the encoding of temporary real numbers.

Nonzero real numbers are encoded in normalized form; that is, the high-order bit of the significand is set. This bit is explicit in the temporary real format

Table 5.5. NDP *Encoding for Temporary Reals*

		CLASS		SIGN	BIASED EXPONENT	SIGNIFICAND
P		NAN		0 · ·	111 ... 111 · ·	1111 ...11 · 1000 ... 01
O S		Infinity		.	111 ... 111	1000 ... 00
I T	R	Normals		. · ·	111 ... 110 · ·	1111 ... 11 · 1000 ... 00
I V		Unnormals		. · ·	· · 000 ... 001	0111 ... 11 · 0000 ... 00
E	E	Denormals		. · ·	000 ... 000 · ·	0111 ... 11 · 0000 ... 01
	A	Zero		0	000 ... 000	0000 ... 00
	L	Zero		1	000 ... 000	0000 ... 00
N E	S	Denormals		. · ·	· ·	0000 ... 01 · 0111 ... 11
G A		Unnormals		. · ·	000 ... 001 · ·	0000 ... 00 · 0111 ... 11
T I		Normals		. · ·	· · 111 ... 110	1000 ... 00 · 1111 ... 11
V		Infinity		.	111 ... 111	1000 ... 00
E	NAN	Indefinite		.	· 111 ... 111	1100 ... 00
				1	111 ... 111	1111 ... 11
		Bits		79	78 64	63 0

(see Figure 5.6). But, as a floating-point value approaches zero (see positive and negative unnormals and denormals in Table 5.5), the normalized form can no longer be used for encoding the significand.

Unnormal and *denormal* numbers are generically termed *nonnormals*. Denormals can be identified by all zeros in the exponent field. A denormal is the result of a masked underflow exception. It represents a number that is too small for the destination format. By gradually denormalizing the result, the NDP allows computations to continue at the expense of contaminating the final result with a rounding error. An unnormal is, generally, a descendant of a denormal, that is, a denormal that has grown bigger during numerical processing. The denormal format prevents a denormal from masquerading as a normal number.

The *infinity* encoding can be produced intentionally by the programmer or can be the result of the masked response to the zerodivide or overflow exceptions. In the temporary real format, the infinities can be identified by all bits set in the exponent field while only the leading bit is set in the significand field (see Table 5.5). The encoding for infinity allows signed representations.

The encoding for *zero* can be positive or negative, according to the setting of the sign bit (see Table 5.5). Negative and positive zeros behave identically during computations. The FXAM instruction (see Table 5.3) can be used to determine the sign of a zero value. An unnormal with a significand of all zeros and a nonzero exponent (but not all 1s) is sometimes called a *pseudo zero*.

The designation *NAN* stands for not a number. A special type of NAN, called *indefinite*, is the masked response to an invalid exception (see Table 5.5). Whenever a NAN enters into a computation, it propagates and contaminates the result. A NAN can be identified in the temporary real format by all bits set in the exponent field and at least 1 bit set in the significand field. The special NAN called indefinite has the 2 high-order bits of the significand set, and all other significand bits clear.

5.6 Programming the NDP

To the programmer, the NDP appears as an extension to the internal registers and the instruction set of the central processor. Assembly language programs that use the NDP usually include opcodes from the instruction sets of both processors. NDP instruction mnemonics are identified in the source by the initial letter F.

The addressing modes available in the NDP are a subset of those of the main CPU. For example, NDP addressing does not allow arithmetic operations on memory variables, as in the 80x86 instruction set.

Some NDP instructions allow the stack registers to be designated explicitly, in the ST(i) form, while in others the stack top operand is assumed. In addition, some instructions can have memory variables as operands; for example,

```
FADD                    ; Implicit destination operand
FADD    S_REAL          ; Explicit source operand
FADD    ST,ST(3)        ; Destination and source operands
```

The leftmost operand is called the *destination*, and the rightmost operand is the *source*. Source operands supply data for the operation but are not altered during execution. The destination operand is replaced with the result.

The programmer must take into account that some NDP instructions change all previous ST designations; for example, loading data into a NDP stack register (FLD or FILD instructions) automatically pushes all previous values in the stack by one stack register.

5.6.1 The NDP Instruction Set

NDP instructions are usually classified into the following groups:

1. Data transfer instructions
2. Arithmetic instructions
3. Comparison instructions
4. Transcendental instructions
5. Constant instructions
6. Processor control instructions

Table 5.6 contains the opcodes, descriptions, and examples of all NDP instructions.

5.6.1.1 Data Transfer Instructions. Data transfer instructions move numeric data between stack registers and between the registers and memory. Any of the seven data formats listed in Table 5.4 can be read from memory. All numerical input is converted to the temporary real format as the values are loaded into the NDP. Data transfer instructions automatically update the tag word that corresponds to the stack register accessed. The following are data transfer instructions.

FLD source (load real number)

FST destination (store real number)

FSTP destination (store real number and pop stack)

FXCH destination (exchange registers)

FILD source (integer load)

FIST destination (integer store)

FISTP destination (integer store and pop stack)

FBLD source (packed decimal load)

FBSTP destination (packed decimal store and pop)

Table 5.6. *80x87 Instruction Set Reference*

	DESCRIPTION	EXAMPLES	
FABS	Calculate absolute value of ST.	FABS	
FADD	Add source to destination with results in destination.	FADD FADD FADD FADD	ST,ST(2) S_REAL L_REAL
FADDP	Add and pop stack.	FADDP	ST(2),ST
FBLD	Load packed BCD onto stack.	FBLD	BCD_NUM
FBSTP	Store stack top as a packed BCD and pop stack.	FBSTP	BCD_NUM
FCHS	Change sign of stack top element.	FCHS	
FCLEX FNCLEX	Clear exception flags, IR flag, and busy flag in the status word.	FCLEX FNCLEX	
FCOM	Compare stack top with source operand (stack register or memory). If no source, ST(1) is assumed.	FCOM FCOM FCOM FCOM	ST(2) S_REAL L_REAL
FCOMP	Compare stack top with source and pop stack (see FCOM).	FCOMP FCOMP FCOMP FCOMP	ST(2) S_REAL L_REAL
FCOMPP	Compare stack top with ST(1) and pop stack twice. Both operands are discarded.	FCOMPP	
FCOS (80387)	Calculate cosine of stack top and return value in ST. $\|ST\| < 2^{63}$ Input in radians.	FCOS	
FDECSTP	Decrement stack top pointer field in the status word. If field = 0, then it will change to 7.	FDECSTP	
FDISI FNDISI (8087)	Disable interrupts by setting mask. No action in 80287 and 80387.	FDISI FNDISI	
FDIV	Divide destination by source with quotient in destination. If no destination specified, ST is assumed.	FDIV FDIV FDIV FDIV	ST,ST(2) ST(4),ST S_REAL L_REAL
FDIVP	Divide destination by source with quotient in destination and pop stack (see FDIV).	FDIVP	ST(3),ST
FDIVR	Divide source by destination with quotient in destination. If no destination is specified, ST is assumed. Reverse divide.	FDIVR FDIVR FDIVR FDIVR	ST,ST(2) ST(3),ST S_REAL L_REAL
FDIVRP	Divide source by destination with quotient in destination and pop stack (see FDIVR).	FDIVRP	ST(4),ST

(continued)

Table 5.6. *80x87 Instruction Set Reference (Continued)*

	DESCRIPTION	EXAMPLES	
FENI FNENI (8087)	Enable interrupts by clearing the mask in the control register. No action in 80287 and 80387.	FENI FNENI	
FFREE	Change destination stack register and tag field to EMPTY.	FFREE	ST(2)
FIADD	Add integer in memory to stack top with sum in stack top.	FIADD FIADD	S_INTEGER W_INTEGER
FICOM	Compare integer in memory with stack top.	FICOM FICOM	S_INTEGER W_INTEGER
FICOMP	Compare integer in memory with stack top and pop stack. Stack top element is discarded.	FICOMP FICOMP	S_INTEGER W_INTEGER
FIDIV	Divide stack top by integer memory variable. Quotient in stack top.	FIDIV FIDIV	S_INTEGER W_INTEGER
FIDIVR	Divide integer memory variable by stack top. Quotient in stack top.	FIDIVR FIDIVR	S_INTEGER W-INTEGER
FILD	Load word, short, or long integer onto stack top. Loaded number is converted to temporary real.	FILD FILD FILD	S_INTEGER W_INTEGER L_INTEGER
FIMUL	Multiply integer memory variable by stack top. Product in stack top.	FIMUL FIMUL	S_INTEGER W_INTEGER
FINCSTP	Add 1 to stack top field in the status word. If field = 7, then it will change to 0.	FINCSTP	
FINIT FNINIT	Initialize processor. Control word is set to 3FFH. Stack registers are tagged EMPTY and all exception flags are cleared.	FINIT FNINIT	
FIST	Round stack top to integer, as per RC field in the status word, and store in integer memory variable.	FIST FIST	S_INTEGER W_INTEGER
FISTP	Round stack top to integer, as per RC field in the status word, store in variable, and pop stack.	FISTP FISTP FISTP	S_INTEGER W_INTEGER L_INTEGER
FISUB	Subtract integer memory variable from stack top. Difference to stack top.	FISUB FISUB	S_INTEGER W_INTEGER
FISUBR	Subtract stack top from integer memory variable. Difference to stack top.	FISUBR FISUBR	S_INTEGER W_INTEGER
FLD	Load real memory variable or stack register onto stack top. Value is converted to temporary real.	FLD FLD FLD FLD	S_REAL L_REAL TEMP_REAL ST(2)
FLDCW	Load memory variable (word) onto the control register.	FLDCW	CTRL_WORD

(continued)

Table 5.6. *80x87 Instruction Set Reference (Continued)*

	DESCRIPTION	EXAMPLES
FLDENV	Load 14-byte environment from memory storage area.	FLDENV MEM_14
FLDLG2	Load logarithm base 10 of 2 onto stack top. Constant is accurate to 64 bits (19 digits).	FLDLG2
FLDLN2	Load logarithm base e of 2 onto stack top. Constant is accurate to 64 bits (19 digits).	FLDLN2
FLDL2E	Load logarithm base 2 of e onto stack top. Constant is accurate to 64 bits (19 digits).	FLDL2E
FLDL2T	Load logarithm base 2 of 10 onto stack top. Constant is accurate to 64 bits (19 digits).	FLDL2T
FLDPI	Load π onto stack top. Constant is accurate to 64 bits (19 digits).	FLDPI
FLDZ	Load 0 onto stack top. Constant is accurate to 64 bits (19 digits).	FLDZ
FLD1	Load +1.0 onto stack top. Constant is accurate to 64 bits (19 digits).	FLD1
FMUL	Multiply reals. Destination by source with product in destination.	FMUL ST,ST(2) FMUL ST(1),ST FMUL S_REAL FMUL L_REAL
FMULP	Multiply reals and pop stack. See FMUL.	FMULP ST(2),ST
FNOP	Floating-point no operation.	FNOP
FPATAN	Partial arctangent. Calculates Arctan = (y/x), x is ST and y is ST(1). x and y must observe $0 < y < x < +\infty$. Stack is popped. x and y are destroyed. φ in radians.	FPATAN
FPREM	Partial remainder. Performs modulo division of the stack top by ST(1), producing an exact result. Sign is unchanged. Formula used: Part. rem. = ST − ST(1) ∗ quotient.	FPREM
FPREM1 80387	Calculates IEEE-compatible partial remainder. See FPREM	FPREM1
FPTAN	Partial tangent. Calculates y/x = Tan φ . φ at ST, must be in the range $0 \leq \varphi < \pi/4$. y is returned in ST and x in ST(1). φ is destroyed. Input in radians.	FPTAN

(continued)

Table 5.6. *80x87 Instruction Set Reference (Continued)*

	DESCRIPTION	EXAMPLES
FRNDINT	Round stack top to an integer.	FRNDINT
FRSTOR	Restore state from 94-byte memory area previously written by a FSAVE or FNSAVE.	FRSTOR MEM_94
FSAVE FNSAVE	Save state (environment and stack registers) to a 94-byte area in memory.	FSAVE MEM_94
FSCALE	Scale variable. Add scale factor, integer in ST(1), to exponent of ST. Provides fast multiplication (division if scale is negative) by powers of 2. Range of factor is $-32{,}768 \le$ ST(1) $< 32{,}768$.	FSCALE
FSETPM (80287)	Set protected-mode addressing for 80287 systems. Interpreted as FNOP in 80387.	FSETPM
FSIN (80387)	Calculate sine of stack top and return value in ST. $|ST| < 2^{63}$. Input in radians.	FSIN
FSINCOS (80387)	Calculate sine and cosine of ST. Sine appears in ST and cosine in ST(1). $|ST| < 2^{63}$. Input in radians. Tangent = sine/cosine.	FSINCOS
FSQRT	Calculate square root of stack top.	FSQRT
FST	Store stack top in another stack register or in a real memory variable. Rounding is according to RC field of control word.	FST ST(3) FST S_REAL FST L_REAL
FSTCW FNSTCW	Store control register in a memory variable (word).	FSTCW CTRL_WORD
FSTENV FNSTENV	Store 14-byte environment into memory storage area. See FLDENV.	FSTENV MEM_14
FSTP	Store stack top in another stack register or in a real memory variable and pop stack. Rounding is according to RC field in control word.	FSTP ST(2) FSTP S_REAL FSTP L_REAL FSTP TEMP_REAL
FSTSW FNSTSW	Store status register in memory variable (word).	FSTSW STAT_WORD
FSUB	Subtract source from destination with difference in destination.	FSUB ST,ST(3) FSUB ST(1),ST FSUB S_REAL FSUB L_REAL
FSUBP	Subtract source from destination with difference in destination and pop stack.	FSUBP ST(2),ST

(continued)

Table 5.6. *80x87 Instruction Set Reference (Continued)*

	DESCRIPTION	EXAMPLES
FSUBR	Subtract destination from source with difference in destination.	FSUBR ST,ST(1) FSUBR ST(3),ST FSUBR S_REAL FSUBR L_REAL
FSUBRP	Subtract destination from source with difference in destination and pop stack.	FSUBRP ST(3),ST
FTST	Compare stack top with 0 and set condition codes.	FTST
FUCOM (80387)	Unordered compare. Operates like FCOM except that no invalid operation if one operand is NAN.	FUCOM FUCOM ST(2) FUCOM S_REAL FUCOM L_REAL
FUCOMP (80387)	Unordered compare and pop. Operates like FCOMP except that no invalid operation if one operand is a NAN.	FUCOMP FUCOMP ST(2) FUCOMP S_REAL FUCOMP L_REAL
FUCOMPP (80387)	Unordered compare and pop twice. Operates like FCOMPP except that no invalid operation if one operand is a NAN.	FUCOMPP
FWAIT	Alternative mnemonic for WAIT. Must be used with Intel emulators.	FWAIT
FXAM	Examine stack top and report if positive, negative, NAN, denormal, unnormal, normal, zero, or empty in condition codes (Table 5.3).	FXAM
FXCH	Swap contents of stack top and another stack register. If no explicit register, ST(1) is used.	FXCH ST(2) FXCH
FXTRACT	Decompose stack top into exponent and significand. The exponent is found at ST and the significand at ST(1).	FXTRACT
FYL2X	Calculate z = log base 2 of x. x is the value at ST and y at ST(1). Stack is popped, and z is found in ST. Operands must be in the range $0 < x < \infty$ and $-\infty < y < +\infty$	FYL2X
FYL2XP1	Calculate z = log base 2 of (x + 1). x is in ST and must be in the range $0 < |x| < (1 - \sqrt{2}/2)$. y is in ST(1) and must be in the range $-\infty < y < \infty$. Stack is popped, and z is found in ST.	FYL2XP1

5.6.1.2 Arithmetic Instructions.   Arithmetic instructions perform the basic calculations of addition, subtraction, multiplication, division, and square root. In addition, some operations to perform auxiliary numeric manipulations are included in this group. The following are arithmetic operations.

1. Addition
FADD
FADD source
FADD destination, source (add real numbers)
FADDP destination, source (add real numbers and pop stack)
FIADD source (add integers)

2. Subtraction
FSUB
FSUB source
FSUB destination, source (subtract real numbers)
FSUBP destination, source (subtract real numbers and pop stack)
FISUB source (subtract integers)

3. Multiplication
FMUL
FMUL source
FMUL destination, source (multiply real numbers)
FMULP destination, source (multiply real numbers and pop stack)
FIMUL source (multiply integers)

4. Normal division
FDIV
FDIV source
FDIV destination, source (divide real numbers)
FDIVP destination, source (divide real numbers and pop stack)
FIDIV source (divide integers)

5. Reversed division
FDIVR
FDIVR source
FDIVR destination, source (reversed division of real numbers)
FDIVRP destination, source (reversed division and pop stack)
FIDIVR source (reversed division of integers)

6. Square root
FSQRT

7. Other numeric operations
FSCALE (scale)
FPREM (partial remainder)
FRNDINT (round to integer)
FXTRACT (extract exponent and significand)
FABS (absolute value)
FCHS (change sign)

5.6.1.3 Comparison Instructions. Comparison instructions test the stack registers and report the results in the condition flags of the status register. The FSTSW (store status word) instruction can be used to transfer the condition codes to memory so that they can be examined.

1. Compare two numeric operands
FCOM
FCOM source (compare real numbers)
FCOMP (compare and pop)
FCOMP source (compare real numbers and pop stack)
FCOMPP (compare reals and pop stack twice)
FICOM source (compare integers)
FICOMP source (compare integers and pop)
FUCOM, FUCOMP, and FUCOMPP are 80387 versions of the compare instruction.

2. Compare with zero
FTST (compare stack top with zero)

3. Examine stack register and report tag, sign, and normalization
FXAM

Table 5.3 lists the interpretation of the condition codes after the execution of the compare instructions.

5.6.1.4 Transcendental Instructions. These instructions perform the basic calculations necessary for the computation of trigonometric, logarithmic, and exponential functions. Normally, they are used in routines that reduce the numerical input to the range of the instruction and adjust the results, if necessary. The trigonometric instructions require input in radians. Section 5.6.4 includes code samples that use transcendental functions in the computation of elementary functions. The following are transcendental instructions.

FPTAN (partial tangent)
FPATAN (partial arc tangent)
F2XM1 (2 to the x minus 1)
FYL2X (log base 2 of x)
FYL2XP1 (log base 2 of x plus 1)

80387 systems include the transcendental instructions
FSIN (sine)
FCOS (cosine)
FSINCOS (sine/cosine)

5.6.1.5 Constant Instructions. These instructions are used in loading constant values frequently required in numerical calculations. All the constant instructions operate on the stack top register. The instructions in this group are a convenience, since they are not strictly necessary and perform no numerical processing. Constants can also be created by the programmer by defining numerical data in memory. However, built-in numerical constants load more rapidly than those defined in memory, which leads to faster execution. The following are constant instructions.

FLDZ (load the value $+0.0$)
FLD1 (load the value $+1.0$)
FLDPI (load π)
FLDL2T (load log base 2 of 10)
FLDL2E (load log base 2 of e)
FLDLG2 (load log base 10 of 2)
FLDLN2 (load log base e of 2)

5.6.1.6 Processor Control Instructions. Processor control instructions perform no numerical computations, but are provided as means of setting up the processor for a desired mode of operation, reading the state of the processor during computations, and making adjustments in the stack registers. The following are processor control instructions.

FINIT (initialize processor)
FDISI (disable interrupts in 8087 systems)
FLDCW source (load control word)
FSTCW destination (store control word)
FSTSW destination (store the status word)
FCLEX (clear exceptions)
FSAVE destination (save NDP environment and register stack)
FRSTOR source (restore environment and register stack)

FSTENV destination (save environment only)

FLDENV source (restore environment)

FINCSTP (increment stack top pointer)

FDECSTP (decrement stack top pointer)

FFREE destination (change the register's tag to empty)

5.6.2 Conversion Routines

One of the major difficulties in programming, in low-level languages, the numeric data processor is converting conventional representations of numbers into a floating-point format that can be loaded into the NDP, and vice versa. User input and output is usually presented in ASCII decimals or scientific notation, for example,

$$\$1,334,234.78$$
or $$-2.3456712 \, E + 13$$

Before computations can proceed, a conversion routine must transform the ASCII string into one of the formats that can be loaded onto the NDP. By the same token, after the computations conclude, the results appear in the NDP stack registers encoded in the temporary real format. To make these numbers meaningful to the user, it is necessary to perform a reverse conversion into ASCII decimals or other conventional representations. The following conversion routines are listed in Appendix A:

1. ASCII_TO_FPD. Assembly language procedure for converting an ASCII decimal number into a floating-point decimal string

2. INPUT_NDP. Assembly language procedure for loading a floating-point decimal string into the NDP stack top register

3. OUTPUT_NDP. Assembly language procedure for storing the NDP stack top register in a floating-point decimal string

5.6.3 Conditional Branching

All control transfer instructions are part of the main processor's instruction set. Conditional branching is a form of control transfer instruction that executes or not depending on the condition of the processor's status flags. Since conditional jumps depend on the state of the CPU flags, it is not possible to directly branch on the NDP's condition codes. However, the condition codes can be transferred to the CPU flag register, as in the following code fragment. Bit movement in conditional branching is shown in Figure 5.7.

```
; Code to transfer the NDP condition codes onto the CPU flag
; register after comparing the third stack register (ST(2))
; with the stack top
        FCOM  ST(2)              ; Compare and set condition
                                 ; code bits
        FSTSW STATUS_87          ; Store NDP status register in
                                 ; a memory variable (word)
        FWAIT                    ; Wait for NDP to conclude
        MOV   AX,STATUS_87       ; Status register to AX
        SAHF                     ; Move high byte of status
                                 ; register (condition codes)
                                 ; to CPU flags
; CPU conditional jump instruction can now be coded
```

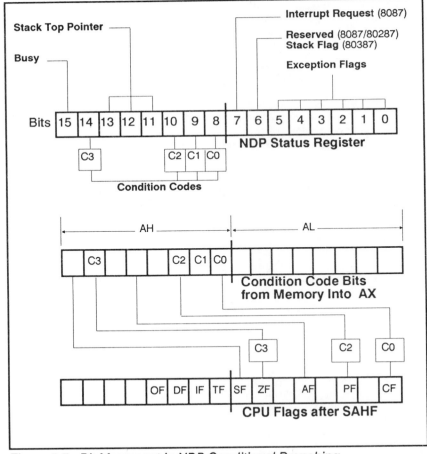

Figure 5.7. *Bit Movement in NDP Conditional Branching*

Table 5.7. *NDP Condition Codes and CPU Conditional Jumps*

INSTRUCTION	CONDITION CODES				INTERPRETATION
	C3	C2	C1	C0	
FCOM, FCOMP, FCOMPP, FICOM, FICOMP, FUCOM, FUCOMP, FUCOMPP	0	0	?	0	ST > source
	0	0	?	1	ST < source
	1	0	?	0	ST = source
	1	1	?	1	ST not comparable
	ZF	PF		CF	
	FLAGS AFTER SAHF				

OPCODE	FLAGS	TRANSFER CONDITION
JB	CF = 1	Taken if ST < source or not comparable
JBE	(CF or ZF) = 1	Taken if ST ≤ source or not comparable
JA	(CF or ZF) = 0	Taken if ST > source
JAE	CF = 0	Taken if ST ≥ source
JE	ZF = 1	Taken if ST = source or not comparable
JNE	ZF = 0	Taken if ST ≠ source

The bit movement from the NDP status register to the CPU flag register takes place as shown in Figure 5.7. The action of some conditional jump instructions is shown in Table 5.7.

5.6.4 Trigonometric Functions

Another difficulty frequently encountered by programmers of 8087 and 80287 systems is that the trigonometric functions sine, cosine, and tangent cannot be obtained directly. The 80387 corrects this problem with the instructions FSIN, FCOS, and FSINCOS (see Table 5.6).

However, the 8087/80287 instruction set allows obtaining a sine-cosine ratio through the use of the partial tangent (FPTAN) or partial arc tangent (FPATAN) instructions. All other trigonometric functions can be calculated from this ratio. One limitation is that the input value for these functions, in radian measure, must be previously scaled to the first octant. The following code fragment contains routines that allow calculation of the sine, cosine, and tangent functions using the 8087 instruction set as well as for converting degrees to radians. All procedures assume that a valid input is already loaded into the NDP stack top.

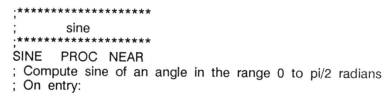

```
;********************
;        sine
;********************
SINE    PROC   NEAR
; Compute sine of an angle in the range 0 to pi/2 radians
; On entry:
```

```
;          ST  =  a  valid  angle  in  radians
;          STATUS_WORD  =a  word-size  memory  variable  defined  as
;                        follows:
;                        STATUS_WORD    DW        0
; On  exit:
;          ST  =  sine  of  angle
; Formula  for  finding  radius  of  r
;  a) if  0  >  r  <  pi/4 ... sine  =  sine  r
;  b) if  pi/4  >  r  <pi/2   sine  =  cos (pi/4 - remainder of r - pi/4)
;
; Find  case  a  or  b
; using  pi/4  as  a  modulus  for  a  partial  remainder  operation
;                          |    ST(0)    |    ST(1)    |    ST(2)
;                          ;    r        |    Empty    |    Empty
          FCLEX
          FLDPI         ;    pi       |    r        |
          FDIV    FOUR  ;    pi/4     |    r        |
          FXCH          ;    r        |    pi/4     |
          FPREM         ;    REM      |    pi/4     |
          FSTSW STATUS_WORD
          FWAIT
;
; Condition  code  C1  is  bit  9  of  the  status  word
; If  C1  =  1,  then  use  formula  b,  else  use  formula  a
; Load  high  byte  of  status  word
          MOV    AH,BYTE  PTR  STATUS_WORD+1
          TEST   AH,00000010B          ; Condition code C1
          JNZ    SINE_FOR_B            ; Bit set indicates b
; Use  formula  a  for  sine
          FSTP   ST(1)  ;    REM      |    Empty    |
          CALL   GET_SINE
          RET
;
SINE_FOR_B:
;                          |    ST(0)    |    ST(1)    |    ST(2)
;                          |    REM      |    pi/4     |
          FXCH          ;    pi/4     |    REM      |
          FSUB ST,ST(1);    pi/4     |    REM      |    REM
          FSTP ST(1)  ;    pi/4     |    REM      |    Empty
          CALL  GET_COS
          RET
;
SINE  ENDP
;
;***************
;      cosine
;***************
;
```

```
COSINE          PROC  NEAR
; Compute cosine of an angle in the range 0 to pi/2
; radians, which is 0 to 90 degrees
; On entry:
;           ST = a valid angle in radians
;           STATUS_WORD = a word-size memory variable defined
;                              as follows:
;                         STATUS_WORD    DW        0
; On exit:
;           ST = sine of angle
; Formulas for finding radius of r
; a) If 0 > r <pi/4 then cos = cos r
; b) il pi/4 > r <pi/2 then cos = sine (pi/4 − reminder of r − pi/4)
;
; Find case a or b
; using pi/4 as a modulus for a partial remainder operation
;                         |  ST(0)    |    ST(1)    |    ST(2)
                         ;    r       |   Empty     |   Empty
        FCLEX
        FLDPI          ;   pi        |    r        |
        FDIV   FOUR  ;   pi/4      |    r        |
        FXCH           ;    r        |   pi/4      |
        FPREM          ;   REM       |   pi/4      |
        FSTSW STATUS_WORD
        FWAIT
;

; Condition code C1 is bit 9 of the status word
; If C1 = 1, then use formula b, else use formula a
; Load high byte of status word
        MOV   AH,BYTE PTR STATUS_WORD+1
        TEST  AH,00000010B              ; Condition code C1
        JNZ   COS_FORM_B                ; Bit set indicates b
; Use formula a for sine
        FSTP  ST(1)  ;    REM      |   Empty     |
        CALL  GET_COS
        RET
;
COS_FORM_B:
;                         |  ST(0)    |    ST(1)    |    ST(2)
;                         |  REM      |   pi/4      |
        FXCH          ;    pi/4     |   REM       |
        FSUB  ST,ST(1); pi/4-REM   |   REM       |
        FSTP  ST(1)  ;  pi/4-REM   |   Empty     |
        CALL  GET_SINE
        RET
COSINE          ENDP
```

```
;********************
;         tangent
;********************
TANGENT PROC        NEAR
; Compute tangent of an angle in the range 0 to pi/2 radians
; On entry:
;       ST = a valid angle in radians
;       STATUS_WORD = A word-size memory variable  defined
;                       as follows:
;                       STATUS_WORD    DW        0
; On exit:
;       ST = tangent of angle
; Formulas for finding tangent of r
;   a) If 0 > r < +pi/4 then tangent = tangent r
;   b) If pi/4 > r < +pi/2 then   tan = cotan (pi/4 - remainder of
;               r - pi/4)
; Find case a or b
; using pi/4 as a modulus for a partial remainder operation
;
;                           |  ST(0)    |  ST(1)    |  ST(2)
;                        ;  r        |  Empty    |  Empty
        FCLEX
        FLDPI           ;  pi       |  r        |
        FDIV   FOUR  ;  pi/4     |  r        |
        FXCH            ;  r        |  pi/4     |
        FPREM           ;  REM      |  pi/4     |
        FSTSW STATUS_WORD
        FWAIT
; Condition code C1 is bit 9 of the status word
; If C1 = 1, then use formula b, else use formula a
; Load high byte of status word
        MOV    AH,BYTE PTR STATUS_WORD+1
        TEST   AH,00000010B             ; Condition code C1
        JNZ    TAN_FORM_B               ; Bit set indicates b
; Use formula a for tangent
;                           |  ST(0)    |  ST(1)    |  ST(2)
        FSTP   ST(1)   ;  REM      |  Empty    |
        FPTAN           ;  y(opp)   |  x(adj)   |
        FXCH            ;  x        |  y        |
        FDIV   ST,ST(1);  tan r     |  ?        |
        FSTP   ST(1)   ;  tan r     |  Empty    |
        RET
TAN_FORM_B:
;                           |  ST(0)    |  ST(1)    |  ST(2)
;                           |  REM      |  pi/4     |
        FXCH            ;  pi/4-REM  |  REM      |
        FSUB   ST,ST(1);  pi/4-REM  |  REM      |
        FSTP   ST(1)   ;  REM       |  Empty    |
```

```
; Use formula b for tangent
;                   |   ST(0)   |   ST(1)   |   ST(2)
        FSTP    ST(1)   ;   REM     |   Empty   |
        FPTAN           ;   y(opp)  |   x(adj)  |
        FDIV    ST,ST(1);  cotan r  |   ?       |
        FSTP    ST(1)   ;   cotan r |   Empty   |
        RET
;
TANGENT ENDP
;
;
;********************
; degrees to radian
;********************
DEG_2_RADS   PROC   NEAR
; Assumes a doubleword constant in memory defined as follows:
; ONE_80         DD      180.0
;
; Convert degrees (in ST) to radians
;                   |   ST(0)   |   ST(1)   |   ST(2)
;                   |   d       |   Empty   |   Empty
        FLD     ONE_80;     180     |   d       |
        FLDPI           ;   pi      |   180     |   d
        FDIV    ST,ST(1);  pi/180  |   180     |   d
        FSTP    ST(1)   ;   pi/180  |   d       |
        FMUL    ST,ST(1);  r        |   d       |
        FSTP    ST(1)   ;   r       |   Empty   |
; Angle in ST is now in radian measure
        RET
DEG_2_RADS   ENDP
;
;
;**********************************
;         auxiliary procedures
;**********************************
GET_SINE      PROC   NEAR
; On entry:
;       ST  = angle in radians in the range 0 to pi/4
; On exit:
;       ST  = sine of angle
; Find sine using formula sin @ = y/SQR(x^2 + y^2)
;                   |   ST(0)   |   ST(1)   |   ST(2)
        FPTAN           ;   x(adj)  |   y(opp)  |
        FMUL    ST,ST(0);  x^2      |   y       |
        FXCH            ;   y       |   x^2     |
        FLD     ST(0)   ;   y       |   y       |   x^2
        FXCH    ST(3)
        FSTP    ST(0)   ;   y       |   x^2     |   y
```

```
                FMUL    ST,ST(0);     y^2        |     x^2        |   y
                FADD    ST,ST(1);   y^2+x^2      |     x^2        |   y
                FSQRT            ;SQ(y^2+x^2)|     x^2        |   y
                FXCH            ;     x^2       |SQ(y^2+x^2)    |   y
                FSTP    ST(0)   ;SQ(y^2+x^2)|      y         |
                FXCH            ;      y        |SQ(y^2+x^2)|
                FDIV    ST,ST(1);    sine r     |      ?         |
                FSTP    ST(1)   ;    sine r     |    Empty       |
                RET
;
GET_SINE        ENDP
;
;
GET_COS PROC            NEAR
; On entry:
;         ST = angle in radians in the range 0 to pi/4
; On exit:
;         ST = cosine of angle
; Find cosine using formula Cos = x / SQR (x^2 + y^2)
;                       |    ST(0)     |     ST(1)      |    ST(2)
                FPTAN          ;   x(adj)    |    y(opp)     |
                FLD     ST(0)  ;    x        |    x          |   y
                FXCH    ST(3)
                FSTP    ST(0)   ;    x        |    y          |   x
                FMUL    ST,ST(0);   x^2       |    y          |   x
                FXCH            ;    y        |   x^2         |   x
                FMUL    ST,ST(0);   y^2       |   x^2         |   x
                FADD    ST,ST(1); y^2+x^2    |   x^2         |   x
                FSQRT           ;SQ(y^2+x^2)|   x^2         |   x
                FXCH            ;   x^2       |SQ(y^2+x^2)|   x
                FSTP    ST(0)   ;SQ(y^2+x^2)|   x           |
                FXCH            ;    x        |SQ(y^2+x^2)|
                FDIV    ST,ST(1);   cosine r  |SQ(y^2+x^2 |
                FSTP    ST(1)   ;   cosine r  |    Empty      |
                RET
;
GET_COS ENDP
```

6

Keyboard and Other
Data Input Devices

6.0 The IBM Keyboards

The keyboard has undergone substantial changes in the various models of the IBM microcomputers. These changes are related to the addition and deletion of certain keys, to the position of some control keys, and to the mechanical and electronic hardware components employed. The number of keys has gone from 83 in the Personal Computer keyboard, to 62 in the PCjr, 78 in the Convertible, 84 in the AT, and 101 in the keyboard for the PS/2 line. Other keys have been moved around several times; for instance, the escape key (labeled Esc), located at the left side of the top row in the Personal Computer and the PCjr, was moved to the right side of this row in the AT, and back to the top right on the PS/2 keyboard (see Figures 6.1 to 6.4). The backslash key has also undergone several relocations. Table 6.1 lists the fundamental characteristics of the IBM micro-computer keyboards.

All IBM keyboards use a dedicated microprocessor which monitors the mechanical key switches, thus freeing the main processor from this time-con-suming task. This chip, called the *keyboard controller*, is an Intel 8048 in the PC, XT, and PCjr and an Intel 8042 in the AT and the PS/2 models.

The keyboard supplied with the original Personal Computer, also used in the PC XT and PC Portable, has 83 keys (see Figure 6.1). The IBM PCjr was initially furnished with a 62-key keyboard, derogatorily called the "Chiclet" keyboard. After some criticism, IBM recalled and replaced it with an improved version (see Figure 6.2).

The original PC AT keyboard has 84 keys (see Figure 6.3). It is characterized by relocated Esc, backslash (\), and Print Screen keys, by a new key labeled Sys Req (system request) intended for use in 80286 protected mode, and by light indicators that reflect the state of the lock keys. Later, IBM made available for the AT an enhanced keyboard with 101 keys. This keyboard is similar in appearance to the keyboard of the PS/2 computers described below, but the connectors that attach the keyboard to the main unit are different.

Table 6.1. *IBM Keyboards*

MACHINE	NUMBER OF KEYS	CONTROLLER	DESCRIPTION
PC PC XT Portable	83	Intel 8048	10 function keys in two columns on left side. Esc key at top left. Fixed typematic rate and keystroke delay.
PCjr	62	Intel 80C48	**Original model:** Battery- powered, cordless. Multistroke function keys. Typematic rate and delay can be increased. **Updated version:** Replacement for original PCjr keyboard. Improved mechanical design.
PC AT XT 286	84	Intel 8042	Relocated < Esc > key. Lighted indicators for lock keys. Sys Req key for protected mode. Programmable typematic rate and keystroke delay.
PS/2	101	Intel 8042	Relocated < Esc > key. Cursor control and editing keypads. 12 function keys. Lighted indicators for lock keys. Programmable typematic rate and keystroke delay.

The microcomputers of the Personal System/2 line are equipped with a keyboard that has 101 keys in the version designed for use in the United States and 102 keys in the models sold outside the United States (see Figure 6.5). This keyboard has a total of 12 function keys, a dedicated keypad for editing and cursor control, and a Pause/Break key. The Esc key has been repositioned, this time to the top left side, as in the original PC keyboard. In the PS/2 keyboard, the Sys Req key is an Alt function of the Print Screen. The Sys Req (system request) function is not used by OS/2 or by any other multitasking operating system presently available.

The various keyboards used in the different models of the IBM microcomputers are not interchangeable. The adapter hardware used for connecting the keyboards to the system units are incompatible, and the electronic components used in the various systems are also different.

6.1 Keyboard Layout

The layout of the various IBM keyboards is shown in Figures 6.1 through 6.5.

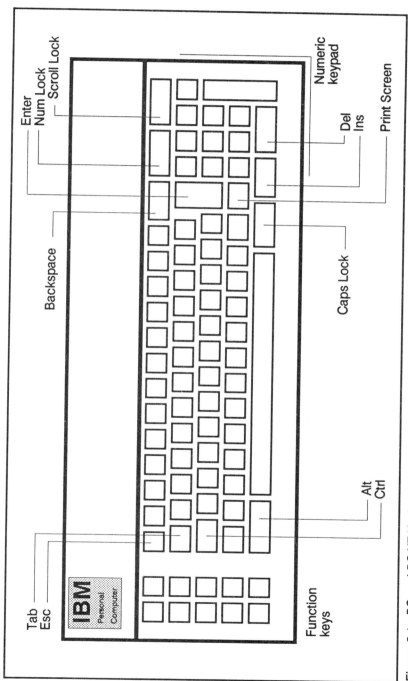

Figure 6.1. *PC and PC XT Keyboard Layout*

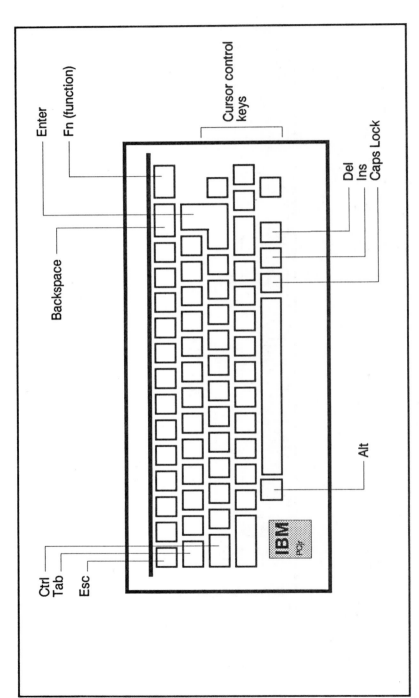

Figure 6.2. *PCjr Keyboard Layout (Updated Version)*

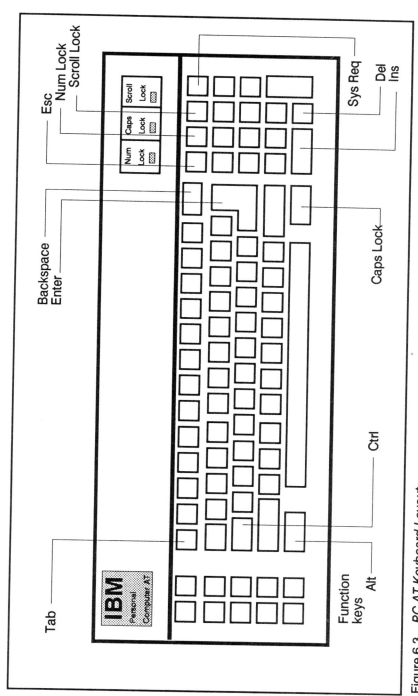

Figure 6.3. *PC AT Keyboard Layout*

239

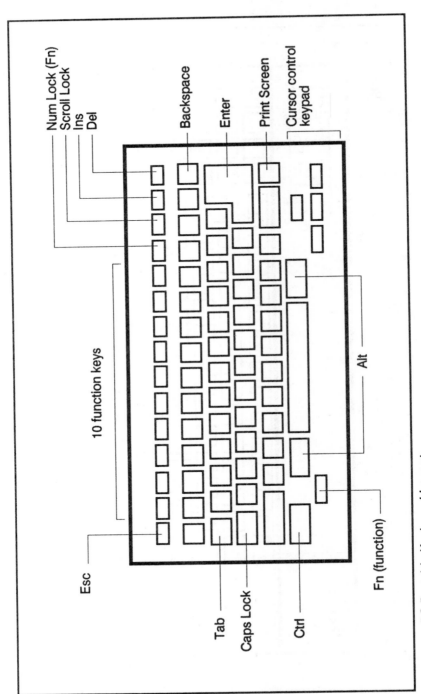

Figure 6.4. *PC Portable Keyboard Layout*

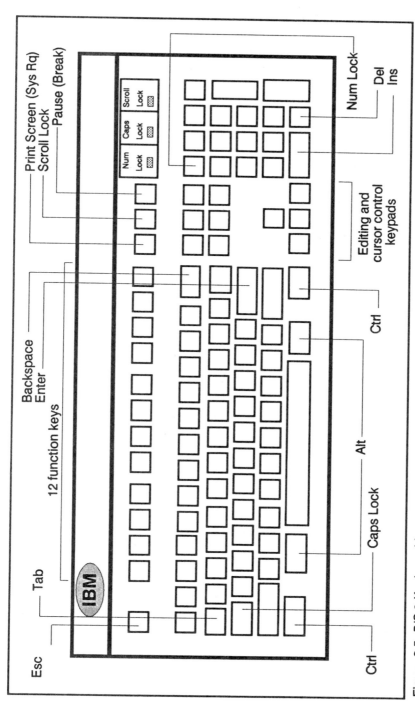

Figure 6.5 *P/S 2 Keyboard Layout*

6.2 Keyboard Operation

Certain fundamental principles of operation have been maintained in the various models of IBM keyboards. In general, the process can be described as follows:

1. Each key operates as a mechanical switch. The keyboard controller detects each time that a switch is closed (key pressed) or opened (key released). The controller, which can be an Intel 8048 or 8042, calculates and stores a code, specific for each key, in a register mapped to port 60H. This code, named the *scan code*, is unrelated to the key's ASCII value.

2. Once the scan code is stored, the keyboard controller generates an interrupt. All IBM systems point this interrupt to a handler located at interrupt 09H. In the PCjr, the interrupt is first directed to the nonmaskable interrupt (NMI) service routine, then to INT 48H for compatibility adjustments, and finally to INT 09H.

3. The service routine for INT 09H is part of the basic input/output system (BIOS). The routine first tests for keys that require special handling (see points 4 and 5 below). If special handling is not required, INT 09H converts the scan codes into ASCII or extended ASCII characters. The ASCII code, as well as the original scan code, is stored in a BIOS buffer area named the keyboard or type-ahead buffer.

4. Some keystrokes require immediate action, for example, the Lock function keys, the Sys Req key, or Hot keys like the print screen or break functions. In these cases the keyboard handler performs the corresponding operations.

5. Other keystrokes not stored in the keyboard buffer are those used in interpreting previous or subsequent keystrokes, for instance, the shift state keys labeled Shift, Ctrl, and Alt, and the Caps Lock key. The INT 09H handler interprets these keys accordingly.

6.2.1 PC and PC XT Keyboard Hardware

The 83-key keyboards of the personal computer, the PC XT, and the PC Portable (see Table 6.1) are equipped with an Intel 8048 controller. This device is not directly accessible to the programmer. However, it is possible to access some keyboard parameters and functions via ports PA (60H) and PC (61H) of the 8255 Programmable Peripheral Interface (see Figure 6.1). The keyboard data ports are described in Figure 6.6.

The keyboard hardware scans all key switches continuously, as described in Section 6.2. In the PC and PC XT, direct keyboard programming consists in reading the scan code (stored at port 60H) and then issuing the keyboard acknowledge by toggling bit 7 of port 61H (see Figure 6.6). The following code fragment shows the processing required for reading the keyboard scan code.

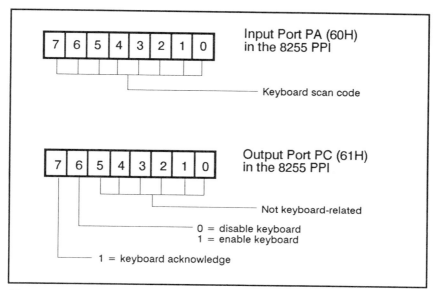

Figure 6.6. *Keyboard Data in PC, XT, and PCjr*

The code is similar to the one used by BIOS interrupt 09H in processing the keyboard interrupt.

```
; Code to read the scan code in PC and PC XT keyboards
;********************
;    read keyboard
;       scan code
;********************
        IN      AL,60H          ; Read scan code at port 60H
        MOV     BL,AL           ; Store scan code in BL
;
;********************
; send acknowledge
;    to 8048 chip
;********************
        IN      AL,61H          ; Read control port
        MOV     AH,AL           ; Save value of port 61H in AH
        OR      AL,80H          ; Set keyboard acknowledge bit
        OUT     61H,AL          ; Send to control port
        XCHG    AH,AL           ; Restore original control
        OUT     61H,AL          ; Send to controller
; BL holds keyboard scan code. Keyboard is reset
```

6.2.2 The PCjr Keyboard Hardware

The PCjr keyboard is equipped with the Intel 80C48 controller, which is similar to the 8048 used in the PC and PC XT. However, there are fundamental differences in the PCjr keyboard processing compared to that of the PC and XT. While in the 83-key keyboards the hardware calculates the scan code and stores it at port 60H (see Section 6.2.1), in the PCjr the task of converting the serial bit stream into a scan code is left to the main processor. The PCjr keyboard processing sequence is as follows:

1. The keyboard interrupt is pointed to the NMI at 02H. This handler deserializes the bit stream and obtains the scan code.

2. The NMI handler passes the scan code to a service routine located at INT 48H. This routine translates the scan code from the PCjr's 62-key keyboard into a scan code compatible with the 83-key keyboard of the PC and PC XT.

3. INT 48H then passes the 83-key-equivalent scan code to the service routine at INT 09H, which performs the standard operations of the keyboard interrupt handler.

The above manipulations ensure that applications that intercept the keyboard handler at INT 09H will operate satisfactorily in the PCjr.

6.2.3 PC AT and PS/2 Keyboard Hardware

One of the innovations introduced by the Personal Computer AT and preserved in the PS/2 line is the use of the Intel 8042 keyboard controller in a programmable environment. The hardware appears to the programmer as follows:

1. A keyboard controller status register (read operations) at port 64H, as shown in Figure 6.7. This byte can be read at any time to determine the present condition of the keyboard hardware.

2. A keyboard controller command register (write operations) at port 64H, as shown in Figure 6.8. Output to this register is used to enable and disable the keyboard, to select the scan code translation mode, to set and reset the system flag bit, and to set the 8042 in the interrupt or poll mode.

3. An output buffer located at port 60H, which is used by the system to read the scan code received from the keyboard or a data byte that results from a system-to-keyboard command. Code that reads the output buffer should do so only if bit 0 of the status register (see Figure 6.7) equals one, indicating data in buffer.

4. An input buffer located at port 60H. Writing to port 60H sends a byte to the keyboard hardware or to the 8042 keyboard controller. 8042 access takes place if the controller is expecting a data byte following a command. Code that writes to the input buffer should first test bit 0 of the status register (see Figure 6.7) to make sure that there is no data in the buffer.

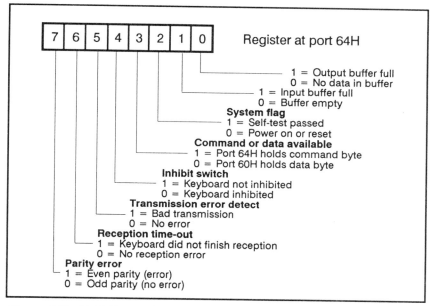

Figure 6.7. *8042 Status Byte at Port 64H (Read Operation)*

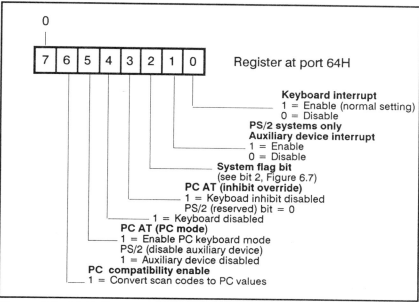

Figure 6.8. *8042 Command Byte at Port 64H (Write Operation)*

Table 6.2. *8042 Keyboard Controller Commands (port 64H)*

	SYSTEM		
CODE	PC AT	PS/2	COMMAND DESCRIPTION
20H	Yes	Yes	Place 8042 command byte in output register (see Figure 6.8).
60H	Yes	Yes	Write command byte (in port 60H) (see Figure 6.8).
A4	No	Yes	Test if password is installed. Results are reported in port 60H. FAH = password installed. F1H = no password.
A5	No	Yes	Initiate load password procedure. Password characters are read from port 60H until 00H is received. Data in scan code form.
A6	No	Yes	Enable password security. Keyboard data is intercepted and compared to the installed password until a match is found.
A7	No	Yes	Disable auxiliary device. Sets bit 5 of the command byte (see Figure 6.8).
A8	No	Yes	Enable auxiliary device. Clears bit 5 of the command byte (see Figure 6.8).
A9	NO	Yes	Test auxiliary device. Results are reported at port 60H as follows: 00H = No error detected 01H = Clock stuck low 02H = Clock stuck high 03H = Data line stuck low 04H = Data line stuck high
AA	Yes	Yes	Self-test. 55H in port 60H if no errors.
AB	Yes	Yes	Interface test. Results reported at port 60H encoded as for command A9.
AC	Yes	No	Diagnostic dump. Dump 16 bytes in 8042 RAM containing input port, output port, and controller's status word.
AD	Yes	Yes	Disable keyboard. Sets bit 4 of the command register (see Figure 6.8).
AE	Yes	Yes	Enable keyboard. Clears bit 4 of the command register (see Figure 6.8).
C0	Yes	Yes	Read input port to port 60H.
C1	No	Yes	Input port bits 0–3 to status bits 4–7.
C2	No	Yes	Input port bits 4–7 to status bits 4–7.
D0	Yes	Yes	Read output port to port 60H. Should be issued when output buffer is empty.
D1	Yes	Yes	Write next data byte to output port at 60H. Note: Bit 0, system reset, should not be 0.

(continued)

Table 6.2. *8042 Keyboard Controller Commands (Continued)*

CODE	SYSTEM		COMMAND DESCRIPTION
	PC AT	PS/2	
D2	No	Yes	Write keyboard output buffer. Next data byte is written to port 60H as if sent by a device. Interrupt occurs.
D3	No	Yes	Write auxiliary device output buffer. Next data byte is writen to port 60H as if sent by a device. Interrupt occurs.
D4	No	Yes	Write to auxiliary device. Next byte placed in port 60H is sent to the auxiliary device.
E0	Yes	Yes	Read test inputs. Read test line T0 to bit 0 of port 60H and line T1 to bit 1. T0 = keyboard clock input. T1 = keyboard data input.
F0-FF	Yes	Yes	Pulse output port (60H). Bits 0–3 of the command byte pulse the corresponding bits of the 8042 output port. Note: Bit 0, system reset, should not be 0.

Several command sets are active in the system. In one set are the commands that can be issued by the system to the 8042 keyboard controller through port 64H, shown in Table 6.2. In another set are the commands that can be issued to the keyboard hardware directly through port 60H, shown in Table 6.3. Finally, there is a set of commands that can be issued by the keyboard hardware. These can be read by the system at port 60H, as shown in Table 6.4.

In programming the AT and PS/2 keyboard it is important to differentiate between commands to the 8042 controller (Table 6.2), which is part of the system board, and those to the keyboard hardware (Table 6.3). The code listing in Section 6.4.2 includes the procedure COM_8042, to write to the 8042 command register, and the procedure COM_2_KBRD, to send a system-to-keyboard command.

Table 6.3. *PC AT and PS/2 System to Keyboard Commands*

	SYSTEM		
CODE	PC AT	PS/2	COMMAND DESCRIPTION
EDH	Yes	Yes	Reset lock state indicator LEDs. The command code is followed by an option byte with the following bit map: 7 6 5 4 3 2 1 0 Scroll Lock Num Lock Caps Lock Reserved (= 0)
EEH	Yes	Yes	Echo (diagnostic aide). Keyboard returns EEH.
EFH to F2H	Yes	No	Invalid command. No action in PC AT.
EFH F1H	No	Yes	Invalid command. No action in PS/2 systems.
F0H	No	Yes	Select alternate scan code set. The command is followed by an option byte as follows: 01H = Select scan code set 1 02H = Select scan code set 2 03H = Select scan code set 3 00H = Report active scan code
F2H	No	Yes	Send 2-byte keyboard identification code.
F3H	Yes	Yes	Set delay and typematic rate. Command code is followed by a parameter (Figure 6.11).
F4H	Yes	Yes	Enable. Keyboard acknowledges, clears buffer, and starts scanning.
F5H	Yes	Yes	Reset power-on conditions, stop scanning, and await instructions.
F6H	Yes	Yes	Set default. Reset power-on state and continue scanning.
F7H to FDH	Yes	No	Reserved command. No operation in PC AT.
F7H to FAH	No	Yes	Set all keys as follows: F7H = All keys typematic F8H = All keys make/break F9H = All keys make FAH = All keys typematic/make/break
FBH to FDH	No	Yes	Set individual key as follows: FBH = Typematic FCH = Make/break FDH = Make On receiving command the keyboard clears the buffer and prepares to receive the scan code of the key desired

(continued)

Table 6.3. *PC AT and PS/2 System to Keyboard Commands (Continued)*

	SYSTEM		
CODE	PC AT	PS/2	COMMAND DESCRIPTION
FEH	Yes	Yes	Resend. Upon error detection the system can send this command to force the keyboard to resend the previous output.
FFH	Yes	Yes	Reset. Resets the keyboard to the power-on state and performs the internal self- test. Output buffer is cleared and default parameters are installed.

Table 6.4. *PC AT and PS/2 Keyboard to System Commands*

	SYSTEM		
CODE	PC AT	PS/2	COMMAND DESCRIPTION
00H	Yes	Yes	Overrun. Character 00H is placed in the last position in the keyboard buffer.
00H	No	Yes	Overrun character for scan code sets 2 and 3. Also used for key error.
83ABH	No	Yes	Keyboard response to command F2H (see Table 6.3) in PS/2 systems. 83ABH is the keyboard ID code.
AAH	Yes	Yes	Basic Assurance Test (BAT) completed. Any other code means that the test failed.
EEH	Yes	Yes	Keyboard response to echo command (see Table 6.3).
F0H	Yes	No	Prefix to scan code after key break. PC AT only.
FAH	Yes	Yes	Keyboard acknowledge to any valid input other than echo or resend commands.
FCH	No	Yes	Basis Assurance Test (BAT) failed. PS/2 systems only.
FDH	Yes	No	Diagnostic failure. Problem detected in the sense amplifier. PC AT only.
FEH	Yes	Yes	Resend. Issued by keyboard after receiving an invalid input.
FFH	No	Yes	Overrun character for scan code set 1. Also used for key error.

The following code fragment shows the processing required for reading the keyboard scan code in the AT and PS/2 keyboards. The code is similar to the one used by BIOS interrupt 09H in processing the keyboard interrupt.

```
; The code uses the procedure named COM_8042 listed in the code
; fragment in Section 6.4.2.
          PUSH   AX              ; Save accumulator register
          MOV    AL,0ADH         ; Code to disable keyboard
          CALL   COM_8042        ; To 8042 controller
;
          CLI                    ; Interrupts off
          MOV    CX,0FFFFH       ; Set up timer counter
WAIT:
          IN     AL,64H          ; 8042 status port
          TEST   AL,00000010B    ; Check for input buffer full
          LOOPNZ WAIT            ; Loop until bit set
                                 ; or timer counter = 0
; Get scan code
          IN     AL,60H          ; Read scan code at 8042 output
                                 ; buffer
          STI                    ; Interrupts reenabled
; The scan code is now in AL.
          MOV    BL,AL           ; Save scan code in BL
; Reenable keyboard
          MOV    AL,0AEH         ; Code to enable keyboard
          CALL   COM_8042        ; To 8042 controller
          .
          .
```

6.3 Key Classification

The keys on the IBM keyboard can be classified in five groups:
1. ASCII keys
2. Function and program control keys
3. Shift state keys
4. Lock state keys
5. Immediate action keys

6.3.1 The ASCII Keys

The ASCII keys correspond approximately to those found on a conventional electric or electronic typewriter (see Figure 6.9). One exception is the key with the symbol for the number one (1). This is due to the traditional use, in typewriter keyboards, of the letter l (ell) to represent the number one, while computer processing requires a numerical symbol.

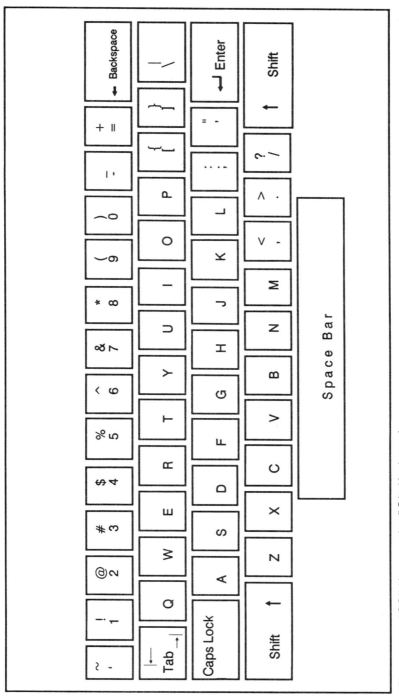

Figure 6.9. ASCII Keys on the PS/2 Keyboard

251

6.3.2 The Function and Program Control Keys

The function keys are labeled F1 to F10 on keyboards of the PC line and F1 to F12 in the PS/2 line. The function keys are intended for use by application software; therefore, their functions have not been standardized. Application can freely assign roles to the function keys. By the same token, to avoid conflicts, system programs and memory-resident utilities should generally abstain from using them.

Other keys and keystroke combinations intended for use by applications are the arrow keys, the Insert (Ins), Delete (Del), Home, End, Page Up (PgUp), and Page Down (PgDn) keys. The keyboard of the PS/2 line provides an individual keypad with the arrow keys and another one with the editing keys mentioned above. In the PC and AT keyboards these functions are found in the numeric keypad, while the PCjr and the PC Portable keyboards require two separate keystrokes to generate some of the program control functions.

6.3.3 The Shift State Keys

This group includes the Shift, Ctrl, and Alt keys. Their purpose is to expand the number of functions that can be assigned to individual keys. For example, an application can assign a function to the code that results from pressing the F1 key, another one to the code that results from pressing F1 while holding the Shift key, a third one to pressing F1 while holding the Ctrl key, and a fourth operation to pressing F1 while holding the Alt key. The Shift key is also used more conventionally to generate uppercase alphabetical characters and the symbols associated with the number keys (see Figure 6.9).

6.3.4 The Lock State Keys

The lock state keys perform a similar function to that of the shift state keys (see Section 6.4.3); that is, they expand the range of possible interpretations of other keystrokes. The difference in their action is that the effect of a shift state key depends on its being held down while the principal key is pressed, while a lock state key enables a permanent interpretation of the principal keystrokes. In the case of a lock state key this interpretation remains active until the key is pressed again. This on/off action is called *toggling*.

Since the effect of a lock state key persists after the key has been released, it is sometimes difficult for the user to determine which state is active. This explains the convenience of light indicators to reflect the state of the lock keys. These indicators [also called the keyboard light-emitting diodes (LEDs)] are found in the PC AT and PS/2 keyboards (see Figures 6.3 and 6.5).

The lock state keys are labeled Caps Lock, Num Lock, and Scroll Lock. The Caps Lock key toggles the alphabetic keys, letters a through z, to upper- and lowercase. This action is similar to the shift lock function on a conventional typewriter keyboard, except that the Caps Lock affects the alphabetic keys only. The Num Lock key toggles between numbers and functions on the numeric keypad. The numeric keypad does not exist in all IBM hardware; for example, there is no numeric keypad in the PCjr and the Portable PC. However, to ensure compatibility, these systems have keystroke combinations that generate the same codes as those obtained from the numeric keypad of the PC, AT, and PS/2 keyboards.

The Scroll Lock function was conceived as a toggle between cursor movements and text window scrolling. Although this action is assumed to refer to the arrow and editing keys, the implementation is left entirely to applications. The only action performed by the keyboard routine is to change the state of a control bit in the BIOS data area.

6.3.5 Immediate Action Keys

The BIOS interrupt service routine at INT 09H provides a few immediate services that are activated by specific keys or keystroke combinations. These functions are transparent to system and application software. For this reason they can be executed by the user at any time. The immediate action keys are often called *hot keys*. The following immediate action services as available in IBM systems:

1. The *reset function* is an immediate action that is activated by the combination keystroke Ctrl/Alt/Del. The keystroke causes a jump to the BIOS startup procedure known as the *warm boot routine*.

2. The *print screen function* is linked to a dedicated key in some systems and to a keystroke combination in others. The corresponding routine is located at BIOS INT 05H. This vector is in conflict with the 80286 BOUND instruction, which uses it to report a register value outside the specified limits.

3. The *pause function* is initiated by a dedicated key on the PS/2 keyboard but requires several keystrokes in other systems. The routine activated by this key consists of a wait-for-keystroke loop internal to the INT 09H handler. The key provides an application-independent wait.

4. The *break function* is a hot key whose action can be defined by the programmer. When the Ctrl/Break keystrokes are received by the keyboard interrupt handler, an INT 1BH is executed. In the default mode, this interrupt returns to the caller without any other action. The programmer can replace this vector with code to perform any desired action.

5. The *system request function* corresponds to a key labeled Sys Req in the AT keyboard (see Figure 6.3). In the PS/2 keyboard this function is assigned as an Alt shift state of the Print Screen key, which is labeled SysRq on its front side (see Figure 6.5). The system request function was conceived as an immediate action for interrupting the task presently executing in 80286 and 80386 protected-mode software. However, because not all keyboards have a dedicated key for the system request function, the designers of the OS/2 operating system preferred to assign the system request function to the Ctrl/Esc and Alt/Esc keystrokes.

Upon detecting the Sys Req keystroke, the PC AT and PS/2 BIOS load the AH register with 85H and execute INT 15H. The AL register holds 00H if the key has been pressed and 01H if it has been released. It is possible to code an interrupt handler to intercept INT 15H, service 85H, which gains control when the Sys Req keystroke is detected. However, this handler has limited portability and could be in conflict with future uses of the system request function.

6.4 Typematic Action

Occasionally, a typist finds it necessary to repeat several keystrokes, for example, a succession of dashes to draw a horizontal line. With mechanical keyboards this repetition requires pressing and releasing the key for each character desired. With electronically controlled keyboards, like the ones used in computer terminals and in microcomputers, it is possible to detect when a key is being held down by the typist and proceed to automatically repeat the corresponding character. IBM refers to this operation as a *typematic action*.

Several factors must be considered in implementing typematic action. In the first place, when a key is pressed, it makes and breaks the circuit several times before establishing a firm contact. This effect, called *key bounce*, is neutralized by waiting a few milliseconds for the key action to stabilize. Another factor to consider is that an average typist normally holds down each key a fraction of a second before releasing it. For this reason, the keystroke processing logic must be able to differentiate between the normal delay of individual keystrokes and a key that has been held down intentionally. This is achieved by measuring the time during which the key's circuit remains closed and by comparing the elapsed time with a norm for individual keystrokes.

In implementing typematic action, the processing logic first determines that a key is being held down intentionally, then starts repeating the character at a certain rate. The sequence of repeated characters is sometimes called a *typematic burst*. If the burst rate is too fast, the typist will not be able to release the key to end the sequence at the desired point. On the other hand, if the typematic burst is too slow, the typist will have to wait excessively long for each character repetition. The initial delay and the burst rate are the two variables of typematic action. The ideal values of these variables are usually a matter of personal preference. Typematic action is shown graphically in Figure 6.10.

6.4.1 Variations in Typematic Action

All IBM keyboards have some form of typematic action, but it is not always implemented in the same manner. The IBM PC and PC XT keyboards have a delay period of approximately 500 ms (one-half second) and a burst rate of approximately 10 keystrokes per second. In these keyboards, delay and burst rate are fixed and cannot be reprogrammed. The PCjr provides reprogramming of the typematic parameters to increase the delay or slow down the burst rate. Since the default parameters of the PCjr are similar to those of the PC and PC XT, it is hard to imagine a user who could profit from this option.

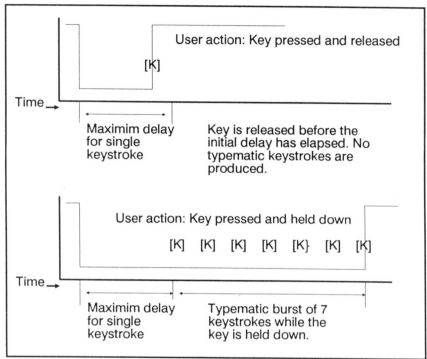

Figure 6.10. *Typematic Action*

The PC AT was the first IBM machine that allowed diminishing the delay and increasing the burst rate by reprogramming the keyboard hardware. The AT delay can be set at 250, 500, 750, and 1000 ms and the burst rate varied between a maximum of 30 and a minimum of 2 characters per second (cps). The default values are the same as the fixed parameters of the PC and PC XT. The keyboards of the PS/2 line are also reprogrammable within the same range as the PC AT. In addition, the quick reference diskette provided with computers of the PS/2 line allows selecting a normal or fast keyboard speed. However, the fast speed installed in this manner is considerably slower than the maximum rate.

6.4.2 Changing the Typematic Parameters

In systems that allow changing the typematic rate this operation can be performed either by using a BIOS service or by programming the controller registers directly. The AT BIOS dated 11-15-85 and after, the BIOS in the PC XT 286, as well as the PS/2 BIOS, contain service number 3, of INT 16H, which allows setting the delay and the typematic rate within the scope mentioned above for the PC AT. The bit map of the data byte for setting the typematic parameters in the PC AT and PS/2 systems is shown in Figure 6.11.

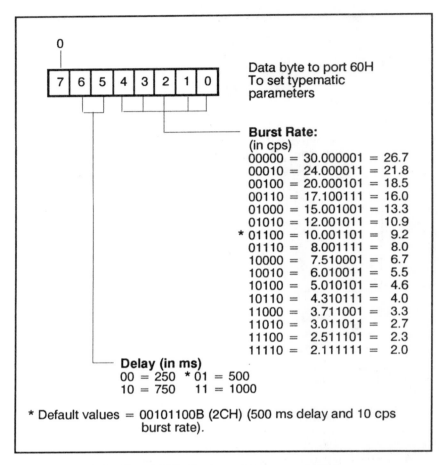

Figure 6.11. *PC AT and PS/2 Keyboard Command F3H*

In IBM and IBM-compatible machines equipped with AT-type keyboard hardware, the typematic parameters can also be changed by issuing system command code FEH to the 8042 keyboard controller. The command port for the 8042 keyboard controller is located at address 64H. This way of setting the typematic parameters can be used in systems in which the BIOS does not support service number 3 of INT 16H. Figure 6.11 shows the bit map of the 8042 command register to set the typematic parameters. The following code fragment performs the necessary operations:

```
; Code to set the delay and typematic rate in AT and PS/2
; systems using direct access to the keyboard controller
; registers at ports 60H and 64H.
;
```

```
; The default value is 00101100B (2CH), for a 500 ms delay and a
; 10.0 CPS burst rate.
; The new value installed by this program is 00000100B (04H)
; for a 250 ms delay and a 20 CPS burst rate.
;
; The procedures COM_8042 and COM_2_KBRD allow access to the
; controller's port 64H and to the keyboard hardware at port 60H.
;
; Disable keyboard interface using command code ADH
        MOV     AL,0ADH
        CALL    COM_8042        ; Send command to port 64H
; Send command code F3H to set delay and typematic rate
        MOV     AL,0F3H
        CALL    COM_2_KBRD  ; Keyboard command to port
                            ; 60H
; Code 04H sets 250 ms delay and 20 CPS burst rate. See bit map
; in Figure 6.11.
        MOV     AL,04H
        CALL    COM_2_KBRD
; Reenable keyboard using command code AEH
        MOV     AL,0AEH
        CALL    COM_8042
; Send command to clear output buffer and restart scanning.
        MOV     AL,0F4H
        CALL    COM_2_KBRD

            .
            .
            .
;*************************************************************
;                      procedures
;*************************************************************
COM_8042     PROC  NEAR
; Issue command to 8042 keyboard controller port 64H
; On entry:
;           AL = command code
        PUSH AX                 ; Save command code
        CLI                     ; Interrupts off
        MOV     CX,0FFFFH       ; Set counter
TEST_4_FULL:
        IN      AL,64H          ; Read STATUS port
        TEST    AL,00000010B    ; Input buffer full?
        LOOPNZ          TEST_4_FULL   ; Loop if CX not zero and if
                                ; zero flag = 0
; Input buffer is empty, send command
        POP     AX              ; Restore entry value (in AL)
        OUT     64H,AL          ; Send command
        STI                     ; Reenable interrupts
```

```
            RET
COM_8042      ENDP
;
COM_2_KBRD  PROC  NEAR
; Write a command or data byte to the keyboard hardware at
; port 60H
; On entry:
;          AL = data byte to write
; Set ES to BIOS data area
            MOV   CX,40H         ; Offset 0400H segment base
            MOV   ES,CX
;
            MOV   BH,AL          ; Save entry AL in BH
            MOV   BL,03          ; Counter for repeat effort
REPEAT_3:
            CLI                  ; Interrupts off
; Make sure that bits 4 and 5 of the keyboard flag byte at
; 0040:0097H are cleared. The function of these bits is:
;          bit 4 = Acknowledgment received
;          bit 5 = Resend receive flag
;
            MOV   AL,01001111B   ; Mask to clear bits 4 and 5
            AND   ES:[0097H],AL
TEST_FULL:
            IN    AL,64H         ; Read STATUS port
            TEST  AL,00000010B   ; Input buffer full?
            LOOPNZ TEST_FULL     ; Loop if CX not zero and if
                                 ; zero flag = 0
            MOV   AL,BH          ; Recover entry value to write
            OUT   60H,AL         ; Write byte to port 60H
            STI                  ; Reenable interrupts
; Wait for keyboard flag bit 4 (Acknowledge) ON
            MOV   CX,6656        ; Cycles to wait
WAIT_4_FLAGS:
            TEST  BYTE PTR ES:[0097H],00010000B
; Exit if bit 4 is set
            JNZ   EXIT_WRITE
            LOOP  WAIT_4_FLAGS
; 6656 cycles elapsed and bits not set. Repeat 3 times
            DEC   BL             ; BL primed to 3
            JNZ   REPEAT_3
; Operation failed after 3 tries. Set keyboard TRANSMIT ERROR
; flag and exit
            OR    BYTE PTR ES:[0097H],10000000B      ; Bit 7 set
EXIT_WRITE:
            RET
COM_2_KBRD  ENDP
```

Table 6.5. *Personal Computer and PC XT Keyboard MAKE Codes*

KEY	SCAN CODE	KEY	SCAN CODE
Esc	01H	1	02H
2	03H	3	04H
4	05H	5	06H
6	07H	7	08H
8	09H	9	0AH
0	0BH	-	0CH
=	0DH	Backspace	0EH
Tab	0FH	Q	10H
W	11H	E	12H
R	13H	T	14H
Y	15H	U	16H
I	17H	O	18H
P	19H	[	1AH
]	1BH	Enter	1CH
Ctrl	1DH	A	1EH
S	1FH	D	20H
F	21H	G	22H
H	23H	J	24H
K	25H	L	26H
;	27H	'	28H
'	29H	Left Shift	2AH
\	2BH	Z	2CH
X	2DH	C	2EH
V	2FH	B	30H
N	31H	M	32H
,	33H	.	34H
/	35H	Right Shift	36H
Print Screen	37H	Alt	38H
Spacebar	39H	Caps Lock	3AH
F1	3BH	F2	3CH
F3	3DH	F4	3EH
F5	3FH	F6	40H
F7	41H	F8	42H
F9	43H	F10	44H
Num Lock	45H	Scroll Lock	46H

(continued)

Table 6.5. *Personal Computer and PC XT Keyboard MAKE Codes*
(Continued)

KEY	SCAN CODE	KEY	SCAN CODE
Home	47H	Up Arrow	48H
Pg Up	49H	-	4AH
Left Arrow	4BH	5 (keypad)	4CH
Right Arrow	4DH	+	4EH
End	4FH	Down Arrow	50H
Pg Dn	51H	Ins	52H
Del	53H		

6.5 The Keyboard Scan Codes

The key codes stored by the keyboard hardware for processing by the Interrupt 09H handler, called *scan codes*, are not in ASCII or any other standard format. It is the INT 09H handler that must translate the scan codes into standardized ASCII values. For the same reason, routines that intercept the INT 09H handler to filter keystrokes or to provide customized handling will retrieve from port 60H the raw scan code mentioned above. Sections 6.2.1 and 6.2.3 contain code fragments to obtain the keyboard scan codes in the PC XT and the AT and PS/2 keyboard hardware.

All IBM systems provide the means for distinguishing between the action of closing or opening a key switch. The closing action is usually referred to as a *make code*, while releasing a key generates a code called the *break scan code*. In the PC XT the break code is the make code with the high bit set, as shown in Tables 6.5 and 6.6, respectively. This also applies to the scan codes in the PCjr after processing by INT 48H (see Section 6.2.2). In the PC AT the value F0H indicates that the following scan code corresponds to a break operation. Table 6.7 lists the keyboard make scan codes for the PC AT.

In the PS/2 keyboard the programmer can select among three scan code sets. Although the system default is scan code set 2, the BIOS initializes scan code set 1 as active. In set number 1 the break codes are reported as for the PC and PC XT keyboard; that is, the break code is the make code with the high bit set. Several keys, which did not exist in previous keyboards, are preceded by the code E0H. The Pause key is not typematic and does not generate a break code. The scan codes for the Pause key are all generated on the make keystroke. Table 6.8 lists the PS/2 keyboard make scan codes.

Table 6.6. *Personal Computer and PC XT Keyboard BREAK Codes*

KEY	SCAN CODE	KEY	SCAN CODE
Esc	81H	1	82H
2	83H	3	84H
4	85H	5	86H
6	87H	7	88H
8	89H	9	8AH
0	8BH	-	8CH
=	8DH	Backspace	8EH
Tab	8FH	Q	90H
W	91H	E	92H
R	93H	T	94H
Y	95H	U	96H
I	97H	O	98H
P	99H	[	9AH
]	9BH	Enter	9CH
Ctrl	9DH	A	9EH
S	9FH	D	A0H
F	A1H	G	A2H
H	A3H	J	A4H
K	A5H	L	A6H
;	A7H	'	A8H
'	A9H	Left Shift	AAH
\	ABH	Z	ACH
X	ADH	C	AEH
V	AFH	B	B0H
N	B1H	M	B2H
,	B3H	.	B4H
/	B5H	Right Shift	B6H
Print Screen	B7H	Alt	B8H
Spacebar	B9H	Caps Lock	BAH
F1	BBH	F2	BCH
F3	BDH	F4	BEH
F5	BFH	F6	C0H
F7	C1H	F8	C2H
F9	C3H	F10	C4H
Num Lock	C5H	Scroll Lock	C6H

(continued)

Table 6.6. *Personal Computer and PC XT Keyboard BREAK Codes*
(Continued)

KEY	SCAN CODE	KEY	SCAN CODE
Home	C7H	Up Arrow	C8H
PgUp	C9H	-	CAH
Left Arrow	CBH	5 (keypad)	CCH
Right Arrow	CDH	+	CEH
End	CFH	Down Arrow	D0H
PgDn	D1H	Ins	D2H
Del	D3H		

6.6 Intercepting Keystrokes

Customized keystroke handlers frequently intercept the keyboard scan code before it is processed by the BIOS service routine at INT 09H. This technique, sometimes described as a keystroke filter, usually has one of the following purposes:

1. To suppress a hot key, for example, to filter the Print Screen key so that this function is not performed by the handler.

2. To create a new hot key that will perform a customized function not implemented in the system software. For example, upon detecting that the Ctrl and F1 keys have been simultaneously pressed, a memory-resident utility can dump to a disk file a bit image of the video display screen.

3. To produce a customized action on a certain keystroke or keystroke combination. For example, a memory-resident utility can enable the Caps Lock state upon detecting the Enter key and can toggle the system to lowercase upon detecting the ; key. This operation is convenient for writing code and comments in assembly language programs.

The fundamental task of a customized keystroke handler is to intercept the keystroke before it reaches the BIOS keyboard service routine at INT 09H. This is usually done by replacing the vector for the original handler with the address of the filter routine. The program named FASTKBD discussed in Section 6.7.1 and listed in Appendix B illustrates this technique. However, versions of the AT BIOS dated June 10, 1985, and after, the BIOS of the PC XT model 286, of the PC Convertible, and of the PS/2 computers, provide a keyboard intercept at INT 15H. This service is requested with an entry value of AH = 79. The programmer can use INT 15H to intercept any desired scan code. The intercepted code can then be modified, discarded, or allowed to pass to the original handler at INT 09H. One advantage of this method is that it does not require accessing the keyboard hardware.

Table 6.7. *Personal Computer AT Keyboard MAKE Codes*

KEY	SCAN CODE	KEY	SCAN CODE
Esc	01H	1	02H
2	03H	3	04H
4	05H	5	06H
6	07H	7	08H
8	09H	9	0AH
0	0BH	-	0CH
=	0DH	Backspace	0EH
Tab	0FH	Q	10H
W	11H	E	12H
R	13H	T	14H
Y	15H	U	16H
I	17H	O	18H
P	19H	[	1AH
]	1BH	Enter	1CH
Ctrl	1DH	A	1EH
S	1FH	D	20H
F	21H	G	22H
H	23H	J	24H
K	25H	L	26H
;	27H	'	28H
'	29H	Left Shift	2AH
\	2BH	Z	2CH
X	2DH	C	2EH
V	2FH	B	30H
N	31H	M	32H
,	33H	.	34H
/	35H	Right Shift	36H
Print Screen	37H	Alt	38H
Spacebar	38H	Caps Lock	3AH
F1	3BH	F2	3CH
F3	3DH	F4	3EH
F5	3FH	F6	40H
F7	41H	F8	42H
F9	43H	F10	44H
Num Lock	45H	Scroll Lock	46H

(continued)

Table 6.7. *Personal Computer AT Keyboard MAKE Codes (Continued)*

KEY	SCAN CODE	KEY	SCAN CODE
Home	47H	Up arrow	48H
PgUp	49H	-	4AH
Left Arrow	4BH	5 (keypad)	4CH
Right Arrow	4DH	+	4EH
End	4FH	Down Arrow	50H
PgDn	51H	Ins	52H
Del	53H	Sys Req	54H

Note: PC AT BREAK codes are the MAKE codes preceded by F0H.

6.6.1 Keyboard Enhancers

Programs sometimes called *keyboard enhancers* provide complex keystroke filtering and execute custom operations. Enhancers are based on the notion that it is possible to increase software performance by manipulating the user's keystrokes. For example, we have seen that the delay and typematic rates cannot be changed in the PC and XT keyboards. However, it is possible for a memory-resident utility to take over the keystroke repetition function. When correctly implemented, the resulting keyboard action appears to a user as if the typematic delay and burst rate had been effectively changed.

The FASTKBD program listed in Appendix B is a memory-resident utility that reprograms the system timer and intercepts the keyboard and the timer interrupts so as to implement keystroke repetition in software. The operations are particularly useful in computers with nonprogrammable keyboards, such as the PC and PC XT. The program operates in relation to the four arrow keys and the Del key. The left shift key acts as a "turbo" keystroke by doubling the burst rate. Although the sample listing is in the form of a TSR, the basic coding can be used in other types of executable code. FASTKBD allows the user to vary the delay and the burst rate, within certain limits, by entering values in the command tail.

Table 6.8. *PS/2 Keyboard MAKE Codes for Scan Code Set No. 1*

KEY	SCAN CODE	KEY	SCAN CODE
Esc	01H	1	02H
2	03H	3	04H
4	05H	5	06H
6	07H	7	08H
8	09H	9	0AH
0	0BH	-	0CH
=	0DH	Backspace	0EH
Tab	0FH	Q	10H
W	11H	E	12H
R	13H	T	14H
Y	15H	U	16H
I	17H	O	18H
P	19H	[	1AH
]	1BH	Enter	1CH
Ctrl	1DH	A	1EH
S	1FH	D	20H
F	21H	G	22H
H	23H	J	24H
K	25H	L	26H
;	27H	'	28H
`	29H	Left Shift	2AH
\	2BH	Z	2CH
X	2DH	C	2EH
V	2FH	B	30H
N	31H	M	32H
,	33H	.	34H
/	35H	Right Shift	36H
Print Screen	E0H 2AH E0H 37H	Alt	38H
Spacebar	39H	Caps Lock	3AH
F1	3BH	F2	3CH
F3	3DH	F4	3EH
F5	3FH	F6	40H
F7	41H	F8	42H
F9	43H	F10	44H

(continued)

Table 6.8. *PS/2 Keyboard MAKE Codes for Scan Code Set No. 1*
(Continued)

KEY	SCAN CODE	KEY	SCAN CODE
Num Lock	45H	Scroll Lock	46H
Home	47H	Up Arrow	48H
PgUp	49H	-	4AH
Left Arrow	4BH	5 (keypad)	4CH
Right Arrow	4DH	+	4EH
End	4FH	Down Arrow	50H
PgDn	51H	Ins	52H
Del	53H		

Editing Keypad		**Cursor Keypad**	
Insert	E6H 52H	Left Arrow	E0H 4BH
Delete	E0H 53H	Up Arrow	E0H 48H
Home	E0H 47H	Down Arrow	E0H 50H
End	E0H 4FH	Right Arrow	E0H 4DH
Page Up	E0H 49H		
Page Down	E0H 51H		

New Keys In Ps/2 Keyboard

Right Alt	E0H 38H	F11	57H
Right Ctrl	E0H 1DH	F12	58H
Keypad Enter	E0H 1CH	Keypad /	E0H 35H
Pause	E1H 1DH 45H E1H 9DH C5H		

6.7 Alternative Input Devices

Some configurations of the IBM microcomputers can receive and process input
originating in devices different from the keyboard. The following are some
alternative input devices used in IBM systems:

1. Mouse

2. Track ball

3. Touchpad or digitizer

4. Scanner

The first three mechanisms listed above are usually classified as *pointing devices*. Several independent vendors have developed and marketed pointing devices compatible with the IBM microcomputers of the PC line. These devices are typically packaged to include an interface card and the necessary software. One such device is the Microsoft mouse.

IBM systems of the PC line do not provide integrated hardware or software support for alternative input devices; on the other hand, all models of the PS/2 line contain a pointing device port. IBM manufactures a mouse for the PS/2 computers which includes a software driver. This mouse does not require special adapters since it is connected to the PS/2 pointing device port.

6.7.1 PS/2 Auxiliary Device Port

All models of the PS/2 line include an auxiliary device port. This port is accessed via a 6-pin miniature DIN connector identical to the one used for the keyboard. The signals and voltage are the same in both connectors. The connector sockets are located at the back of the system unit.

Like the keyboard, the auxiliary device port is coupled to the 8042 keyboard controller described in Section 6.2.3. The auxiliary device port can be used with any serial input device compatible with the Intel 8042. IBM and other vendors manufacture a serial mouse for PS/2 systems that connects to the auxiliary device port. In operation, the PS/2 serial mouse is compatible with application software written for the Microsoft mouse.

The auxiliary device function of the 8042 can be enabled by clearing bit 5 of the 8042 command byte (see Figure 6.8). In PS/2 systems, the 8042 can be programmed to generate an interrupt when the auxiliary device places data in the port's output buffer. This function is controlled by bit 1 of the 8042 command byte at port 64H (see Figure 6.8). This interrupt is assigned to request line number 12 (IRQ12) of the second 8259-A interrupt controller and vectored through interrupt 74H (see Table 3.13).

In PS/2 systems, BIOS service number 194 (C2H), of INT 15H, provides the means for initializing and programming a pointing device. These services are especially appropriate for interfacing with and controlling a PS/2 serial mouse attached to the auxiliary device port. Subservice number 7 simplifies the initialization and creation of an interrupt intercept routine that automatically gains control when pointing device data become available.

7

Communications

7.0 IBM Communications Hardware

Computer communications refers to the exchange of data between computers and terminals and to the transmission of data to processing devices. In theory, the definition includes data transmission to any type of peripheral equipment and through any type of internal or external, wired or wireless data path.

In this sense it is correct to refer to communications between a computer and devices such as the keyboard, the video display, the diskette, the hard disk drive, or even a satellite in space, as data communications. However, in the present chapter, adopting the more common treatment of this subject, the discussion regarding communication facilities concentrates on the serial port, the parallel port, and the various modems. The communications protocols and standards are discussed with the corresponding hardware elements. Intersystem communications are mentioned in relation to local area networks.

Table 7.1. *Communications Hardware in the IBM Microcomputers*

SYSTEM	DEVICE
Personal Computer and PC XT	Parallel printer adapter. Monochrome display and printer adapter. Asynchronous communications adapter (serial port). Optional external and internal modems.
IBM PCjr	Parallel printer adapter. Built-in serial port. Optional external and internal modems.
Personal Computer AT	Serial/parallel adapter. Optional internal and external modems.
Personal System/2	Built-in parallel port. Built-in serial port. Built-in auxiliary device port (mouse). Optional internal and external modems.

Independent vendors furnish additional cards or devices that serve as communications ports for the IBM microcomputers. Some of these cards provide either a parallel or a serial port, or both. These devices are more popular for machines of the PC line, since serial and parallel ports are part of the standard hardware in the models of the PS/2 line (see Table 7.1). Modems are not a standard component in any IBM microcomputer and must be purchased separately in the form of internal or external options.

In the PC line the parallel port is output-only and is used almost exclusively as a printer interface. This limitation was corrected in the PS/2 line, in which the parallel port is bidirectional. Normally, the serial port follows the RS-232-C communications protocol, but serial cards for newer standards are also available.

7.1 Serial Communications

Serial communications take place by transmitting and receiving data in a stream of consecutive electrical pulses that represent bits. The Electronic Industries Association (EIA) has sponsored the development of several standards for serial communications, for example, RS-232-C, RS-422, RS-423, and RS-449. In this designation the characters RS stand for the words Recommended Standard. The simplest to implement and most used serial communications standard is the RS-232-C voltage level convention.

7.1.1 The RS-232-C Standard

This standard for serial communications was developed jointly by the EIA, the Bell Telephone System, and modem and computer manufacturers. The RS-232-C standard has achieved such widespread acceptance that its name is often used as a synonym for the serial port.

The RS-232-C convention specifies that, with respect to ground, a voltage more negative than minus 3 V is interpreted as a 1 bit and a voltage more positive than $+3$ V as a 0 bit. Serial communications according to RS-232-C require that the transmitter and the receiver agree on a communications protocol. The following terminology refers to the RS-232-C communications protocol:

1. *Baud period*. The rate of transmission measured in bits per second. The transmitter and the receiver clocks must be synchronized to the same baud period. The word *baud* was chosen to honor the nineteenth-century French scientist and inventor J. M. E. Baudot.

2. *Marking state*. The time period during which no data is being transmitted. During the marking period the transmitter holds the line at a steady high voltage.

3. *Start bit*. The low bit which indicates that data transmission is about to start. The low state that occurs during the start bit is called the *spacing state*.

4. *Character bits*. The data stream composed of 5, 6, 7, or 8 bits that encode the character transmitted. The least significant bit (LSB) is the first one transmitted.

4. *Parity bit.* An optional bit, transmitted following the character bits, used in checking for transmission errors. If *even parity* is chosen, the transmitter sets or clears the parity bit so as to make the sum of the character's 1 bits and the parity bit an even number. In *odd parity* the parity bit makes the sum of 1 bits an odd number. If parity is not correct, the receiver sets an error flag in a special register. This register can be read by the central processing unit.

5. *Stop bits.* One or more high bits inserted in the stream following the character bits or the parity bit, if there is one. The stop bit or bits ensure that the receiver will have enough time to make ready for the next character.

Figure 7.1 shows the different elements in a serial communications bit stream. The time period separating characters is variable. The transmitter holds the line voltage high (marking state) until it is ready to send. The start bit (spacing state) is used to signal the start of a new character. This mode of operation, in which the characters are independent from each other, is called *asynchronous communications*. The start bit is also used by the receiver to resynchronize with the transmitter. This compensates for drifts and small errors in the baud rate.

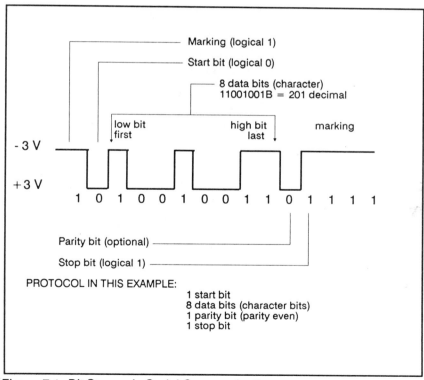

Figure 7.1. *Bit Stream in Serial Communications*

In the RS-232-C protocol the transmission-reception parameters are selected from a range of standard values. The following are the most common ones in the IBM microcomputers:

Baud rate: 50, 110, 300, 600, 1200, 2400, 4800, 9600, and 19200

Data bits: 5, 6, 7, or 8.

Parity bit: Odd, even, or no parity.

Stop bits: 1, 1.5, or 2.

RS-232-C defines data terminal equipment (DTE) and data circuit-terminating equipment (DCE), sometimes called data communications equipment. According to the standard the DTE designation includes both terminals and computers, and DCE refers to modems, transducers, and other devices. The serial port in IBM microcomputers is defined as DTE.

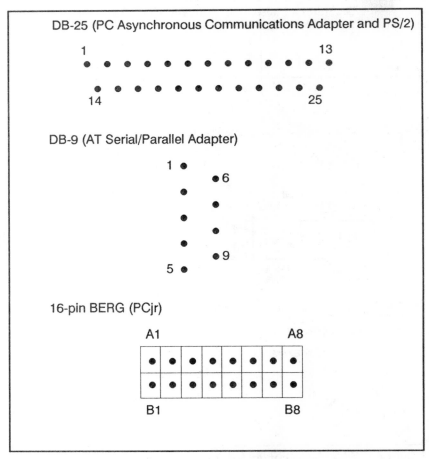

Figure 7.2. *Contact Numbers on IBM Serial Connectors*

7.1.1.1 Connectors and Wiring. The RS-232-C standard requires a specific hardware connector with 25 pins, called a *D-shell connector*, or DB-25. But not all IBM serial ports use the DB-25 connector. The PCjr serial port uses a 16-position BERG connector and the PC AT Serial/Parallel Adapter uses a 9-pin D-shell connector. Figure 7.2 shows the pin numbering on DB-25, DB-9, and 16-pin BERG connectors. The diagram corresponds to the male connectors, as seen from the back of the system units.

The function assigned to each pin varies in the different connectors. Table 7.2 lists the assignation of the RS-232-C lines in the different hardware. Table 7.3 defines some common RS-232-C circuits.

Table 7.2. *Definition of Common RS-232-C Lines*

CONNECTOR			FUNCTION	CODE NAME	DIRECTION
DB-25	DB-9	BERG			
1		B2	Ground	G	
2	3	A4	Transmit data	TD	Output
3	2	A8	Receive data	RD	Input
4	7	A3	Request to send	RTS	Output
5	8	A7	Clear to send	CTS	Input
6	6	A6	Data set ready	DSR	Input
7	5	B1	Chassis ground	G	
8	1	A5	Carrier detect	CD	
20	4	A2	Data terminal ready	DTR	Output
22	9		Ring indicator	RI	Input

Table 7.3. *Definition of Common RS-232-C Circuits*

SIGNAL NAME	DIRECTION	PURPOSE
Control signals		
Request to send	DTE ⇒ DCE	DTE wishes to send
Clear to send	DTE ⇐ DCE	Response to request to send
Data set ready	DTE ⇐ DCE	DCE ready to operate
Data terminal ready	DTE ⇒ DCE	DTE ready to operate
Ring indicator	DTE ⇐ DCE	DTE receiving telephone ringing signal
Carrier detect	DTE ⇐ DCE	DTE receiving a carrier signal
Data signals		
Transmitted data	DTE ⇒ DCE	Data generated by DTE
Received data	DTE ⇐ DCE	Data generated by DCE

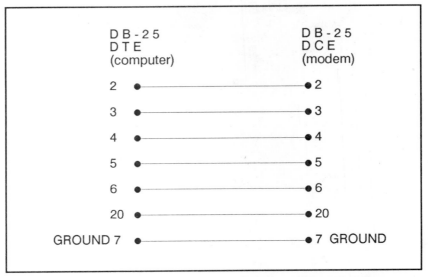

Figure 7.3. *Wiring Diagram for RS-232-C DTE to DCE in IBM Systems*

The RS-232-C standard has earned the reputation of being excessively flexible. This flexibility has determined that interfacing with RS-232-C devices often requires customized wiring. However, in connecting devices that correspond with the DTE and DCE designation, respectively — for instance, a computer to a modem — the required wiring is straight-through. This means that pin number 2 in the computer is connected to modem pin number 2, pin 3 to pin 3, and so forth. Figure 7.3 shows the necessary connections for IBM systems.

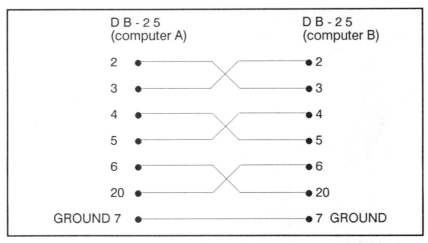

Figure 7.4. *Wiring Diagram for RS-232-C Null Modem in IBM Systems*

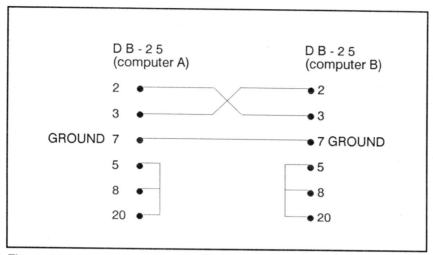

Figure 7.5. *Alternative Wiring for IBM RS-232-C Null Modem*

On the other hand, connecting similar devices, for example, a computer to a computer or a terminal to a terminal, requires crossed wiring. This connecting scheme, which ensures that the receiving lines are coupled to the transmitting lines, is known as a *null modem*. Figures 7.4 through 7.7 show several null modem wiring diagrams for the various serial connectors used in IBM systems.

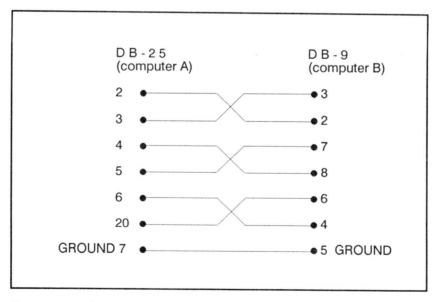

Figure 7.6. *RS-232-C Wiring Diagram for DB-25 to DB-9 Null Modem*

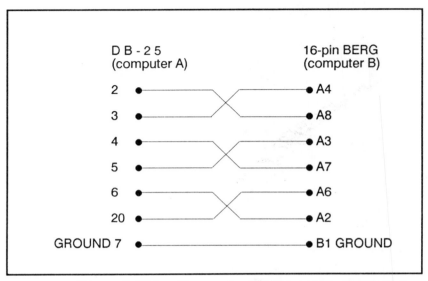

Figure 7.7. *RS-232-C Wiring Diagram for DB-25 to 16-pin BERG Null Modem*

7.2 Implementations of the Serial Port

IBM microcomputers show considerable variations in the implementation of the serial port. In the various models of the PC line the serial port is furnished in an optional adapter card known as the Asynchronous Communications Adapter. The PCjr comes equipped with a built-in serial port. The PC AT serial port is furnished as an optional adapter card, known as the Serial/Parallel Adapter, while in all models of the PS/2 line the serial port is standard equipment. In all systems the IBM serial port follows the EIA RS-232-C standard, although there are variations in the connecting hardware (see Section 7.1.1.1).

7.2.1 The Serial Communications Controllers

The fundamental element of the serial port is an integrated circuit communications controller. The 8250 universal asynchronous receiver and transmitter (UART), or a functionally equivalent chip, is used in the IBM Asynchronous Communications Adapter of the PC line, in the PCjr, and in the non-Micro Channel computers of the PS/2 line (Models 25 and 30). The Serial/Parallel Adapter in the PC AT is equipped with the NS-16450 chip, and the Micro Channel models of the PS/2 line with the NS-16550. Fortunately, the various serial communications controllers listed above have similar architectures and appear almost identical to the programmer.

In operation, the transmitter portion of the controller converts an 8-bit data value, placed by the processor in the adapter's output port, into a serial bit stream formatted according to the RS-232-C protocol. During the transmission operation the controller inserts the necessary start, stop, and parity bits. On the other hand, the controller can also decode an incoming bit stream and place the data byte in the adapter's input port, where it can be read by the processor. During the reception operation the chip uses the start, stop, and parity bits to synchronize the transmission, to identify the data bits, and to check for errors.

In serial communications, if the hardware device is capable of simultaneously transmitting and receiving data, it is said to operate in *full duplex* mode. The term *half duplex* is used to describe serial communications that must take place alternatively, that is, in one direction at a time. All the serial communications controllers used in the IBM microcomputers are capable of full duplex operation. Figure 7.8 is a diagram of the internal elements in the serial communications controllers used in the IBM microcomputers.

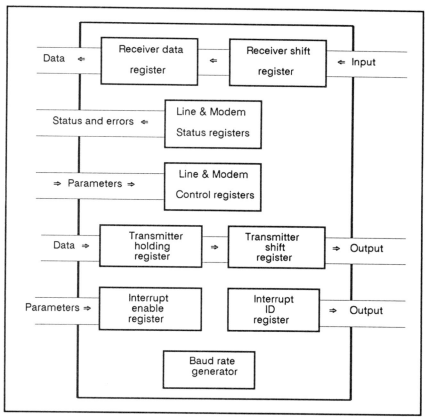

Figure 7.8. *Registers and Functions of the IBM Serial Communications Controllers NS8250 (UART), NS16450 (PC AT), and NS16550 (PS/2)*

Table 7.4. *Internal Register Mapping of the Serial Communications Controller in the IBM Microcomputers (except the PCjr)*

REGISTER NAME	REGISTER CODE NAME	PORT ADDRESS		FUNCTION
		COM1	COM2	
Transmitter holding register	THR	3F8H	2F8H	Output
Receiver data register	RDR	3F8H	2F8H	Input
Baud rate divisor (LSB)	BRDL	3F8H	2F8H	Output
Baud rate divisor (MSB)	BRDH	3F9H	2F9H	Output
Interrupt enable register	IER	3F9H	2F9H	Output
Interrupt ID register	IID	3FAH	2FAH	Input
Line control register	LCR	3FBH	2FBH	Output
Modem control register	MDC	3FCH	2FCH	Output
Line status register	LST	3FDH	2FDH	Input
Modem status register	MSR	3FEH	2FEH	Input

The IBM serial communications controllers (8250 UART, NS-16450, and NS-16550) appear to the programmer as 10 internal registers. These registers are accessible to the CPU through as many ports. IBM systems allow the use of more than one serial communications device by mapping each device to a different set of seven ports. In all IBM microcomputers, except the PCjr, if the serial communications controller is mapped to ports 3F8H to 3FEH, it is said to be configured as communications port number 1, or COM1. If it is mapped to ports 2F8H to 2FEH, then it is said to be configured as COM2. Table 7.4 shows the internal registers of the IBM serial communications controllers when configured as COM1 and COM2. Table 7.5 shows register mapping in the IBM PCjr.

Some IBM hardware allows more than one serial port in a system. For example, changing jumper J1 on the AT's Serial/Parallel Adapter determines the mapping and designation of the serial port. In one setting, the serial port becomes COM1 and the first digit of the port's address becomes 3 (see Table 7.5). In the alternate setting the port is designated as COM2 and the first digit of the address becomes 2. Serial port mapping and designation for the PCjr can be seen in Table 7.6.

These possible variations in the serial port can be the source of uncertainty regarding the number of serial ports installed in a system and their address mapping. In any case, the BIOS initialization routines store the base address of the first serial port (COM1) at memory locations 400H in the BIOS data area. If additional ports are implemented, their base addresses are stored at memory locations 402H, 404H, and 406H, respectively. One or more of these fields is initialized to zero if the system contains less than four serial ports, but the BIOS does not initialize valid ports following a zero address value.

Table 7.5. *Internal Register Mapping of the 8250 UART in the IBM PCjr*

REGISTER NAME	REGISTER CODE NAME	INTERNAL MODEM	SERIAL PORT	FUNCTION
Transmitter holding register	THR	3F8H	2F8H	Output
Receiver data register	RDR	3F8H	2F8H	Input
Baud rate divisor (LSB)	BRDL	3F8H	2F8H	Output
Baud rate divisor (MSB)	BRDH	3F9H	2F9H	Output
Interrupt enable register	IER	3F9H	2F9H	Output
Interrupt ID register	IID	3FAH	2FAH	Input
Line control register	LCR	3FBH	2FBH	Output
Modem control register	MDC	3FCH	2FCH	Output
Line status register	LST	3FDH	2FDH	Input
Modem status register	MSR	3FEH	2FEH	Input

Note: If the PCjr internal modem is installed, the serial port is logically COM2 and the modem is COM1. With no modem, the serial port is COM1. In the PCjr the serial port's base address is always 2F8H.

Table 7.6. *Divisor Values for Programming the Baud Rate Generator*

BAUD RATE	PC-AT and PS/2 CLOCK SPEED, 1.8432 MHz			PCjr CLOCK SPEED, 1.7895 MHz		
	DECIMAL	HEX	% ERROR	DECIMAL	HEX	% ERROR
50	2304	900H	0	2337	8BDH	.008
75	1536	600H	0	1491	5D3H	.017
110	1047	417H	.026	1017	3F9H	.023
134.5	857	359H	.058	832	340H	.054
150	768	300H	0	746	2EAH	.050
300	384	180H	0	373	175H	.050
600	192	C0H	0	186	BAH	.218
1200	96	60H	0	93	5DH	.218
1800	64	40H	0	62	3EH	.218
2000	58	3AH	.690	56	38H	.140
2400	48	30H	0	47	2FH	.855
3600	32	20H	0	31	1FH	.218
4800	24	18H	0	23	17H	1.291
7200	16	10H	0	– NOT RECOMMENDED –		
9600	12	CH	0	– NOT RECOMMENDED –		
19200	6	6H	0	– NOT RECOMMENDED –		

The following code fragment shows how to obtain and save the address of the four possible serial ports:

```
DATA    SEGMENT
;
COM1_BASE    DW    0000H    ; Storage for COM1 base address
COM2_BASE    DW    0000H    ; Storage for COM2 base address
COM3_BASE    DW    0000H    ; Storage for COM3 base address
COM4_BASE    DW    0000H    ; Storage for COM4 base address
;
DATA    ENDS
;
CODE    SEGMENT
        ASSUME          CS:CODE
        .
        .
; Obtain base address of serial ports from BIOS data area
        PUSH    DS              ; Save program's DS
        XOR     AX,AX           ; AX = 0
        MOV     DS,AX           ; Data segment zero for BIOS
        MOV     DX,DS:0400H     ; Base address of COM1
        MOV     CX,DS:0402H     ; Base address of COM2
        MOV     BX,DS:0404H     ; Base address of COM3
        MOV     AX,DS:0406H     ; Base address of COM4
        POP     DS              ; Restore program's DS
        MOV     COM1_BASE,DX        ; Store COM1
        MOV     COM2_BASE,CX        ; Store COM2
        MOV     COM1_BASE,BX        ; Store COM3
        MOV     COM2_BASE,AX        ; Store COM4
; The code can now check each stored port address for a zero
; value to determine the number of valid ports
        .
        .
```

7.2.2 The Controller's Registers

The internal architecture of the various serial communications controllers used in the IBM microcomputers (8250 UART, NS-16450, and NS-16550) appears almost identical to the programmer. The CPU can gain access to the controller registers through the corresponding ports (see Tables 7.5 and 7.6).

The Transmitter Holding Register. The transmitter holding register contains the character ready to be sent. During a transmission operation the LSB in the holding register is the first one sent.

The Receiver Data Register. The receiver data register, also called the *receiver buffer register*, holds the character received.

The Baud Rate Divisor Registers. The baud rate divisor registers, also called the *divisor latch registers,* are used to program the baud rate generator in the serial communications controller. One baud rate divisor register (BRDL) stores the least significant byte (see Tables 7.5 and 7.6), and the following register (BRDH) stores the most significant byte. The following formula is for calculating the value of the divisor that will generate a given baud rate:

$$D = \frac{Ck}{16 * Br}$$

where D = desired divisor
      Ck = clock speed in Hz
      Br = baud rate desired

The clock speed (Ck) is 1,843,200 Hz in all IBM microcomputers except the PCjr. In the PCjr the clock speed is 1,789,500 Hz.

Table 7.6 lists the values required for the baud rate divisor in order to obtain the more common baud rates. A separate listing is provided for the PCjr due to its different clock speed.

Setting the baud rate in the serial communications controllers requires programming the baud rate divisor registers. However, observation of Tables 7.5 and 7.6 shows that the baud rate divisor least significant byte register is mapped to the same address as the transmitter holding register and the receiver data register, while the baud rate divisor most significant byte is mapped to the same address as the interrupt enable register. For this reason, in order to select the baud rate divisor registers, it is first necessary to set bit 7 of the line control register (see "The Line Control Register" later in this section). Due to this, its high bit is often called the *divisor latch access bit,* or DLAB. When the DLAB bit of the line control register is clear (bit equals zero), access can be gained to the transmitter holding register, the receiver data register, and the interrupt enable register.

The following code fragment illustrates setting the baud rate of the first serial port (COM1) to 1200 baud (Bd) in a non-PCjr system. The code assumes that a valid address for the first serial port has been previously stored in a variable named COM1_BASE (see code fragment in Section 7.2.1). Note that the divisor values would be different for the IBM PCjr.

```
        MOV    DX,COM1_BASE       ; See previous code fragment
        ADD    DX,3          ; Line control register is at
                             ; base address + 3
        IN     AL,DX         ; Read contents of LC register
        JMP    SHORT $+2     ; I/O delay
        OR     AL,80H        ; To set the divisor latch access
                             ; bit (DLAB)
        OUT    DX,AL         ; To line control register
        JMP    SHORT $+2     ; I/O delay
;
        MOV    AL,60H        ; LSB for 1200 Bd (Table 7.7)
```

```
MOV    DL,0F8H        ; Address of divisor's LSB
OUT    DX,AL          ; AL to baud rate divisor LSB
JMP    SHORT $+2      ; I/O delay
MOV    AL,0H          ; MSB for 1200 Bd (see table)
MOV    DL,0F9H        ; Address of divisor's MSB
OUT    DX,AL          ; AL to Bd rate divisor MSB
JMP    SHORT $+2      ; I/O delay
; Bd rate is now set for 1200 Bd
.
.
.
```

The Interrupt Enable Register. The serial communications controller allows four types of interrupts. The interrupt enable register (IER) permits activating one or more of these interrupt sources. Serial communication interrupts also require setting bit 3 of the modem control register (see "The Modem Control Register" later in this section) and that the CPU's interrupt system be active. Figure 7.9 shows the bit map of the IER.

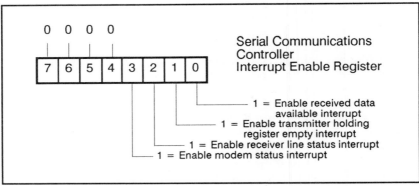

Figure 7.9. *The Interrupt Enable Register*

As can be seen in Table 7.5, the IER and the baud rate divisor (MSB) share the same address. This is why, in order to obtain access to the IER, the high bit of the line control register (DLAB) must be clear. The following code fragment shows how to enable the received data available interrupt in the serial communications controller. The code assumes that a valid address for the first serial port has been previously stored in the variable COM1_BASE (see code fragment in Section 7.2.1).

```
MOV    DX,COM1_BASE      ; See code in Section 7.2.1
ADD    DX,3              ; Line control register is at
                         ; base address + 3
IN     AL,DX             ; Read contents of LC register
JMP    SHORT $+2         ; I/O delay
AND    AL,7FH            ; To clear DLAB
```

```
        OUT    DX,AL           ; To line control register
        JMP    SHORT $+2       ; I/O delay
; The line control register high bit is now clear. This selects
; the interrupt enable register
        MOV    DL,0F9H          ; IER address
        MOV    AL,1H            ; Receiver data available bit
                                ; see Table 7.9
        OUT    DX,AL
        JMP    SHORT $+2       ; I/O delay
; Interrupt enable register set for data available interrupts
        .
        .
        .
```

In IBM microcomputer systems the communications interrupt, originating in the serial line designated as COM1, is linked to the hardware interrupt line IRQ4. This line is vectored through interrupt 0CH. The interrupts originating in the serial line designated COM2 are linked to IRQ3 and to interrupt vector 0BH. The serial port in the IBM PCjr is always linked to the IRQ3 line and to vector 0BH.

The Interrupt Identification Register. The interrupt identification register (IID) stores a priority code that makes possible the identification of one or more pending interrupts. The possible interrupt sources depend on setting the IER discussed previously in this section. Bit 0 of the interrupt ID register will be clear if there is a pending interrupt. Polling routines can use this bit to determine whether there is an interrupt condition that requires service. The bit map of the interrupt ID register is shown in Figure 7.10.

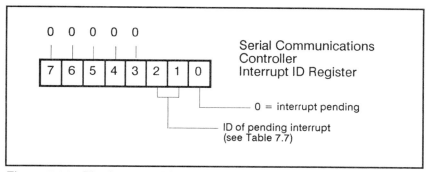

Figure 7.10. *The Interrupt Identification Register*

Bits 1 and 2 of the interrupt ID register contain the priority code that permits the identification of the pending interrupt. This code is also called the *interrupt priority level.* The parameters of the serial communications interrupt are shown in Table 7.7.

Table 7.7. *Interrupt Priority, Type, Cause, and Reset Action in the Serial Communications Controller*

INTERRUPT ID BITS		INTERRUPT PRIORITY LEVEL	TYPE	POSSIBLE CAUSES	RESETTING ACTION
2	1				
1	1	1	Receiver line status.	Overrun error. Parity error. Framing error. Break interrupt.	Read the line status register.
1	0	2	Received data available.	Data in register.	Read receiver data register.
0	1	3	Transmitter holding register empty.	No data in register.	Read interrupt ID register or write THR.
0	0	4	Modem status.	Clear to send. Data set ready. Ring indicator. Received line signal detect.	Read modem status register.

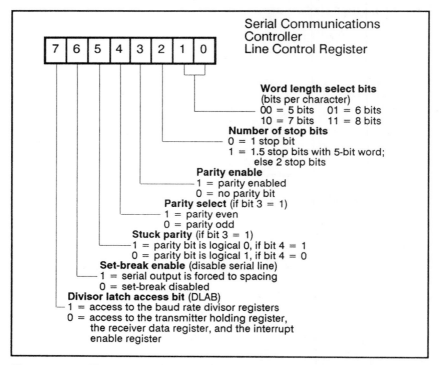

Figure 7.11. *The Line Control Register*

The Line Control Register. The high bit of the line control register (LCR), often called the divisor latch access bit (DLAB), is used to select between various registers mapped to the same address. If the DLAB bit is set, then read or write operations to the registers mapped to the base address (3F8H or 2F8H) will access the baud rate divisor LSB register. Also, read and write operations to the base address plus one (3F9H or 2F9H) will access the baud rate divisor LSB register (see Tables 7.5 and 7.6). On the other hand, if the DLAB bit is clear, write operations to the base address will access the transmitter holding register and read operations will access the receiver data register. In this case read and write operations to the base address plus one will access the interrupt enable register.

The other bit fields in the LCR are used in relation to the RS-232-C communications protocol. The function of the individual bits can be seen in Figure 7.11.

The break control bit (bit 6 in Figure 7.11) can be used to selectively enable and disable terminals in a communications network.

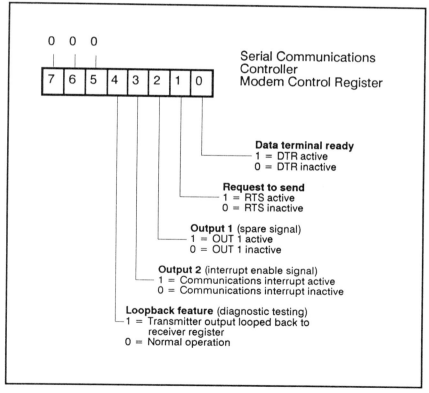

Figure 7.12. *The Modem Control Register*

Table 7.8. *Initialization of the Modem Control Register*

BITS 7 6 5 4 3 2 1 0	HEX	PURPOSE
0 0 0 0 0 0 1 1	03H	DTR and RTS active for normal communications in systems with or without a modem. No interrupts.
0 0 0 0 1 0 1 1	0BH	DTR and RTS active for normal communications in systems with or without a modem. Interrupts active.

The Modem Control Register. The modem control register (MCR) is used in setting the handshake protocol when communicating with a modem or with a device that emulates a modem. Figure 7.12 is a bit map of the MCR.

Bits 0 and 1 of the MCR control the data-terminal-ready (DTR) and the request-to-send (RTS) signals that appear on pin numbers 20 and 4 of the connector (see Table 7.3). When these bits are set, the DTR and RTS signals become active. Bit 3 of this register controls the output 2 signal. This signal allows the interrupts generated by the communications controller to reach the interrupt controller. Programs that use communications interrupts must set this bit. Bit 4 provides a loopback feature that can be used in testing the communications controller or the operation of portions of a serial communications program. The MCR is normally initialized as shown in Table 7.8.

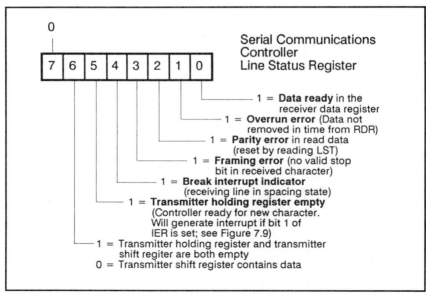

Figure 7.13. *The Line Status Register*

The Line Status Register. The line status register (LSR) provides the CPU with information regarding the state of the data transfer operations. Figure 7.13 shows a bit map of this register.

Bits 1, 2, 3, and 4 reflect specific error conditions that can occur during serial communications. The error bits of the LSR are reset when the receiver data or the line status registers are read by the CPU. Bit 0 of the LSR can be used to determine if a character is ready at the receiver data register. Bit 0 is reset when the character is removed from the receiver data register. Bit 5 indicates that the transmitter holding register is ready to accept a new character. No new character should be input until bit 5 equals 1. This bit is reset when the transmitter holding register is loaded. If bit 1 of the interrupt enable register is set (see Figure 7.9), an interrupt is generated when bit 5 of the LSR changes to a logical 1.

The following code fragment tests the LSR for error conditions, data ready, and transmitter holding register empty and then branches to the corresponding routine. The code assumes that a valid address for the first serial port has been previously stored in the variable COM1_BASE (see code fragment in Section 7.2.1).

```
        MOV    DX,COM1_BASE
CHECK_LINE:
        MOV    DL,0FDH          ; Line status register offset
        IN     AL,DX            ; Read byte
        JMP    SHORT $+2        ; I/O delay
        TEST   AL,00011110B     ; Test error bits 1, 2, 3 or 4
        JNZ    ERROR            ; Error condition, take action
        TEST   AL,00000001B     ; Data ready ?
        JNZ    RECEIVE          ; Take action
        TEST   AL,00100000B     ; THR empty ?
        JNZ    SEND             ; Yes, take action
        JMP    CHECK_LINE       ; Continue looping
        .
        .
        .
; Code at labels ERROR, RECEIVE, and SEND will handle
; processing in each case
```

The Modem Status Register. The modem status register (MSR) provides the CPU with information regarding the state of the control lines from the modem or modemlike device. The first 4 bits of this register are set to logical 1 whenever a modem control line changes state. Figure 7.14 shows a bit map of this register.

When set, bits 0, 1, 2, and 3 of the MSR generate a modem status interrupt if bit 3 of the interrupt enable register is also set (see Figure 7.9).

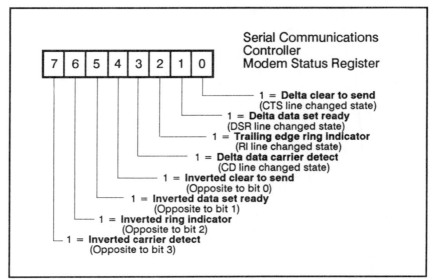

Figure 7.14. *The Modem Status Register*

7.3 Programming Serial Communications

The asynchronous serial communications controllers used in the IBM micro-computers can be initialized, set up, and controlled in many different ways. However, the fundamental problem that must be solved by the communications software is frequently related to the synchronization of sender and receiver. Synchronization techniques can be based on polling, handshake, or interrupts.

7.3.1 Polling

Polling techniques consist of a time loop during which the receiving device checks the status of the data register. The polling frequency must be short enough to ensure that the transmitting device will not send a new character before the previous one has been removed by the receiver. Consequently, the slower the baud rate, the longer the polling frequency that will satisfy this requirement. The processing tasks that the receiver must perform between polling cycles is another factor to be considered in polling. Failure to remove the received data results in an overrun error, as the old data byte in the receiver register is overwritten by a new one.

At sufficiently slow baud rates it is possible to design communications routines based on polling that will satisfactorily perform simple operations. However, programs that execute at the higher baud rates or that must perform more elaborate processing, require other means of synchronization. In addition, polling techniques need an *intelligent* receiver and are usually not possible in regard to *dumb* devices, such as printers and terminals.

7.3.2 Handshaking

Handshake techniques make it possible for the receiver to suspend the transmission when the characters cannot be processed faster than the transmission rate. A typical example of handshaking is in the communications setup between a computer and a serial printer. In this case, the printer may force the computer into a wait state until the previous character has been printed or if other circumstances require it, such as an out-of-paper condition. Handshaking can be implemented using hardware or software techniques.

7.3.2.1 Hardware Handshaking. In serial communications, hardware handshaking is based on the RS-232-C control signals (see Tables 7.3 and 7.4). A simple handshake protocol can be established using the data-set-ready and data-terminal-ready signals. For example, a serial printer (DTE) will raise the data-terminal-ready line to inform the computer (DCE) that it is ready to receive. If the printer wants to suspend transmission, it will lower data terminal ready to a negative voltage. The clear-to-send (CTS) and request-to-send (RQS) lines can be used as a subsidiary handshake.

Handshaking between data communications equipment (DCE) and data terminal equipment (DTE) usually requires straight-through connections, as discussed in Section 7.1.1.1 (see also Figure 7.3). This means that, in the case of a serial printer, the printer's DTR signal becomes DSR at the computer and the printer's RQS becomes the computer's CTS. The flowchart of Figure 7.15 illustrates the handshake logic used by the sending device (DTE). In the case of Figure 7.15, the sender tests both the DSR and the CTS lines.

7.3.2.2 Software Handshaking. Some serial communications setups do not use the control lines required for hardware handshaking. For example, the null modem wiring shown in Figure 7.5 permits connecting two IBM computers through the serial port using only the transmit data and receive data lines. Several software handshake protocols have been developed to allow serial communications when the RS-232-C control signals are not available.

The XON/XOFF convention uses the character 13H (XOFF) to signal to the transmitting device to stop sending characters and the character 17H (XON) to signal that transmission can take place. The flowchart of Figure 7.16 illustrates the software handshake logic used by the sending device (DTE). In addition to the XON and XOFF codes, the routine also uses a transmission flag (see TRM flag in Figure 7.16). The sending device initializes the TRM flag ON at the start of the transmission. This flag allows the assumption that the receiving device is initially ready. The TRM flag is turned OFF by the XOFF code. Ultimately, it is the TRM flag that determines whether the sending device can transmit a character.

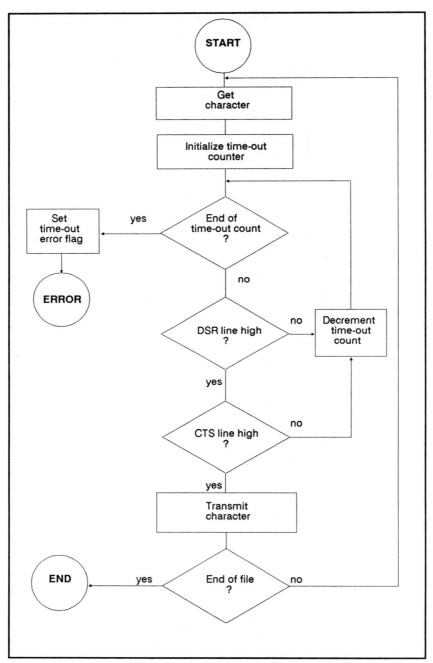

Figure 7.15. *Hardware Handshaking Flowchart (Sending Device)*

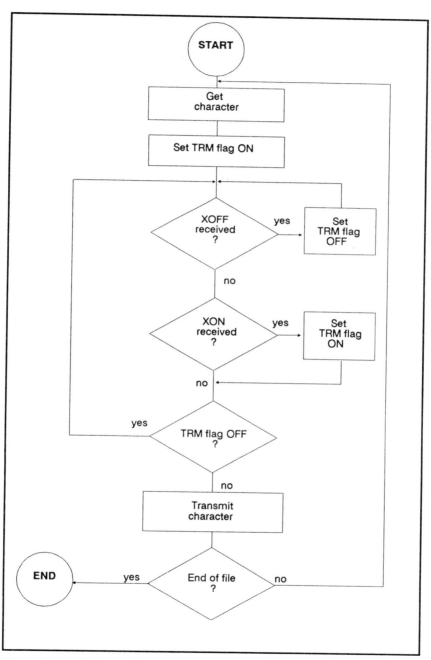

Figure 7.16. *Software Handshaking Flowchart (Sending Device)*

7.3.3 Interrupts

Serial communications programs that make use of hardware interrupts allow greater freedom of operation to the transmitting and receiving devices. Interrupt-driven communications programs can operate more efficiently and use higher baud rates than programs that rely on polling or handshaking techniques. All serial communications controllers used in the IBM microcomputers support hardware interrupts.

It can be demonstrated that, without some form of synchronization during data transmission, communications programs on the IBM microcomputers lose characters when operating at speeds above 1200 Bd. The calculations are based on the following fact: when the chore of monitoring the serial line for new characters is left to the receiver, as in polling methods, the program must remove the received character from the data register before the next one arrives. Failure to do so will result in an overrun error, as the old data byte is overwritten by the new one.

The frequency with which the program must monitor the line for new data can be estimated by dividing the baud rate by the number of bits in each character transmitted. In a typical encoding each character will contain one start bit, seven data bits, one parity bit, and one stop bit. This makes a total of 10 bits per character. Dividing the baud rates by the 10 bits required to represent each character gives the following approximate transmission speeds, in characters per second (cps):

Baud rate	Speed
300	30
600	60
1200	120
2400	240
4800	480

Consequently, a receiver operating at 2400 Bd will have to monitor the communications line at a minimum frequency of 240 times per second to prevent reception errors. This leaves the CPU with less than 1/240 of a second in which to store, display, or otherwise manipulate the received character.

The IBM serial communications controllers make possible the generation of several hardware interrupts during the communications cycle (see Figures 7.9 and 7.10 and Table 7.8). Of these, the received data available interrupt is probably the most used one. This interrupt can be described as a way of giving the microprocessor a "tap on the shoulder" to let it know that data is available on the serial line. The CPU can then interrupt whatever it is doing long enough to remove the character from the receiver data register and store it in a dedicated buffer. The characters can remain in the buffer until the CPU has time to perform the required processing.

The program named TERM232.ASM, listed in Appendix C, is an example of the use of interrupts in serial communications. The code contains routines to set up and enable the received data available interrupt and to install an interrupt handler that will process, as a background task, the characters received on the serial communications line. In addition, the program also demonstrates the operations required for initializing and displaying the RS-232-C protocol.

7.3.4 Character and File Transfer

According to the RS-232-C standard, serial communications programs can transfer data encoded in units of 5- to 8-bit lengths. But in IBM microcomputer systems only the 7- and 8-bit word lengths are in use. The ASCII encoding of character data (see Figure 4.3) comprises the range from 20H to 7FH. This makes it possible to encode all the ASCII characters in 7 bits.

Programs that operate exclusively with character data can improve their performance by adopting a protocol that uses seven data bits per character word. The usual control codes, in the range 00H to 1FH, can also be transmitted with this convention. For example, the XON/XOFF software handshaking protocol (see Section 7.3.2.2) can be used with a 7-bit transmission format.

However, transferring program code, graphic symbols, and other binary data in the range 0 to FFH requires 8-bit characters. This range prohibits the use of embedded control codes, since all possible values are used in encoding data. The simplest solution to this problem consists of adopting protocols that transmit data, not as individual characters, but in blocks of a predefined size. These blocks usually include headers with handshake characters, which are used to establish the communications line, and conclude with checksum characters used in detecting transmission errors.

The XMODEM file transfer protocol, developed in 1977 by Ward Christensen and later modified by Keith Petersen, has gained considerable popularity in the microcomputer field. In the XMODEM convention, data is transferred in 132-byte blocks, formatted as shown in Table 7.9.

Table 7.9. *Block Format in the XMODEM Protocol*

OFFSET	CODE OR RANGE	CONTENTS AND FUNCTION
0	01H	Start-of-header character (SOH).
1	0 to FFH	Block number. Starts with number 1. After FFH wraps around to 0H.
2	0 to FFH	1s complement of the block number 255 minus block number.
3 to 130	0 to FFH	Block of 128 data bytes
131	0 to FFH	LSB of sum of all data bytes (checksum).

   The XMODEM convention also implements handshaking. According to the protocol, data transmission cannot begin until the sender receives a character 15H (called *NAK*, or *negative acknowledge*) from the receiver. At this time the sender can transmit one 132-byte block (see Table 7.9). The code 06H (called *acknowledge*, or *ACK*) is issued by the receiver to acknowledge each block received correctly. If the receiver detects errors, it uses the code 15H (NAK) to request from the transmitter to resend the block. At the end of the transmission the transmitter sends the code 04H (called *EOT*, or *end of transmission*).

7.3.5 Buffers

Communications programs frequently use dedicated memory areas, called *buffers*, to store the characters that have been received or that are ready for transmission. For example, serial communications using the XMODEM protocol (see Section 7.3.4) require 128-byte storage areas for the data blocks used by this convention. Buffers are sometimes classified as input or output according to their use during reception or transmission.

   Another type of data structure sometimes associated with communications software is called a circular or wraparound buffer. Data operations in circular buffer are described as occurring in a first-in first-out (FIFO) pattern. This means that data items are removed in the same order in which they were stored. Figure 7.17 illustrates the operation of a 15-byte circular buffer.

   The buffer pointers in Figure 7.17 are labeled BUFFER_HEAD and BUFFER_TAIL. In coding, these pointers would be memory variables that indicate offsets into the circular buffer. In Step 1 (Figure 7.17) the BUFFER_HEAD variable shows that 6 characters have been received and stored in the buffer, while the BUFFER_TAIL variable shows that no character has yet been removed. Steps 2, 3, and 4 show various stages in the reception and removal of the characters. In Step 3 the BUFFER_HEAD pointer has reached the end of the buffer, and in Step 4 it has wrapped around to the start of the buffer. It is this action that makes the buffer appear circular, or endless. In Step 5 the BUFFER_TAIL pointer has reached the value of the BUFFER_HEAD pointer. This condition indicates that there are no characters pending to be removed from the buffer.

   The program named TERM232.ASM, listed in Appendix C, illustrates the use of a circular buffer in a communications program. In this case the buffer, named CIRC_BUF, is 20 bytes long. The buffer pointers are word-size variables named DATA_IN and DATA_OUT. The interrupt service routine in the TERM232 program manages the DATA_IN pointer while storing the data received during the data ready interrupt. The code in the main program tests the value of the buffer pointers (DATA_IN and DATA_OUT) to determine if there are new data in the buffer. If there is, the DATA_OUT pointer indicates the offset of the data item to be removed.

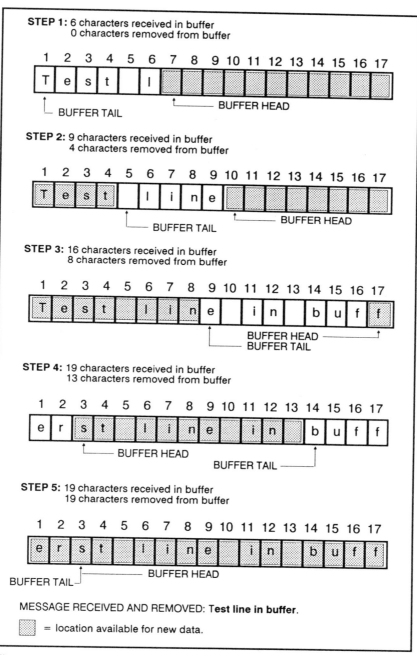

Figure 7.17. *Circular or Wraparound Buffer Operation*

7.4 Parallel Communications

Serial communication methods transmit data consecutively, in the form of electrical pulses over the same physical line. In parallel communications the data bits are transmitted simultaneously, over different lines. The most obvious advantage of parallel data transmission is a higher speed. The disadvantages are that more connecting elements are required in the physical interface and that parallel transmission is more sensitive to noise and interference. In spite of this high-speed capability, microcomputer systems have traditionally used the parallel port primarily as a printer output.

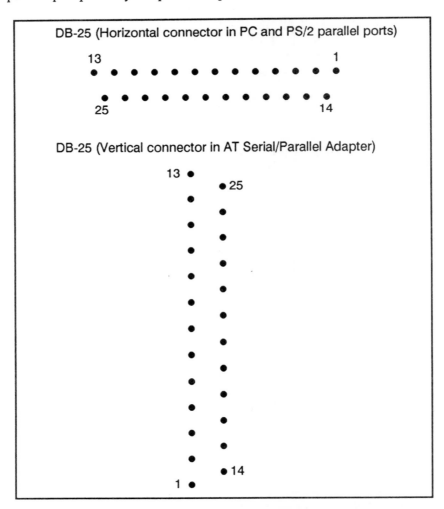

Figure 7.18. *Contact Numbers on IBM Parallel Port Connectors*

7.4.1 The Centronics Printer Interface

While serial communications have been regulated by several generally adopted standards, parallel communications are not well standardized. The *Centronics Printer Interface*, which was developed by a printer manufacturer, is the convention most frequently associated with parallel communications.

The Centronics convention establishes the use of 36-pin connectors, but the IBM implementations use the 25-pin D-shell. In this respect, the printer ports in the IBM microcomputers are nonstandard. Figure 7.18 shows the contact numbering on the IBM parallel port connectors. Figure 7.19 is a wiring diagram for an IBM printer cable using a DB-25 male connector at the computer end and a 36-pin Amphenol male connector at the printer end.

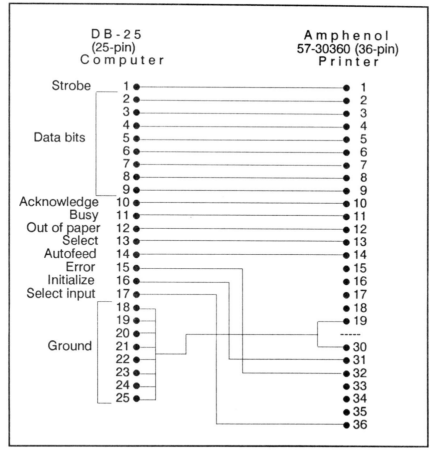

Figure 7.19. *Wiring Diagram for Parallel Printer (Centronics Standard)*

Table 7.10. *Centronics Printer Interface Lines in IBM Systems*

	DB-25 PIN NUMBER	DIRECTION		VOLTAGE	SIGNAL NAME	
		PC*	PS/2			
	1	⇒	⇔	-	STROBE	
C	2	⇒	⇔	+	Data bit number 0	
	3	⇒	⇔	+	Data bit number 1	P
O	4	⇒	⇔	+	Data bit number 2	
	5	⇒	⇔	+	Data bit number 3	R
M	6	⇒	⇔	+	Data bit number 4	
	7	⇒	⇔	+	Data bit number 5	I
P	8	⇒	⇔	+	Data bit number 6	
	9	⇒	⇔	+	Data bit number 7	N
U	10	⇐	⇐	-	Acknowledge (ACK)	
	11	⇐	⇐	-	Busy	T
T	12	⇐	⇐	+	Out of paper (PE)	
	13	⇐	⇐	+	Select (SLCT)	E
E	14	⇒	⇒	-	Autofeed (XT)	
	15	⇐	⇐	-	Error	R
R	16	⇒	⇒	-	Initialize printer (INIT)	
	17	⇒	⇒	-	Select input (SLCT IN)	
	18–25				Ground	

* PC systems include the non-Micro Channel models of the PS/2 line (Models 25 and 30).

The Centronics convention establishes lines and signals for data transmission and handshaking. Table 7.10 shows the designation of the Centronics lines in IBM microcomputer systems. The lines on adapter pins 2 to 9 contain the 8 bits that form the transmitted character. The *strobe* line is used to pulse the character to the printer.

Several lines are used by the printer to report its status. By holding high the *busy* line, the printer informs the computer that it cannot receive a new character. When it has finished receiving a character and is ready for the next one, the printer pulses the *acknowledge* line. The *select* line informs the sender that the printer is selected (active), and the *out -of- paper* line informs the sender that the printer is not available due to this condition.

The control lines to activate printer functions are designated *autofeed, initial-ize,* and *select input.* When the autofeed function is set, the printer automatically executes a line feed after each line is printed. The initialize line activates internal printer initialization routines. The select input line is used to select and deselect individual printers. The *error* line reports that the printer has encountered an error condition.

7.5 Implementations of the Parallel Port

The implementation of the parallel port has changed in the various IBM microcomputer lines and models. In the PC line the parallel port is supplied in the form of several optional adapters, while in the PS/2 line the parallel port is a standard component. The BIOS and DOS designations for the parallel port use the characters LPT (Line PrinTer) followed by the port number; for example, LPT1 and LPT2 designate the first and second parallel ports. A maximum of three parallel ports is allowed in a system (except as noted in Section 7.6.1). The address mapping of the parallel ports is not consistent with the BIOS/DOS designation in LPTx form. Table 7.11 shows the parallel port parameters in different IBM microcomputer hardware.

Table 7.11. *The Parallel Port in the IBM Microcomputers*

SYSTEM	BIOS NAME	BASE ADDRESS	CHARACTERISTICS
PC and PC XT	LPT1	3BCH	Monochrome display and printer adapter (used alone)
	LPT1	378H	Printer adapter (used alone)
	LPT2	378H	Printer adapter with monochrome display and printer adapter
PC AT	LPT1	378H	Serial/parallel adapter configured as port 1
	LPT2	278H	Serial/parallel adapter configured as port 2
PCjr	LPT1	378H	Parallel printer attachment
PS/2 Models 25 and 30	LPT1	378H	Built-in parallel port
PS/2 Micro Channel systems	LPT1	3BCH	Built-in parallel port set up as parallel port 1
	LPT2	378H	Built-in parallel port set up as parallel port 2
	LPT3	278H	Built-in parallel port set up as parallel port 3

7.5.1 Parallel Port Extended Mode

In PS/2 systems with Micro Channel architecture the parallel port supports bidirectional communications (see Table 7.11). However, the parallel port in PC systems and non-Micro Channel models of the PS/2 line allow only unidirectional transmission on the Strobe and data lines. This limitation of PC and PS/2 non-Micro Channel systems probably results from the traditional notion that the parallel port is only a printer interface.

In the PS/2 Micro Channel systems the bidirectional operation of the parallel port, also called the *extended mode*, is selected during the programmable option select function (POS). POS register 2, at port I/O address 102H, contains the Option Select Data Byte 1. When bit 7 of this byte is set, the parallel port is unidirectional and emulates the parallel port in PC systems. When bit 7 of the Option Select Data Byte 1 is clear, the parallel port supports bidirectional operation and is said to be in extended mode.

In extended mode (bidirectional operation) the direction of data transmission is controlled by bit 5 of the parallel port control port (see Section 7.5.2). When this bit is set, the parallel port is in read mode and data from an external device is available in the port's data register. When the direction control bit is clear, the port is in the write mode and the read function is disabled. Bit 5 of the control register is not used in the unidirectional parallel port of non-Micro Channel systems.

7.5.2 Parallel Port Registers

The parallel port appears as a set of three registers accessible to the programmer. The registers are designated as a *data* register, a *status* register, and a *control* register. The registers are mapped to a base port address (see Table 7.12 and Section 7.5) that can take the values 3BCH, 378H, and 278H according to the system configuration. The data register is located at the base port address, while the status register is at the base address plus 1, and the control register at the base address plus 2.

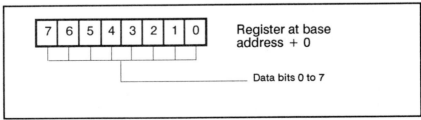

Figure 7.20. *The Data Register of the Parallel Port Controller*

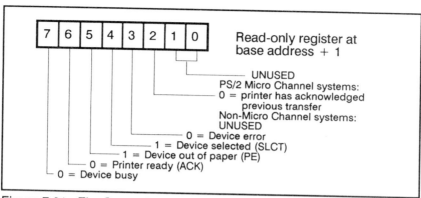

Figure 7.21. *The Status Register of the Parallel Port Controller*

The Data Register. The data register is located at the port's base address. This register is shown in Figure 7.20. A write operation to the data register stores the data internally. This operation is sometimes called *latching* the data, and the register is referred to as the *data latch*. Note that latching data in the data register does not send it to an external device. The data transmission through the parallel port requires pulsing the Strobe line, as described in Section 7.6.3.

In non-Micro Channel systems (the PC line and PS/2 Models 25 and 30) reading the data register produces the last byte that was written to the register. In Micro Channel systems operating in extended mode (see Section 7.5.1) reading the data register can produce a data byte latched by an external device. This form of read operation requires that bit 5 of the control register be set (see Figure 7.22). If bit 5 of the control register is not set, the read operation produces the same result in extended mode as in the PC compatibility mode.

The Status Register. The status register is located at the port's base address plus 1. This is a read-only register which can be used by the CPU to obtain the current status of the signal lines that go from the printer or device to the computer. Figure 7.21 shows a bit map of the status register. Note bits 3, 6, and 7, which correspond with the busy, ACK, and error lines. Because these lines are implemented using a negative voltage (see Table 7.11), their active condition is reported with a 0 bit.

The Control Register. The control register is located at the port's base address plus 2. This is a read-write register. The write function is used in setting the state of the signal lines that go from the computer to the printer or device. The read function can be used by the processor to obtain the value of the last byte written to the register. Figure 7.22 shows a bit map of the control register.

Bit 5 of the control register, sometimes called the data direction control bit, is meaningful in Micro Channel systems only (see Section 7.5.1). The direction control bit is write-only; consequently, this bit does not report a meaningful value during read operations.

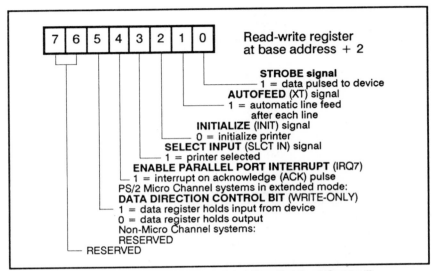

Figure 7.22. *The Control Register of the Parallel Port Controller*

7.6 Programming the Parallel Port

Programs that access the parallel port can do so using the services provided by the BIOS and DOS or by programming the port registers directly. Direct programming operations consist of obtaining the address of the available ports, initializing the parallel device (usually a printer), and sending and receiving data through the port.

7.6.1 Obtaining the Parallel Port Address

The BIOS system initialization routines store the base address of the first parallel port (LPT1) at memory location 408H in the BIOS data area. The base addresses of the two possible additional parallel ports (LPT2 and LPT3) are stored at 40AH and 40CH, respectively. In the models of the PC line, the address of a fourth parallel port (LPT4) can be found at address 40EH, but this location in reserved in PS/2 systems. One or more of these fields is initialized to zero if the system contains fewer than the maximum number of allowed parallel ports; however, the BIOS does not initialize valid ports following a zero value. The following code fragment shows the processing for retrieving the address of three parallel ports from the BIOS storage:

```
DATA   SEGMENT
;
LPT1_BASE      DW      0000H ; Storage for LPT1 base address
LPT2_BASE      DW      0000H ; Storage for LPT2 base address
LPT3_BASE      DW      0000H ; Storage for LPT3 base address
;
DATA   ENDS
;
;
CODE   SEGMENT
       ASSUME          CS:CODE
       .
       .
       .
; Obtain base address of parallel ports from BIOS data area
       PUSH   DS              ; Save program's DS
       XOR    AX,AX           ; AX = 0
       MOV    DS,AX           ; Data segment zero for BIOS
       MOV    DX,DS:0408H     ; Base address of LPT1
       MOV    CX,DS:040AH     ; Base address of LPT2
       MOV    BX,DS:040CH     ; Base address of LPT3
       POP    DS              ; Restore program's DS
       MOV    LPT1_BASE,DX    ; Store LPT1
       MOV    LPT2_BASE,CX    ; Store LPT2
       MOV    LPT3_BASE,BX    ; Store LPT3
; The code can now check each stored port address for a zero
; value to determine the number of valid ports
       .
       .
       .
```

7.6.2 Initializing the Parallel Port

Initializing the parallel port consists of setting the bit fields in the port's control register (see Figure 7.22). In addition, bit 2 of the control register (INIT) initializes the parallel device. This line must be held low for a minimum of one-twentieth of a second. The following code fragment shows the required coding for initializing the first parallel port (LPT1). The code assumes that a valid address for the first parallel port has been previously stored in the variable LPT1_BASE (see code fragment in Section 7.6.1).

```
       MOV    DX,LPT1_BASE ; See previous code fragment
       ADD    DX,2         ; Control register is at
                           ; base address + 2
       MOV    AL,00001000B ; Bit 2 = 0 (INIT ON)
                           ; and bit 3 = 1 (SLCT IN)
       OUT    DX,AL        ; Write to control port
```

```
        JMP    SHORT $+2   ; I/O delay
; Time delay using BIOS time-of-day clock service INT 1AH
        MOV    AH,0        ; Request to read timer counter
        INT    1AH         ; BIOS timer service
; DX = low order byte of timer counter
        ADD    DX,2        ; Add 2 time cycles to present
                           ; timer count
        MOV    BX,DX       ; Move final count to BX
DELAY_20:
        INT    1AH         ; Call service again
        CMP    DX,BX       ; Compare to final count
        JB     DELAY_20    ; Repeat if time not elapsed
; Reset control register to default value
        MOV    AL,00001100B  ; Bit 2 = 1 (INIT OFF)
                             ; and bit 3 = 1 (SLCT IN)
        OUT    DX,AL
        JMP    SHORT $+2   ; I/O delay
; Parallel port LPT1 is initialized
        .
        .
        .
```

Programs can initialize other functions on the parallel port by setting or clearing the corresponding bits in the control register (see Figure 7.22). For example, in Micro Channel systems operating in extended mode (see Section 7.5.1), bit 5 of the control register can be set to enable data input from a device.

7.6.3 Sending Data Through the Parallel Port

Writing to the data register, located at the port's base address, stores a byte of data in the register. However, to actually transmit the latched data, the Strobe bit of the control register (see Figure 7.22) must be held high during a minimum of 5 μs. The following code fragment illustrates the process of latching the character byte, checking the device busy bit in the status register and pulsing the Strobe bit in the control register. The code assumes that a valid address for the first parallel port has been previously stored in the variable LPT1_BASE (see code fragment in Section 7.6.1).

```
; Character to be sent to parallel port is already in AL
        MOV    DX,LPT1_BASE ; Base address of LPT1
        OUT    DX,AL        ; Latch character
        JMP    SHORT $+2    ; I/O delay
; Check BUSY bit in status register for PRINTER READY
        INC    DX           ; Point to status register
CHK_FOR_BUSY:
        IN     AL,DX        ; get printer status byte
        TEST   AL,10000000B ; Printer busy ?
        JZ     CHK_FOR_BUSY ; Repeat until not busy
```

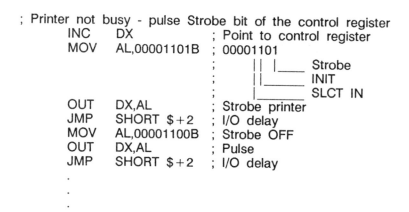

```
; Printer not busy - pulse Strobe bit of the control register
        INC    DX                ; Point to control register
        MOV    AL,00001101B      ; 00001101
                                 ;        || |____ Strobe
                                 ;        ||_____ INIT
                                 ;        |_____ SLCT IN
        OUT    DX,AL             ; Strobe printer
        JMP    SHORT $+2         ; I/O delay
        MOV    AL,00001100B      ; Strobe OFF
        OUT    DX,AL             ; Pulse
        JMP    SHORT $+2         ; I/O delay
        .
        .
        .
```

7.7 Telephone System Communications

Due to their convenience and availability, the telephone lines are often used as a data path in computer communications. But the telephone system is designed for voice communications. In order to transmit digital computer data through the telephone lines, the data must first be converted into an audio signal by a device called a *modulator*. By the same token, the receiving computer must use a demodulator to convert the audio signal into a digital signal. A device that can perform as a modulator/demodulator is called a *modem*.

7.7.1 The Modem

Modems are optional components in all IBM microcomputer systems. They are either internal or external. Internal modems are furnished by IBM and other vendors in the form of an adapter card. The modem card, which is installed in an expansion slot in the conventional manner, usually provides its own serial port. This port can be designated as serial port 1 to 4 (COM1, COM2, COM3, or COM4) according to the system configuration (see Section 7.2.1 and Table 7.5). In systems of the PC line, setting the serial port assignments may require changing mechanical connectors called jumpers. In the PS/2 line port assignations are performed by the programmable options select (POS) function of the system configuration software.

External modems usually require connection to an existing serial port. Both internal and external modems must also be connected to the telephone lines. The telephone system uses four connecting wires. The limited number of lines makes it necessary to use a serial communications protocol. This explains why modems normally access the computer through an RS-232-C port.

Modem communications can take place according to different conventions and baud rates:

1. *300-Bd modems*. At 300 Bd/s the voltage signals are converted into audible tones following a convention known as *frequency key shifting*, or FKS. According to the Bell 103 protocol the originator logical 0 tone has a frequency of 1070 Hz and the logical 1 tone 1270 Hz. The answerer logical 0 tone has a frequency of 2025 Hz and the logical 1 tone 2225 Hz.

2. *1200-Bd modems*. The Bell 212A protocol establishes the conventions for modem communications at 1200 Bd/s. The communications techniques at this baud rate are based on phase modulation, which consists of manipulating the carrier signal so that 2 bits can be transmitted simultaneously in each direction. This accounts for a transmission speed rated at 1200 Bd, while the line frequency is of 600 Bd. The method, known as *phase shift keying*, or PSK, uses two carrier signals: the originator transmits at 1200 Hz and the answerer at 2400 Hz.

3. *2400-Bd modems*. Yet another protocol, known as CCITT V.22 (developed by the Cooperative Committee for International Telephony and Telegraphy of the United Nations) establishes the conventions for modem transmissions at 2400 Bd. This technique, based on creating 3 amplitudes and 12 phase angles, is known as *phase amplitude modulation*, or PAM. The resulting 36 states make possible the transmission of 6 simultaneous data bits. Consequently, although the line frequency is at 600 Bd, the transmission rate is rated at 2400 Bd/s.

4. *9600- and 19,200- Bd modems*. Techniques that combine data compression with PAM make possible modem transmissions at 9600 Bd and even higher rates. The present international standards for high-speed modem communications are CCITT V.29 and V.32.

7.7.2 Programming the Modem

While some modems provide their own serial port (internal modems), others must be connected to a serial port available in the system (external modems). Programming the modem consists of transmitting and receiving specific codes and data through the modem's serial port. Serial communications and programming were discussed starting with Section 7.1.

7.7.3 The Hayes Command Set

In recent years, a company named Hayes Microcomputer Products has gained considerable approval in the field of modem design and manufacturing. This has created a de facto standard whereby most modems by other manufacturers are offered as being *Hayes-compatible*. However, there are some notable exceptions to this rule. For example, the optional Internal Modem furnished by IBM for the PCjr does not use the Hayes command set. Table 7.12 lists some common modem commands in the Hayes system.

Table 7.12. *Frequently Used Modem Commands (Hayes System)*

COMMAND	EXAMPLE	DESCRIPTION
A/	A/	Repeat last command (redial last number).
<w> + + + <w>	+ + +	Escape sequence. Switch from online to command mode. <w> is 1-s wait
B<p>	AT B0<cr>	Enable communications protocol <p> can be: 0 = CCITT V.22 international 1 = Bell 212A protocol
D<s><n>	AT DT 727-6319	Dialing command. Subcommmmands <s> can be: , = pause (default time 2 s) T = dial using touch tones P = dial using rotary (pulse) tones W = wait for dial tone ; = return to command mode at end of line (voice call dialing) <n> = telephone number with optional "-" and "()" symbols
E<p>	AT E0 <cr>	Echo characters in command mode <p> can be: 0 = do not echo 1 = echo (default)
H<p>	AT H0<cr>	Hook control <p> can be: 0 = hang-up (on hook) 1 = pick-up (off hook)
O	AT O	Online. Return modem to online mode after escape or voice.
S<n> = <p>	AT S0 = 3 <cr>	Set modem register <n> = register number <p> = value installed in register
S <n>?	AT S0? <cr>	Report contents of modem register number <n>
V<p>	AT V1<cr>	Verbal response mode. <p> can be: 0 = numerical result codes 1 = verbal (text) result codes

Note: <cr> = carriage return code 0DH.

7.7.3.1 Modem States.

While in operation, the Hayes-compatible modem must be in one of two states. These states, or modes, are known as the *on-line* and the *local command* modes. While in the local command mode, the modem can receive command codes through its serial interface with the computer. The commands activate modem functions; for example, a command can make the modem dial a telephone number using touch tones. When the modem finishes executing a command, it sends a response message through the serial line.

Once a connection is established, the modem goes automatically into the on-line mode. In the on-line mode, data sent through the serial line is transmitted by the modem and is not interpreted as a command. A modem in the on-line mode can be either the originator or the answerer. To establish a connection between modems, one must be an originating modem and the other one an answering modem.

7.7.3.2 The AT Command Format. Most modem command codes in the Hayes command set are preceded by the code letters AT (attention). The modem also uses these code letters to adjust the baud rate, word length, and parity values for the transmission. Commands are entered in a command line that can contain up to 40 characters (excluding spaces and AT codes).

A command line can include multiple commands and can contain embedded spaces and the conventional symbols commonly used in writing telephone numbers. For example, the parenthesis characters can be used to enclose the area code and the dash to separate the first three from the last four digits. The following command line instructs the modem to dial a telephone number using touch tones:

AT DT (406) 727-6319 < cr >

Each AT command line must be terminated with a carriage return control code (0DH). In the above example the carriage return is represented by the characters < cr > .

7.7.3.3 Exceptions. Two modem commands in the Hayes command set do not require the AT preface and the carriage return terminator codes. The first one, the *escape* command, is used to instruct a modem, in the on-line mode, to return to the command mode. The command format consists of a 1-s initial guard time, followed by the Hayes escape code " + + + " and another 1-s guard time wait. The guard times surrounding the escape code are designed to prevent the modem from accidentally interpreting the data values " + + + " as an escape sequence. The other command that does not require the standard preface and epilogue is the one to repeat the previous command line. The command code for the repeat command is A/.

7.7.4 Hayes Result Codes

In the Hayes system, commands that terminate in the carriage return code generate a standard modem response in the form of a numeric or text message. This response is sometimes called the *command result code*. The V command (see Table 7.13) allows selecting a numeric or text mode for the screen message. The text response is often called the *verbal* response mode. Table 7.13 lists the result codes to modem commands.

Table 7.13. *Result Codes to Hayes Modem Commands*

CODE NO.	TEXT	DESCRIPTION
0	OK	Command line executed with no errors.
1	CONNECT	Modem connected.
2	RING	Incoming call detected.
3	NO CARRIER	Carrier signal not detected or lost.
4	ERROR	Error in command line. Invalid command or character limit exceeded.
5	CONNECT 1200	Modem connected at 1200 Bd/s.
6	NO DIALTONE	No dial tone detected.
7	BUSY	Busy signal.
8	NO ANSWER	Number dialed not answered.
9		Message not implemented.
10	CONNECT 2400	Modem connected at 2400 Bd/s.

7.7.5 Modem Registers

The Hayes system uses a set of 28 internal registers, sometimes called the *S-registers*, which are accessible to the programmer via the S = and S? modem commands (see Table 7.12). The S-registers are numbered S0 to S27, and each register holds 8 bits of data. Since the Hayes system is not a formal standard, the number of modem registers implemented and their default contents vary in modems by different manufacturers. Table 7.14 shows the modem registers most frequently used and their typical default values.

Table 7.14. *Modem Registers, Typical Use*

NO.	RANGE	DEFAULT VALUE	CONTENTS
S0	0–255	0	Number of rings before answering. 0 = no auto answer.
S1	0–255	0	Counter for incoming rings. Cleared automatically after 8 s.
S2	0–127	" + "	Escape code character.
S3	0–127	0DH	Command line and modem response terminator character
S4	0–127	0AH	Line feed character. Send after a verbal response string.
S5	0–127	08H	Backspace character.
S6	0–255	2	Wait time for dial tone (seconds).

(continued)

Table 7.14. *Modem Registers, Typical Use (Continued)*

NO.	RANGE	DEFAULT VALUE	CONTENTS
S7	0–255	30	Wait time for carrier signal (seconds).
S8	0–255	2	Pause upon comma symbol in dial command (seconds.)
S9	0–255	6	Response time after carrier detect signal (in one-tenth of a second)
S10	0–255	14	Wait time to hang-up after carrier is lost (in one-tenth of a second)
S11	0–255	70	Duration and spacing of touch tones (in one-hundreth of a second)
S12	0–255	50	Guard time before and after escape sequence (in one-fiftieth of a second)
S14	0–255	10001010B	7 6 5 4 3 2 1 0 Bits 1 = echo ON 0 = results ON 1 = verbal results 0 = use pulse tones 1 = originate
S18	0–255	0	Duration of self-test (seconds)
S21	0–255	00000000B	7 6 5 4 3 2 1 0 Bits 00 = DTR ignored 0 = DCD always ON 0 = long space disconnect OFF
S22	0–255	00001000B	7 6 5 4 3 2 1 0 Bits SPEAKER VOLUME: 00 = low 01 = low 10 = medium 11 = high SPEAKER ON/OFF: 00 = off 01 = on if no carrier 10 = always on 11 = off while dialing 1 = wait for dialtone 1 = call progress ON 0 = CONNECT only (no CONNECT 1200, etc) MAKE/BREAK RATIO: 0 = 39:61 1 = 39:67

(continued)

Table 7.14. *Modem Registers, typical use (Continued)*

NO.	RANGE	DEFAULT VALUE	CONTENTS
S23	0–255	00000101B	7 6 5 4 3 2 1 0 Bits

Bit layout for S23:

```
7 6 5 4 3 2 1 0  Bits
          └ 1 = obey RDL request
          MODEM BPS:
          00 = 0-300
          01 = not used
          10 = 1200
          11 = 2400
          PARITY:
          00 = even parity
          01 = space parity
          10 = odd parity
          11 = no parity
          GUARD TONES:
          00 = no guard tones
          01 = 1800 Hz guard tones
          10 = not used
          11 = 550 Hz guard tones
```

7.8 Local Area Networks

The benefit of sharing computer resources is related to the cost of computer hardware and to the need of sharing data and software. The concept of distributed processing, on the other hand, is based on the advantages of providing independent computing power to the individual human elements in a system. Microcomputer technology has made possible combining the best of both worlds in networks of workstations that have individual processing power and yet are able to share information and hardware.

A *local area network*, or LAN, is an arrangement of physically connected microcomputers, operating within a limited area for the purpose of sharing information and resources. The area of operation of a LAN is generally limited to less than 1 mi. Although there is presently very little standardization regarding LANs, the particular identity of a LAN is based on the fact that each unit is a "smart" terminal, equipped with its own processor, memory, and logic. A network of dumb terminals connected to a central processor does not satisfy the generalized definition of a LAN, even if the central processor is a microcomputer.

7.8.1 The LAN's Physical Elements

Because of the lack of protocols and standards it is difficult to make valid generalizations regarding LANs. However, the following elements seem to be present in most systems:

1. *Workstations*. A standard microcomputer is a typical LAN workstation. Although it is possible to configure a system using dedicated workstations with minimum processing resources, the greater practical use of LANs is in linking, for use within an organization, the already existing microcomputers, software, and peripherals. In this case, each network workstation is also capable of operating as an independent microcomputer. In many LAN systems the networking capabilities are provided in the form of a plug-in adapter card and a LAN software package.

2. *LAN servers*. A network server is a hardware-software device that controls and assigns the shared resources. LAN systems often use nondedicated servers; for example, a microcomputer equipped with a hard disk drive can perform the functions of a file server. In this case the file server manages the disk files and directories and controls access to the hard disk drive by the workstations. Typically, the fastest and most advanced microcomputer in a network will be assigned the functions of a file server. Another type of server, called a *print* (or laser print) *server*, controls the spooling of documents to be printed and their eventual assignation to one or more printers.

3. *LAN cabling*. The workstations, servers, and peripherals in a LAN must be physically connected to each other. Several cable and connector options are available for LAN systems. The profusion of connecting hardware reflects the absence of standards in this field. The least expensive option is the *twisted pair cable* used for telephone systems. Twisting the wires distributes the environment noise evenly between the two elements in the pair but does not eliminate the noise. In network applications the cables are usually 22- or 24-gage. *Coaxial cable*, like that used for cable television, is also used in LANs. Although more expensive than twisted pair cable, coaxial cable can be used to transmit data faster and over longer distances. Finally, *fiber-optic cable* and hardware are also used to transmit network data. Although the most expensive option, fiber-optic technology is virtually immune from noise and interference. This makes transmissions over several miles of cable possible. In addition, the fiber-optic signal is protected from unauthorized reception, which can be a factor in networks that require absolute security.

4. *Baseband and broadband networks*. Coaxial cable network systems can be implemented in two forms: in the baseband design, supported by Xerox and Digital Equipment Corporation, the cable has a single, high-speed channel that is very efficient for data transmission but cannot carry integrated voice, data, and video signals. On the other hand, broadband systems can carry integrated signals but require amplifiers and the installation hardware is more complex and expensive.

7.8.2 LAN Topology

LANs can assume different geometric patterns. These patterns, often called the network's *architecture* or *topology*, are unrelated to the cabling system used by the network and to other hardware components.

1. *The star*. The star design emulates the arrangement used in telephone networks in which a central switching station provides service to several

customers or workstations. In the star topology all data are processed and controlled by a central computer. Since each workstation is cabled to the central computer, adding a new workstation requires a single cable. The STARLAN network, by AT&T, is an example of this technology.

2. *The bus.* In contrast with the individual cabling scheme used in the star topology, the bus network topology is based on a common line shared by all workstations. This design simplifies cabling and connections, but since all workstations share the network bus, each station must check all messages on the bus in order to identify those addressed to it. Although the bus topology is the least expensive to implement, it does suffer from signal interference and from inherent security flaws.

3. *The ring.* This third network topology, designed to combine the advantages of the star and bus designs, consists of a ring of interconnected workstations. The ring topology ensures that every workstation has equal access to the network. This plan is particularly convenient when the several workstations in the network are of approximately equal complexity and have the same access privileges. The IBM Token Ring Network is an example of this topology.

8

Auxiliary Storage

8.0 Main and Auxiliary Storage

Because that part of main memory (primary storage) which can be accessed by the user is volatile, scarce, and costly, computer systems often require other means of data storage. The alternatives to storing data in the system's main memory are usually called *auxiliary or secondary storage*. Larger computer systems can trace auxiliary storage hardware to mechanical encoding and decoding devices, such as those employed in the punched card and punched tape systems so extensively used in the 1950s and 1960s. By the advent of microcomputers in the late 1970s, magnetic storage had almost totally superseded mechanical storage, the reason being that magnetic data storage technology often provides greater convenience and faster access to the information. Figure 8.1 lists the more popular forms of computer data storage.

The traditional definition is that auxiliary storage serves as an extension of the system's main memory and that programs and data residing in auxiliary storage devices must be moved into main memory for manipulation and execution. This concept is based on the idea that auxiliary storage serves as a long-term, nonvolatile, information storage medium, but not as a substitute for main memory. However, as data storage devices have become more efficient, the conventional concepts of auxiliary storage have changed. Fast access technologies allow software to move portions of code and data to main memory as needed. These blocks, sometimes called *overlays*, can reside successively in the same area of main memory. By overlaying code and data a program is able to reduce the main memory area required for its execution.

In the IBM microcomputers, auxiliary storage devices are based, almost exclusively, on magnetic and optical technology, while main memory consists of read-only memory (ROM) and random-access memory (RAM) storage (see Chapter 3). Magnetic storage devices can be subclassified into two groups: devices that can access an individual data item directly (*direct access*) and those in which it is necessary to cross over other stored data in order to reach the desired item (*sequential access*). A typical example of a direct access device is a disk or diskette system and one of sequential storage is a magnetic tape storage system. Optical devices store information on concentric disk areas, somewhat similar to those of magnetic disks. For this reason they should be considered direct access devices. At the present stage of technological development, access time is usually greater in optical drives than in the magnetic counterparts.

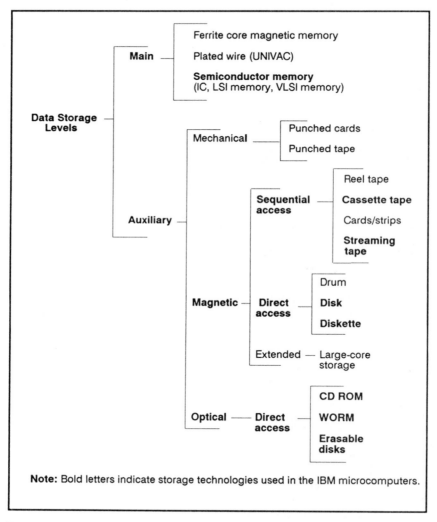

Figure 8.1. *Main and Auxiliary Data Storage*

8.0.1 Direct Access Storage Devices

Direct access storage devices can be compared to a turntable record player in which the user can rapidly access any portion of a recording by positioning the tone arm on the desired point of the recorded surface. Sequential access storage devices, on the other hand, can be compared to a cassette recorder, in which the user must cross over previous recordings in order to access a specific part of the tape. The main advantage of a direct access device is its greater average access speed to individual data items.

In IBM microcomputers direct access storage devices can use magnetic or optical technologies. Although magnetic devices are still by far more popular, optical technology is no longer limited to compact disk (CD ROM) playback systems. Presently available are write-once–read-many times (WORM) optical drives, which furnish an alternative mass storage medium, as well as erasable optical disks, which may evolve as an alternative to the diskette drive.

8.0.2 Sequential Access Storage Devices

The original IBM PC and the PCjr have a connector for a conventional cassette recorder. The BIOS in these machines, as well as in the AT, provides the following services:

1. *BIOS service number 0, INT 15H.* Cassette motor ON.
2. *BIOS service number 1, INT 15H.* Cassette motor OFF.
3. *BIOS service number 2, INT 15H.* Read data blocks from cassette.
4. *BIOS service number 3, INT 15H.* Write data blocks to cassette.

However, the cassette interface never obtained commercial significance and was discontinued with the PC XT.

Another sequential access magnetic storage device sometimes used in the IBM microcomputers is known as a *streaming tape drive.* The most common use of streaming tape drives is as a fast and relatively inexpensive means for backing up hard disk drives. At a typical rate of 5 Mbytes/min, a streaming tape drive can back up or restore a 60-Mbyte hard disk in approximately 12 min. The sequential access feature of this device severely limits its use in other forms of data storage.

8.1 Diskette Storage

A popular medium for microcomputer data storage consists of a thin, polyester disk coated with a metal oxide similar to that used in magnetic tapes. These magnetic disks are known as diskettes, floppy disks, floppies, and microdisks. Diskettes are manufactured in 8, 5¼, and 3½-in diameters. The 8-in diskette size is not used in the IBM microcomputers. The 5¼-in diskettes are used in all IBM microcomputers of the PC line except the PC convertible, which uses 3½-in diskettes. All models of the PS/2 line use the 3½-in diskette size. The

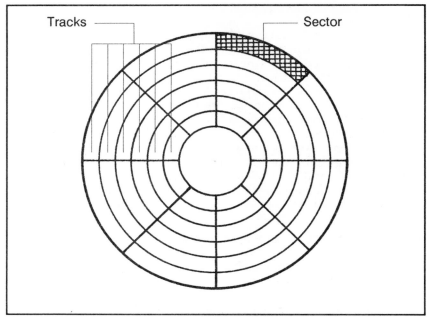

Figure 8.2. *Tracks and Sectors on the Surface of a Diskette or Disk*

3½-in diskettes come in a rigid plastic case and are sometimes called microdisks, microdiskettes, and micro floppy disks.

Information is stored on the magnetic surface of a diskette in a pattern of concentric circles called *tracks*. Each track is divided into areas called *sectors*. The read-write mechanism, similar to the ones used in tape recorders, can be moved from track to track by a stepper motor while the diskette spins on its axis. Figure 8.2 shows the pattern of tracks and sectors on a diskette surface.

Diskette sectoring can be based on physical or magnetic divisions of the diskette's surface. The physical type of division is called *hard-sectoring*, and the magnetic divisions are called *soft-sectoring*. All IBM microcomputer diskette systems use soft-sectoring. IBM soft-sector technology uses one small hole near the center of the diskette, which is sensed by a photodiode as the start of the first sector. Thereafter, a special bit pattern identifies the start and end of the remaining sectors in each track.

8.1.1 DOS Storage Structures

In the IBM microcomputers the structuring and programming of diskette and disk devices is left almost entirely to operating system software. To ensure compatibility with DOS, OS/2 has maintained the same disk and diskette storage structures and formats. For this reason, magnetic media formatted in either

Table 8.1. *Diskette Storage Formats in the IBM Microcomputers*

STORAGE MEDIA	SIDES	TRACKS	SECTORS	BYTES PER SECTOR	CAPACITY	DOS
5¼-in floppy disk SS/DD/48 TPI	1	40	8	512	160K	1.1
	1	40	9	512	180K	1.2+
5¼-in floppy disk DS/DD/48 TPI	2	40	8	512	320K	2.0
	2	40	9	512	360K	2.0+
5¼-in floppy disk DS/QD/96 TPI	2	80	15	512	1.2 Mbytes	3.0+
3½-in microdisk DS/DD/135 TPI	2	80	9	512	720K	3.0+
3½-in microdisk DS/HD/135 TPI	2	80	18	512	1.4 Mbytes	3.0+

system can be read and written by the other one. References to DOS data structures in the present chapter can be considered applicable to OS/2, unless noted otherwise. Table 8.1 shows the diskette storage formats used in the IBM microcomputers.

The patterns and densities used for storing magnetic data on the diskette's surface have changed in the different IBM microcomputers. The original diskette drives, operating under DOS versions 1.1 and 1.2, were equipped with a single read-write head, therefore only one side of the diskette contained data (see Table 8.1). With the introduction of DOS 2.0, the single-sided drives were substituted by double-sided diskettes and drives. These drives are equipped with a recording head for each diskette surface. The magnetic track density on the diskette's surface has gone from 48 tracks per inch in the drives of the PC line (double density), to 96 tracks per inch in the PC AT (quad density), and to 135 tracks per inch the 3½-in microdisks of the PC convertible and the PS/2 line. The amount of data recorded in each sector has remained at 512 bytes for all IBM disk and diskette systems (see Table 8.1).

8.2 Diskette System Hardware

The hardware required for the operation of a diskette storage system consists of the following elements:

1. A removable magnetic media (the diskette itself).

2. A diskette drive mechanism furnished with rotational and stepper motors, and with other mechanisms required to hold and spin the diskette and to move the recording head or heads along the diskette tracks.

3. A drive controller containing the programmable and nonprogrammable electronic components necessary to operate the device.

Table 8.2. *Removable Magnetic Media for the IBM Microcomputers*

DISKETTE SIZE	TYPE	SYSTEMS	FORMATTED CAPACITY	MEDIA SPECIFICATIONS
5¼-in	1	PC	160K or 180K	Single side, double density, soft sectors
	2	PC, PC XT, PCjr	320K or 360K	Double side, double density, soft sectors
	3	PC AT	1.2 Mbytes	High-capacity double side, quad density, soft sectors
3½-in	4	PS/2 Model 25 Model 30	720K	Double side, double density, 1.0-Mbyte capacity
	5	PS/2 Micro Channnel	1.4 Mbytes	Double side, high-density 2.0-Mbyte capacity

8.2.1 Removable Magnetic Media

There are several types of diskettes used in the IBM microcomputers. The most obvious difference is between the 5¼-in diskettes and the 3½-in microdisks; however, there are other variations in diskettes of the same size. Table 8.2 lists the five types of diskettes used in the IBM microcomputers.

8.2.2 The Diskette Drive

The diskette drive is an electromechanical device for recording data on the diskette's surface and for reading the recorded data. The various diskette drives used in the IBM microcomputers vary according to media type, number of read-write heads, drive size, recording technology, and performance. Table 8.3 lists the most popular IBM diskette drives of the 5¼ and 3½-in types as well as the compatible controller for each drive.

All IBM microcomputer diskette drives are capable of performing the following fundamental operations:

1. Spin the diskette on its axis at a fixed number of revolutions per minute.

2. Move the recording head in the direction of the diskette's center in discrete intervals or steps.

3. Move the recording head into contact with the diskette surface (load) at read-write time and away from the surface (unload) during positioning operations. This maneuver is designed to prevent excessive friction and disk wear.

4. Provide signals to the controller regarding the status of the drive and the installed media, for example:

a. A track zero sensor informs the controller when the recording head is positioned over track number zero.

b. An index sensor generates a signal every time that the diskette's sector hole passes over a phototransistor.

c. A write-protect sensor detects if the media has been mechanically protected from write operations.

Table 8.3. *Diskette Drives in the IBM Microcomputers*

MEDIA SIZE	DESIGNATION	SYSTEM	COMPATIBLE CONTROLLER
5¼ inch	5¼-in Diskette Drive (single-side)	PC	5¼-in Diskette Drive Adapter
	5¼-in Diskette Drive (double-side)	PC, XT	5¼-in Diskette Drive Adapter
	5¼-in Slimline Diskette Drive	PC, XT, Portable	5¼-in Diskette Drive Adapter
	5¼-in PCjr Diskette Drive	PCjr	PCjr Diskette Drive Adapter
	Double-Sided Diskette Drive	AT	Fixed Disk and Diskette Drive Adapter
	High Capacity Diskette Drive	AT	Fixed Disk and Diskette Drive Adapter
	PS/2 External Diskette Drive	Model 25 Model 30	5¼-in External Diskette Drive Adapter
		Micro Channel	5¼-in External Diskette Drive Adapter/A
3½ inch	720K Diskette Drive	PC Convertible	Diskette Drive Controller (on system board)
		Model 25 Model 30	Diskette Drive Interface (on system board)
	1.4-Mbyte Diskette Drive	PS/2 Micro Channel	Diskette Drive Controller (on system board)
	External Diskette Drive Model 001	PC, XT, Portable	Diskette Drive Adapter
	External Diskette Drive Model 002	AT XT 286	Model 002 Adapter Card
	Internal Diskette Drive	Specific models of the PC line	3½-in Internal Diskette Drive Adapter Card

All IBM systems allow more than one physical diskette drive to be connected to the controller. This is achieved by means of a jumper or selector, located on the drive, which is set to a specific drive number. The drive is enabled when the controller emits the corresponding command containing the drive's number. When a drive is not selected, it ignores all signals on the interface.

8.2.3 The Diskette Drive Controller

The operation and command of a diskette drive is done through the electronic circuitry and the programmable chips contained in the diskette drive controller. In the IBM microcomputers of the PC line the controller is furnished as an adapter card that fits in a standard or in a special-purpose slot, while in the PS/2 line the diskette drive controller elements are part of the motherboard. In most systems the diskette drive controller is a dedicated device, but in the PC AT the diskette drive controller is part of the Fixed Disk and Diskette Adapter.

The following are the fundamental functions of the diskette drive controller:

1. To select the disk drive that will be enabled for the particular operation (see Section 8.2.2).

2. To select the desired recording head. This function is active in double-sided systems only.

3. To issue the sequence of commands necessary for moving the recording head to any desired track.

4. To monitor the data on a track until a specific sector is located under the recording head.

5. To issue commands to load and unload the recording head (see Section 8.2.2).

6. To read data stored on the diskette's surface and write data onto the diskette's surface.

7. To detect errors caused by defective media, by electromagnetic noise, or by mechanical defects in the system.

8.2.3.1 The 5¼-in Diskette Adapter   This is the diskette drive controller for the PC, the XT, and the IBM Portable Computer. This adapter, which fits into one of the expansion slots in the system unit, can manage up to four diskette drives. Of these four drives two must be internal and two external. The internal 5¼-in drives can be single-sided or double-sided, normal size or slimline. The external drives are designated as A and B and the internal drives as C and D.

A 34-pin, keyed, edge connector and the corresponding ribbon cable provides the interface with the internal drives. A 37-pin D-shell connector on the adapter, accessible from the rear of the system unit, provides an interface with the external drives. Figure 8.3 shows the pin numbering on the adapter's D-shell connector and Table 8.4 describes the functions of the adapter's external connector pins.

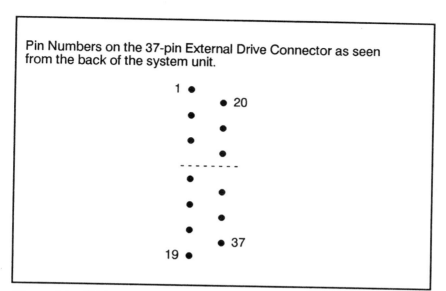

Pin Numbers on the 37-pin External Drive Connector as seen
from the back of the system unit.

Figure 8.3. *IBM 5¼-in Diskette Drive Adapter*

Table 8.4. *External Drive Connector Pinout on the IBM 5¼-in Diskette Drive Adapter*

	PIN NUMBERS	SIGNAL DIRECTION	SIGNAL DESCRIPTION	
	1–5		Unused	
	6	⇒	Index	A
	7	⇐	Motor enable C	
D	8	⇐	Drive select D	D
	9	⇐	Drive select C	
R	10	⇐	Motor enable D	A
	11	⇐	Direction of stepper motor	
I	12	⇐	Step pulse	P
	13	⇐	Write data	
V	14	⇐	Write enable	T
	15	⇒	Track zero	
E	16	⇒	Write protect	E
	17	⇒	Read Data	
	18	⇐	Select head number 1	R
	20–37		GROUND	

8.2.3.2 The PCjr Diskette Drive Adapter. This is the diskette drive controller used in the IBM PCjr. It fits in a special slot on the motherboard and is attached to the single disk drive through a ribbon cable. No external port is provided. Functionally, the PCjr controller is similar to the 5¼-in Diskette Drive Controller of the PC and XT, described previously, and both use the NEC 765 floppy disk controller chip.

According to the IBM documentation, the PCjr controller supports a single, double-sided, internal disk drive. However, Rapport Corporation and other manufacturers have made available a second diskette drive for the PCjr which makes use of the original controller. This is accomplished by substituting the original ribbon cable with one that can interface with both drives. This alteration is possible because the diskette services in the PCjr BIOS support four disk drives, and the coding is compatible with the one in PC and XT BIOS.

8.2.3.3 The Fixed Disk and Diskette Drive Adapter. One of the functions of this dual-purpose adapter used in the PC AT is to serve as a diskette drive controller. The card fits into one of the expansion slots in the system unit. The diskette functions in the controller are designed for double-density drives with write precompensation and are equipped with analog circuits for driving the clock and for data recovery. This limits the hardware that is compatible with the AT's adapter to double-sided and high-capacity diskette drives (see Table 8.3).

The adapter supports storage formats of 160K, 180K, 320K, 360K, and 1.2 Mbytes per diskette. No connector for external drives is provided. The adapter can manage a total of three drives: two diskettes and one hard disk or two hard disks and one diskette drive. A difficulty frequently encountered with this adapter is that diskettes which have been written by a high-capacity drive cannot be reliably read in the conventional drives used in the other systems of the PC line. This is true even if the diskette was originally formatted in a standard drive.

8.2.3.4 The PC Convertible Diskette Controller. This controller is not furnished in an adapter card but is part of the motherboard. The floppy disk controller chip is a NEC 765 similar to the one used in several other diskette controllers of the PC line. The system supports two internal, 3½-in diskette drives with 720K capacity per diskette.

8.2.3.5 The Models 25 and 30 Diskette Drive Interface. This controller, also called the *diskette gate array*, is part of the motherboard logic in the PS/2 Models 25 and 30. The controller supports two internal, 3½-in, 720K capacity diskette drives, which are connected through a ribbon cable. No connector for external drives is provided.

8.2.3.6 The PS/2 Micro Channel Diskette Drive Controller. With slight variations this controller is used in all the Micro Channel models of the PS/2 line. The controller supports two internal, 3½-in, diskette drives. The drive can operate with low- and high-density 3½-in microdisks. Either type can be formatted to 720K for compatibility with the Model 25, Model 30, and PC Convertible drives. High-density microdisks can be formatted to 1.4 Mbytes.

Since the diskette controller cannot detect low-density media, it is possible to format a low-density diskette to the 1.4-Mbyte mode. However, according to the technical documentation, high data density cannot be reliably used with low-density microdisks. The connectors for attaching the diskette drives to the controller vary in the different systems. In Models 50 and 70 the drives are coupled to the system bus through a card edge connector while the Models 60 and 80 use a ribbon cable.

8.3 The NEC 765 Floppy Disk Controller

IBM has used the same floppy disk controller chip in all the models of the PC and the PS/2 line. This floppy disk controller, or FDC, is the NEC 765. The Intel 8272A FDC is identical to the NEC chip.

The NEC 765 is capable of operating in single density (FM mode) and double density (MFM mode), although all IBM microcomputer diskette drives use double-density recording. Data records can be of 128, 256, 512, and 1024 bytes (IBM systems under DOS use 512 bytes per sector). The controller chip can drive up to four drives of 8-, 5¼-, or 3½-in media size.

Data transfers with the NEC 765 can take place using or not using direct memory access (DMA). DMA operations are described in Chapter 3, starting in Section 3.2.1. In the non-DMA mode, the FDC interrupts the CPU as each data byte is transferred. In DMA operation the CPU sends a command to the FDC and the data transfer takes place under the supervision of the DMA controller, while the CPU is free to perform other tasks. Note that the PCjr is the only IBM microcomputer that does not implement DMA.

Table 8.5. *NEC 765 Floppy Disk Controller Commands*

NO.	DESCRIPTION	NO.	DESCRIPTION
1	Specify characteristics	9	Write data
2	Sense drive status	10	Write deleted data
3	Sense interrupt status	11	Read track
4	Seek (move to track)	12	Read ID
5	Recalibrate	13	Scan equal
6	Format track	14	Scan high or equal
7	Read data	15	Scan low or equal
8	Read deleted data	16	Invalid (no operation)

8.3.1 NEC 765 Commands

The NEC 765 Floppy Disk Controller can execute 15 valid commands, as shown in Table 8.5.

Commands to the FDC consist of several successive bytes transmitted through the FDC data register (see Section 8.3.2). The first byte contains the command codes. The remaining command bytes, which can make a total of 2 to 9 bytes per command, contain data required for the operation. FDC commands can be described as consisting of three phases:

1. *Command Phase*. In this phase the FDC receives the sequence of bytes that constitute a command. The controller enters the command phase after a RESET or following the conclusion of a previous command.
2. *Execution Phase*. In this phase the FDC performs the required operations. The controller enters the execution phase immediately after receiving the last byte in the command.
3. *Result Phase*. At the conclusion of the execution phase, some FDC commands report to the CPU the results of the performed operations. In these commands, the controller will not return to the command phase until this data is read by the CPU.

Tables 8.6 to 8.21 describe the command format for all NEC 765 Floppy Disk Controller commands.

Table 8.6. *NEC 765 SPECIFY CHARACTERISTICS Command*

PHASE	NO.	BITS								COMMENTS
		7	6	5	4	3	2	1	0	
COMMAND	0	0	0	0	0	0	0	1	1	Command code
	1	SRT	SRT	SRT	SRT	HUT	HUT	HUT	HUT	Timer settings (see CODES)
	2	HLT	HLT	HLT	HLT	HLT	HLT	HLT	ND	
EXECUTION	Install load-unload times and stepping rates									
RESULT	No result phase									
CODES	**SRT** (step rate time) Time interval between stepper pulses. Range: 1 to 16 ms. **HUT** (head unload time) Time interval from end of read or write to head unloaded. Range: 16 to 240 ms. **HLT** (head load time) Time interval from after head load to before read or write. Range 2 to 254 ms. **ND** (non-DMA mode) When set, FDC operates in non-DMA mode.									

Table 8.7. *NEC 765 SENSE DRIVE STATUS Command*

PHASE	NO.	BITS								COMMENTS
		7	6	5	4	3	2	1	0	
COMMAND	0	0	0	0	0	0	1	0	0	Command code
	1	0	0	0	0	0	HD	US1	US0	
EXECUTION	Obtain status of disk drive selected in USx field									
RESULT	0	Status register 3								Status information
CODES	**HD** (head number) Recording head 0 or 1. **US0/US1** (unit select) Disk drive select value. Range is 0 to 3 and matches bits 0 and 1 of the Digital Output Register.									

Table 8.8. *NEC 765 SENSE INTERRUPT STATUS Command*

PHASE	NO.	BITS								COMMENTS
		7	6	5	4	3	2	1	0	
COMMAND	0	0	0	0	0	1	0	0	0	Command code
EXECUTION	Read interrupt cause into ST0 bits 5, 6, and 7									
RESULT	0	Status register 0								Status information
	1	Present cylinder number								
NOTE	Bits: 5 6 7 0 1 1 = Ready line changed state or polarity. 1 0 0 = Normal termination of SEEK or RECALIBRATE command. 1 1 0 = Abnormal termination of SEEK or RECALIBRATE command.									

Table 8.9. *NEC 765 SEEK Command*

PHASE	NO.	BITS								COMMENTS
		7	6	5	4	3	2	1	0	
COMMAND	0	0	0	0	0	1	1	1	1	Command code
	1	0	0	0	0	0	HD	US1	US0	
	2	New cylinder number								Seek data
EXECUTION	Position recording head over new cylinder									
RESULT	No result phase									
CODES	**HD** (head number) Recording head 0 or 1. **US0/US1** (unit select) Disk drive select value. Range is 0 to 3 and matches bits 0 and 1 of the Digital Output Register.									

Table 8.10. *NEC 765 RECALIBRATE Command*

PHASE	NO.	BITS								COMMENTS
		7	6	5	4	3	2	1	0	
COMMAND	0	0	0	0	0	0	1	1	1	Command code
	1	0	0	0	0	0	0	US1	US0	
EXECUTION	Retract recording head to track No. 0									
RESULT	No result phase									
CODES	**HD** (head number) Recording head 0 or 1. **US0/US1** (unit select) Disk drive select value. Range is 0 to 3 and matches bits 0 and 1 of the Digital Output Register.									

Table 8.11. *NEC 765 FORMAT A TRACK Command*

PHASE	NO.	BITS								COMMENTS
		7	6	5	4	3	2	1	0	
COMMAND	0	0	MFM	0	0	1	1	0	0	Command code
	1	0	0	0	0	0	HD	US1	US0	
	2	Data bytes per sector (N)								
	3	Sectors per track								
	4	Gap length								
	5	Data bits								
EXECUTION	Detect index hole and format track									
RESULT	0	Status register 0								Status information returned after execution
	1	Status register 1								
	2	Status register 2								
	3	Cylinder number (C)								Sector information after command execution
	4	Head address (H)								
	5	Sector number (R)								
	6	Data bytes per sector (N)								
CODES	**MFM** (modified frequency modulation) Double density. **HD** (head number) Recording head 0 or 1. **US0/US1** (unit select) Disk drive select value. Range is 0 to 3 and matches bits 0 and 1 of the Digital Output Register.									

Table 8.12. *NEC 765 READ DATA Command*

PHASE	NO.	BITS								COMMENTS
		7	6	5	4	3	2	1	0	
COMMAND	0	MT	MFM	SK	0	0	1	1	0	Command code
	1	0	0	0	0	0	HD	US1	US0	
	2	Cylinder number						(C)		Sector information passed with the command
	3	Head address						(H)		
	4	Sector number						(R)		
	5	Data bytes per sector						(N)		
	6	End of track								
	7	Gap length								
	8	Data length								
EXECUTION	Read data from multiple sectors									
RESULT	0	Status register 0								Status information returned after execution
	1	Status register 1								
	2	Status register 2								
	3	Cylinder number						(C)		Sector information after command execution
	4	Head address						(H)		
	5	Sector number						(R)		
	6	Data bytes per sector						(N)		
CODES	**MT** (multitrack) Select multitrack operation for dual-sided diskettes. Each cylinder is treated as a single track. **MFM** (modified frequency modulation) Double density. **SK** (skip) Skip sectors with deleted data. **HD** (head number) Recording head 0 or 1. **US0/US1** (unit select) Disk drive select value. Range is 0 to 3 and matches bits 0 and 1 of the Digital Output Register.									

Table 8.13. *NEC 765 READ DELETED DATA Command*

PHASE	NO.	BITS								COMMENTS
		7	6	5	4	3	2	1	0	
COMMAND	0	MT	MFM	SK	0	1	1	0	0	Command code
	1	0	0	0	0	0	HD	US1	US0	
	2	Cylinder number (C)								Sector information passed with the command
	3	Head address (H)								
	4	Sector number (R)								
	5	Data bytes per sector (N)								
	6	End of track								
	7	Gap length								
	8	Data length								
EXECUTION	Read data from multiple sectors									
RESULT	0	Status register 0								Status information returned after execution
	1	Status register 1								
	2	Status register 2								
	3	Cylinder number (C)								Sector information after command execution
	4	Head address (H)								
	5	Sector number (R)								
	6	Data bytes per sector (N)								
CODES	**MT** (multitrack) Select multitrack operation for dual-sided diskettes. Each cylinder is treated as a single track. **MFM** (modified frequency modulation) Double density. **SK** (skip) Skip sectors with deleted data. **HD** (head number) Recording head 0 or 1. **US0/US1** (unit select) Disk drive select value. Range is 0 to 3 and matches bits 0 and 1 of the Digital Output Register.									

Table 8.14. *NEC 765 WRITE DATA Command*

PHASE	NO.	BITS								COMMENTS
		7	6	5	4	3	2	1	0	
COMMAND	0	MT	MFM	0	0	0	1	0	1	Command code
	1	0	0	0	0	0	HD	US1	US0	
	2	Cylinder number (C)								Sector information passed with the command
	3	Head address (H)								
	4	Sector number (R)								
	5	Data bytes per sector (N)								
	6	End of track								
	7	Gap length								
	8	Data length								
EXECUTION	Write data to multiple sectors									
RESULT	0	Status register 0								Status information returned after execution
	1	Status register 1								
	2	Status register 2								
	3	Cylinder number (C)								Sector information after command execution
	4	Head address (H)								
	5	Sector number (R)								
	6	Data bytes per sector (N)								
CODES	**MT** (multitrack) Select multitrack operation for dual-sided diskettes. Each cylinder is treated as a single track. **MFM** (modified frequency modulation) Double density. **HD** (head number) Recording head 0 or 1. **US0/US1** (unit select) Disk drive select value. Range is 0 to 3 and matches bits 0 and 1 of the Digital Output Register.									

Table 8.15. *NEC 765 WRITE DELETED DATA Command*

PHASE	NO.	BITS								COMMENTS
		7	6	5	4	3	2	1	0	
COMMAND	0	MT	MFM	0	0	1	0	0	1	Command code
	1	0	0	0	0	0	HD	US1	US0	
	2	Cylinder number (C)								Sector information passed with the command
	3	Head address (H)								
	4	Sector number (R)								
	5	Data bytes per sector (N)								
	6	End of track								
	7	Gap length								
	8	Data length								
EXECUTION	Write data to multiple sectors									
RESULT	0	Status register 0								Status information returned after execution
	1	Status register 1								
	2	Status register 2								
	3	Cylinder number (C)								Sector information after command execution
	4	Head address (H)								
	5	Sector number (R)								
	6	Data bytes per sector (N)								
CODES	**MT** (multitrack) Select multitrack operation for dual-sided diskettes. Each cylinder is treated as a single track. **MFM** (modified frequency modulation) Double density. **HD** (head number) Recording head 0 or 1. **US0/US1** (unit select) Disk drive select value. Range is 0 to 3 and matches bits 0 and 1 of the Digital Output Register.									

Table 8.16. *NEC 765 READ TRACK* Command

PHASE	NO.	BITS								COMMENTS
		7	6	5	4	3	2	1	0	
COMMAND	0	0	MFM	SK	0	0	0	1	0	Command code
	1	0	0	0	0	0	HD	US1	US0	
	2	Cylinder number (C)								Sector information passed with the command
	3	Head address (H)								
	4	Sector number (R)								
	5	Data bytes per sector (N)								
	6	End of track								
	7	Gap length								
	8	Data length								
EXECUTION	Read all sectors in track									
RESULT	0	Status register 0								Status information returned after execution
	1	Status register 1								
	2	Status register 2								
	3	Cylinder number (C)								Sector information after command execution
	4	Head address (H)								
	5	Sector number (R)								
	6	Data bytes per sector (N)								
CODES	**MFM** (modified frequency modulation) Double density. **SK** (skip) Skip sectors with deleted data. **HD** (head number) Recording head 0 or 1. **US0/US1** (unit select) Disk drive select value. Range is 0 to 3 and matches bits 0 and 1 of the Digital Output Register.									

Table 8.17. *NEC 765 READ ID Command*

PHASE	NO.	7	6	5	4	3	2	1	0	COMMENTS
		BITS								
COMMAND	0	0	MFM	0	0	1	0	1	0	Command code
	1	0	0	0	0	0	HD	US1	US0	
EXECUTION	Read first ID field following the index hole									
RESULT	0	Status register 0								Status information returned after execution
	1	Status register 1								
	2	Status register 2								
	3	Cylinder number (C)								Sector information after command execution
	4	Head address (H)								
	5	Sector number (R)								
	6	Data bytes per sector (N)								
CODES	**MFM** (modified frequency modulation) Double density. **HD** (head number) Recording head 0 or 1. **US0/US1** (unit select) Disk drive select value. Range is 0 to 3 and matches bits 0 and 1 of the Digital Output Register.									

Table 8.18. *NEC 765 SCAN EQUAL Command*

PHASE	NO.	BITS								COMMENTS
		7	6	5	4	3	2	1	0	
COMMAND	0	MT	MFM	SK	1	0	0	0	1	Command code
	1	0	0	0	0	0	HD	US1	US0	Sector information passed with the command
	2	Cylinder number (C)								
	3	Head address (H)								
	4	Sector number (R)								
	5	Data bytes per sector (N)								
	6	End of track								
	7	Gap length								
	8	Data length								
EXECUTION		Scan disk to match system data								
RESULT	0	Status register 0								Status information returned after execution
	1	Status register 1								
	2	Status register 2								
	3	Cylinder number (C)								Sector information after command execution
	4	Head address (H)								
	5	Sector number (R)								
	6	Data bytes per sector (N)								
CODES		**MT** (multitrack) Select multitrack operation for dual-sided diskettes. Each cylinder is treated as a single track. **MFM** (modified frequency modulation) Double density. **SK** (skip) Skip sectors with deleted data. **HD** (head number) Recording head 0 or 1. **US0/US1** (unit select) Disk drive select value. Range is 0 to 3 and matches bits 0 and 1 of the Digital Output Register.								

Table 8.19. *NEC 765 SCAN HIGH OR EQUAL Command*

PHASE	NO.	BITS								COMMENTS
		7	6	5	4	3	2	1	0	
COMMAND	0	MT	MFM	SK	1	1	1	0	1	Command code
	1	0	0	0	0	0	HD	US1	US0	
	2	Cylinder number (C)								Sector information passed with the command
	3	Head address (H)								
	4	Sector number (R)								
	5	Data bytes per sector (N)								
	6	End of track								
	7	Gap length								
	8	Data length								
EXECUTION		Scan disk for data equal or higher than system's								
RESULT	0	Status register 0								Status information returned after execution
	1	Status register 1								
	2	Status register 2								
	3	Cylinder number (C)								Sector information after command execution
	4	Head address (H)								
	5	Sector number (R)								
	6	Data bytes per sector (N)								
CODES		**MT** (multitrack) Select multitrack operation for dual-sided diskettes. Each cylinder is treated as a single track. **MFM** (modified frequency modulation) Double density. **SK** (skip) Skip sectors with deleted data. **HD** (head number) Recording head 0 or 1. **US0/US1** (unit select) Disk drive select value. Range is 0 to 3 and matches bits 0 and 1 of the Digital Output Register.								

Table 8.20. *NEC 765 SCAN LOW OR EQUAL Command*

PHASE	NO.	BITS								COMMENTS
		7	6	5	4	3	2	1	0	
COMMAND	0	MT	MFM	SK	1	1	0	0	1	Command code
	1	0	0	0	0	0	HD	US1	US0	
	2	Cylinder number (C)								Sector information passed with the command
	3	Head address (H)								
	4	Sector number (R)								
	5	Data bytes per sector (N)								
	6	End of track								
	7	Gap length								
	8	Data length								
EXECUTION		Scan disk for data equal or lower than system's								
RESULT	0	Status register 0								Status information returned after execution
	1	Status register 1								
	2	Status register 2								
	3	Cylinder number (C)								Sector information after command execution
	4	Head address (H)								
	5	Sector number (R)								
	6	Data bytes per sector (N)								
CODES		**MT** (multitrack) Select multitrack operation for dual-sided diskettes. Each cylinder is treated as a single track. **MFM** (modified frequency modulation) Double density. **SK** (skip) Skip sectors with deleted data. **HD** (head number) Recording head 0 or 1. **US0/US1** (unit select) Disk drive select value. Range is 0 to 3 and matches bits 0 and 1 of the Digital Output Register.								

Table 8.21. *NEC 765 INVALID Command*

PHASE	NO.	BITS								COMMENTS
		7	6	5	4	3	2	1	0	
COMMAND	0	?	?	?	?	?	?	?	?	Invalid codes
EXECUTION		No operation								
RESULT	0	Status register 0								ST0 = 80

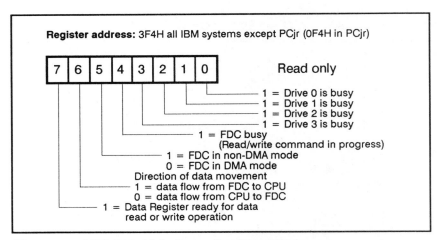

Figure 8.4. *NEC 765 Main Status Register Bit Map*

8.3.2 Floppy Disk Controller Registers

The transfer of information between the FDC and the system take place through two 8-bit registers. One of these registers is designated as the *main status register* and the other one as the *data register*. The main status register, which is read-only, provides information regarding the status of each diskette drive in the system. The data register is used in issuing commands to the FDC and in obtaining command results (see Section 8.3.1). Figure 8.4 shows the bit map of the FDC main status register.

The data register is used for issuing multiple-byte commands to the Floppy Disk Controller and for reading command results (see Tables 8.6 to 8.21). During the command phase, the program sends all command bytes successively through the data register. After the last command byte is received, the controller automatically enters the execution phase. At the conclusion of the execution phase, the program must read all result bytes in the specific command. The FDC will not be ready for a new command until the last result byte is read from the data register.

The result of an FDC command, except for those commands that do not have a result phase, is reported in 1 to 7 bytes which are read by the CPU at the controllers's data register port. The first one, two, or three of these result bytes correspond with the status registers (see Tables 8.6 to 8.21). The status registers are numbered from 0 to 3 and are, sometimes, referred to as ST 0, ST 1, ST 2, and ST 3. Figures 8.5 to 8.8 show the bit maps of the status registers.

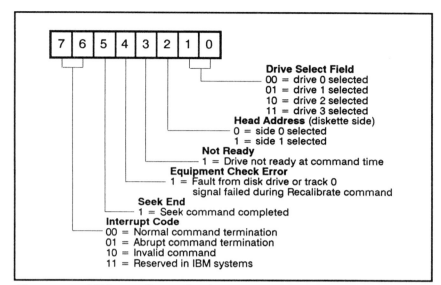

Figure 8.5. *NEC 765 Status Register 0*

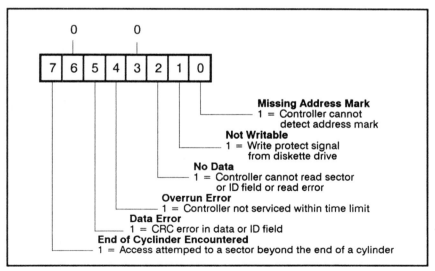

Figure 8.6. *NEC 765 Status Register 1*

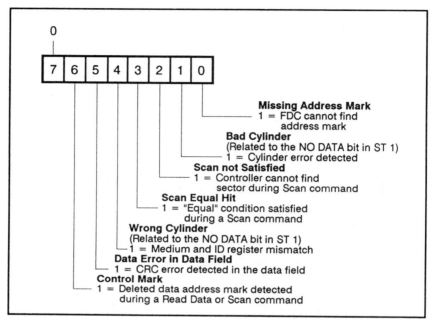

Figure 8.7. *NEC 765 Status Register 2*

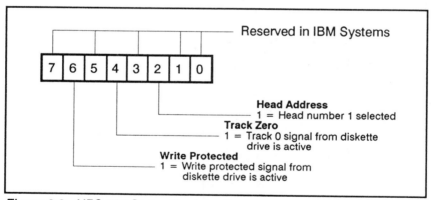

Figure 8.8. *NEC 765 Status Register 3*

8.4 Other Diskette Controller Registers

In addition to the NEC 765, or the equivalent Intel 8272A Floppy Disk Controller, the diskette controllers in the IBM microcomputers contain other electronic components and programmable registers. These additional registers are used to show the status of the diskette signals and lines and to set the control parameters for the operation of the diskette drives.

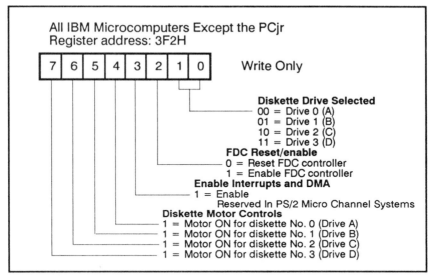

Figure 8.9. *The Diskette Controller's Digital Output Register*

8.4.1 The Digital Output Register

All IBM diskette controllers have a programmable register, named the *digital output register*, which can be written by the program to control the drive motors, to select drives, and to enable and disable special features.

The functions of the individual bits in this register are not identical in all systems. Figure 8.9 shows the bit map of the digital output register in all IBM microcomputers except the PCjr. Figure 8.10 shows the bit functions of the digital output register in the PCjr.

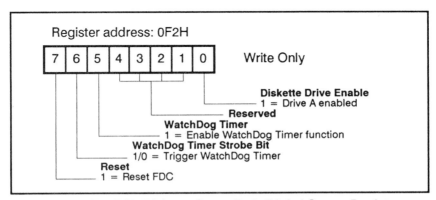

Figure 8.10. *The PCjr Diskette Controller's Digital Output Register*

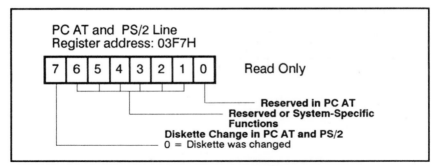

Figure 8.11. *The Diskette Controller's Digital Input Register*

The PCjr is the only IBM microcomputer that does not use DMA. For this reason, programming diskette read and write operations is different in the PCjr than in the other IBM systems. The PCjr WatchDog Timer is a 1- to 3-s timing device connected to the diskette interrupt line (IRQ6). The WatchDog Timer can be used by a program to break out of an endless loop due to a hardware malfunction during a diskette data transfer. Bits 5 and 6 of the PCjr's digital output register (see Figure 8.10) allow enabling and triggering the WatchDog Timer function.

8.4.2 The Digital Input and Configuration Control Registers

Some IBM diskette controllers and drives contain registers not implemented in other systems. For example, the digital input register of the PC AT and the PS/2 line is a read-only register mapped to port 037FH. Figure 8.11 shows the map of the digital input register.

The IBM microcomputers of the PS/2 line also implement an output function at port 037FH. This function, designated as the *configuration control register*, is used to set the data transfer parameters. Figure 8.12 shows the bit map of the configuration control register for the Models 25 and 30. Figure 8.13 shows the configuration control register in the Micro Channel systems.

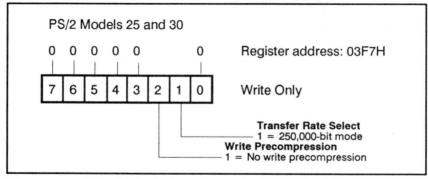

Figure 8.12. *PS/2 Diskette Controller's Configuration Control Register*

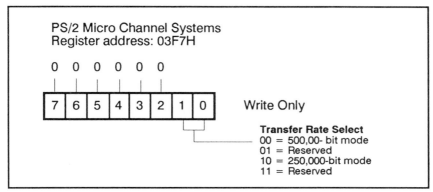

Figure 8.13. *PS/2 Diskette Controller's Configuration Control Register*

8.5 Programming the NEC 765 Floppy Disk Controller

Few programs require performing diskette operations by accessing the controller directly, since the services provided in the DOS and BIOS are usually sufficient and more convenient. The exceptions to this rule are operating system software and programs that use unconventional manipulations of the floppy disk controller (FDC) to obstruct unauthorized copying of diskettes.

Programming the NEC 765 FDC consists of issuing the commands listed in Tables 8.6 to 8.21. These commands are executed by reading the main status register (see Figure 8.4) and by reading and writing to the data register. The port mapping of these registers in the IBM microcomputers can be seen in Table 8.22.

Read and write operations to the data register must be synchronized by examining bits 6 and 7 of the main status register (see Figure 8.4). During write operations (command phase) the program must check that bit 6 of the main status register is clear (indicating flow from the CPU to the FDC) and that bit 7 is set (indicating that the data register is ready). This test must be performed before sending each byte in the command code. During read operations (result phase) the program must test that bit 6 of the main status register is set (indicating flow from the FDC to the CPU). This test must be performed before reading each result byte.

Table 8.22. *Mapping of Diskette Controller Registers (IBM systems)*

SYSTEM	DIGITAL OUTPUT REGISTER	NEC 765 OR INTEL 8272A	
		DATA	MAIN STATUS
All IBM micros (except PCjr)	3F2H	3F5H	3F4H
PCjr	0F2H	0F5H	0F4H

Table 8.23. *IBM Diskette Drive Parameter Table*

(Address at vector for INT 1EH)

OFFSET	BYTES	DESCRIPTION
0	2	Drive specification bytes
2	1	Count of timer ticks to wait before turning diskette motor OFF
3	1	Code for bytes per sector: 00 = 128 bytes 01 = 256 bytes 02 = 512 bytes (IBM standard format) 03 = 1024 bytes
4	1	Number of sectors per track
5	1	Gap length parameter
6	1	Data length parameter
7	1	Gap length for format
8	1	Fill byte to use during format
9	1	Head settle time (in milliseconds)
10	1	Motor start-up time (in 1/8 s)

8.5.1 Diskette Data in BIOS

An examination of Tables 8.6 to 8.21 reveals that many FDC commands require technical data regarding the setup and parameters of the diskette system. For example, the READ DATA command of Table 8.12 needs the number of data bytes per sector, the end of track value, the gap length, and the data length. These parameters are in addition to the variables in the command codes and the sector information.

During the initialization routines of the POST, the IBM BIOS determines and stores the basic parameters of the diskette system. This data, sometimes called the diskette table, is stored in an 11-byte area whose address is located by the vector for interrupt 1EH. Table 8.23 shows the parameters stored in the diskette table.

The procedure named FETCH_PARAM listed in Section 8.5.2 provides a sample of the coding necessary to retrieve any desired parameter from the BIOS diskette table. Several Floppy Disk Controller routines listed in Section 8.5.3 make use of this primitive.

8.5.2 Diskette System Primitives

The lower layer of software for controlling diskette operations is made up of the elementary routines required for directly accessing the diskette drive hardware and the Floppy Disk Controller. Typical diskette primitives are routines to turn a specific drive motor on, to turn it off, to output a data byte to the FDC, and to read a data byte from the FDC. In addition to the services that operate the diskette hardware, the primitives must also include auxiliary procedures, such as timing routines and routines to check diskette status registers and to obtain parameters from the diskette table.

Since primitive routines are hardware-dependent, their application is limited to compatible systems and devices. In the IBM microcomputers it is possible to achieve a certain level of portability in diskette software by using the system-specific parameters stored in the diskette table (see Table 8.23). Other factors that favor the portability of the code are the generalized use of the NEC 765 Floppy Disk Controller (see Section 8.3) and the consistency in the mapping of the essential ports and registers.

On the other hand, there are fundamental differences in the diskette hardware and other support components used in the various models and lines of IBM microcomputers. For example, the diskette system in the IBM PCjr uses the same NEC controller as other members of the PC and PS/2 lines, but, because the PCjr does not have DMA, the controller must be initialized and operated in a different, noncompatible manner. Other differences are diskette drive hardware, media types and formats, and the availability of the auxiliary status and control ports and registers discussed in Section 8.4.2.

Due to these hardware differences, the diskette primitives and device driver routines listed in this chapter should be considered generic samples. The programmer may have to make some adjustments and modifications to ensure that the code operates in the system or systems for which it is intended.

```
;********************************
;          output to FDC
;********************************
OUTPUT_NEC PROC NEAR
; Output byte to the NEC 765 or Intel 8272A FDC
; On entry:
;          AH = byte to output
;
; On exit:
;          Carry clear if successful
;          Carry set if no output
;
        PUSH   BX              ; Save input registers
        PUSH   CX
        PUSH   DX
        MOV    DX,03F4H        ; main status register
                               ; (except in PCjr)
```

```
;********************
;    test direction
;********************
        MOV    BH,2           ; Times to repeat direction test
                              ; loop
SET_DIR_LOOP:
        XOR    CX,CX          ; Set up counter
TEST_DIR:
        IN     AL,DX          ; Get status byte from register
        JMP    SHORT $+2      ; I/O delay
        TEST   AL,01000000B   ; Bit 6 is direction of data flow
        JZ     OK_DIR         ; Data flow from CPU to FDC if
                              ; bit is clear
        LOOP   TEST_DIR       ; Loop waiting for direction bit
        DEC    BH             ; Decrement high counter
        JNZ    SET_DIR_LOOP;  Repeat loop if not zero
; Time lapse exhausted for direction test loop
;
;********************
;      error exit
;********************
OUTPUT_ERROR:
        STC
        JMP    OUTNEC_EXIT    ; Restore registers and return
;
;********************
;    test status
;********************
OK_DIR:
        MOV    BH,2           ; High counter for status
        XOR    CX,CX          ; Set up counter
TEST_STAT:
        IN     AL,DX          ; Get status byte from register
        JMP    SHORT $+2      ; I/O delay
        TEST   AL,10000000B   ; Bit 7 is data register ready
                              ; for read or write operation
        JNZ    OK_STATUS      ; Output if ready
        LOOP   TEST_STAT      ; Loop waiting for status bit
        DEC    BH             ; Decrement high counter
        JNZ    TEST_STAT      ; Repeat loop if not zero
; Time lapse exhausted for status bit test
        JMP    OUTPUT_ERROR          ; Error exit
;
;********************
;      output
;********************
OK_STATUS:
```

```
        MOV     AL,AH           ; Byte to output to AL
        INC     DX              ; DX = 03F5H (FDC data register)
        OUT     DX,AL           ; Output byte
        JMP     SHORT $+2       ; I/O delay
        CLC                     ; No error
OUTNEC_EXIT:
        POP     DX
        POP     CX
        POP     BX
        RET
;
OUTPUT_NEC ENDP


;********************************
;           input from FDC
;********************************
INPUT_NEC    PROC  NEAR
; Input a byte from the NEC 765 or Intel 8272A FDC
; On exit:
;           AL = byte read from FDC
;
        MOV     DX,3F4H         ; FDC main status register
FDC_IN:
        IN      AL,DX           ; Get byte from port
        JMP     SHORT $+2       ; I/O delay
        TEST    AL,01000000B    ; Data flow from FDC to CPU
        JNZ     INPUT_READY     ; Go if ready
BAD_INPUT:
        STC                     ; Error flag
        RET
RET
; Read data register
INPUT_READY:
        INC     DX              ; DX = FDC data register
        IN      AL,DX           ; Read byte
        CLC                     ; No error
        RET
;
INPUT_NEC    ENDP


;********************************
;       fetch diskette parameter
;********************************
FETCH_PARAM         PROC  NEAR
; Fetch diskette system parameter from disk table pointed at by
```

```
; the vector stored at INT 1EH
; Logical address of vector is 0000:0078H (78H = 1EH * 4)
; On entry:
;          AL = offset of parameter desired
; On exit:
;          AL = parameter from disk table
;
          PUSH  SI              ; Save SI
          PUSH  DS              ; Save present data segment
          PUSH  AX              ; Save entry values
          MOV   AX,0            ; Point to segment base of
                                ; interrupt vector table
          MOV   DS,AX           ; Segment base to DS
          MOV   DI,78H          ; Offset of vector 1EH
          MOV   SI,DS:[DI]      ; Set up SI as offset pointer to
                                ; diskette parameter table
          INC   DI
          INC   DI              ; Bump to segment of vector 1EH
          MOV   AX,DS:[DI]      ; Get word
          MOV   DS,AX           ; Set DS to base of diskette
                                ; parameter table
          POP   AX              ; Restore input value
          MOV   AH,0            ; Clear high byte for add
          ADD   SI,AX           ; Add parameter offset to pointer
          MOV   AL,DS:[SI]      ; Parameter into AL
          POP   DS              ; Restore segment register
          POP   SI
          RET
;
FETCH_PARAM          ENDP


;*******************************
;          diskette motor ON
;*******************************
MOTOR_ON   PROC  NEAR
; Turn on drive motor
; On entry:
;          AL    =    0 (drive A)
;                     1 (drive B)
;                     2 (drive C)
;                     3 (drive D)
; Routine sets bit 2 (enable FDC) and bit 3 (enable interrupts
; and DMA) of the digital output register
;
; Transfer corresponding motor mask to AL high nibble
          MOV   CL,AL           ; Rotate count to CL
```

```
        MOV   CH,00010000B  ; Mask for drive A
        ROL   CH,CL         ; Rotate mask
        OR    AL,CH         ; Or mask into AL
        OR    AL,00001100B  ; Set bits 2 and 3
; AL now holds the bit pattern for the DOR. Note that bits
; 1 and 0 are set on entry
        MOV   DX,3F2H       ; Address of DOR in all IBM
                            ; systems except PCjr
        OUT   DX,AL         ; Write byte and MOTOR ON
        JMP   SHORT $+2
; Programs for AT and PS/2 computers should use service number
; 90H of BIOS INT 15H at this time to notify the operating
; system of a WAIT-FOR-DEVICE condition. AL should be FDH for
; a diskette drive motor start wait.
;
;******************
;   get motor delay
;******************
        MOV   AL,10         ; Offset of motor wait in
                            ; diskette table
        CALL  FETCH_PARAM   ; Use procedure
; AL now holds required motor wait in 1/8 s. For example, if
; AL = 8 motor delay is 1 s
; Convert 8 per second factor to 18 per second factor required
; by the BIOS time-of-day clock at INT 1AH
; Approximate formula is: (x*9)/4
        MOV   AH,0          ; Clear high byte
        MOV   CL,9          ; Multiplier for conversion
        MUL   CL            ; Multiply
        MOV   CL,4          ; Divisor for conversion
        DIV   CL            ; Divide
        INC   AL            ; Safety margin for conversion
; AL now holds approximately 1/18-s delay periods
        MOV   BL,AL         ; Counter to BL
        MOV   BH,0          ; Clear high byte
        CALL  DELAY_18TH    ; Delay routine
        RET
;
MOTOR_ON     ENDP


;******************************
;        delay using INT 1AH
;******************************
DELAY_18TH   PROC  NEAR
; Delay routine using BIOS time-of-day service of INT 1AH
; On entry:
```

```
;            BX = Desired delay in 1/18-s periods
;
        PUSH    AX
        PUSH    DX
        MOV     AH,0           ; BIOS service request number
        INT     1AH            ; for timer service
; DX holds low portion of counter
        ADD     BX,DX          ; Add present value to delay
;********************
;     delay
;********************
WAIT_FOR_CNT:
        INT     1AH            ; Continue calling counter
        CMP     DX,BX          ; until count expires
        JB      WAIT_FOR_CNT
; Delay executed
        POP     DX             ; Restore registers
        POP     AX
        RET
;
DELAY_18TH    ENDP


;********************************
;        diskette motor OFF
;********************************
MOTOR_OFF    PROC  NEAR
; Turn off all diskette drive motors
; Routine sets bit 2 (enable FDC) and bit 3 (enable interrupts
; and DMA) of the digital output register
;
        MOV     DX,3F2H        ; Address of DOR in all IBM
                               ; systems except PCjr
        MOV     AL,00001100B   ; Bits 2 and 3 ON, all others
                               ; OFF
        OUT     DX,AL          ; Write byte and MOTOR ON
        JMP     SHORT $+2
        RET
;
MOTOR_OFF    ENDP


;********************************
;    wait for INT 6 (diskette)
;********************************
WAIT_FOR_INT6        PROC  NEAR
; Wait for diskette interrupt (IRQ6) to occur by monitoring
```

```
; the interrupt flag bit (bit 7) of the diskette status byte
; stored at logical address 0040:003EH
;
; A time-out loop is provided for error detection
; On exit:
;               Carry flag clear if interrupt occurred
;               Carry flag set if time-out error
;
; Save registers used by routine
          PUSH   ES
          PUSH   SI
          PUSH   AX
          PUSH   BX
          PUSH   CX
          PUSH   DX
;*******************
;     set up BIOS
;         pointer
;*******************
          MOV    AX,40H         ; AX to BIOS data area
          MOV    ES,AX          ; and move to ES
          MOV    SI,003EH       ; SI to offset of byte
          STI                   ; Make sure interrupts ON
; Programs for AT and PS/2 computers should use service number
; 90H of BIOS INT 15H at this time to notify the operating
; system of a WAIT-FOR-DEVICE condition. AL should be 01H for
; a diskette time-out wait.
;*******************
;   set up time-out
;         counter
;*******************
          XOR    CX,CX          ; Set low-level counter
          MOV    BL,4           ; and high-level counter
;*******************
; wait for interrupt
;*******************
WAIT_INT6:
          MOV    DL,ES:[SI]     ; Get byte from BIOS data area
          TEST   DL,10000000B   ; Is high bit set?
          JNZ    INT6_OCCURRED     ; Exit if bit 7 set
          LOOP   WAIT_INT6      ; Continue testing
          DEC    BL             ; Decrement high counter
          JNZ    WAIT_INT6      ; Restart loop
; Time-out error. Probable cause is drive not ready
          STC                   ; Carry set
          JMP    EXIT_INT6
          RET
```

```
INT6_OCCURRED:
        AND     DL,01111111B  ; Clear bit 7
        MOV     ES:[SI],DL    ; in BIOS diskette status byte
        CLC                   ; No error flag
EXIT_INT6:
        POP     DX            ; Restore registers
        POP     CX
        POP     BX
        POP     AX
        POP     SI
        POP     ES
        RET
WAIT_FOR_INT6       ENDP


;********************************
;       milliseconds timer
;********************************
MILLI_TIMER   PROC  NEAR
; Timer in 1/1000-s intervals
; On entry:
;           BX = time delay in milliseconds
;
;*******************
;   initial count
;*******************
READ_COUNTER:
; Read initial count for each 1-ms delay
; Timer channel 0 at port 40H
        MOV     AL,00000110B  ; 0 0 0 0 0 1 1 0
                              ;   _____
                              ;   | |   |   | |_ binary mode
                              ;   | |   |   |_____ mode 3
                              ;   | |   |_____ latch
                              ;   | |_____ channel 0
        OUT     43H,AL        ; To counter command port
        JMP     SHORT $+2     ; I/O delay
; Read LSB then MSB
        IN      AL,40H
        JMP     SHORT $+2
        MOV     DL,AL
        IN      AL,40H
        JMP     SHORT $+2
        MOV     DH,AL
; DX holds timer counter value
        SUB     DX,1190       ; Subtract 1-ms delay count
```

```
;********************
;   loop for 1 ms
;********************
ONE_MS:
        MOV     AL,06H          ; Latch for read code
        OUT     43H,AL          ; To counter command port
        JMP     SHORT $+2       ; I/O delay
; Read LSB then MSB
        IN      AL,40H          ; Port for channel 0
        JMP     SHORT $+2
        MOV     CL,AL           ; LOB to DL
        IN      AL,40H          ; Read HOB
        JMP     SHORT $+2
        MOV     CH,AL           ; HOB to DH
; CX holds timer counter value
;+DX holds terminal count for 1-ms delay
        CMP     CX,DX           ; Compare counts
        JA      ONE_MS          ; Wait until DX <CX
;********************
;    repeat BX ms.
;********************
        DEC     BX              ; Milliseconds counter
        JNZ     READ_COUNTER            ; Continue if count not finished
        RET
;
MILLI_TIMER     ENDP
```

8.5.3 Diskette System Drivers

The routines and procedures to execute FDC commands, to obtain command results, and to set up the DMA chip and other support devices constitute a second level of diskette operation software. The following code fragment contains four drivers: one to set up the DMA controller for diskette read or write transfers, one to perform SEEK command, one to perform the READ DATA command, and one to obtain the result bytes after the execution of a FDC command. These driver routines frequently call the primitives listed in Section 8.5.2 to perform input/output and for other support operations.

```
;******************************
;     set up DMA controller
;     for diskette operations
;******************************
DISKETTE_DMA            PROC  NEAR
; Set up DMA chip for diskette/memory operations
; On entry:
;           AL = 0 for read operation
;           AL = 1 for write operation
```

```
;       DS:SI = Buffer address for read or write data
;          DI = Bytes to read or write (not less than 2)
;
        PUSH   SI              ; Save registers
        PUSH   DI
        PUSH   AX
        PUSH   BX
        PUSH   CX
        PUSH   DX
        CLI                    ; Interrupts off
;********************
;    set DMA mode
;********************
        MOV    AH,AL           ; Input to AH
        MOV    AL,46H          ; Assume a read operation
        CMP    AH,0            ; Is it read?
        JE     DMA_DO1         ; Yes, write read mode byte
        MOV    AL,4AH          ; Write mode byte
DMA_DO1:
        OUT    12,AL           ; Output read/write byte
        JMP    SHORT $+2       ; I/O delay
        OUT    11,AL

;
;********************
;    set address
;********************
; Calculate 20-bit physical address from DS:SI
        MOV    AX,SI           ; Offset of buffer to AX
        MOV    BX,DS           ; Segment of buffer to BX
        MOV    CL,4            ; Rotate 4 times to get page
        ROL    BX,CL           ; Rotate BX
        MOV    DL,BL           ; BL to DL
        AND    DL,00001111B    ; Clear high nibble of DL
        AND    BL,11110000B    ; and low nibble of BL
        ADD    AX,BX           ; Add segment and offset to
                               ; form 16 bits of physical add
        JNC    PAGE_OK         ; DL is OK for page if no carry
        INC    DL
PAGE_OK:
        OUT    4,AL            ; Send low byte of offset
        JMP    SHORT $+2       ; I/O delay
        MOV    AL,AH           ; High byte of offset to AL
        OUT    4,AL            ; Send it
        JMP    SHORT $+2       ; I/O delay
        MOV    AL,DL           ; Page to AL
        OUT    81H,AL          ; To DMA page register
```

```
;*******************
;    set byte count
;*******************
; DI = number of bytes to transfer to memory
        MOV     AX,DI       ; Byte count to AX
        DEC     AX          ; DMA set up is to 1 less
                            ; than number of bytes to
                            ; transfer
        OUT     5,AL        ; Low byte of count
        JMP     SHORT $+2   ; I/O delay
        MOV     AL,AH       ; High count to AL
        OUT     5,AL        ; High byte of count
        JMP     SHORT $+2   ; I/O delay
        STI                 ; Interrupts ON
;********************
;   enable DMA Ch. 2
;********************
        MOV     AL,2        ; Load channel number
        OUT     10,AL       ; To DMA port 10
        POP     DX          ; Restore register
        POP     CX
        POP     BX
        POP     AX
        POP     DI
        POP     SI
        RET
;
DISKETTE_DMA            ENDP


;******************************
;       perform SEEK command
;******************************
SEEK_COMMAND        PROC  NEAR
; Move recording head to desired track
; On entry:
;           DH = drive number
;           DL = track number (cylinder)
;           CH = head number (0 or 1)
;
        PUSH    CX              ; Save registers
        PUSH    DX
; Set bit 2 of the second command byte (in DH) if head number 1
        CMP     CH,0            ; No action if head number 0
        JE      HEAD_OK         ; Leave DH bit 2 clear
        OR      DH,00000100B    ; Set bit 2
HEAD_OK:
```

```
; 1
        MOV     AH,0FH          ; SEEK command code
        CALL    OUTPUT_NEC      ; To FDC
; 2
        MOV     AH,DH           ; Drive number
        CALL    OUTPUT_NEC      ; To FDC
; 3
        MOV     AH,DL           ; Track number
        CALL    OUTPUT_NEC      ; To FDC
;
        CALL    WAIT_FOR_INT6           ; Wait for command execution
        JNC     OK_SEEK                 ; Interrupt occurred
; SEEK operation error
        STC                     ; Error flag
        JMP     SEEK_EXIT
;********************
; head settle wait
;********************
OK_SEEK:
        MOV     AL,9            ; Parameter for head settle time
        CALL    FETCH_PARAM     ; Get value from diskette table
; AL holds head settle time in milliseconds
        MOV     BL,AL           ; To BL
        MOV     BH,0            ; Clear high byte of counter
        CALL    MILLI_TIMER     ; Delay head settle time
        CLC                     ; No error
SEEK_EXIT:
        POP     DX              ; Restore register
        POP     CX
        RET
;
SEEK_COMMAND            ENDP


;********************************
;       perform READ command
;********************************
READ_COMMAND           PROC    NEAR
; Read diskette data from one or more sectors in a diskette track
; On entry:
;               DH = drive number
;               DL = track number (cylinder)
;               CH = head number (0 or 1)
;               CL = starting sector number
;
; Note: The number of sectors read by this procedure is
; determined by the DMA setup
```

```
;
;
; Set bit 2 of the second command byte (in DH) if head number 1
        CMP     CH0             ; No action if head number 0
        JE      HEAD_OK0        ; Leave DH bit 2 clear
        OR      DH,00000100B    ; Set bit 2
HEAD_OK0:
;********************
;   send command
;********************
; 0
        MOV     AH,66H          ; = 01100110 for first code
        CALL    OUTPUT_NEC
; 1
        MOV     AH,DH           ; Second command byte
        CALL    OUTPUT_NEC
; 2
        MOV     AH,DL           ; Track number
        CALL    OUTPUT_NEC
; 3
        MOV     AH,CH           ; Head number (0 or 1)
        CALL    OUTPUT_NEC
; 4
        MOV     AH,CL           ; Starting sector number
        CALL    OUTPUT_NEC
; Follow four technical parameters obtained from diskette table
; 5
        MOV     AL,3            ; Offset 3 is bytes per sector
        CALL    FETCH_PARAM     ; Get from table
        MOV     AH,AL           ; Move to AH
        CALL    OUTPUT_NEC
; 6
        MOV     AL,4            ; Offset 4 is end of track
        CALL    FETCH_PARAM     ; Get from table
        MOV     AH,AL           ; Move to AH
        CALL    OUTPUT_NEC
; 7
        MOV     AL,5            ; Offset 5 is gap length
        CALL    FETCH_PARAM     ; Get from table
        MOV     AH,AL           ; Move to AH
        CALL    OUTPUT_NEC
; 8
        MOV     AL,6            ; Offset 6 is data length
        CALL    FETCH_PARAM     ; Get from table
        MOV     AH,AL           ; Move to AH
        CALL    OUTPUT_NEC
        RET
READ_COMMAND            ENDP
```

```
;*******************************
;       get command results
;*******************************
COM_RESULT PROC  NEAR
; Read 7 bytes of command results into the caller's buffer
; On entry:
;          DS:DI --> 7-byte caller's buffer
;
; Make sure previous command has concluded the execution phase
          CALL   WAIT_FOR_INT6
          JNC    INPUT_RDY    ; Continue if interrupt
          RET                 ; Carry set to signal error
INPUT_RDY:
          MOV    BL,7         ; Maximum bytes to read
;******************
;    read 7 bytes
;******************
INPUT_7:
          CALL   INPUT_NEC    ; Call read FDC primitive
          JNC    OK_READ      ; No error
BAD_RESULT:
          STC                 ; Error flag
          RET                 ; Exit
OK_READ:
          MOV    [DI],AL      ; Place byte in buffer
          INC    DI           ; Bump buffer pointer
;
;******************
;    delay
;******************
          MOV    CX,20        ; Load delay count
DELAY_20:
          LOOP   DELAY_20     ; Kill time to wait for FDC
;******************
;   test for BUSY
;******************
          MOV    DX,03F4H     ; FDC main status register
          IN     AL,DX        ; Get status
          TEST   AL,00010000B ; Bit 4 is FDC busy
          JZ     EXIT_RESULT  ; FDC finished
          DEC    BL           ; Counter for 7 bytes cannot
                              ; go to zero
          JNZ    INPUT_7
          JMP    BAD_RESULT   ; Error exit
;******************
;       exit
;******************
```

```
EXIT_RESULT:
        CLC                 ; No error returned
        RET
COM_RESULT  ENDP
```

8.5.4 Developing Diskette System Software

The driver routines in Section 8.5.3 are of a higher level than the primitive routines in Section 8.5.2. However, both primitives and drivers should be considered the building blocks of diskette operation software. For example, the code to read or write a diskette track requires the following steps:

1. Turn the diskette motor on.
2. Perform a seek operation to the track to be read or written.
3. Set up the DMA controller to the destination buffer for the read or write operation and for the number of bytes in the transfer.
4. Perform the read or write command.
5. Store the command results and examine the data for operation errors. Bits 6 and 7 of the status register 0 will be clear if the command is executed correctly (see Figure 8.5). Take the necessary action if error conditions are detected.
6. Turn the diskette motor off.

The following code fragment illustrates the use of the primitives and drivers listed in Sections 8.5.2 and 8.5.3 in performing a diskette read for diskette head number 0, track number 1, and sector number 1, in drive A.

```
DATA   SEGMENT
; Binary data for diskette side, track, and sector
HEAD            DB      0
TRACK           DB      1
SECTOR          DB      1

;*******************
;       buffers
;*******************
DIRECT_512      DB      512 DUP ('?')
                DB      0FFH
;
RESULTS_BUF DB          7 DUP (00H)
                DB      0FFH
;
DATA   ENDS
        .
        .
        .

CODE  SEGMENT
```

```
        ASSUME        CS:CODE
        .
        .
        .
; 1. Motor ON
        MOV   AL,0              ; Drive A
        CALL  MOTOR_ON
;
; 2. SEEK
        MOV   DH,0              ; Drive A
        MOV   DL,TRACK          ; Track number to SEEK
        MOV   CH,HEAD           ; Head number
        CALL  SEEK_COMMAND
; The code can examine the carry flag to detect possible
; errors returned by the SEEK_COMMAND procedure
;
; 3. Set up DMA
        MOV   AL,0              ; DMA read operation
        LEA   SI,DIRECT_512     ; Destination buffer for data
        MOV   DI,512            ; Bytes to read
        CALL  DISKETTE_DMA
;
; 4. READ
        MOV   DH,0              ; Drive A
        MOV   DL,TRACK          ; Track number to read
        MOV   CH,HEAD           ; Head number
        MOV   CL,SECTOR         ; Starting sector
        CALL  READ_COMMAND
;
; 5. Results
        LEA   DI,RESULTS_BUF           ; Destination buffer for results
        CALL  COM_RESULT
;
; After the result bytes are read, the code can examine bits 6
; and 7 of the first result byte (status register 0) to check
; for normal command termination.
;
 6. Motor OFF
        CALL  MOTOR_OFF
;
; At this point the buffer named DIRECT_512 will contain 512
; bytes of data read from diskette drive A, head 0, track 1,
; sector 1, if the FDC and DMA operations executed successfully.
        .
        .
        .
```

8.6 Hard Disk Storage

The hard disk system is a direct access, magnetic storage device with nonremovable media. The hard disk device differs from a diskette drive in the following ways:

1. The hard disk drive uses several magnetically coated, metal disks as recording media, instead of the individual, plastic media used by diskette systems. The individual disks are usually called *platters* in hard disk systems.

2. The metal disks of a hard disk form part of the drive mechanism and, normally, are not removable from the drive.

3. The drive motor in a hard disk rotates constantly, while the diskette drive motor is turned on prior to every data access operation and off after the data has been read or written.

4. Most hard disk drives are formatted by the manufacturer.

The advantages and disadvantages of hard disks over diskette systems are a direct result of their different structures. One substantial advantage of diskette storage is that the recording media can be easily moved to other compatible devices and machines, which provides a convenient method of data exchange. On the other hand, the metal-based, nonremovable, media used in hard disk drives allow a design in which the platters rotate constantly and at a higher rate than is possible in diskette mechanisms. This, in turn, makes possible more compact magnetic storage patterns, higher data transfer speeds, as well as faster access times.

The differences between hard disks and diskette systems can be summarized by stating that hard disk drives offer better performance than diskette systems at the price of lesser portability of the stored data. The typical performance improvement of hard disks over diskette drives is in the ratio of 10:1. An additional mechanical advantage of hard disk over diskette systems is that the recording heads of a hard disk drive do not touch the magnetic surface of the platters.

Hard disk drives are usually called *fixed disk drives* in IBM literature. The term *Winchester drive* refers to an external hard disk drive. The original version of the Winchester drive was equipped with 8-in-diameter platters. The word "Winchester" probably originated in the fact that the device had two 30-Mbyte platters, reminiscent of the Winchester 30-30 rifle.

8.7 Hard Disk Hardware

A hard disk drive was offered as an option for the first time with the introduction of the Personal Computer XT. But not all models of the IBM microcomputers that followed the XT can support the hard disk option. For example, the PC Portable, the PCjr, and the PC Convertible cannot normally be equipped with an internal hard disk drive. Nevertheless, third-party manufacturers have offered internal and external hard disk options for some of these models.

Non-IBM sources have proliferated in the hard disk market. Companies like Seagate (formerly Shugart), Computer Memories Incorporated (CMI), and Tandon Corporation have gained considerable popular favor in this field. Alternative options for the conventional hard disk drive are external drives, drives mounted on adapter cards, and platterless drives with battery-operated RAM memories.

The discussion of hard disk hardware in the following sections refers exclusively to the devices offered by IBM. Due to its specialized character, and to considerable variations in the hardware, the programming of hard disk drives and controllers is not considered in this book.

8.7.1 The XT 10-Mbyte Fixed Disk

The 10-Mbyte Fixed Disk Drive and its adapter card, the Fixed Disk Adapter, was the first microcomputer hard disk system offered by IBM. The drive uses two nonremovable, 5¼-in metal disks. The entire mechanism is sealed in a dustproof enclosure in which the rotating platters serve as an air turbine to force circulation through a scrubbing filter. Table 8.24 shows the formatted capacity of the hard drive. Table 8.25 lists the technical specifications.

Table 8.24. *Storage Format of the IBM 10-Mbyte Fixed Disk Drive (Personal Computer XT)*

PLATTERS	HEADS	CYLINDERS PER SIDE	SECTORS PER CYLINDER	BYTES PER SECTOR	TOTAL BYTES
2	4	306	17	512	10,653,696

Table 8.25. *Technical Specifications of the IBM 10-Mbyte Fixed Disk Drive (Personal Computer XT)*

RPM	TRACK DENSITY, tracks/in	ACCESS TIME, ms	AVERAGE LATENCY, ms	DESIGN LIFE, h	TRANSFER RATE, bits/s	RECORDING MODE
3600	345	85*	8.33	8000	5M	MFM

* Average time for heads to move from one to another cylinder, including the head settling time before a read operation.

The 10-Mbyte Fixed Disk Drive requires an adapter card that fits into one of the system slots. The drive and the adapter are connected through a ribbon cable. The Fixed Disk Adapter can drive one or two 10-Mbyte Fixed Disk Drives. The adapter contains a ROM module that provides a low-level programming interface with the hard disk drive. These services are accessed through BIOS INT 13H (see Chapter 9).

8.7.2 The AT 20-Mbyte Hard Disk

The IBM PC AT was marketed in two versions, one of them equipped with a 20-Mbyte hard disk drive. However, the Fixed Disk and Diskette Adapter are standard equipment in both versions. Therefore, updating an AT not furnished with a hard drive requires only adding the drive mechanism and performing the necessary initialization routines.

The 20-Mbyte Fixed Disk Drive uses two nonremovable, 5¼-in metal disks. As in the 10-Mbyte XT drive, the drive mechanism is sealed in a dustproof enclosure. The higher capacity of the AT drive is the result of a greater track density. Table 8.26 shows the formatted capacity of the AT 20-Mbyte hard drive. Table 8.27 lists the technical specifications.

Table 8.26. *Storage Format of the IBM 20-Mbyte Fixed Disk Drive (Personal Computer AT)*

PLATTERS	HEADS	CYLINDERS PER SIDE	SECTORS PER CYLINDER	BYTES PER SECTOR	TOTAL BYTES
2	4	615	17	512	21,411,840

Table 8.27. *Technical Specifications of the IBM 20-Mbyte Fixed Disk Drive (Personal Computer AT)*

RPM	TRACK DENSITY, tracks/in	ACCESS TIME, ms	AVERAGE LATENCY, ms	DESIGN LIFE, h	TRANSFER RATE, bits/s	RECORDING MODE
3573	750	45*	8.4	na	5M	MFM

* Average time for heads to move from one to another cylinder, including the head settling time before a read operation.

The Fixed Disk and Diskette Drive Adapter is required for the operation of the 20-Mbyte Fixed Disk Drive. The Fixed Disk Drive Adapter and the 10-Mbyte Fixed Disk Drive used in the PC XT are not compatible with the AT. The Fixed Disk and Diskette Drive Adapter must be installed in one of the six 62- or 36-pin slots of the AT input/output channel.

The hard disk functions of the adapter support up to two fixed disks, with up to 16 recording heads and 1024 cylinders per side. In the PC AT, the hard disk services are part of system BIOS. These services are described in Chapter 9.

Table 8.28. *Hard Disk Drives for the PS/2 Line*

MACHINE MODEL	FURNISHED	CAPACITY Mbytes	COMMENTS
25	Optional	20	With integral or separate adapter card
30-021	Standard	20	80 ms, ST 506 controller
50-021	Standard	20	80 ms, ST 506 controller
	Optional	60	27 ms, ST 506 controller
50-031	Standard	30	39 ms, ST 506 controller
	Optional	60	
50-061	Standard	60	
50Z-131	Standard	30	39 ms, ST 506 controller
50Z-061	Standard	60	27ms, ESDI controller
60-041	Standard	44	33 ms, ST 506 controller
60-071	Standard	70	30 ms, ESDI controller
	Optional	115	28 ms, ESDI controller
70-E61	Standard	60	27 ms, ESDI controller
70-121		120	23 ms, ESDI controller
70-A21		120	
P70-061	Standard	60	27 ms, ESDI controller
P70-121	Standard	120	23 ms, ESDI controller
80-041	Standard	44	40 ms, ST 506 controller
80-071	Standard	70	30 ms, ESDI controller
	Optional	115	28 ms, ESDI controller
	Optional	314	23 ms, ESDI controller
80-111	Standard	115	
	Optional	314	
80-311		314	

8.7.3 PS/2 Hard Disk Systems

All models of the PS/2 line support hard disk storage devices. The drives range from 20- to 314-Mbyte capacity and from 80 to 23 ms average access time. Table 8.28 lists the basic characteristics of the hard disk drives available for each PS/2 system.

There are major differences in the form of implementation of the hard disk hardware in PS/2 systems. For example, the optional hard disk drive for Model 25 can be purchased with an integral or a separate adapter card. Model 30 is equipped with a dedicated slot for the installation of the hard disk and controller, while the system board contains the interface circuits. In Models 50, 60, and 80 the hard disk plugs into its controller card plugs, which, in turn, plug into a Micro Channel slot, while in Model 70 the controller is integrated with the drive. Table 8.29 lists the parameters of some hard disks of the PS/2 line.

Table 8.29. *Storage Format and Technical Specifications for Several Hard Disk Systems for the PS/2 Line*

CAPACITY Mbytes	NO. OF HEADS	CYLINDERS PER SIDE	SECTORS	BYTES PER SECTOR	ACCESS TIME	USED IN
20	4	612	17	512	80 ms	Model 30 Model 50
44	7	733	17	512	33 ms	Model 60 Model 80
70	7	583	36	512	30 ms	Model 60 Model 80
115	7	915	36	512	28 ms	Model 60 Model 80

Two forms of interface are used in IBM microcomputer hard disk systems. The traditional standard is called Modified Frequency Modulation (MFM), or ST-506. A newer standard, named the Enhance Small Device Interface (ESDI) is used by IBM in 60-Mbyte and larger drives (see Table 8.28). The services in the IBM BIOS support 32 types of hard disk drives of different configurations and parameters, as listed in Table 8.30.

Table 8.30. *IBM Hard Disk Types and Parameters*

TYPE NO.	NO. OF HEADS	CYLINDER PER SIDE	PRECOMPENSATION DURING WRITE	LANDING ZONE	DEFECT MAP
0	No hard disk drive installed				
1	4	306	128	305	No
2	4	615	300	615	No
3	6	615	300	615	No
4	8	940	512	940	No
5	6	940	512	940	No
6	4	615	None	615	No
7	8	462	256	511	No
8	5	733	None	733	No
9	15	900	None	901	No
10	3	820	None	820	No
11	5	855	None	855	No
12	7	855	None	855	No
13	8	306	128	319	No

(continued)

Table 8.30. *IBM Hard Disk Types and Parameters (Continued)*

TYPE NO.	NO. OF HEADS	CYLINDER PER SIDE	PRECOMPENSATION DURING WRITE	LANDING ZONE	DEFECT MAP
14	7	733	None	733	No
15			R E S E R V E D		
16	4	612	All cylinders	633	No
17	5	977	300	977	No
18	7	977	None	977	No
19	7	1024	512	1023	No
20	5	733	300	732	No
21	7	733	300	732	No
22	5	733	300	733	No
23	4	306	All cylinders	336	No
24	4	612	305	663	No
25	4	306	None	340	No
26	4	612	None	670	No
27	7	698	300	732	Yes
28	5	976	488	977	Yes
29	4	306	All cylinders	340	No
30	4	611	306	663	Yes
31	7	732	300	732	Yes
32	5	1023	None	1023	Yes
33 to 255			R E S E R V E D		

Notes:
Types 0 to 14 are supported by the original PC AT.
Types 0 to 23 are supported by the AT BIOS dated 6-10-85 or later.
Types 0 to 24 are supported by the PC XT Model 286.
Types 0 to 26 are supported by PS/2 Models 25 and 30.
Types 0 to 32 are supported by PS/2 Micro Channel systems.

8.7.4 Hard Disk Parameters

Some configurations of the IBM microcomputers store the parameters for the hard disk drive in accessible memory areas or in a reserved area of the drive itself. Tables 8.31 and 8.32 list two hard disk parameter areas documented by IBM.

Table 8.31. *Fixed Disk Drive Parameter Table for PS/2 Micro Channel Systems*

OFFSET	DATA SIZE	VALUE	CONTENTS
0	Word	41	Length of this table
2	Area		String of 22 ASCII characters: "IBM HARDFILE TYPE xxx"
24	Byte		Type code
25	Word		Maximum number of cylinders
27	Byte		Maximum number of heads
28	Word	0000H	Reserved
30	Word		Cylinder to start write precompensation
32	Byte	00H	Reserved
33	Byte		Control byte: 7 6 5 4 3 2 1 0 bits — More than 8 heads (PC AT only) — Defect map installed — Disable retries
34	Area		3 bytes Reserved
37	Word		Landing zone
39	Byte		Sectors per track
40	Byte		Reserved

Note: This table is located at head 0, track 0, sector 2.

Table 8.32. *PC XT Fixed Disk Drive Parameter Table*

OFFSET	DATA SIZE	BIOS DATE	VALUES	CONTENTS
0	Word	11/10/82	306 375	Maximum number of cylinders
		01/08/86	306 612 615	
2	Byte	11/10/82	2 8 6 4	Maximum number of heads
		01/08/86	4 8	
3	Word	11/10/82	306 375 128	Current cylinder number to start reduced write
		01/08/86	306 612 615	
5	Word	11/10/82	000 256	Cylinder to start write precompensation
		01/08/86	000 300 128	
7	Byte		0BH	Maximum ECC burst data length
8	Byte	11/10/82	00 05	Control byte
		01/08/86	05	
9	Byte	11/10/82 01/08/86	0CH 0CH 20H 18H	Standard time-out
10	Byte		0B4H	Time-out for format operation
11	Byte		28H	Time-out for check drive
12	Area		00H	4 bytes Reserved

Note: The address of this table is stored at the vector for Interrupt 41H.

9

The IBM BIOS

9.0 The Basic Input/Output System

The basic input/output system, or BIOS, is a system program designed to provide the following functions:

1. Start up the computer when the power is turned on. This function is often called *booting*, from the image of a machine lifting itself up by its bootstraps.

2. Test the microprocessor, memory, and fundamental hardware components for satisfactory operation. The portion of the BIOS that performs this operation is called the *Power-on Self-Test*, or POST.

3. Store critical system data in dedicated memory areas that can be accessed by programs. The locations of these special areas have remained unchanged in the different lines and models of IBM microcomputers.

4. Provide an interface with the system hardware in the form of services that can be accessed through software interrupts.

5. Provide users and programmers with information regarding the memory size as well as the installed options and other hardware configuration parameters. Also provide them with the services to print the screen, to time external events, and to report the current values in the time and date counters.

The BIOS program is contained in one or more ROM chips located on the motherboard. Supplementary BIOS chips can also be found in some IBM and third-party adapter cards. The initialization routines in the BIOS POST provide the means for installing additional system-level drivers. This function allows the designers of hardware devices intended for the IBM microcomputers with the alternative of replacing or complementing the original BIOS services. The option of having customized routines that become part of the system's software core has been described as an *open architecture*.

IBM published listings of the BIOS code up to the introduction of the PS/2 line. These listings are found in the IBM Technical Reference Manual for each machine model of the PC line and for the adapters equipped with ROM BIOS chips (see Bibliography). Other companies have developed programs similar to the IBM BIOS; for example, Phoenix Technologies furnishes a BIOS that has been used in many IBM-compatible machines.

9.0.1 BIOS Versions

Since the release of the original IBM Personal Computer, with BIOS dated April 24, 1981, IBM has made numerous changes in the BIOS code. In the first place, each new machine model has been equipped with its particular version of BIOS adapted to the characteristics of the hardware. In addition, the BIOS in some specific machines has been subject to one or more updates. Table 9.1 lists BIOS versions and updates.

Table 9.1. *Versions of IBM BIOS*

LINE	MACHINE	MODEL CODE	SUBMODEL CODE	BIOS DATE	REVISION
PC	Personal Computer	FFH	-- -- --	04/24/81 10/19/81 10/27/82	-- -- --
	PC XT	FEH FBH	-- 00 00	11/08/82 01/10/86 05/09/86	-- 01 02
	PCjr	FDH	--	05/01/83	--
	PC AT	FCH	-- 00 01	01/10/84 06/10/85 11/15/85	-- 01 00
	PC XT Model 286	FCH	02	04/21/86	00
	PC Convertible	F9H	00	09/13/85	00
PS/2	Model 25	FAH	01	06/27/87	00
	Model 30	FAH	00	09/02/86	00
	Model 50	FCH	04	02/13/87	00
	Model 60	FCH	05	02/13/87	00
	Model 70 –Type 1 Type 2 Type 3	F8H	09 04 0D	04/11/88	00
	Model 80	F8H	01	10/07/87	00

The machine's model code (see Table 9.1) is stored at BIOS logical address F000:FFFEH. The submodel code is obtained using service number 192 of interrupt 15H (INT 15H) as seen in Tables 9.34 and 9-35). The BIOS date is stored in 8 bytes starting at address F000:FFF5H. The following code fragment shows how to obtain and display the BIOS date.

```
; Display 8 characters of BIOS release date stored at F000:FFF5
        MOV    AX,0F000H     ; Segment address for BIOS
                             ; date storage area
        MOV    ES,AX         ; To ES
        MOV    SI,0FFF5H      ; Offset of BIOS date
        MOV    CX,8          ; Counter for 8 characters
DISPLAY_8:
        MOV    AL,ES:[SI]     ; Get character
        PUSH   SI            ; Save pointer
        PUSH   CX            ; And counter
        MOV    AH,14         ; BIOS teletype service
        MOV    BX,0          ; Using page zero
        INT    10H           ; BIOS video service
        POP    CX            ; Restore counter
        POP    SI            ; and pointer
        INC    SI            ; Bump pointer
        LOOP   DISPLAY_8     ; Display 8 characters
```

9.0.2 The IBM ABIOS

The BIOS in the IBM microcomputers is designed to operate in the 8086/8088 environment or in the real mode of the 80286 and 80386 chips. This BIOS does not contain multitasking provisions, nor services for executing in protected mode or for managing memory above 1 Mbyte. To correct this problem, PS/2 machines that support multitasking in protected mode are equipped with an advanced version of BIOS designated as ABIOS. In this case the conventional BIOS is sometimes called the Compatibility BIOS, or CBIOS.

ABIOS services can be useful only to operating system programs running in PS/2 Micro Channel machines. Instead of ABIOS, other multitasking software use the more powerful, portable, and versatile services provided by the operating system itself. In the case of the OS/2 operating system these services are generically known as the *Application Programming Interface*, or API. Due to this limited application, ABIOS services and programming are not discussed in this book.

9.1 Additional ROM

The entry routines of the BIOS program serve to test the microprocessor, the ROM and RAM chips, to check for stuck keyboard keys, and to examine and initialize various critical hardware components in the system. This portion of the BIOS code is usually called the Power-on Self-Test, or POST.

The microprocessors of the Intel 80x86 family used in the IBM microcomputers, the 8086, 8088, 80286, and 80386, power up by executing the instruction located 15 bytes from the highest memory address. In the 8086/8088 this address is FFFF0H, in the 80286 it is FFFFF0H, and in the 80386 the address is FFFFFF0H. System initialization is automatically accomplished by placing, at this address, a jump to the first instruction of the BIOS, which is the start of the POST. Therefore, it is possible to create a customized BIOS by replacing the original chip or chips with others (typically EPROMs) containing a jump or call to the replacement initialization code.

9.1.1 Adapter ROM

As soon as the POST has established hardware reliability, the code initializes the interrupt vector table with the segment and offset addresses of the various BIOS service routines and data tables. Once these default vectors are in place, the POST scans certain reserved memory addresses for the presence of ROM modules contained in adapter cards.

The memory designated as the start of adapter ROM extends for 64K starting at address C00000H. The first 32K of this area, from C0000H to C7FFFH, is reserved for modules that require initialization, for example, video adapter ROM. The area from C8000H to DFFFFH is reserved for conventional ROM modules contained in adapter cards.

In either case, scanning for adapter ROM proceeds in 2K increments from the start address. This means that for conventional ROM modules, in the range C8000H to DFFFFH, there are 15 possible start locations. At these locations a valid adapter ROM module must have a specific signature recognized by the POST. The encoding must be as follows:

1. *Offset 0*. This byte must be 55H.

2. *Offset 1*. This byte must be AAH.

3. *Offset 2*. This byte is an indicator of the length of the ROM module, measured in 512-byte blocks. For example, the value 8 indicates that the module length is 4096 bytes (512 * 8 = 4096). The maximum number of 512-byte blocks allowed is 127, which means that the module code can extend 65,024 bytes.

4. *Offset 3*. The module's executable code starts at this offset. The *POST* transfers control to the module's ROM by executing a far call to this address. The adapter should return control to the POST by performing a far return instruction.

Table 9.2. *ROM Parameters for Some IBM Adapters*

ADAPTER NAME	ROM LENGTH	START ADDRESS
Enhanced Graphics Adapter	16K	C0000H
Fixed Disk Adapter	8K	C8000H
Cluster Adapter	32K	D0000H

The POST performs a checksum of all bytes in the ROM module to check its integrity. The two low-order bytes of the checksum must be 00H; if not, the module is tagged as invalid and control is not transferred.

No provisions have been made in the POST for identifying modules with conflicting addresses. The length and location of the ROM code in some IBM adapters have been documented. Table 9.2 lists these parameters for three popular adapters. However, there is always a possibility of installing two or more adapters with conflicting ROMs.

Upon receiving control, the adapter ROM performs the required initialization operations. These can include testing the functionality of one or more devices, updating the BIOS tables and control areas to reflect the new status, installing new interrupt handlers, and replacing or intercepting interrupts already installed. Although the typical handler returns control to the BIOS after performing this initialization, it is also possible for the adapter ROM code to seize control of the system at this time.

9.1.2 System Board Expansion ROM

The system board in the IBM Personal Computer contains an empty socket for a 64K ROM chip. This socket, labeled U28, can be used to install up to 64K of additional ROM, sometimes called *expansion ROM*. The ROM installed in the spare socket must be formatted as for an adapter ROM module (see Section 9.2.1). In PC systems, the POST tests for expansion ROM extend from C8000H to F4000H, in 2K increments. The ROM chip in the spare socket is mapped to address F4000H.

No empty ROM socket is provided in the PC XT, but the PC AT system board contains two empty sockets, labeled U17 and U37, respectively, which can be used to install additional system ROM. The PC AT POST code checks addresses E0000H and EFFFFH for a valid signature. The signature code for a valid system board's additional ROM is identical to that of an adapter ROM module described in Section 9.1.1. Because the length byte is not used in the additional ROM encoding, the signature code (55FFH) is usually followed by an empty byte. As in the adapter ROM modules, executable code starts at offset 3 of the additional ROM chip.

9.1.3 The PCjr Cartridge ROM

The concept of expansion ROM was taken one step further in the design of the IBM PCjr. This microcomputer is equipped with two external slots in which the user can insert a ROM cartridge without removing the machine's cover. Each cartridge can hold up to 64K. PCjr ROM cartridges are mapped starting at address D0000H, at 32K intervals. Addresses F0000H and F8000H are reserved for cartridges that replace the system ROM. The cartridge ROM must be formatted as follows:

1. *Offset 0.* This byte must be 55H.
2. *Offset 1.* This byte must be AAH.
3. *Offset 2.* This byte is an indicator of the length of the ROM in the cartridge, measured in 512-byte blocks. For example, the value 8 indicates that the module length is 4096 bytes (512 * 8 = 4096).
4. *Offset 3, 4, and 5.* The 3 bytes starting at offset 3 can contain a jump to the module's executable code. If no initialization is required, this area can contain, instead, a far return instruction. The jump instruction is used if the cartridge ROM must initialize hardware devices or if it retains execution. The reason for requiring this jump is that the byte at offset 6 must be null.
5. *Offset 6.* This byte must be 00H.
6. *Offset 7 to end-of-cartridge.* This area contains the executable code.
7. *End-of-cartridge.* The two last bytes in the cartridge ROM are reserved for the cycle redundancy check performed by the POST. Their value is adjusted during cartridge manufacture to ensure a zero checksum.

9.2 The Interrupt Vector Table

The interrupt system and its hardware components are discussed in Section 3.2.2. However, the operation of an interrupt system also requires a table of addresses for the various enabled hardware, software, and internal interrupts. In systems using the Intel microprocessors of the iAPX 86 family, as is the case in the IBM microcomputers, this table of addresses must be located in the first 1K of the memory space, which extends from 00000H to 00400H.

The interrupt vector table is initialized during the BIOS POST. As the POST executes its hardware reliability tests, it stores in the vector table the addresses of the corresponding service routines implemented in the BIOS. Table 3-10 lists the interrupt codes and purpose of most of IBM interrupt·service routines. The actual addresses of the service routines are different in the various versions of BIOS.

This table of addresses, usually called the *interrupt vector table*, requires two words for each entry: the low-order word holds the offset of the service routine, and the high order word holds the segment base. Because there are 256 possible interrupt handlers, the table extends 1024 bytes, or 1K (256 * 4 = 1024). The offset of each vector can be obtained by multiplying the interrupt type times four. For example, the vector for the print screen interrupt, which is type 05H, is located at offset 14H in the vector table, because 05H * 04H = 14H.

The programmer can replace an interrupt service routine with a new one by inserting the address of the new routine in the corresponding position in the vector table. The following code fragment shows the necessary steps for inserting the address of a handler corresponding to interrupt type 60H:

```
; Take over INT 60H by inserting the offset and segment address
; of the service routine in the interrupt vector table
        MOV    AX,0000H        ; Start of interrupt vector table
        MOV    ES,AX           ; To ES via AX
        MOV    DI,180H         ; Pointer to the offset of
                               ; INT 60H (60H * 4H = 180H)
        MOV    AX,OFFSET HEX60_INT ; Offset of service routine
        MOV    ES:[DI],AX      ; to vector table
        INC    DI              ; Bump pointer to next position
        INC    DI              ; in the vector table
        MOV    AX,SEG HEX60_INT      ; Segment of service routine
        MOV    ES:[DI],AX      ; to vector table
        .
        .
        .
;******************************************************************
;             INT 60H service routine
;******************************************************************
;
HEX60_INT:
        .
        .
```

Programs often need to intercept an existing interrupt handler in order to perform an operation or a test, and later return execution to the original service routine. In this case the code must retrieve the address of the original routine from the vector table before installing its own intercept. The original address can be moved to the program's own space, and execution can be transferred to the original handler using a far jump instruction. The following code fragment shows one way to perform these operations:

```
;**********************
; retrieve old vector
;**********************
;
; Set ES:DI to the offset of INT 08H in the vector table
        MOV    AX,0000H        ; Start of interrupt vector table
        MOV    ES,AX           ; To ES via AX
        MOV    DI,20H          ; Pointer to the offset of
                               ; INT 08H (08H * 4H = 20H)
        MOV    AX,ES:[DI]      ; Offset into AX
        INC    DI              ; Bump pointer to next position
        INC    DI              ; in the vector table
        MOV    BX,ES:[DI]      ; Segment into BX
```

```
;********************
;  save old vector
;   in memory
;********************
; BX --> Segment address of installed interrupt handler
; AX --> Offset address of installed interrupt handler
; OLD_VECTOR_08 is a doubleword in the program's code segment
        MOV    SI,OFFSET CS:OLD_VECTOR_08
        MOV    CS:[SI],AX        ; Save offset of original handler
        MOV    CS:[SI+2],BX   ; and segment
; OLD_VECTOR_08 now holds the address of original service
; routine. The code can now proceed to install the address of
; its own service routine in the vector table, as shown in the
; previous code sample.
        .
        .
; The new interrupt handler can transfer execution to the
; original handler using the following code:
        STC                                ; Continue processing
        JMP    DWORD PTR CS:OLD_VECTOR_08
        .
        .
;
;*********************************************
;         code segment data
;*********************************************
OLD_VECTOR_08       DD     0      ; Pointer to original INT 08H
                                  ; interrupt service routine
```

Programmers working the DOS environment can also use service numbers 53 and 37 of INT 21H for this purpose. Service number 53 allows obtaining, from the vector table, the address of an installed service routine while service number 37 is used to install the address of a new routine in the table. These services, in addition to being convenient, keep DOS informed of changes in the interrupt system.

9.3 BIOS Data Areas

The BIOS reserves certain memory areas for storing hardware parameters, addresses, and other system information. Functions and services in BIOS and adapter ROM often use this area for variables and for status data. System programs and applications can access this data to read the stored parameters and, sometimes, to update or modify these values. The following sections contain tables showing the contents of these special BIOS areas.

9.3.1 Communications and Printer Data

Table 9.3. *Serial Ports Data in BIOS*

LOGICAL ADDRESS	DATA SIZE	CONTENTS
0040:0000	Word	Base address of serial port 1 (COM1)
0040:0002	Word	Base address of serial port 2 (COM2)
0040:0004	Word	Base address of serial port 3 (COM3)
0040:0006	Word	Base address of serial port 4 (COM4)

Note: Nonexisting ports are initialized to zero. No valid port can appear in the table after a zero value.

Table 9.4. *Parallel Ports Data in BIOS*

LOGICAL ADDRESS	DATA SIZE	CONTENTS
0040:0008	Word	Base address of parallel port 1 (LPT1)
0040:000A	Word	Base address of parallel port 2 (LPT2)
0040:000C	Word	Base address of parallel port 3 (LPT3)
0040:000E	Word	PC line: Base address of parallel port 4 (LPT4) PS/2 line: Reserved

Note: Nonexisting ports are initialized to zero. No valid port can appear in the table after a zero value.

9.3.2 Optional System Equipment Data

Table 9.5. *Optional Equipment Data in BIOS*

LOGICAL ADDRESS	DATA SIZE	CONTENTS
0040:0010	Word	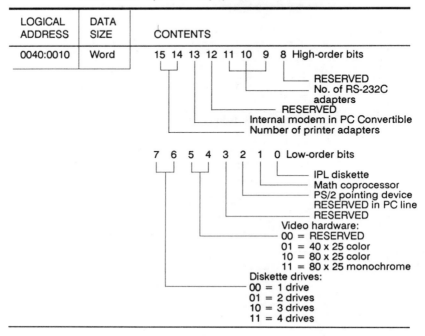

Table 9.6. *Miscellaneous Data Area in BIOS*

LOGICAL ADDRESS	DATA SIZE	CONTENTS
0040:0012	Byte	PC Convertible: Power-on Self Test status All others: RESERVED

9.3.3 Memory Size Data

Table 9.7. *Memory Size Data Area in BIOS*

LOGICAL ADDRESS	DATA SIZE	CONTENTS
0040:0013	Word	K of memory installed (range 0 to 640)
0040:0015	Word	RESERVED

9.3.4 Keyboard Data

Table 9.8. *Keyboard Data Area 1 in BIOS*

LOGICAL ADDRESS	DATA SIZE	CONTENTS
0040:0017	Byte	7 6 5 4 3 2 1 0 bits └ Right shift pressed └ Left shift pressed └ Ctrl key pressed └ Alt key pressed └ Scroll Lock locked └ Num Lock locked └ Caps Lock locked └ Insert ON
0040:0018	Byte	7 6 5 4 3 2 1 0 bits └ Left Ctrl pressed └ Left Alt pressed └ Sys Req key pressed └ Pause locked └ Scroll Lock key pressed └ Num Lock key pressed └ Caps Lock key pressed └ Ins key pressed
0040:0019	Byte	Alternate keypad entry
0040:001A	Word	Keyboard buffer head pointer
0040:001C	Word	Keyboard buffer tail pointer
0040:001E	Area	32-byte keyboard buffer

9.3.5 Diskette Data

Table 9.9. *Diskette Data in BIOS*

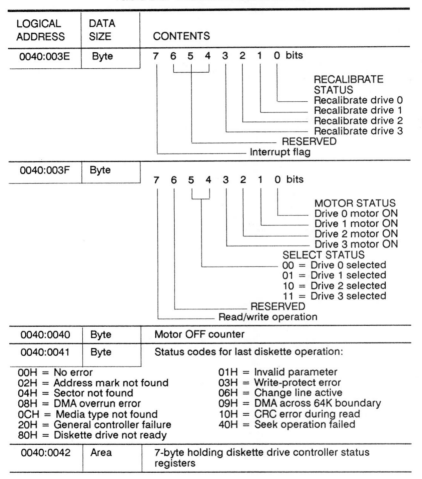

LOGICAL ADDRESS	DATA SIZE	CONTENTS
0040:003E	Byte	7 6 5 4 3 2 1 0 bits RECALIBRATE STATUS Recalibrate drive 0 Recalibrate drive 1 Recalibrate drive 2 Recalibrate drive 3 RESERVED Interrupt flag
0040:003F	Byte	7 6 5 4 3 2 1 0 bits MOTOR STATUS Drive 0 motor ON Drive 1 motor ON Drive 2 motor ON Drive 3 motor ON SELECT STATUS 00 = Drive 0 selected 01 = Drive 1 selected 10 = Drive 2 selected 11 = Drive 3 selected RESERVED Read/write operation
0040:0040	Byte	Motor OFF counter
0040:0041	Byte	Status codes for last diskette operation: 00H = No error 01H = Invalid parameter 02H = Address mark not found 03H = Write-protect error 04H = Sector not found 06H = Change line active 08H = DMA overrun error 09H = DMA across 64K boundary 0CH = Media type not found 10H = CRC error during read 20H = General controller failure 40H = Seek operation failed 80H = Diskette drive not ready
0040:0042	Area	7-byte holding diskette drive controller status registers

9.3.6 Video Data

Table 9.10. *Video Display Data Area 1 in BIOS*

LOGICAL ADDRESS	DATA SIZE	CONTENTS
0040:0049	Byte	Active display mode
0040:004A	Word	Number of display columns
0040:004C	Word	Length of video buffer (in bytes)
0040:004E	Word	Starting address in video buffer
0040:0050	Word	Cursor position in display page 1
0040:0052	Word	Cursor position in display page 2
0040:0054	Word	Cursor position in display page 3
0040:0056	Word	Cursor position in display page 4
0040:0058	Word	Cursor position in display page 5
0040:005A	Word	Cursor position in display page 6
0040:005C	Word	Cursor position in display page 7
0040:005E	Word	Cursor position in display page 8
0040:0060	Word	Cursor type
0040:0062	Byte	Number of active display page
0040:0063	Word	CRT controller base address
0040:0065	Byte	Current setting of register 3x8H
0040:0066	Byte	Current setting of register 3x9H

9.3.7 System and Timer Data

Table 9.11. *System Data Area 1 in BIOS*

LOGICAL ADDRESS	DATA SIZE	CONTENTS
0040:0067	Dword	PC line: RESERVED PS/2 Micro Channel: Entry point for system reset code (see Table 9.12)
0040:006B	Byte	RESERVED

Table 9.12. *System Timer Data in BIOS*

LOGICAL ADDRESS	DATA SIZE	CONTENTS
0040:006C	Dword	Timer counter
0040:0070	Byte	Timer overflow. If not zero, count has passed 24 h

Table 9.13. *System Data Area 2 in BIOS*

LOGICAL ADDRESS	DATA SIZE	CONTENTS
0040:0071	Byte	Break key state (not zero if key pressed)
0040:0072	Word	Reset flag code:

1234H	Bypass memory test	
4321H	PS/2 Micro Channel systems: preserve memory during reset	
5678H	PC Convertible: system suspended	
9ABCH	PC Convertible: manufacturing test mode	
ABCDH	PC Convertible: system POST loop mode	

9.3.8 Fixed Disk Data

Table 9.14. *Fixed Disk Data in BIOS*

LOGICAL ADDRESS	DATA SIZE	CONTENTS
0040:0074	Byte	Status codes for last fixed disk operation: (All systems except IBM ESDI Adapter/A)

00H = No error	01H = Invalid function request
02H = Address mark not found	03H = Write-protect error
04H = Sector not found	05H = Reset failed
07H = Drive activity failed	08H = DMA overrun in operation
09H = Data boundary error	0AH = Bad sector detected
0BH = Bad track detected	0DH = Invalid sector count (in format command)
0EH = Control data address mark	0FH = DMA arbitration level out of range
10H = ECC or CRC error	11H = ECC corrected data error
20H = General controller failure	40H = Seek operation failed
80H = Time-out error	AAH = Drive not ready
BBH = Undefined error	CCH = Write fault
E0H = Status register or error register is zero	
FFH = Sense operation failed	

LOGICAL ADDRESS	DATA SIZE	CONTENTS
0040:0074	Byte	IBM ESDI Adapter/A = RESERVED
0040:0075	Byte	Number of fixed disk drives
0040:0076	Byte	All systems except PC XT = RESERVED PC XT = Fixed disk drive control
0040:0077	Byte	All systems except PC XT = RESERVED PC XT = Fixed disk drive controller port

9.3.9 Supplementary Data

Table 9.15. *Printer Time-Out Data in BIOS*

LOGICAL ADDRESS	DATA SIZE	CONTENTS
0040:0078	Byte	Printer no. 1 time-out value
0040:0079	Byte	Printer no. 2 time-out value
0040:007A	Byte	Printer no. 3 time-out value
0040:007B	Byte	PC, XT, & AT = Printer no. 4 time-out value All others: RESERVED

Table 9.16. *Serial Port Time-Out Data in BIOS*

LOGICAL ADDRESS	DATA SIZE	CONTENTS
0040:007C	Byte	Serial port no. 1 time-out value
0040:007D	Byte	Serial port no. 2 time-out value
0040:007E	Byte	Serial port no. 3 time-out value
0040:007F	Byte	Serial port no. 4 time-out value

Table 9.17. *Keyboard Data Area 2 in BIOS*

LOGICAL ADDRESS	DATA SIZE	CONTENTS
0040:0080	Word	Keyboard buffer start pointer
0040:0082	Word	Keyboard buffer end pointer

Table 9.18. *Video Display Data Area 2 in BIOS*

LOGICAL ADDRESS	DATA SIZE	CONTENTS
0040:0084	Byte	Number of screen rows minus 1
0040:0085	Word	Character height (bytes per character)
0040:0087	Byte	Video control states
0040:0088	Byte	Video control states
0040:0089	Word	RESERVED

9.3.10 Diskette and Fixed Disk Control Area

Table 9.19. *Diskette and Fixed Disk Drives Control Area in BIOS*

LOGICAL ADDRESS	DATA SIZE	CONTENTS
0040:008B	Byte	7 6 5 4 3 2 1 0 bits —————— RESERVED —————— Last diskette step rate selected —————— Last diskette data rate selected 00 = 500K/s 01 = 300K/s 10 = 250K/s 11 = RESERVED
0040:008C	Byte	Fixed disk drive controller status
0040:008D	Byte	Fixed disk drive controller error status
0040:008E	Byte	Fixed disk drive interrupt control
0040:008F	Byte	RESERVED
0040:0090	Byte	Drive 0 media state
0040:0091	Byte	Drive 1 media state

Bit map for bytes 0040:0090 and 0040:0091

7 6 5 4 3 2 1 0 bits

- Drive or media state:
  - 000 = 360K diskette or disk not established
  - 001 = 360K diskette or 1.2-Mbyte disk not established.
  - 010 = 1.2-Mbyte diskette or disk not established
  - 011 = 360K diskette or disk established
  - 101 = 1.2-Mbyte diskette or disk established
  - 110 = RESERVED
  - 111 = None of the above
- RESERVED
- Media established
- Double stepping required
- Diskette data rate:
  - 00 = 500K/s   01 = 300K /s
  - 10 = 250K/s   11 = RESERVED

LOGICAL ADDRESS	DATA SIZE	CONTENTS
0040:0092	Word	RESERVED
0040:0094	Byte	Current cylinder on drive 0
0040:0095	Byte	Current cylinder on drive 1

Note: The area from 0040:008B to 0040:0095 is RESERVED in the PC, PCjr, PC XT BIOS date 11/08/82, and PC Convertible.

9.3.11 Supplementary Keyboard Data

Table 9.20. *Keyboard Data Area 3 in BIOS*

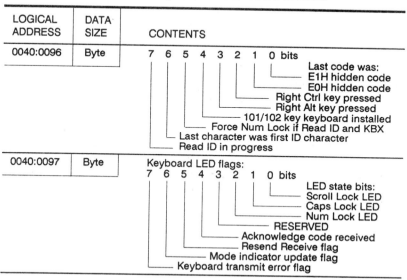

LOGICAL ADDRESS	DATA SIZE	CONTENTS
0040:0096	Byte	7 6 5 4 3 2 1 0 bits Last code was: E1H hidden code E0H hidden code Right Ctrl key pressed Right Alt key pressed 101/102 key keyboard installed Force Num Lock if Read ID and KBX Last character was first ID character Read ID in progress
0040:0097	Byte	Keyboard LED flags: 7 6 5 4 3 2 1 0 bits LED state bits: Scroll Lock LED Caps Lock LED Num Lock LED RESERVED Acknowledge code received Resend Receive flag Mode indicator update flag Keyboard transmit error flag

9.3.12 Miscellaneous Data

Table 9.21. *Miscellaneous Data Area in BIOS*

LOGICAL ADDRESS	DATA SIZE	CONTENTS
0040:00AC	Area	From 0040:00AC to 0040:00FF is RESERVED
0050:0000	Word	Print screen status (INT 05H) 00 = print screen not active 01 = print screen in progress 02 = error during screen print operation

9.4 User Accessible BIOS Interrupts

Certain BIOS interrupts are interesting to the programmer because they perform critical system functions or because they can be intercepted or replaced. The interrupt vectors discussed in the following sections exclude the BIOS programmer functions which appear starting at Section 9.6.

9.4.1 The NMI Vector (INT 02H)

The nonmaskable interrupt (NMI) was originally intended for dealing with disastrous situations, such as power failures. However, the NMI line has been used in different models of the IBM microcomputers to signal various non-catastrophic events. For example, in the PCjr the NMI line is attached to the keyboard interrupt. In the PC and the PC XT the NMI interrupt handles system board parity errors, parity errors in the I/O channel, and the 8087 error exception.

In the PC AT the NMI line handles system board parity errors and parity errors in the I/O channel. In this case, the coprocessor interrupt is vectored through INT 13H, which, in turn, redirects it to the NMI interrupt. This manipulation is necessary to achieve compatibility with software developed for previous systems. The NMI handler should read the coprocessor's status register to determine if the interrupt was caused by a coprocessor exception. If this is not the case, control should be returned to the BIOS NMI handler.

In PS/2 Micro Channel systems the nonmaskable interrupt (NMI) is used to signal a parity error, a channel check, a system channel time-out, or a system WatchDog Timer time-out. These conditions are assigned the error codes 110, 111, 112, and 113, respectively, which are displayed by the handler. The coprocessor error exception is also vectored to the NMI and should be handled in the same manner as for the PC AT.

9.4.2 The Print Screen Vector (INT 05H)

When the Print Screen key is pressed, the BIOS handler at INT 05H is given control by the keyboard routine. The action of this handler is to scan the screen and transmit the characters to the parallel printer port. Additional requests are ignored if the screen is currently being printed.

The status of the print screen function is stored in the BIOS data word at address 0050:0000H (see Table 9.21).

9.4.3 The System Timer Vector (INT 08H)

The handler at vector 08H controls the interrupts originating in channel 0 of the system timer. The POST routines initialize this timer channel to generate an interrupt approximately every 18.2 times per second. The handler maintains a count of the interrupts occurred in the doubleword located at logical address 0040:006CH. The byte located at address 0040:0070H is used to signal an overflow of the main counter after 24 h of operation. These storage locations are listed in Table 9.12.

An additional function of the system timer interrupt is to decrement the diskette motor-off counter located at BIOS logical address 0040:0040H. When the counter reaches zero, the handler turns off the diskette drive motor and updates the motor status flags at 0000:003FH. These locations can be seen in Table 9.9.

Every tick of the system timer calls software interrupt 1CH. This vector, sometimes called the *user timer tick*, provides a way for a program to receive control approximately every 55 ms. Since INT 1CH is called after the system timer routine has updated the internal controls, the user handler need not return execution to INT 08H and can exit with a simple IRET instruction.

9.4.4 The Keyboard Interrupt Handler (INT 09H)

Every keyboard make or break action on a key switch generates an interrupt vectored through INT 09H. The action of this handler is different for the different types of keys and has been described in detail in Chapter 6, starting at Section 6.3.

Certain specific keystrokes produce immediate action or are linked to separate interrupt handlers. For example, the Ctrl-Alt-Del sequence in the handler resets the flag at BIOS address 0040:0096H (see Table 9.13) to the value 1234H and jumps to the start of the BIOS POST routine. This system resetting action is often referred to as a *warm boot*.

The Pause key or keystroke combination causes the handler to execute an internal wait loop until an ASCII key is pressed. The Print Screen keystroke generates an interrupt 05H as described in Section 9.5.2. The System Request key, labeled SysRq or Sys Req, is recognized by the PC XT BIOS dated 01/10/86 and later, by the PC AT, the PC XT Model 286, the PC Convertible, and the PS/2 systems. In these systems this keystroke causes an INT 15H, with AH = 133.

The PC AT BIOS dated 06/10/85 and later, the PC Model 286, the PC Convertible, and the PS/2 systems execute a keyboard intercept interrupt after reading the scan code. This action, vectored through INT 15H, AH = 79, allows a simple way to intercept a keystroke and absorb or replace the scan code.

9.4.5 ROM BASIC Loader (INT 18H)

This BIOS interrupt transfers control to the BASIC program in ROM.

9.4.6 Bootstrap Loader (INT 19H)

This interrupt is used by a system program to gain control at the conclusion of the BIOS POST routines. Applications can use this entry to reboot the disk operating system. Once the interrupt is executed, diskette or disk track 0, sector 1, is loaded to logical address 0000:7C00H and execution is transferred to the loaded code. At transfer time the DL register holds the diskette or hard disk drive number where the bootstrap code was read.

9.5 The BIOS Programmer Functions

The IBM BIOS provides an extensive set of services or functions which allow the programmer to access many devices without directly addressing the hardware components. These functions are vectored through software interrupts. Some individual interrupts contain more than one service. For example, INT 10H, which is devoted to video functions, provides up to 28 different services. In this case the caller selects the specific function, or sub function, in the BIOS service by passing information to the BIOS routine in the microprocessor registers.

For example, BIOS service number 0, of INT 10H, can be used to set any video mode available in the hardware. The service number is passed in the AH register and the desired mode in the AL register. The following code fragment shows the calling procedure:

```
; Use BIOS video function (INT 10H) to set alphanumeric mode
; number 7
        MOV     AH,0        ; BIOS service number
        MOV     AL,7        ; Desired video mode
        INT     10H
```

This specific BIOS service does not report success or error conditions to the caller, but the user's routine can inspect the BIOS data byte at address 0040:0049H (see Table 9.10) to determine if the desired action took place. Table 9.22 lists the BIOS programmer functions.

Table 9.22. *BIOS Programmer Functions*

INTERRUPT VECTOR	DESCRIPTION	REFERENCE TABLES
INT 10H	Video functions	9.24 and 9.25
INT 11H	Equipment determination	9.26
INT 12H	Memory size determination	9.27
INT 13H	Diskette functions	9.28 and 9.29
INT 13H	Hard disk functions	9.30 and 9.31
INT 14H	Serial communications functions	9.32 and9. 33
INT 15H	System services	9.34 and9. 35
INT 16H	Keyboard functions	9.36 and 9.37
INT 17H	Printer functions	9.38 and 9.39
INT 1AH	System-timer functions	9.40 and 9.41
INT 70H	Real-time clock interrupt	9.42

9.5.1 Video Functions (INT 10H)

Table 9.23. *Index to BIOS Video Functions — Interrupt 10H*

SERVICE REQUEST NUMBER	D E S C R I P T I O N
AH = 0	Set video mode
AH = 1	Set cursor type (determine top and bottom lines)
AH = 2	Set cursor position (screen row and column)
AH = 3	Read cursor position (screen row and column)
AH = 4	Read light pen position
AH = 5	Select display page (in multipage systems)
AH = 6	Scroll text up or initialize window
AH = 7	Scroll text down or initialize window
AH = 8	Read character and attribute at cursor position
AH = 9	Write character and attribute at cursor position
AH = 10	Write character (no attribute) at cursor position
AH = 11	Set color palette in CGA, EGA, VGA, and PCjr
AH = 12	Write pixel (in graphics modes)
AH = 13	Read pixel (in graphics modes)
AH = 14	Write character at cursor using teletype style
AH = 15	Get current video mode
AH = 16	Set color palette
AH = 17	Character generator
AH = 18	Alternate function select
AH = 19	Write string (PC XT BIOS 01/10/86 and later)
AH = 26	Read/write display combination codes
AH = 27	Read functionality and state information

Table 9.24. *BIOS Interrupt 10H — Video Functions*

SERVICE NUMBER (IN AH)	ON ENTRY	ON EXIT	DESCRIPTION
0	AL	Nothing	Set video mode (in AL)
1	CX	Nothing	Set cursor type

```
0  1  2   4  3  2  1   0  CL bits
L__|__|   L__|__|__|__|
       |                        Top cursor line
       |_____ RESERVED (must be 0)

0  1  2   4  3  2  1   0  CH bits
L__|__|   L__|__|__|__|
       |                        Bottom cursor line
       |_____ RESERVED (must be 0)
```

SERVICE NUMBER (IN AH)	ON ENTRY	ON EXIT	DESCRIPTION
2	DX-BH	Nothing	Set cursor position DH = row number (0-based) DL = column number (0-based) BH = page number (0-based)
3	BH	CX-DX	Read cursor position BH = page number (0-based)

Returns:
DH = current cursor row (0-based)
DL = current cursor column (0-based)
CH = cursor start line
CL = cursor end line

SERVICE NUMBER (IN AH)	ON ENTRY	ON EXIT	DESCRIPTION
4	Nothing	AH-CH-BX DX	Read light pen position Returns: AH = 01 if valid value in registers

CH = light pen pixel row (0 to 199)
BX = light pen pixel column (0 to 639)
DH = character row (0 to 24)
DL = character column (0 to 79)
Note: The light pen function is not available in the
PC convertible and the PS/2 line.

SERVICE NUMBER (IN AH)	ON ENTRY	ON EXIT	DESCRIPTION
5	AL	Nothing	Select display page (except PCjr) AL = page number
5	AL-BX	BX	Select diplay page in PCjr AL = page number

BL = microprocessor page register
BH = CRT page register
Returns:
BH = microprocessor page register selected
BL = CRT page register selected
Note: This function is not legal in single-page video systems.

SERVICE NUMBER (IN AH)	ON ENTRY	ON EXIT	DESCRIPTION
6	AL-BH-CX DX	Nothing	Scroll page up or initialize AL = number of lines to scroll AL = 0 to initialize window

BH = attribute for initialization
CH/CL = row/column of upper left corner of window
DH/DL = row/column of lower right corner of window

(continued)

Table 9.24. *BIOS Interrupt 10H — Video Functions (Continued)*

SERVICE NUMBER (IN AH)	ON ENTRY	ON EXIT	DESCRIPTION
7	AL-BH-CX DX	Nothing	Scroll page down or initialize AL = number of lines to scroll AL = 0 to initialize window
	BH = attribute for initialization CH/CL = row/column of upper left corner of window DH/DL = row/column of lower right corner of window		
8	BH	AX	Read character and attribute at present cursor position
	BH = page number (0-based) Returns: AL = character AH = attribute		
9	AL-BX-CX	Nothing	Write character and attribute at current cursor position
	AL = character to write (in ASCII) BL = attribute (character color in graphics modes) BH = display page (0-based) CX = count of characters to repeat Note: The repeat count (in CX) is valid only for the same row. This function can be used to display text while in a graphics mode.		
10	AL-BH-CX	Nothing	Write character at current cursor position (no attribute)
	AL = character to write (in ASCII) BH = display page (0-based) CX = count of characters to repeat Note: The repeat count (in CX) is valid only for the same row.		
11	BX	Nothing	Set color palette in CGA systems (See also service number 16)
	BH = color ID (0 or 1) If BH = 0, set background color for 320 x 200 graphics modes or border color in alpha modes. Set foreground color in 640 x 200 graphics modes. BL must be in the range 0 to 31. BL = color value		
12	AL-CX-DX	Nothing	Write pixel in graphics modes AL = pixel color requested
	If bit 7 of AL is set, then color is XORed with pixel contents. CX = pixel column DX = pixel row		
13	CX-DX	AL	Read pixel in graphics modes CX = pixel column
	DX = pixel row Returns: AL = color value of pixel read		

(continued)

Table 9.24. *BIOS Interrupt 10H — Video Functions (Continued)*

SERVICE NUMBER (IN AH)	ON ENTRY	ON EXIT	DESCRIPTION
14	AL-BX	Nothing	Write character in teletype mode (at current cursor position)

AL = character code in ASCII
BH = display page
BL = foreground color in graphics modes
Note: Carriage return (0DH), line feed (0AH), backspace (08H), and bell (07H) codes are intepreted as commands. Line wrapping and screen scrolling are provided.

15	Nothing	AX-BH	Get current video mode

Returns:
AL = active mode
AH = number of screen columns
BH = active video page (0 based)

16	AL-BL ES:DX	ES:DX	Set color palette (EGA/VGA BIOS extension)

PCjr, EGA, AND PS/2 SYSTEMS
AL = 0 to set individual palette registers
    BL = register to set BH = color value
AL = 1 to set overscan register (border color)
    BH = color value
AL = 2 to set palette and overscan registers
    ES:DX -> 17-byte table:
        bytes 0–15 = palette register values
        byte 16 = border color value
AL = 3 to toggle intensity and blinking attribute
    BL = 0 to enable intensity
    BL = 1 to enable blinking

PS/2 MICRO CHANNEL SYSTEMS
AL = 4 to 6 RESERVED
AL = 7 to read individual palette registers
    BL = register to set (range 0 to 15)
    Returns: BL = value read
AL = 8 to read overscan register (border color)
    Returns: BL = value read
AL = 9 to read all palette and overscan registers
    ES:DX -> 17-byte table:
        bytes 0–15 = palette register values
        byte 16 = border color value
AL = 16 to set individual color registers
    BX = color register to set
    DH = red value to set
    CH = green value to set
    CL = blue value to set
AL = 17 RESERVED
AL = 18 to set a block of color registers
    ES:DX -> table of color values in the sequence
    red, green, blue, red, green . . .
    BX = first color register to set
    CX = count of color registers to set

(continued)

Table 9.24. *BIOS Interrupt 10H — Video Functions (Continued)*

SERVICE NUMBER (IN AH)	ON ENTRY	ON EXIT	DESCRIPTION
16	(continued)		

AL = 19 to set color page
    BL = 0 to select paging mode
        BH = 0 selects 4 register blocks of 64 registers
        BH = 1 selects 16 register blocks of 16 registers
    BL = 1 select page
        BH = page number (0 based)
      64-register block mode:
        BH = 00H selects first block of 64 registers
        01H selects second block of 64 registers
        03H selects third block of 64 registers
        04H selects fourth block of 64 registers
      16-register block mode:
        BH = block number of 16 color registers
        (range 0 to 15)
AL = 20 RESERVED
AL = 21 to read individual color registers
    BX = color register to read
    Returns:
    DH = red value read
    CH = green value read
    CL = blue value read
AL = 22 RESERVED
AL = 23 to read a block of color registers
    ES:DX - > table of values in red, green, blue sequence
    BX = first color register to read
    CX = number of color registers to read
    Returns: ES:DX pointer

PS/2 MICRO CHANNEL SYSTEMS
AL = 24 RESERVED
AL = 25 RESERVED
AL = 26 to read the color page state
    Returns:
    BL = current paging mode
    BH = current page
AL = 27 to sum color values to gray shades
    BX = first color register to sum
    CX = number of color registers to sum

PS/2 NON-MICRO CHANNEL SYSTEMS
AL = 0 to set color registers to 8 consistent colors
    BX = 0712H
AL = 1 RESERVED
AL = 2 RESERVED
AL = 3 to toggle intensity and blinking attribute
    BL = 0 to enable intensity
    BL = 1 to enable blinking
AL = 4 to 7 RESERVED
AL = 16 to set individual color registers
    BX = color register to set
    DH = red value to set
    CH = green value to set
    CL = blue value to set

(continued)

Table 9.24. *BIOS Interrupt 10H — Video Functions (Continued)*

SERVICE NUMBER (IN AH)	ON ENTRY	ON EXIT	DESCRIPTION
16	(continued)		

AL = 17 RESERVED
AL = 18 to set a block of color registers
    ES:DX -> table of color values in the sequence
    red, green, blue, red, green, ...
    BX = first color register to set
    CX = count of color registers to set
AL = 19 RESERVED
AL = 20 RESERVED
AL = 21 to read individual color registers
    BX = color register to read
    Returns:
    DH = red value read
    CH = green value read
    CL = blue value read
AL = 22 RESERVED
AL = 23 to read a block of color registers
    ES:DX -> table of values in red, green, blue sequence
    BX = first color register to read
    CX = number of color registers to read
    Returns: ES:DX pointer
AL = 24 to 26 RESERVED
AL = 27 to sum color values to gray shades
    BX = first color register to sum
    CX = number of color registers to sum

| 17 | AL-BX-CX DX-ES:BP | CX-DL ES:BP | Character generator (EGA/VGA BIOS extension) |

EGA SYSTEMS

AL = 0 to load user-defined character set
    ES:BP -> user character table
    CX = count of characters to store
    DX = offset of first character to load
    BL = block to load (range 0 to 3 — see note)
    BH = count of bytes per character
AL = 1 to load ROM 8 x 14 character set
    BL = block to load (range 0 to 3 — see note)
AL = 2 to load ROM 8 x 8 character set
    BL = block to load (range 0 to 3 — see note)
AL = 3 to set block specifier in alpha modes
    Create 512-character set if more than 64K
    EGA memory

    7 6 5 4 3 2 1 0 BL bit map

    Block number (range 0 to 3) if attribute byte bit 3 = 0
    Block number (range 0 to 3) if attribute byte bit 3 = 1
    must be 0 in EGA

Note: Each EGA character set is called a block. There is one block for each 64K of EGA memory.

(continued)

Table 9.24. *BIOS Interrupt 10H — Video Functions (Continued)*

SERVICE NUMBER (IN AH)	ON ENTRY	ON EXIT	DESCRIPTION
17	(continued)		

AL = 16 to load user-defined character set after mode reset
ES:BP -> user character table
CX = count of characters to store
DX = offset of first character to load
BL = block to load (range 0 to 3 — see note)
BH = count of bytes per character
AL = 17 to load ROM 8 x 14 character set after mode reset
BL = block to load (range 0 to 3 — see note)
AL = 18 to load ROM 8 x 8 character set after mode reset
BL = block to load (range 0 to 3 — see note)
AL = 32 to set vector for INT 1FH to point to user-defined
8 x 8 character set
ES:BP holds address of user table
AL = 33 to set vector for INT 43H to point to user-defined
character set
ES:BP holds address of user table
CX = bytes per character
BL = character rows per screen
BL = 0 for user defined set
DL = number of rows (if BL = 0)
DL = 1 for 14 rows
DL = 2 for 25 rows
DL = 3 for 43 rows
AL = 34 to set vector for INT 43H to point to ROM table
of 8 x 14 characters
BL = character rows per screen (see AL = 33)
AL = 35 to set vector for INT 43H to point to ROM table
of 8 x 8 characters
BL = character rows per screen (see AL = 33)
AL = 36 to set vector for INT 43H to point to ROM table
of 8 x 16 characters
BL = character rows per screen (see AL = 33)
AL = 48 to obtain EGA register information
BH = font pointer
BH = 0 to obtain pointer to current INT 1FH
BH = 1 to obtain pointer to current INT 43H
BH = 2 to obtain pointer to ROM 8 x 14 set
BH = 3 to obtain pointer to ROM 8 x 8 set
BH = 4 to obtain pointer to upper half of
ROM 8 x 8 set
BH = 5 to obtain pointer to ROM 9 x 16
alternate set
Returns:
CX = bytes per character in font
DL = number of rows
ES:BP -> character table

PS/2 MICRO CHANNEL SYSTEMS
AL = 0 to load user-defined character set
ES:BP -> user character table
CX = count of characters to store
DX = offset of first character to load
BL = block to load (range 0 to 3 — see note)
BH = count of bytes per character

(continued)

Table 9.24. *BIOS Interrupt 10H — VIDEO FUNCTIONS (Continued)*

SERVICE NUMBER (IN AH)	ON ENTRY	ON EXIT	DESCRIPTION
17	(continued)		

AL = 1 to load ROM 8 x 14 character set
    BL = block to load (range 0 to 7 — see note)
AL = 2 to load ROM 8 x 8 character set
    BL = block to load (range 0 to 7 — see note)
AL = 3 to set block specifier in alpha modes
    Create 256- or 512-character set

```
7  6  5  4  3  2  1  0   BL bit map
|__|     |  |  |  |  |
               Block number (range 0 to 7)
               if attribute byte bit 3 = 0
            Block number (range 0 to 7)
            if attribute byte bit 3 = 1
       must be 0 in VGA
```

Note: Each character set is called a block. There are 8 blocks in VGA systems.

AL = 4 to load ROM 8 x 16 character set
    BL = block to load (range 0 to 7)
AL = 16 to load user-defined character set after mode reset
    ES:BP -> user character table
    CX = count of characters to store
    DX = offset of first character to load
    BL = block to load (range 0 to 7)
    BH = count of bytes per character
AL = 17 to load ROM 8 x 14 character set after mode reset
    BL = block to load (range 0 to 7)
AL = 18 to load ROM 8 x 8 character set after mode reset
    BL = block to load (range 0 to 7)
AL = 32 to set vector for INT 1FH to point to user-defined
    8 x 8 character set
    ES:BP holds address of user table
AL = 33 to set vector for INT 43H to point to user-defined
    character set
    ES:BP holds address of user table
    CX = bytes per character
    BL = character rows per screen
        BL = 0 for user defined set
    DL = number of rows (if BL = 0)
        DL = 1 for 14 rows
        DL = 2 for 25 rows
        DL = 3 for 43 rows
AL = 34 to set vector for INT 43H to point to ROM table
    of 8 x 14 characters
    BL = character rows per screen (see AL = 33)
AL = 35 to set vector for INT 43H to point to ROM table
    of 8 x 8 characters
BL = character rows per screen (see AL = 33)
AL = 36 to set vector for INT 43H to point to ROM table
    of 8 x 16 characters
    BL = character rows per screen (see AL = 33)

(continued)

Table 9.24. *BIOS Interrupt 10H — Video Functions (Continued)*

SERVICE NUMBER (IN AH)	ON ENTRY	ON EXIT	DESCRIPTION
17	(continued)		

AL = 48 to obtain VGA register information
    BH = font pointer
    BH = 0 to obtain pointer to current INT 1FH
    BH = 1 to obtain pointer to current INT 43H
    BH = 2 to obtain pointer to ROM 8 x 14 set
    BH = 3 to obtain pointer to ROM 8 x 8 set
    BH = 4 to obtain pointer to upper half of
        ROM 8 x 8 set
    BH = 5 to obtain pointer to ROM 9 x 16 alternate set
Returns:
    CX = bytes per character in font
    DL = number of rows
    ES:BP -> character table

PS/2 NON-MICRO CHANNEL SYSTEMS
AL = 0 to load user-defined character set
    ES:BP -> user character table
    CX = count of characters to store
    DX = offset of first character to load
    BL = block to load (range 0 to 3 —see note)
    BH = 16 bytes per character (400 scan lines)
AL = 1 RESERVED
AL = 2 to load ROM 8 x 8 character set
    BL = block to load (range 0 to 4 —see note)
AL = 3 to set block specifier in alpha modes
    Create 256- or 512-character set
    7 6 5 4 3 2 1 0 BL bit map

                      Block number (range 0 to 3)
                      if attribute byte bit 3 = 0
                      Block number (range 0 to 3)
                      if attribute byte bit 3 = 1
                      must be 0 in MCGA
Note: Each character set is called a block. There are
        4 blocks in an MCGA system.
AL = 4 to load ROM 8 x 16 character set
    BL = block to load (range 0 to 7)
AL = 16 to 18 RESERVED
AL = 20 RESERVED
AL = 32 to set vector for INT 1FH to point to user-defined
    8 x 8 character set
    ES:BP holds address of user table
AL = 33 to set vector for INT 43H to point to user-defined
    character set
    ES:BP holds address of user table
    CX = bytes per character
    BL = character rows per screen
        BL = 0 for user-defined set
    DL = number of rows (if BL = 0)
        DL = 1 for 14 rows
        DL = 2 for 25 rows
        DL = 3 for 43 rows
AL = 34 RESERVED

(continued)

Table 9.24. *BIOS Interrupt 10H — Video Functions (Continued)*

SERVICE NUMBER (IN AH)	ON ENTRY	ON EXIT	DESCRIPTION

17	(continued)		AL = 35 to set vector for INT 43H to point to ROM table of 8 x 8 characters
			   BL = character rows per screen (see AL = 33)
			AL = 36 to set vector for INT 43H to point to ROM table of 8 x 16 characters
			   BL = character rows per screen (see AL = 33)
			AL = 48 to obtain MCGA Register information
			   BH = font pointer
			      BH = 0 to obtain pointer to current INT 1FH
			      BH = 1 to obtain pointer to current INT 43H
			      BH = 2 to obtain pointer to ROM 8 x 14 set
			      BH = 3 to obtain pointer to ROM 8 x 8 set
			      BH = 4 to obtain pointer to upper half of ROM 8 x 8 set
			      BH = 5 to obtain pointer to ROM 9 x 16 alternate set
			Returns:
			   CX = bytes per character in font
			   DL = number of rows
			   ES:BP -> character table

18	BX-CX	AX-BX	Alternate select

EGA AND PS/2 MICRO CHANNEL SYSTEMS
BL = 16 to return VGA/EGA information
Returns:
   BH = 0 if color mode active
   BH = 1 if monochrome mode active
   BL = 0 if 64K of video memory
   BL = 1 if 128K of video memory
   BL = 2 if 192K of video memory
   BL = 3 if 256K of video memory (VGA)
   BL = 4 to 256 RESERVED
   CH = Feature control register bit settings
   CL = Switch setting on EGA card or equivalent VGA functions
   BL = 32 to activate alternate print-screen routine

PS/2 MICRO CHANNEL SYSTEMS
BL = 48 to change the number of scan lines in an alpha mode (usually for MDA, CGA, and EGA compatibility)
AL = 0 for 200 scan lines (CGA-compatible)
AL = 1 for 350 scan lines (EGA-compatible)
AL = 2 for 400 scan lines (MDA-compatible)
BL = 49 to control default palette during mode reset
AL = 0 enables default palette during mode changes
AL = 1 disables default palette during mode changes
Returns:
   AL = 18 if function supported
   BL = 50 to disable the video function
   AL = 0 to enable
   AL = 1 to disable

(continued)

Table 9.24. *BIOS Interrupt 10H — Video Functions (Continued)*

SERVICE NUMBER (IN AH)	ON ENTRY	ON EXIT	DESCRIPTION
18	(continued)		

BL = 51 to activate summing to gray shades, as follows:
    30% gray for red, 59% for green, and 11% for blue
    Gray shades are displayed at the next mode change
AL = 0 to enable summing
AL = 1 to disable summing
Returns:
    AL = 18 if function supported
    BL = 52 Enable cursor emulation by scaling cursor to
        present character height
    AL = 0 to enable cursor emulation
    AL = 1 to disable cursor emulation
Returns:
AL = 18 if function supported

PS/2 NON-MICRO CHANNEL SYSTEMS
BL = 48 RESERVED
BL = 49 to control default palette during mode reset
AL = 0 enables default palette during mode changes
AL = 1 disables default palette during mode changes
Returns:
    AL = 18 if function is supported
    BL = 50 to disable the video function
    AL = 0 to enable
    AL = 1 to disable
Returns:
    AL = 18 if function supported
    BL = 51 to activate summing to gray shades,
    as follows:
    30% gray for red, 59% for green, and 11% for blue
    Gray shades are displayed at the next mode change
    AL = 0 to enable summing
    AL = 1 to disable summing
Returns:
    AL = 18 if function supported

ALL PS/2 SYSTEMS
BL = 53 to control motherboard and external adapter video
    systems in address or port conflict
AL = 0 is initial command for external adapter OFF
AL = 1 is initial command for system board video ON
AL = 2 is to set active adapter OFF
AL = 3 is to set inactive adapter ON
ES:DX -> 128-byte switch state save area
Returns:
    AL = 18 if function is supported
    BL = 54 to blank screen
    AL = 0 to turn screen ON
    AL = 1 to turn screen OFF

(continued)

Table 9.24. *BIOS Interrupt 10H — Video Functions (Continued)*

SERVICE NUMBER (IN AH)	ON ENTRY	ON EXIT	DESCRIPTION
19	AL-CX-DX BX-ES:BP	Nothing	Write string

PC XT BIOS 01/10/86 AND LATER, AT, EGA, PC CONVERTIBLE, AND PS/2 SYSTEMS
AL = 0 to display characters only and cursor not moved
AL = 1 to display characters only and cursor to string end
AL = 2 to display character/attributes and cursor not moved
AL = 3 to display character/attributes and cursor to end of string
BL = attribute if AL = 0 or 1
BH = page number (0-based)
CX = Character count (attributes not included)
DH = start row for string display
DL = start column for string display
ES:BP -> string in memory

26	AL	AL-BX	Read and write display combination code

ALL PS/2 SYSTEMS
AL = 0 to READ display combination codes
Returns:
    AL = 26 if function is supported
    BL = display system code, as follows:
    0 = no display   1 = monochrome with 5151
    2 = CGA with 5153/4   3 = RESERVED
    4 = EGA with 5153/4   5 = EGA with 5151 (mono)
    6 = PGS with 5175 (color) 7 = PS/2 MC with mono
    8 = PS/2 MC with color 9 and 10 = RESERVED
    11 = PS/2 not MC mono 12 = PS/2 not MC color
    13 to 256 = RESERVED
    BH = Alternate display code
AL = 1 to WRITE display code combination
BL = display system code (see AL = 0)
BH = alternate display code

27	BX ES:DI	BX ES:DI	Read functionality/state information

ALL PS/2 SYSTEMS
BX = implementation type
    ES:DI -> 64-byte buffer
Returns:
BX = 0 for implementation type 0
ES:DI -> 64-byte buffer formatted as follows:

Offset	Size	Contents
0	Word	Offset of static functionality table
2	Word	Segment of static functionality table
4	Byte	Active video mode
5	Word	Number of character columns
7	Word	Size of video buffer (in bytes)
9	Word	Starting address of video buffer
11 to 26	Area	8 words of cursor position (row/column format) for video pages 0 to 7
27	Byte	Cursor start line
28	Byte	Cursor end line

(continued)

Table 9.24. *BIOS Interrupt 10H — Video Functions (Continued)*

SERVICE NUMBER (IN AH)	ON ENTRY	ON EXIT	DESCRIPTION
27	(continued		

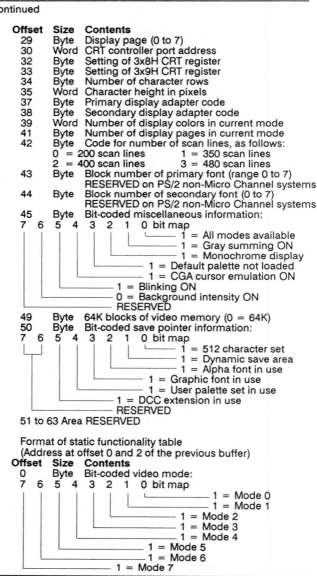

Offset Size   Contents
29   Byte   Display page (0 to 7)
30   Word   CRT controller port address
32   Byte   Setting of 3x8H CRT register
33   Byte   Setting of 3x9H CRT register
34   Byte   Number of character rows
35   Word   Character height in pixels
37   Byte   Primary display adapter code
38   Byte   Secondary display adapter code
39   Word   Number of display colors in current mode
41   Byte   Number of display pages in current mode
42   Byte   Code for number of scan lines, as follows:
       0 = 200 scan lines   1 = 350 scan lines
       2 = 400 scan lines   3 = 480 scan lines
43   Byte   Block number of primary font (range 0 to 7)
             RESERVED on PS/2 non-Micro Channel systems
44   Byte   Block number of secondary font (0 to 7)
             RESERVED on PS/2 non-Micro Channel systems
45   Byte   Bit-coded miscellaneous information:
       7 6 5 4 3 2 1 0 bit map
                              1 = All modes available
                              1 = Gray summing ON
                              1 = Monochrome display
                           1 = Default palette not loaded
                           1 = CGA cursor emulation ON
                        1 = Blinking ON
                        0 = Background intensity ON
                        RESERVED
49   Byte   64K blocks of video memory (0 = 64K)
50   Byte   Bit-coded save pointer information:
       7 6 5 4 3 2 1 0 bit map
                              1 = 512 character set
                              1 = Dynamic save area
                              1 = Alpha font in use
                           1 = Graphic font in use
                           1 = User palette set in use
                        1 = DCC extension in use
                        RESERVED
51 to 63 Area RESERVED

Format of static functionality table
(Address at offset 0 and 2 of the previous buffer)
Offset Size   Contents
0   Byte   Bit-coded video mode:
       7 6 5 4 3 2 1 0 bit map
                              1 = Mode 0
                              1 = Mode 1
                           1 = Mode 2
                           1 = Mode 3
                           1 = Mode 4
                        1 = Mode 5
                        1 = Mode 6
                        1 = Mode 7

                                                              (continued)

Table 9.24. *BIOS Interrupt 10H — Video Functions (Continued)*

SERVICE NUMBER (IN AH)	ON ENTRY	ON EXIT	DESCRIPTION
27	(continued		

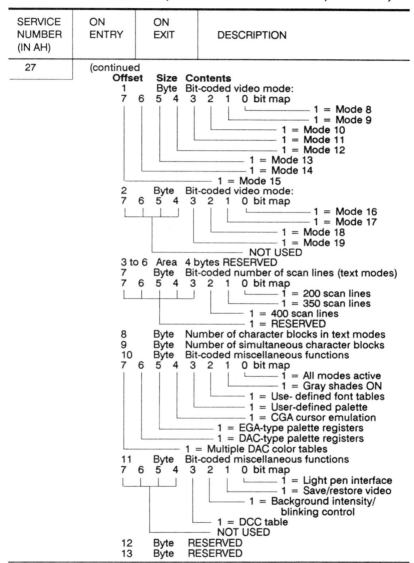

| | | | (continued) |

(continued)

Table 9.24. *BIOS Interrupt 10H — Video Functions (Continued)*

SERVICE NUMBER (IN AH)	ON ENTRY	ON EXIT	DESCRIPTION
27	(continued		

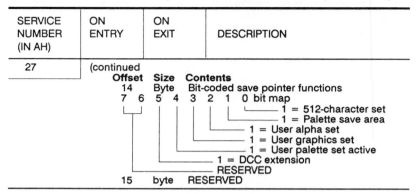

9.5.2 Equipment Determination (INT 11H)

Table 9.25. *BIOS Interrupt 11H — Equipment Determination*

SERVICE NUMBER (IN AH)	ON ENTRY	ON EXIT	DESCRIPTION
Not Required	Nothing	AX	Return system devices as in BIOS data area 0040:0010 (see Table 9.5)

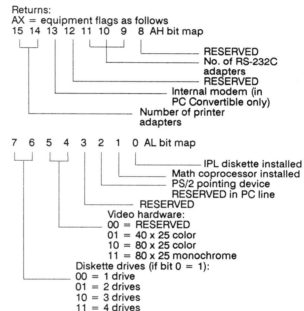

```
Returns:
AX = equipment flags as follows
15 14 13 12 11 10  9  8 AH bit map
```
- RESERVED
- No. of RS-232C adapters
- RESERVED
- Internal modem (in PC Convertible only)
- Number of printer adapters

```
 7  6  5  4  3  2  1  0 AL bit map
```
- IPL diskette installed
- Math coprocessor installed
- PS/2 pointing device
- RESERVED in PC line
- RESERVED
- Video hardware:
  - 00 = RESERVED
  - 01 = 40 x 25 color
  - 10 = 80 x 25 color
  - 11 = 80 x 25 monochrome
- Diskette drives (if bit 0 = 1):
  - 00 = 1 drive
  - 01 = 2 drives
  - 10 = 3 drives
  - 11 = 4 drives

9.5.3 Memory Size Determination (INT 12H)

Table 9.26. *BIOS Interrupt 12H — Memory Size Determination*

SERVICE NUMBER (IN AH)	ON ENTRY	ON EXIT	DESCRIPTION
Not Required	Nothing	AX	Determine the amount of system RAM up to 640K minus the memory used in the extended BIOS data area

Returns:
AX = number of contiguous 1K memory blocks

9.5.4 Diskette Functions (INT 13H)

Table 9.27. *Index to BIOS Diskette Functions — Interrupt 13H*

SERVICE REQUEST NUMBER	DESCRIPTION
AH = 0	Reset diskette system
AH = 1	Read status of last diskette operation
AH = 2	Read diskette sectors into memory
AH = 3	Write diskette sectors into memory
AH = 4	Verify diskette sectors
AH = 5	Format diskette track
AH = 6	RESERVED FOR FIXED DISK
AH = 7	RESERVED FOR FIXED DISK
AH = 8	Read diskette drive parameters
AH = 9 to 20	RESERVED FOR FIXED DISK
AH = 21	Read device type
AH = 22	Diskette change line status
AH = 23	Set device type for format operation
AH = 24	Set diskette media type for format operation

Table 9.28. *BIOS Interrupt 13H — Diskette Functions*

SERVICE NUMBER (IN AH)	ON ENTRY	ON EXIT	DESCRIPTION
0	DL	AH-cf	Reset diskette system

    DL = drive number (0-based)
        Note: Bit 7 must be 0 for diskette operations.
    Returns:
        Carry flag set (cf = 1) if status is not 0
        Carry flag clear (cf = 0) if status is 0 (no error)
        AH = diskette status:
            00H - no error
            80H - diskette drive not ready
            40H - seek operation failed
            20H - general failure of diskette controller
            10H - CRC error during read operation
            0CH - media type not found
            09H - attempt to DMA across 64K
            08H - DMA overrun error
             06H - diskette change line active
            04H - sector not found
            03H - write protect error
            02H - address mark not found
            01H - invalid parameter

| 1 | DL | AH-cf | Read status of last diskette operation |

    DL = drive number (0-based)
        Note: Bit 7 must be 0 for diskette operations.
    Returns:
        Carry flag set (cf = 1) if status is not 0
        Carry flag clear (cf = 0) if status is 0
        AH = diskette status as in service number 0 of
            INT 13H

| 2 | AL-CX-DX ES:BX | AX-cf | Read diskette sectors into memory |

    DL = drive number (0-based)
        Note: Bit 7 must be 0 for diskette operations.
    DH = head number (0-based)
    CH = track number (0-based)
    CL = sector number
    AL = number of sectors to read
    ES:BX -> address of buffer
    Returns:
        Carry flag set (cf = 1) if status is not 0
        Carry flag clear (cf = 0) if status is 0 (no error)
        AL = number of sectors actually transferred
        AH = diskette status as in service number 0, INT 13H

| 3 | AL-CX-DX ES:BX | AX-cf | Write diskette sectors into memory |

    DL = drive number (0-based)
        Note: Bit 7 must be 0 for diskette operations.
    DH = head number (0-based)
    CH = track number (0-based)

(continued)

Table 9.28. *BIOS Interrupt 13H — Diskette Functions (Continued)*

SERVICE NUMBER (IN AH)	ON ENTRY	ON EXIT	DESCRIPTION
3	(continued)		

CL = sector number
AL = number of sectors to write
    Note: Not required in PC XT Model 286.
ES:BX - > address of buffer
Returns:
    Carry flag set (cf = 1) if status is not 0
    Carry flag clear (cf = 0) if status is 0 (no error)
    AL = number of sectors actually transferred
    AH = diskette status as in service number 0, INT 13H

| 4 | AL-CX-DX ES:BX | AX-cf | Verify diskette sectors |

DL = drive number (0-based)
    Note: Bit 7 must be 0 for diskette operations.
DH = head number (0-based)
CH = track number (0-based)
CL = sector number
AL = number of sectors to verify
ES:BX - > address of buffer
    Note: Not required for AT BIOS dated 11/15/85
    and later, PC XT 286, PC Convertible, and PS/2.
Returns:
    Carry flag set (cf = 1) if status is not 0
    Carry flag clear (cf = 0) if status is 0 (no error)
    AL = number of sectors actually transferred
    AH = diskette status as in service number 0, INT 13H

| 5 | AL-CH-DX ES:BX | AH-cf | Format diskette track |

DL = drive number (0-based)
    Note: Bit 7 must be 0 for diskette operations.
DH = head number (0-based)
CH = track number (0-based)
AL = number of sectors to format
    Note: Not required for PC XT Model 286.
ES:BX - >address of buffer
Returns:
    Carry flag set (cf = 1) if status is not 0
    Carry flag clear (cf = 0) if status is 0 (no error)
    AH = diskette status as in service number 0, INT 13H

| 8 | DL | AX-BX-CX DX-ES:DI | Read diskette drive parameters |

PC, PC XT, PCjr, and AT BIOS dated 01/10/85
Returns:
    Carry flag set (cf = 1) if error
    AH = status of operation
    AH = 1 if invalid command

(continued)

Table 9.28. *BIOS Interrupt 13H — Diskette Functions (Continued)*

SERVICE NUMBER (IN AH)	ON ENTRY	ON EXIT	DESCRIPTION
8	(continued)		

ALL OTHER SYSTEMS
DL = drive number (0-based)
Returns:
    ES:DI -> 11-byte parameter block as in Table 8.23
    CH = low 8 bits of 10-bit value of maximum number
        of tracks
    CL bits 6 and 7 = high 2 bits of value of maximum
        number of tracks
    CL bits 0 to 5 = maximum sectors per track
    DH = maximum head number (sides)
    DL = number of drives intalled
    BH = 0
    BL = drive type as follows:
        01H - 360K, 5¼-in, 40 tracks
        02H - 1.2 Mbytes, 5¼in, 80 tracks
        03H - 720K, 3½-in, 80 tracks
        04H - 1.44 Mbytes, 3½-in, 80 tracks
    AX = 0
    Note: if the requested drive (in DL) is not installed,
    AX, BX, CX, and DX are zero.

| 21 | DL | AH-cf | Read device type (Also read DASD type, DASD = Direct Access Storage Device) |

**PC XT BIOS 01/10/86 AND LATER, PC Model 286,
PC CONVERTIBLE, AND PS/2 SYSTEMS**
DL = drive number (0 based)
    Note: Bit 7 must be 0 for diskette operations.
Returns:
    Carry flag clear (cf = 0) if no error
    AH = 00H if drive not present
    1H if no change line available
    2H if change line available
    3H RESERVED FOR FIXED DISK
ALL OTHER SYSTEMS
Returns:
    Carry flag clear (cf = 0) if no error
    AH = status of operation
    AH = 1H if invalid command

| 22 | DL | AH-cf | Diskette change line status |

**PC XT BIOS 01/10/86 AND LATER, PC Model 286,
PC CONVERTIBLE, AND PS/2 SYSTEMS**
DL = drive number (0 based)
    Note: Bit 7 must be 0 for diskette operations.
Returns:
    Carry flag clear (cf = 0) if AH = 0 (no error)
    AH = 0H diskette change signal not active
        01H invalid diskette parameter
        06H diskette change signal active
        80H if diskette drive not ready

(continued)

Table 9.28. *BIOS Interrupt 13H — Diskette Functions (Continued)*

SERVICE NUMBER (IN AH)	ON ENTRY	ON EXIT	DESCRIPTION
22	(continued)		

ALL OTHER SYSTEMS
Returns:
    Carry flag clear (cf = 0) if no error
    AH = status of operation
    AH = 1H if invalid command
    Carry flag set (cf = 1) if error

23	DL-AL	AH-cf	Set device type for format

Also set DASD type for format
(DASD = Direct Access Storage Device)

**PC XT BIOS 01/10/86 AND LATER, PC Model 286,
PC CONVERTIBLE, AND PS/2 SYSTEMS**
DL = drive number (0-based)
    Note: Bit 7 must be 0 for diskette operations.
AL = 00H - invalid request
    01H - 320/360K diskette in 360K drive
    02H - 360K diskette in 1.2-Mbyte drive
    03H - 1.2-Mbyte diskette in 1.2-Mbyte drive
    04H - (AT BIOS before 06/10/85): invalid request
        All others: 720K diskette in 720K drive
    05H to 0FFH - invalid request
Returns:
    Carry flag set (cf = 1) if error
    AH = status of operation (see service no. 0, INT 13H)

ALL OTHER SYSTEMS
Returns:
    Carry flag clear (cf = 0) if no error
    AH = status of operation (see service no. 0, INT 13H)
    AH = 1H if invalid command
    Carry flag set (cf = 1) if error

24	CX-DL	AH-cf ES:DI	Set diskette media type for format operation)

**PC XT BIOS 01/10/86 AND LATER, PC Model 286,
PC CONVERTIBLE, AND PS/2 SYSTEMS**
DL = drive number (0-based)
    Note: Bit 7 must be 0 for diskette operations.
    CH = low 8 bits of a 10-bit track number (0-based)
    CL bits 6 and 7 = high 2 bits of track number
    CL bits 0 to 5 = sectors per track
Returns:
    ES:DI - > 11-byte parameter block as in Table 8.23
    Carry flag clear (cf = 0) if no error
    AH = status of operation (see service no. 0, INT 13H)
ALL OTHER SYSTEMS
Returns:
    Carry flag clear (cf = 0) if no error
    AH = status of operation (see service no. 0,
        INT 13H)
AH = 1H if invalid command
    Carry flag set (cf = 1) if error

9.5.5 Hard Disk Functions (INT 13H)

Table 9.29. *Index to BIOS Hard Disk Functions — Interrupt 13H*

SERVICE REQUEST NUMBER	D E S C R I P T I O N
AH = 0	Reset disk system
AH = 1	Read status of last disk operation
AH = 2	Read disk sectors into memory
AH = 3	Write disk sectors into memory
AH = 4	Verify disk sectors
AH = 5	Format disk cylinder
AH = 6	Format disk cylinder and set bad sector flags
AH = 7	Format drive starting at desired cylinder
AH = 8	Read disk drive parameters
AH = 9	Initialize drive pair characteristics
AH = 10	RESERVED FOR DIAGNOSTICS
AH = 11	RESERVED FOR DIAGNOSTICS
AH = 12	Seek
AH = 13	Alternate disk reset
AH = 14	RESERVED FOR DIAGNOSTICS
AH = 15	RESERVED FOR DIAGNOSTICS
AH = 16	Test drive ready
AH = 17	Recalibrate
AH = 18 to 20	RESERVED FOR DIAGNOSTICS
AH = 21	Read device type (also read DASD type)
AH = 22 to 24	RESERVED FOR DISKETTE
AH = 25	Park heads
AH = 26	Format unit in IBM ESDI Fixed Disk Drive Adapter/A

Table 9.30. *BIOS Interrupt 13H - Hard Disk Functions*

SERVICE NUMBER (IN AH)	ON ENTRY	ON EXIT	DESCRIPTION
0	DL	AH-cf	Reset disk system

DL = drive number (0-based)
   Note: Bit 7 must be 1 for disk operations.
   Note: The reset operation requires that the lower 7 bits of DL be less than or equal to the number of hard disk drives installed in the system.
Returns:
   Carry flag set (cf = 1) if status is not 0
   Carry flag clear (cf = 0) if status is 0 (no error)
   AH = disk status, as follows:
      00H - no error
      01H - invalid function request
      02H - address mark not found
      03H - write protect error
      04H - sector not found
      05H - reset failed
      07H - drive parameter activity failed
      08H - DMA overrun during operation
      09H - DMA boundary error
      0AH - bad sector flag detected
      0BH - bad cylinder detected
      0DH - invalid number of sectors on format
      0EH - control data address mark detected
      0FH - DMA arbitration level out of range
      10H - ECC or CRC error
      11H - ECC corrected data error
      20H - general controller failure
      40H - Seek operation failed
      80H - time-out
      BBH - undefined error
      CCH - write fault on selected drive
      E0H - status error/error register = 0
      FFH - sense operation failed

| 1 | DL | AH-cf | Read status of last disk operation |

DL = drive number (0 based)
   Note: Bit 7 must be 1 for disk operations.
Returns:
   Carry flag set (cf = 1) if status is not 0
   Carry flag clear (cf = 0) if status is 0
   AH = disk status as in service number 0

| 2 | AL-CX-DX ES:BX | AX-cf | Read disk sectors into memory |

DL = drive number (0 based)
   Note: Bit 7 must be 1 for disk operations.
DH = head number (0 based)
CH = low 8 bits of a 10-bit cylinder number
CL bits 6 and 7 = high 2 bits of cylinder number
CL bits 0 to 5 = sector number
AL = number of sectors to read
ES:BX -> address of buffer

(continued)

Table 9.30. *BIOS Interrupt 13H — Hard Disk Functions (Continued)*

SERVICE NUMBER (IN AH)	ON ENTRY	ON EXIT	DESCRIPTION
2	(continued)		

Returns:
        Carry flag set (cf = 1) if status is not 0
        AH = disk status as in service number 0

3	AL-CX-DX ES:BX	AX-cf	Write disk sectors into memory

DL = drive number (0-based)
        Note: Bit 7 must be 1 for disk operations.
DH = head number (0-based)
CH = low 8 bits of a 10-bit cylinder number
CL bits 6 and 7 = high 2 bits of cylinder number
CL bits 0 to 5 = sector number
AL = number of sectors to read
ES:BX -> address of buffer
Returns:
        Carry flag set (cf = 1) if status is not 0
        AH = disk status as in service number 0

4	AL-CX-DX ES:BX	AX-cf	Verify disk sectors

DL = drive number (0-based)
        Note: Bit 7 must be 1 for disk operations.
DH = head number (0-based)
CH = low 8 bits of a 10-bit cylinder number
CL bits 6 and 7 = high 2 bits of cylinder number
CL bits 0 to 5 = sector number
AL = number of sectors to verify
ES:BX -> address of buffer
Returns:
        Carry flag set (cf = 1) if status is not 0
        AH = disk status as in service number 0

5	AL-CX-DX ES:BX	AH-cf	Format disk cylinder

DL = drive number (0-based)
        Note: Bit 7 must be 1 for disk operations.
DH = head number (0-based)
CH = low 8 bits of a 10-bit cylinder number
CL bits 6 and 7 = high 2 bits of cylinder number
AL = interleave factor in PC XT systems
Returns:
        Carry flag set (cf = 1) if status is not 0
        AH = disk status as in service number 0

PC AT, PC XT Model 286, and PS/2 SYSTEMS
ES:BX -> 512-byte buffer
Returns:
ES:BX -> 512-byte buffer

(continued)

Table 9.30. *BIOS Interrupt 13H — Hard Disk Functions (Continued)*

SERVICE NUMBER (IN AH)	ON ENTRY	ON EXIT	DESCRIPTION
5	(continued)		

The first two bytes in the buffer contain F and N for the first cylinder, as follows:
> F = 00H if sector is good
> 80H if sector is bad
> N = sector number

The remaining pairs of buffer bytes contain F and N for the other sectors in the formatted cylinder.

IBM ESDI FIXED DISK ADAPTER
Returns:
> Carry flag set (cf = 1) if error
> AH = disk status as in service number 0
> 01H if invalid function request

6	AL-CX-DX	AH-cf	Format disk cylinder and set bad sector flags

PC XT
DL = drive number (0-based)
> Note: Bit 7 must be 1 for disk operations.

DH = head number (0-based)
CH = low 8 bits of a 10-bit cylinder number
CL bits 6 and 7 = high 2 bits of cylinder number
AL = number of sectors to read
Returns:
> Carry flag set (cf = 1) if status is not 0
> AH = disk status as in service number 0

PC AT, PC XT Model 286, PS/2 SYSTEMS, and IBM ESDI FIXED DISK
Returns:
> Carry flag set (cf = 1) if error
> AH = disk status as in service number 0
> 01H if invalid function request

7	AL-CX-DL	AH-cf	Format drive starting at desired cylinder

DL = drive number (0-based)
> Note: Bit 7 must be 1 for disk operations.

CH = low 8 bits of a 10-bit cylinder number
CL bits 6 and 7 = high 2 bits of cylinder number
AL = interleave factor
Returns:
> Carry flag set (cf = 1) if status is not 0
> AH = disk status as in service number 0

8	AL-CX-DX	AH-cf	Read disk drive parameters

DL = drive number (0-based)
> Note: Bit 7 must be 1 for disk operations.

Returns:
DL = number of drives in system
DH = maximum value for head number (0 to 63)

(continued)

Table 9.30. *BIOS Interrupt 13H - — Hard Disk Functions* *(Continued)*

SERVICE NUMBER (IN AH)	ON ENTRY	ON EXIT	DESCRIPTION
8	(continued)		
			CH = low 8 bits of a 10-bit cylinder number CL bits 6 and 7 = high 2 bits of cylinder number CL bits 0 to 5 = maximum sector number
9	DL	AH-cf	Initialize drive pair characteristics

			DL = drive number (0-based)
			    Note: Bit 7 must be 1 for disk operations.
			Returns:
			    Carry flag set (cf = 1) if status is not 0
			    AH = disk status as in service number 0
			Note: The vector for INT 41H points to the parameter table
			    for drive 0 and INT 46H points to the parameter table
			    for drive 1, except in the IBM ESDI Fixed Disk Adapter
			    in which the data is obtained from the drive.

12	DX-CX	AH-cf	Seek

			DL = drive number (0-based)
			    Note: Bit 7 must be 1 for disk operations.
			DH = head number (0-based)
			CH = low 8 bits of a 10-bit cylinder number
			CL bits 6 and 7 = high 2 bits of cylinder number
			Returns:
			    Carry flag set (cf = 1) if status is not 0
			    AH = disk status as in service number 0

13	DL	AH-cf	Alternate disk reset

			DL = drive number (0-based)
			    Note: Bit 7 must be 1 for disk operations.
			Returns:
			    Carry flag set (cf = 1) if status is not 0
			    AH = disk status as in service number 0
			Note: Alternate reset is not implemented in the IBM ESDI
			Fixed Disk Adapter/A

16	DL	AH-cf	Test drive ready
			DL = drive number (0-based) Note: Bit 7 must be 1 for disk operations. Returns: Carry flag set (cf = 1) if status is not 0 AH = disk status as in service number 0
17	DL	AH-cf	Recalibrate

			DL = drive number (0-based)
			    Note: Bit 7 must be 1 for disk operations.
			Returns:
			    Carry flag set (cf = 1) if status is not 0
			    AH = disk status as in service number 0

(continued)

Table 9.30. *BIOS Interrupt 13H -— Hard Disk Functions (Continued)*

SERVICE NUMBER (IN AH)	ON ENTRY	ON EXIT	DESCRIPTION
21	DL	AH-CX-DX cf	Read device type (Also read DASD type; DASD = Direct Access Storage Device)

PC AT, PC Model 286, and PS/2 SYSTEMS
DL = drive number (0-based)
    Note: Bit 7 must be 0 for diskette operations.
Returns:
    Carry flag clear (cf = 0) if no error
    AH = 00H if drive not present
        1H RESERVED FOR DISKETTE
        2H RESERVED FOR DISKETTE
        3H hard disk installed
    CX-DX = number of 512-byte blocks

PC XT
Returns:
    Carry flag clear (cf = 0) if no error
    AH = status of operation
    AH = 1H if invalid command

| 25 | DL | AH-cf | Park heads |

PS/2 SYSTEMS
DL = drive number (0-based)
    Note: Bit 7 must be 1 for disk operations.
Returns:
    Carry flag set (cf = 1) if status is not 0
    AH = disk status as in service number 0

PC XT
Returns:
    Carry flag clear (cf = 0) if no error
    AH = status of operation
    AH = 1H if invalid command

| 26 | AL-CL-DL ES:BX | Nothing | Format unit in IBM ESDI Fixed Disk Adapter/A Note: This service can take more than1 h to execute. |

DL = drive number (0 based)
    Note: Bit 7 must be 1 for disk operations.
AL = relative block address (RBA) defect table block
    count, as follows:
AL = 0 if no RBA table in format request
    AL larger than 0 if RBA table is used
ES:BX -> RBA table if AL larger than 0
CL = format modifier bits

(continued)

Table 9.30. *BIOS Interrupt 13H -— Hard Disk Functions (Continued)*

SERVICE NUMBER (IN AH)	ON ENTRY	ON EXIT	DESCRIPTION
26	(continued)		

```
        7  6  5  4  3  2  1  0  CL bit map
        L__|__|                     L___ Ignore primary defect map
                                  L_____ Ignore secondary defect map
                              L_____ Update secondary defect map
                          L_____ Perform extended surface analysis
                     L Periodic interrupt (can be used to display
                       progress of format operation)
                       INT 15H (AH = 0FH) is executed as the format
                       phase is completed for each cylinder.
                       AL holds the phase code as follows:
                           AL = 0 is RESERVED
                           AL = 1 is surface analysis phase
                           AL = 2 is formatting phase
                       Calling program must clear the carry flag
                         before returning so that format can continue
                L__ Must be 0
```

9.5.6 Serial Communications Functions (INT 14H)

Table 9.31. *Index to BIOS Serial Communications Functions —*
Interrupt 14H

SERVICE REQUEST NUMBER	DESCRIPTION
AH = 0	Initialize the serial port
AH = 1	Send character
AH = 2	Receive character
AH = 3	Read status
AH = 4	Extended initialize for PS/2 systems
AH = 5	Extended serial port control for PS/2 systems

Table 9.32. *BIOS Interrupt 14H — Serial Port Functions*

SERVICE NUMBER (IN AH)	ON ENTRY	ON EXIT	DESCRIPTION
0	AL-DX	AX	Initialize serial port

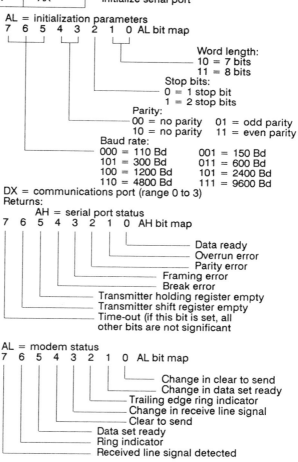

AL = initialization parameters
7 6 5 4 3 2 1 0 AL bit map

Word length:
10 = 7 bits
11 = 8 bits
Stop bits:
0 = 1 stop bit
1 = 2 stop bits
Parity:
00 = no parity 01 = odd parity
10 = no parity 11 = even parity
Baud rate:
000 = 110 Bd 001 = 150 Bd
101 = 300 Bd 011 = 600 Bd
100 = 1200 Bd 101 = 2400 Bd
110 = 4800 Bd 111 = 9600 Bd

DX = communications port (range 0 to 3)
Returns:
AH = serial port status
7 6 5 4 3 2 1 0 AH bit map

Data ready
Overrun error
Parity error
Framing error
Break error
Transmitter holding register empty
Transmitter shift register empty
Time-out (if this bit is set, all
other bits are not significant

AL = modem status
7 6 5 4 3 2 1 0 AL bit map

Change in clear to send
Change in data set ready
Trailing edge ring indicator
Change in receive line signal
Clear to send
Data set ready
Ring indicator
Received line signal detected

| 1 | AL-DX | AX | Send character |

AL = character to send
DX = communications port (range 0 to 3)
Returns:
AH = line status (see service number 0)
AL is preserved

(continued)

Table 9.32. *BIOS Interrupt 14H — Serial Port Functions (Continued)*

SERVICE NUMBER (IN AH)	ON ENTRY	ON EXIT	DESCRIPTION
2	DX	AX	Receive character

DX = communications port (range 0 to 3)
Returns:
    AL = character received
    AH = line status (see service number 0)
Note: This service waits for a character

3	DX	AX	Read status

DX = communications port (range 0 to 3)
Returns:
    AL = modem status (see service number 0)
    AH = line status (see service number 0)

4	AL-BX-CX DX	AX	Extended initialize for PS/2 systems

AL = 00H for no break
    01H for break
BH = parity, as follows:
    0 for no parity, 1 for odd, 2 for even, 3 for stick parity
    odd, and 4 for stick parity even
BL = stop bits, as follows:
    0 for one stop bit, 1 for two stop bits if word length is
    6, 7 or 8 bits and $1\frac{1}{2}$ bits if word length is 5 bits
CH = word length, as follows:
    0 for 5-bit word length, 1 for 6 bits, 2 for 7 bits, and 3
    for 8 bits
CL = baud rate, as follows:
    0 for 110 Bd, 1 for 150 Bd, 2 for 300 Bd,
    3 for 600 Bd, 4 for 1200 Bd, 5 for 2400 Bd,
    6 for 4800 Bd, 7 for 9600 Bd and 8 for 19,200
    Bd
DX = communications port (range 0 to 3)
Returns:
    AL = modem status (see service number 0)
    AH = line status (see service number 0)

5	AL-DX	BL-AX	Extended serial port control for PS/2 systems

AL = 0 to read modem control register
AL = 1 to write modem control register
DX = communications port (range 0 to 3)
Returns:
BL = modem control register
7 6 5 4 3 2 1 0 BL bit map

```
|___|___|  | | | | |_____ 1 = data terminal ready
              | | | |_____ 1 = request to send
              | | |_____ 1 = out1
              | |_____ 1 = out2
              |_____ 1 = loop
|_____ RESERVED
```

AL = modem status (see service number 0)
AH = line status (see service number 0)

9.5.7 System Services (INT 15H)

Table 9.33. *Index to BIOS System Functions — Interrupt 15H*

SERVICE REQUEST NUMBER	DESCRIPTION
AH = 0	Cassette motor ON
AH = 1	Cassette motor OFF
AH = 2	Read blocks from cassette
AH = 3	Write blocks to cassette
AH = 4 to 14	RESERVED
AH = 15	Periodic interrupt in IBM ESDI Fixed Disk Adapter/A
AH = 16 to 32	RESERVED
AH = 33	Power-on self-test error log
AH = 34 to 63	RESERVED
AH = 64	Read/modify profiles in PC Convertible
AH = 65	Wait for external event in PC Convertible
AH = 66	Request system power off in PC Convertible
AH = 67	Read system status in PC Convertible
AH = 68	Activate/deactivate internal modem in PC Convertible
AH = 69 to 78	RESERVED
AH = 79	Keyboard intercept
AH = 80 to 127	RESERVED
AH = 128	Device open
AH = 129	Device close
AH = 130	Program termination
AH = 131	Event wait
AH = 132	Joystick support
AH = 133	System request key pressed
AH = 134	Wait
AH = 135	Move block
AH = 136	Extended memory size determination
AH = 137	Switch processor to protected mode
AH = 138 to 143	RESERVED

(continued)

Table 9.33. *Index to BIOS System Functions (Continued)*

SERVICE REQUEST NUMBER	DESCRIPTION
AH = 144	Device busy
AH = 145	Interrupt complete
AH = 146 to 191	RESERVED
AH = 192	Return system configuration parameters
AH = 193	Return extended BIOS data area segment address
AH = 194	BIOS interface for pointing device
AH = 195	Enable and disable WatchDog Timer
AH = 196	Programmable option select
AH = 197 to 255	RESERVED

Table 9.34. BIOS Interrupt 15H — System Functions

SERVICE NUMBER (IN AH)	ON ENTRY	ON EXIT	DESCRIPTION
0	Nothing	AH-cf	Cassette motor ON

PC and PCjr
Returns:
    AH = 0
    Carry flag clear (cf = 0)

1	Nothing	AH-cf	Cassette motor OFF

PC and PCjr
Returns:
    AH = 0
    Carry flag clear (cf = 0)

2	CX ES:BX	DX-cf ES:BX	Read blocks from cassette

PC and PCjr
ES:BX -> variable size data buffer
CX = count of bytes to read (data buffer size)
Returns:
    ES:BX -> address of last byte read plus 1
    DX = count of bytes read
    Carry clear if no error (cf = 0)

PCjr
Returns:
    If carry flag clear (cf = 1), then AH holds error code
    AH = 1 for CRC error
    AH = 2 for lost data during transmission
    AH = 3 for no data found

3	CX ES:BX	cf ES:BX	Write blocks to cassette

PC and PCjr
ES:BX -> variable size data buffer
CX = count of bytes to read (data buffer size)
Returns:
    ES:BX -> address of last byte written plus 1
    CX = 0
    Carry clear if no error (cf = 0)

PCjr
Returns:
    If carry flag clear (cf = 1), then AH holds error code
    AH = 1 for CRC error
    AH = 2 for lost data during transmission
    AH = 3 for no data found

15	AL	cf	Periodic interrupt in IBM ESDI Fixed Disk Adapter/A

AL = phase code, as follows:
    0 is reserved
    1 is surface analysis
    2 is format operation

(continued)

Table 9.34. *BIOS Interrupt 15H — System Functions (Continued)*

SERVICE NUMBER (IN AH)	ON ENTRY	ON EXIT	DESCRIPTION
15	(continued)		

Returns:
    Carry clear to continue format or scan operation
    Carry set to end format or scan operation
    Note: This service receives control upon the completion
of the format or scan operation for each cylinder.

| 33 | AL-BX | AH-BX-cf ES:DI | Power-on self-test error log |

PS/2 MICRO CHANNEL SYSTEMS
AL = 0 to read POST error log
Returns:
    ES:DI -> POST error log
    BX = count of stored error codes
    Carry clear (cf = 0)

AL = 1 to write error code to POST error log
    BX = POST error code to write
    BH holds device code
    BL holds device error
Returns:
    Carry clear if no error (cf = 0)
    Carry set if error code storage is full
    AH = 0 if code successfully stored
    AH = 1 if error code storage is full
    ES:DI -> POST error log
    BX = count of stored error codes
    Carry clear (cf = 0)

| 64 | AL-CX-BX | AL-BX-CX cf | Read/modify profiles in PC Convertible |

AL = 0 to read system profile
    CX-BX = profile information
AL = 1 to modify system profile
    CX-BX = profile information
AL = 2 to read internal modem profile
AL = 3 to modify internal modem profile
    BX = profile information
Returns:
    CX-BX = profile information
    AL = 0 and cf = 0 if operation successful
    AL = 80H and cf = 1 if operation failed

| 65 | AL-BX-DX ES:DI | cf | Wait for external event in PC Convertible |

AL = event type code, as follows:
    0 - return after any event has occurred
    1 - compare values and return if equal
    2 - compare values and return if not equal
    3 - test bit and return if not zero
    4 - test bit and return if zero

(continued)

Table 9.34. *BIOS Interrupt 15H — System Functions (Continued)*

SERVICE NUMBER (IN AH)	ON ENTRY	ON EXIT	DESCRIPTION
65	(continued)		

ES:DI -> byte in user area for event determination, or
DX = port address to read for event determination
    In this case type codes are 11H, 12H, 13H, and 14H
BH = condition compare or mask value
BL = time-out value (in 55-ms units)
   = 0 for no time-out
Returns:
   Carry flag set (cf = 1) if time-out occurred

| 66 | AL | AX | Request system power off in PC Convertible |

AL = 0 to use system profile for suspend/IPL
   determination
AL = 1 to force system suspended mode
Returns:
   AX is modified

| 67 | Nothing | AL | Read system status in PC Convertible |

Returns:
AL = status, as follows:
  7 6 5 4 3 2 1 0 AL bit map

                                     LCD detached
                                     RESERVED
                                  RS-232C/parallel power ON
                            Internal modem power ON
                       Power activated by clock alarm
                  Standby power lost (bad RT clock)
              Operating on external power
         Low battery

| 68 | AL | AL | Activate/deactivate internal modem power in PC Convertible |

AL = 0 to power-off internal modem
AL = 1 to power-on internal modem and configure
   according to system profile
Returns:
   AL = 0 and cf = 0 if operation successful
   AL = 80H and cf = 1 if operation failed

| 79 | AL | AL-cf | Keyboard intercept |

The keyboard intercept is available in the following systems:
PC XT BIOS dated 01/10/86 and 05/09/86
PC AT BIOS dated 06/10/85 and 11/15/85
PC XT Model 286
PC Convertible
PS/2 Systems
The intercept is called by the INT 09H handler to allow the
program to change or absorb a keystroke. The handler can
proceed as follows:
   1. Replace the scan code in AL and clear the carry flag

(continued)

Table 9.34. *BIOS Interrupt 15H — System Functions (Continued)*

SERVICE NUMBER (IN AH)	ON ENTRY	ON EXIT	DESCRIPTION
79	(continued)		

2. Process or ignore the keystroke and return with the carry flag set

The interrupt handler at INT 15H must test AH for a value of 79 before assuming that it is this interrupt.
On entry to INT 15H (AH = 79)
    AL = scan code
    Carry flag set (cf = 1)
Returning to INT 08H:
    AL = new scan code and carry set, or
    AL unchanged and carry clear to ignore scan code

Service number 192 of INT 15H can be used to determine if a system supports the keyboard intercept

128	BX-CX	Nothing	Device open

PC XT BIOS dated 01/10/86 and later, PC AT, PC CONVERTIBLE, and PS/2 SYSTEMS
BX = device identification code
CX = process identification code

129	BX-CX	Nothing	Device close

PC XT BIOS dated 01/10/86 and later, PC AT, PC CONVERTIBLE, and PS/2 SYSTEMS
BX = device identification code
CX = process identification code

130	BX	Nothing	Program termination

PC XT BIOS dated 01/10/86 and later, PC AT, PC CONVERTIBLE, and PS/2 SYSTEMS
BX = device identification code

131	AL-CX-DX ES:BX	cf	Event wait (see also Table 9.41)

PC AT BIOS dated 06/10/85 and later, PC CONVERTIBLE, and PS/2 SYSTEMS
AL = 0 to set interval
ES:BX -> a byte in the caller's data area which will have its high bit set when the interval expires
CX-DX = 976 μs units in interval
AL = 1 to cancel interval
Returns:
    Carry clear (cf = 0) if operation successful
    Carry set (cf = 1) if operation not successful
Note: PS/2 non-Micro Channel systems always return with the carry flag set

(continued)

Table 9.34. *BIOS Interrupt 15H — System Functions (Continued)*

SERVICE NUMBER (IN AH)	ON ENTRY	ON EXIT	DESCRIPTION
132	DX	AX-BX-CX DX-cf	Joystick support

PC XT BIOS dated 01/10/86 and later, PC AT, and PS/2 SYSTEMS
DX = 0 to read current switch settings
Returns:
    AL bits 4 to 7 hold switch setting
    Carry set (cf = 1) if invalid call

DX = 1 to read resistive inputs
Returns:
    AX = A(x) value
    BC = A(y) value
    CX = B(x) value
    DX = B(y) value
    Carry set (cf = 1) if invalid call

| 133 | Nothing | AL | System request key pressed |

PC XT BIOS dated 01/10/86 and later, PC AT, PC CONVERTIBLE and PS/2 SYSTEMS
Returns:
    AL = 0 if key action was make
    AL = 1 if key action was break

| 134 | CX-DX-cf | Nothing | Wait (see also Table 9.43) |

PC AT, PC CONVERTIBLE and PS/2 SYSTEMS
CX-DX = 976-μs units in interval
Returns:
    Carry clear (cf = 0) if function successful
    Carry set (cf = 1) if wait already in progress

| 135 | CX ES:SI | AH-cf-zf | Move block |

PC AT, PC XT Model 286, and PS/2 MICRO CHANNEL SYSTEMS
This service allows a real-mode program to transfer a block of data to and from the 1-Mbyte real-mode limit by switching to protected mode.
CX = number of words in block to be moved
    (maximum count is 8000H)
ES:SI -> location in the global descriptor table built by the routine using this service
Returns:
    AH = 0 if operation successful
        1 if RAM parity error
        2 if other exception interrupt error
        3 if gate address line 20H failed
If AH = 0, then cf = 0 and zf = 1; otherwise cf = 1 and zf = 0.

(continued)

Table 9.34. *BIOS Interrupt 15H — System Functions (Continued)*

SERVICE NUMBER (IN AH)	ON ENTRY	ON EXIT	DESCRIPTION
136	Nothing	AX	Extended memory size determination

PC AT, PC XT Model 286, and PS/2
MICRO CHANNEL SYSTEMS
This service returns the amount of system memory beginning at 100000H.
Returns:
    AX = contiguous 1K memory blocks starting at 100000H

| 137 | ES:DI | AH | Switch processor to protected mode |

PC AT, PC XT Model 286, and PS/2
MICRO CHANNEL SYSTEMS
ES:SI -> Location of GTD previously built by routine
Returns:
    AH = 0 if operation was successful
    In this case all segment registers are changed and so are AL and BP.
Note: The use of this service is usually limited to operating system software.

| 144 | AL | cf | Device busy |

PC XT BIOS dated 01/10/86 and later, PC AT,
PC CONVERTIBLE, and PS/2 SYSTEMS
This service informs the operating system of a device wait.
AL = device type code, as follows:
    0 is disk (time-out) 1 is diskette (time-out)
    2 is keyboard   3 is pointing device (time-out)
    80H is network 4   FCH is PS/2 fixed disk reset
    FDH is diskette motor
    FEH is printer
Returns: Carry set (cf = 1) if wait satisfied

| 145 | Nothing | AL | Interrupt complete |

PC XT BIOS dated 01/10/86 and later, PC AT,
PC CONVERTIBLE, and PS/2 SYSTEMS
Returns:
    AL = device type code as in service 144

| 192 | Nothing | AH-cf ES:BX | Return system configuration parameters |

PC XT BIOS dated 01/10/86 and later, PC AT BIOS dated
06/10/85 and later, PC XT Model 286, PC CONVERTIBLE,
and PS/2 SYSTEMS
Returns:
    ES:BX -> system descriptor table in ROM
    AH = 0
    Carry clear (cf = 0)

(continued)

Table 9.34. *BIOS Interrupt 15H — System Functions (Continued)*

SERVICE NUMBER (IN AH)	ON ENTRY	ON EXIT	DESCRIPTION
192	(continued)		

System descriptor table structure:

Offset:	Data size:	Contents:
0	Word	Byte count of data in table (this item not included)
2	Byte	System identification byte (see model code in Table 9.1)
3	Byte	Submodel code (see Table 9.1)
4	Byte	Revision level (see Table 9.1)
5	Byte	Feature information byte no. 1

```
7  6  5  4  3  2  1  0  bit map
                  |__|____ RESERVED
                     |_____ 1 = Micro Channel system
                  |_____ 1 = extended BIOS data area
               |_____ 1 = wait for external event supported
            |_____ 1 = INT 15H intercept called
         |_____ 1 = real-time clock
      |_____ 1 = 2nd interrupt chip present
   |_____ 1 = hard disk BIOS uses DMA channel 3
```

6	Byte	RESERVED
7	Byte	RESERVED
8	Byte	RESERVED
9	Byte	RESERVED

| 193 | Nothing | ES-cf | Return extended BIOS data area segment address |

PS/2 SYSTEMS
Returns:
ES = extended BIOS data area segment
Carry clear (cf = 0) if no error
Carry set (cf = 1) if error

| 194 | AL-BX | BX-CL-DL ES:BX | BIOS interface for pointing device |

PS/2 SYSTEMS
AL = 0 to enable/disable pointing device
BH = 0 to disable
BH = 1 to enable
Returns:
AH = status of pointing device
AH = 0 for no error
    1 for invalid function call
    2 for invalid input
    3 for interface error
    4 for resend command
    5 for no far call installed
Carry clear (cf = 0) if operation successful

(continued)

Table 9.34. *BIOS Interrupt 15H — System Functions (Continued)*

SERVICE NUMBER (IN AH)	ON ENTRY	ON EXIT	DESCRIPTION
194	(continued)		

AL = 1 to reset pointing device
Returns:
    Status and cf as in service number 0
    If operation successful:
    BX holds device ID or 0
The default pointing device state is as follows:
    Device disabled
    Sample rate of 100 reports per second
    Resolution of 4 counts per millimeter
    Scaling 1:1
    Data package size same as before service call

AL = 2 to set sample rate
    BH holds sample rate value in reports per second
    BH = 0 for 10 reports   BH = 1 for 20 reports
    BH = 2 for 40 reports   BH = 3 for 60 reports
    BH = 4 for 80 reports   BH = 5 for 100 reports
    BH = 6 for 200 reports
Returns:
Status and cf as in service number 0

AL = 3 to set resolution
    BH holds resolution value
    BH = 0 for 1 count per millimeter
          1 for 2 count per millimeter
          2 for 4 count per millimeter
          3 for 8 count per millimeter
Returns:
    Status and cf as in service number 0

AL = 4 to read device type
Returns:
    Status and cf as in service number 0
    BH = device ID (0) if operation successful

AL = 5 to initialize pointing device
    BH = data package size in byte (range 0 to 8)
Returns:
    Status and cf as in service number 0
    The pointing device state is as follows:
        Device disabled
        Sample rate of 100 reports per second
        Resolution of 4 counts per millimeter
        Scaling 1:1

AL = 6 for extended commands
    BH = 0 to return status
        = 1 to set scaling to 1:1
        = 2 to set scaling to 2:1
    If BH = 0, (status operation) was successful:

(continued)

Table 9.34. *BIOS Interrupt 15H — System Functions (Continued)*

SERVICE NUMBER (IN AH)	ON ENTRY	ON EXIT	DESCRIPTION
194	(continued)		

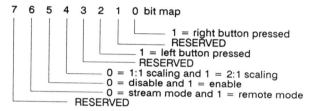

BL = status byte no. 1

```
7  6  5  4  3  2  1  0  bit map
                        1 = right button pressed
                     RESERVED
                  1 = left button pressed
               RESERVED
            0 = 1:1 scaling and 1 = 2:1 scaling
         0 = disable and 1 = enable
      0 = stream mode and 1 = remote mode
   RESERVED
```

CL = status byte no. 2
    0 for 1 count per millimeter
    1 for 2 count per millimeter
    2 for 4 count per millimeter
    3 for 8 count per millimeter

DL = status byte no. 3
    0AH for 10 reports   14H for 20 reports
    28H for 40 reports   3CH for 60 reports
    50H for 80 reports   64H for 100 reports
    C8H for 200 reports
BH = 1 to set scaling to 1:1
    = 2 to set scaling to 2:1
Returns:
    Status and cf as in service number 0

AL = 7 for device driver far call initialization
ES = segment address of user routine
BX = offset of user routine
Returns:
Status and cf as in service number 0

Notes on the pointing device interface routine:
The user routine is installed by communicating the code's
segment and offset address to the BIOS using service
number 7 (device driver far call initialization). The user
routine should be coded as a far procedure. As device data
becomes available, the BIOS transfers execution to the user
routine with the following parameters in the stack:

Stack word:	Contents:
1	Device status
2	x coordinate data
3	y coordinate data
4	z coordinate data

(continued)

Table 9.34. *BIOS Interrupt 15H — System Functions (Continued)*

SERVICE NUMBER (IN AH)	ON ENTRY	ON EXIT	DESCRIPTION
194	(continued)		

Stack word no. 1, low-order byte

```
7  6  5  4  3  2  1  0  bit map
                        └───── 1 = left button pressed
                     └──────── 1 = right button pressed
                  └─────────── RESERVED (must be 0)
               └────────────── RESERVED (must be 1)
            └───────────────── 1 = x data is negative
         └──────────────────── 1 = y data is negative
      └─────────────────────── 1 = x data overflow
   └────────────────────────── 1 = y data overflow
```

Stack word no. 1, high-order byte = 0
Stack word no. 2, low-order byte is x data
Stack word no. 2, high-order byte = 0
Stack word no. 3, low-order byte is y data
Stack word no. 3, high-order byte = 0
Stack word no. 4, low-order byte = 0
Stack word no. 4, high-order byte = 0
Note: The user routine should not pop parameters off the stack before returning

| 195 | AL-BX | cf | Enable and disable WatchDog Timer |

PS/2 MICRO CHANNEL SYSTEMS
AL = 0 to disable WatchDog Timer
AL = 1 to enable WatchDog Timer
BX = WatchDog Timer count (range 1 to 255)
Returns:
    Carry clear (cf = 0) if operation successful
    Carry set (cf = 1) if error

| 196 | AL-BL | AL-DX-cf | Programmable option select |

PS/2 MICRO CHANNEL SYSTEMS
AL = 0 to return POS adapter base register address
Returns:
    AL = 0
    DX = POS adapter base register address

AL = 1 to enable slot for setup
BL = slot number
Returns:
    AL = 1
    BL = slot number

AL = 2 to enable adapter
    Returns:
    AL = 2

Return for all:
    Carry clear (cf = 0) if operation successful
    Carry set (cf = 1) if request failed

9.5.8 Keyboard Functions (INT 16H)

Table 9.35. *Index to BIOS Keyboard Functions — Interrupt 16H*

SERVICE REQUEST NUMBER	DESCRIPTION
AH = 0	Read keyboard
AH = 1	Return keyboard status
AH = 2	Return keyboard flags
AH = 3	Set typematic rate
AH = 4	Keyboard click adjustment
AH = 5	Write to keyboard buffer
AH = 6 to 15	RESERVED
AH = 16	Extended keyboard read
AH = 17	Extended keystroke status
AH = 18	Extended shift key status
AH = 19 to 255	RESERVED

Table 9.36. *BIOS Interrupt 16H — Keyboard Functions*

SERVICE NUMBER (IN AH)	ON ENTRY	ON EXIT	DESCRIPTION
0	Nothing	AX	Read keyboard (wait for key)

Returns:
    AL = ASCII character code
    AH = scan code
    Note: This service waits for a keystroke to become available.

1	Nothing	AX-zf	Return keyboard status

Returns:
    Zero flag set (zf = 1) if no code available
    Zero flag clear (zf = 0) if code available
    AL = ASCII character code
    AH = scan code

2	Nothing	AL	Return keyboard flags

Returns:
    AL = keyboard flags

```
   7  6  5  4  3  2  1  0  AL bit map
                        └──── 1 = right shift key pressed
                     └─────── 1 = left shift key pressed
                  └────────── 1 = Ctrl key pressed
               └───────────── 1 = Alt key pressed
            └──────────────── 1 = Scroll Lock locked
         └─────────────────── 1 = Num Lock locked
      └────────────────────── 1 = Caps Lock locked
   └───────────────────────── 1 = Insert key locked
```

AH = RESERVED

3	AL-BX	Nothing	Set typematic rate

PCjr
AL = 0 to restore default delay and typematic rate
AL = 1 to increase initial delay
AL = 2 to slow the typematic rate by one-half
AL = 3 to increase delay and slow typematic rate by one-half
AL = 4 to turn off typematic action

PC AT BIOS dated 11/15/85 and later, PC XT Model 286, and PS/2 SYSTEMS
AL = 5 to set typematic rate and delay
BL = typematic rate in characters per second (cps)

0 = 30.0 cps	1 = 26.7 cps	2 = 24.0 cps
3 = 21.8 cps	4 = 20.0 cps	5 = 18.5 cps
6 = 17.1 cps	7 = 16.0 cps	8 = 15.0 cps
9 = 13.3 cps	10 = 12.0 cps	11 = 10.9 cps
12 = 10.0 cps	13 = 9.2 cps	14 = 8.6 cps
15 = 8.0 cps	16 = 7.5 cps	17 = 6.7 cps
18 = 6.0 cps	19 = 5.5 cps	20 = 5.0 cps
21 = 4.6 cps	22 = 4.3 cps	23 = 4.0 cps
24 = 3.7 cps	25 = 3.3 cps	26 = 3.0 cps
27 = 2.7 cps	28 = 2.5 cps	29 = 2.3 cps
30 = 2.1 cps	31 = 2.0 cps	
32 to 255 = RESERVED		

(continued)

Table 9.36. *BIOS Interrupt 16H — Keyboard Functions (Continued)*

SERVICE NUMBER (IN AH)	ON ENTRY	ON EXIT	DESCRIPTION
3	(continued)		

BH = delay in milliseconds
    0 = 250 ms   1 = 500 ms   2 = 750 ms
    3 = 1000 ms
    4 to 255 = RESERVED

| 4 | AL | Nothing | Keyboard click adjustment |

PCjr and PC CONVERTIBLE
AL = 0 to set keyboard click OFF
AL = 1 to set keyboard click ON

| 5 | CX | AL | Write to keyboard buffer |

PC AT BIOS dated 11/15/85 and later, PC XT BIOS dated 01/10/86 and later, PC XT Model 286, and PS/2 SYSTEMS
Note: This service writes a character and a scan code to the keyboard buffer as if they had been typed on the keyboard.
CL = ASCII character code to write
CH = scan code to write
Returns:
    AL = 0 if operation successful
    AL = 1 if keyboard buffer full

| 16 | Nothing | AX | Extended keyboard read |

PC AT BIOS dated 11/15/85 and later, PC XT BIOS dated 01/10/86 and later, PC XT Model 286, and PS/2 SYSTEMS
Note: This service extracts a character and a scan code from the keyboard buffer.
Returns:
    AL = ASCII character read from the keyboard buffer
    AH = scan code read from the keyboard buffer

| 17 | Nothing | AX-zf | Extended keystroke status |

PC AT BIOS dated 11/15/85 and later, PC XT BIOS dated 01/10/86 and later, PC XT Model 286, and PS/2 SYSTEMS
Returns:
    Zero flag set (zf = 1) if no code available
    Zero flag clear (zf = 0) if code available
    AL = ASCII character code
    AH = scan code
Note: The keystroke is not removed from the buffer.

(continued)

Table 9.36. *BIOS Interrupt 16H — Keyboard Functions (Continued)*

SERVICE NUMBER (IN AH)	ON ENTRY	ON EXIT	DESCRIPTION
18	Nothing	AX	Extended keyboard flags

PC AT BIOS dated 11/15/85 and later, PC XT BIOS dated 01/10/86 and later, PC XT Model 286, and PS/2 SYSTEMS
Returns:
AL = extended keyboard status flags
7 6 5 4 3 2 1 0   AL bit map

```
                         1 = right shift key pressed
                         1 = left shift key pressed
                      1 = Ctrl key pressed
                      1 = Alt key pressed
                   1 = Scroll Lock locked
                1 = Num Lock locked
             1 = Caps Lock locked
          1 = Insert key locked
```

AH = extended keyboard shift status flags
7 6 5 4 3 2 1 0   AH bit map

```
                         1 = Left Ctrl key pressed
                         1 = Left Alt key pressed
                      1 = Right Ctrl key pressed
                      1 = Right Alt key pressed
                   1 = Scroll Lock key pressed
                1 = Num Lock key pressed
             1 = Caps Lock key pressed
          1 = Sys Req key pressed
```

9.5.9 Printer Functions (INT 17H)

Table 9.37. *Index to BIOS Printer Functions — Interrupt 17H*

SERVICE REQUEST NUMBER	D E S C R I P T I O N
AH = 0	Print character
AH = 1	Initialize printer
AH = 2	Read printer status
AH = 3 to 255	RESERVED

Table 9.38. *BIOS Interrupt 17H — Printer Functions*

SERVICE NUMBER (IN AH)	ON ENTRY	ON EXIT	DESCRIPTION
0	AL-DX	AH	Print character

AL = character to print
DX = printer port number (0-based)
Returns:
    AH = printer status

AH bit map:
- 1 = time-out
- RESERVED
- RESERVED
- 1 = I/O error
- 1 = printer selected
- 1 = out of paper
- 1 = acknowledge
- 1 = printer not busy

| 1 | DX | AH | Initialize printer |

DX = printer port number (0-based)
Returns:
    AH = printer status as in service number 0

| 2 | DX | AH | Read printer status |

DX = printer port number (0-based)
Returns:
    AH = printer status as in service number 0

9.5.10 System Timer Functions (INT 1AH)

Table 9.39. *Index to BIOS System-Timer Functions — Interrupt 1AH*

SERVICE REQUEST NUMBER	DESCRIPTION
AH = 0	Read system-timer counters
AH = 1	Set system-timer counters
AH = 2	Read real-time clock time
AH = 3	Set real-time clock time
AH = 4	Read real-time clock date
AH = 5	Set real-time clock date
AH = 6	Set real-time clock alarm
AH = 7	Reset real-time clock alarm
AH = 8	Set real-time clock power-on mode in PC Convertible
AH = 9	Read real-time clock alarm
AH = 10	Read system-timer day counter
AH = 11	Set system-timer day counter
AH = 12 to 127	RESERVED
AH = 128	Set up sound multiplexer in PCjr
AH = 129 to 255	RESERVED

Table 9.40. *BIOS Interrupt 1AH — System-Timer Functions*

SERVICE NUMBER (IN AH)	ON ENTRY	ON EXIT	DESCRIPTION
0	Nothing	AL-CX-DX	Read system-timer counters

Returns:
   CX = high word of counter
   DX = low word of counter
   AL = 0 if timer has not passed 24 h of counts since last power-on, reset, read, or set operation
   AL = 1 if timer has passed 24 h of counts since last power-on, reset, read, or set operation
   Note: The system timer beats at a rate of approximately 18.2 times per second (1,193,180 / 65,535).

1	CX-DX	Nothing	Set system-timer counters

CX = high word of counter
DX = low word of counter

2	Nothing	CX-DX-cf	Read real-time clock time

AT BIOS dated 06/10/85
Returns:
   CH = hours (in BCD)
   CL = minutes (in BCD)
   DH = seconds (in BCD)
   Carry flag clear (cf = 0) if clock is operating
   Carry flag set (cf = 1) if clock is not operating

PC AT BIOS dated 06/10/85 and later, PC XT Model 286, PC CONVERTIBLE, and PS/2 SYSTEMS
Returns:
   CH = hours (in BCD)
   CL = minutes (in BCD)
   DH = seconds (in BCD)
   DL = 1 for daylight savings time option
   DL = 0 for no daylight savings time option
   Carry flag clear (cf = 0) if clock is operating
   Carry flag set (cf = 1) if clock is not operating

3	CX-DX	Nothing	Set real-time clock time

PC AT, PC XT Model 286, PC CONVERTIBLE and PS/2 SYSTEMS
CH = hours (in BCD)
CL = minutes (in BCD)
DH = seconds (in BCD)
DL = 1 for daylight savings time option
DL = 0 for no daylight savings time option
Note: DL is not used in PS/2 non-Micro Channel systems

4	Nothing	CX-DX-cf	Read real-time clock date

PC AT, PC XT Model 286, PC CONVERTIBLE, and PS/2 SYSTEMS
Returns:
   CH = century (in BCD)
      range is 19 or 20

(continued)

Table 9.40. *BIOS Interrupt 1AH — System-Timer Functions (Continued)*

SERVICE NUMBER (IN AH)	ON ENTRY	ON EXIT	DESCRIPTION
4	(continued)		
	CH = hours (in BCD) CL = year (in BCD) DH = month (in BCD) DL = day (in BCD) Carry flag clear (cf = 0) if clock is operating Carry flag set (cf = 1) if clock is not operating		
5	CX-DX	Nothing	Set real-time clock date
	PC AT, PC XT Model 286, PC CONVERTIBLE and PS/2 SYSTEMS CH = century (in BCD) range is 19 or 20 CL = year (in BCD) DH = month (in BCD) DL = day (in BCD)		
6	CX-DH	cf	Set real-time clock alarm

	PC AT, PC XT Model 286, PC CONVERTIBLE, and PS/2 SYSTEMS
	CH = hours (in BCD)
	CL = minutes (in BCD)
	DH = seconds (in BCD)
	Returns:
	    Carry flag clear (cf = 0) if operation successful
	    Carry flag set (cf = 1) if alarm already set or error
	Note: The alarm function generates an INT 4AH. The program should install an alarm handler at this vector before setting the alarm function with this service.		

7	Nothing	Nothing	Reset real-time clock alarm
	PC AT, PC XT Model 286, PC CONVERTIBLE, and PS/2 SYSTEMS This service cancels an installed real clock alarm.		
8	CX-DH	cf	Set real-time clock power-on mode

	PC Convertible
	CH = hours (in BCD)
	CL = minutes (in BCD)
	DH = seconds (in BCD)
	Returns:
	    Carry flag clear (cf = 0) if operation successful
	    Carry flag set (cf = 1) if alarm already set or error		

(continued)

Table 9.40. *BIOS Interrupt 1AH — System-timer Functions*
(Continued)

SERVICE NUMBER (IN AH)	ON ENTRY	ON EXIT	DESCRIPTION
9	Nothing	CX-DX-cf	Read real-time clock alarm

PC CONVERTIBLE, and PS/2 NON-MICRO CHANNEL SYSTEMS
Returns:
    CH = hours (in BCD)
    CL = minutes (in BCD)
    DH = seconds (in BCD)
    DL = alarm status, as follows:
        1 for alarm not enabled
        2 for alarm enabled but will not power-on system
        3 for alarm enabled and will power-on system
Note: PS/2 non-Micro Channel systems do not support the power-on feature.

10	Nothing	CX	Read system-timer day counter

PC XT BIOS dated 01/10/86 and after and PS/2 SYSTEMS
CX = count of days since 01/01/1980

11	CX	Nothing	Set system-timer day counter

PC XT BIOS dated 01/10/86 and after and PS/2 SYSTEMS
CX = count of days since 01/01/1980
Note: For PC XT BIOS dated 01/10/86 and after and PS/2 non-Micro Channel systems the count is initialized to zero during the POST.

128	AL	Nothing	Set up sound multiplexed in PCjr

PCjr
AL = sound source ("Audio Out" or RF modulator)
    0 for 8253 channel 2
    1 for cassette input
    2 for "Audio In" line in I/O channel
    3 for complex sound generator chip

9.5.11 Real-Time Clock Interrupt (INT 70H)

Table 9.41. *BIOS Interrupt 70H — Real-Time Clock Interrupt*

DESCRIPTION

Real-time clock interrupt to signal an elapsed interval of 976
μs (1024 times per second)

PC AT, PC XT Model 286, and PS/2 SYSTEMS
This interrupt is activated by one of the following actions:
Case 1. Setting the event wait function using service number
131 of INT 15H (see Table 9.34)
Case 2. Setting the wait function using service number 134
of INT 15H (see Table 9.34)
Case 3. Setting the alarm function using service number 6 of
INT 1AH (see Table 9.40)

In cases 1 and 2 the counter in CX-DX is decremented at 976-μs
intervals. When the count reaches zero, the designated memory byte
will have its high bit set. In case 1 the location of this byte is
determined by the program. In case 2 the designated location is in the
BIOS data area at address 0040:00A0. In the alarm function, case 3, the
program must code a handler routine at interrupt 4AH before setting the
function.

The following BIOS data areas are related to the clock interrupt:

Address:	Data size:	Function
0040:0098	Word	Offset of user wait complete flag
0040:009A	Word	Segment of user wait complete flag
0040:009C	Word	Low word of microsecond counter
0040:009E	Word	High word of microsecond counter
0040:00A0	Byte	Wait active flag

```
7  6  5  4  3  2  1  0  bit map
|  |  |  |  |  |  |  |
                  └───── 1 = INT 15H, service no. 134
                         (case 2) wait has occurred
            └─────────── RESERVED
└─────────────────────── 1 = Wait time elapsed in event wait (case 2)
```

Appendix A

Numerical Conversion Routines

1. ASCII_TO_FPD. Procedure for converting an ASCII decimal number into a floating-point decimal string.

2. INPUT_NDP. Procedure for loading a floating-point decimal string into the NDP stack top register.

3. OUTPUT_NDP. Store the NDP stack top register in a floating-point decimal string.

4. Auxiliary procedures:

   a. 10_2_X. Raise the number 10 to a power.
   b. ASC_TO_BIN. Convert a 5-digit ASCII string into a 16-bit binary number.
   c. BIN_TO_ASC. Convert a 16-bit binary into a 5-digit ASCII string
   d. NIBBS_2_DEC. Convert 2 packed BCD digits into 2 decimal digits.
   e. FILL_CALLERS. Fill a buffer supplied by the caller with a 27-byte message.

```
;****************************************************************
;                            publics
;****************************************************************
PUBLIC   ASCII_TO_FPD
PUBLIC   INPUT_NDP
PUBLIC   OUTPUT_NDP

;****************************************************************
;                          data storage
;****************************************************************
ROUT_DATA          SEGMENT
; Temporary storage buffers for conversion routines
```

```
TEMP_REAL          DT      ?
                   DB      0
WORK_BUF           DB      18 DUP (?)
                   DB      0
; NDP caller's environment storage area
STATE_8087         DB      94 DUP (?)
;
; Binary and BCD variables and constants
PACKED_EXP         DT      ?          ; 18-digit BCD exponent
PACKED_SIG         DT      ?          ; 18-digit BCD significand
BINARY_EXP         DW      ?          ; Storage for binary exponent
SIGN_OF_EXP        DB      ?          ; 1 = negative
                                      ; 0 = positive
TEN_TO_17          DT      00100000000000000000
TEN                DW      10
NAN_CODE           DD      0FFFFFFFFH     ; Not a number encoding
INF_NEGATIVE       DD      0FF800000H     ; Negative infinity
INF_POSITIVE       DD      07F800000H     ; Positive infinity
;
USERS_CW           DW      ?          ; Storage for caller's control
                                      ; word
DOWN_CW            DW      17FFH      ; Temporary control word to
                                      ; force
                                      ; rounding down
;
; Text for clearing the caller's buffer. Has 27 characters
FPD_MES            DB      '                      E       '
; Status word storage and error messages
ERROR_AL1          DB      ' NONORMAL                    '
ERROR_AL2          DB      ' INFINITY                    '
ERROR_AL3          DB      ' NOT-A-NUMBER                '
ERROR_AL4          DB      ' EMPTY                       '
NUMBER_0           DB      ' 0.00000000000000000 E+0     '
STATUS_WORD        DW      ?
;
; Intermediate buffer for 5 exponent ASCII digits
EXP_BUFFER         DB      '       ',00H
;
; Storage for entry pointers
ENTRY_SI           DW      0          ; Start of caller's input string
ENTRY_DI           DW      0          ; Start of caller's output
                                      ; buffer
                   DB      0
;
ROUT_DATA          ENDS
;****************************************************************
;                              code
;****************************************************************
CODE    SEGMENT
        ASSUME  CS:CODE
;*****************************|
;       ASCII_TO_FPD         |
;*****************************|
;
ASCII_TO_FPD   PROC    FAR
; Conversion of an ASCII decimal number into floating-point
; decimal string
; On entry:
;          DS:SI --> an ASCII decimal string, terminated in a NULL
; later ES:SI    byte, which holds the caller's ASCII decimal
;                input
;                Note: The caller's buffer may contain the $ sign
;                and commas as formatting symbols. The string
;                terminator (00H) may be preceded by a CR
```

```
;                         (ODH) or LF (OAH) control codes. If the
;                         characters E or e are in the string, the
;                         procedure assumes that the string is already
;                         in floating-point notation.
;
;        DS:DI --> a 27-byte unformatted memory area which will
; later ES:DI     be filled with the floating-point decimal
;                 output
;
; On exit:
;        DS:DI --> the caller's buffer with the input number
;                 reformatted in floating-point decimal format
;                 as follows:
;
;                    sm.mmmmmmmmmmmmmmmmmm ESeeee
; where
; s = sign of number (blank = +)
; m = 18 significand digits
; . = decimal point following the first significand digit
; E = letter E signals the start of the exponent field
; S = + or - sign of exponent
; e = up to four exponent digits
;                 All registers are preserved
;
;********************|
;   save caller's    |
;     segments       |
;********************|
;
        PUSH    DS
        PUSH    ES
; Set ES --> caller's data
        PUSH    DS
        POP     ES
; Set DS to --> routine's data
        MOV     AX,ROUT_DATA
        MOV     DS,AX
        ASSUME  DS:ROUT_DATA
;********************|
;
; save input ptrs.   |
;    in memory       |
;********************|
;
        MOV     ENTRY_SI,SI
        MOV     ENTRY_DI,DI
;********************|
;
;  save input regs.  |
;********************|
;
        PUSH    AX
        PUSH    CX
        PUSH    DX
        PUSH    SI
        PUSH    DI
;********************|
;
;   test for E or e  |
;********************|
; The caller's string may already be in floating-point format
TEST_4_FPF:
        CMP     BYTE PTR ES:[SI],'E'
        JE      STRING_ISFP              ; String in FP format
        CMP     BYTE PTR ES:[SI],'e'
        JE      STRING_ISFP
        CMP     BYTE PTR ES:[SI],' '     ; Less than 20H is
                                         ; end
                                         ; of string
```

```
        JB      NOT_FPF         ; Not floating-point
        INC     SI
        JMP     TEST_4_FPF
;********************
;  move FP input
; to output buffer
;********************
STRING_ISFP:
        MOV     SI,ENTRY_SI     ; Restore input string pointer
; Clear 27 bytes in output buffer
        PUSH    DI              ; Save output pointer
        MOV     CX,27           ; Set up digits counter
PREP_27:
        MOV     BYTE PTR ES:[DI],' '    ; Place blank in buffer
        INC     DI
        LOOP    PREP_27
        POP     DI              ; Restore output buffer pointer
; Move up to 27 digits from input to output buffers. No checks
; are made for an invalid input string
        MOV     CX,27           ; Digits counter
MOVE_INPUT:
        MOV     AL,ES:[SI]      ; Get character
        CMP     AL,' '          ; Less than 20H ends input string
        JB      END_ISTRING     ; End move if terminator
        MOV     ES:[DI],AL      ; Move character to output buffer
        INC     SI              ; Bump pointers
        INC     DI
        LOOP    MOVE_INPUT
END_ISTRING:
        JMP     A2FP_EXIT
;********************
; clear output area
;********************
NOT_FPF:
        MOV     SI,ENTRY_SI     ; Restore input buffer pointer
        PUSH    DI              ; Save output pointer
        LEA     SI,NUMBER_0     ; Zero is default value
        MOV     CX,27           ; Byte to clear
CLEAR_27:
        MOV     AL,[SI]         ; Get message character
        MOV     ES:[DI],AL      ; Place in buffer area
        INC     DI              ; Bump pointers
        INC     SI
        LOOP    CLEAR_27
; Caller's buffer is now formatted. Restore pointer
        MOV     SI,ENTRY_SI     ; Start of caller's buffer
        POP     DI              ; Output buffer start
;********************
;    get sign
;********************
; Find first significant character in the caller's string
; Skip leading blanks, $ and # sign, and other invalid symbols
GET_NB:
        MOV     AL,ES:[SI]      ; Get character
        CMP     AL,'+'          ; Test for + sign
        JAE     FIRST_NB        ; Go if equal or larger
        INC     SI
        JMP     GET_NB
; First nonblank is a symbol or number larger than the + sign
FIRST_NB:
        CMP     AL,'+'          ; Test for +
        JE      SIGN_IS_PLUS
        CMP     AL,'-'          ; Test for -
```

```
                JE          SIGN_IS_MINUS
; First nonblank character is not a sign. Assume a digit and
; force a positive significand
                JMP         IMPLICIT_POS
SIGN_IS_MINUS:
                MOV         BYTE PTR ES:[DI],'-'    ; Set minus sign in
                                                   ; caller's buffer
; Positive numbers are formatted with a leading blank
SIGN_IS_PLUS:
                INC         SI                 ; Bump source pointer
IMPLICIT_POS:
                INC         DI                 ; Bump destination pointers
;*******************|
;    skip leading   |
;       zeros       |
;*******************|
SKIP_ZERO:
; Leading zeros are not significant. Skip them
                CMP         BYTE PTR ES:[SI],'0'   ; Test for 0
                JNE         NOT_LEAD0
                INC         SI                 ; Bump to next digit
                JMP         SKIP_ZERO
;*******************|
; find decimal point|
;*******************|
;   Clear counter for digits preceding the decimal point
NOT_LEAD0:
                MOV         DX,0               ; DX is integer digit counter
                PUSH        SI                 ; Save pointer to caller's
                                               ; leading digit
; Caller's string must end in a NULL byte (00H), but it can have
; other embedded control characters, for example, 0DH
; Test for an integer zero input
                CMP         BYTE PTR ES:[SI],' '   ; Smaller than 20H is
                                                   ; end of input buffer
                JAE         GET_POINT          ; Continue if not end
                JMP         NUM_ISZERO         ; Number is zero
GET_POINT:
                MOV         AL,ES:[SI]         ; Get caller's characters
                CMP         AL,'.'             ; Test for decimal point
                JE          POINT_FOUND
                CMP         AL,','             ; Test for formatting comma
                                               ; in the caller's string
                JE          SKIP_COMMA         ; Ignore comma
                CMP         AL,0               ; String terminator
                JNE         LOOK_4_PT          ; Continue searching
                JMP         NO_POINT           ; No decimal point in string
LOOK_4_PT:
                INC         DX                 ; Count one integer digit
SKIP_COMMA:
                INC         SI                 ; Bump integer digits counter
                JMP         GET_POINT
;*******************|
;    string is a    |
;  decimal fraction |
;*******************|
; If DX = 0, then the caller's string <1 and the EXPONENT IS
;            NEGATIVE or the number is zero
; If DX = 1, then the caller's string is already normalized
;            and the EXPONENT = +0
; If DX > 1, then the caller's string is a number less than or
;            equal to 10 and the EXPONENT IS POSITIVE
;
```

```
POINT_FOUND:
        CMP      DX,1                ; Test for normalized input
        JNE      TEST_4_DX0
;*******************
;    DX = 1
;*******************
; Number is between 1 and 10. Set exponent sign and value
        MOV      SI,ENTRY_DI        ; SI --> start of output buffer
        ADD      SI,22              ;       --> first character after E
; DS:SI --> position for exponent sign in output buffer
        MOV      BYTE PTR ES:[SI],'+'   ; Sign must be +
        INC      SI
        MOV      BYTE PTR ES:[SI],'0'   ; Set zero exponent
; Move exponent digits from conversion buffer into output buffer
        JMP      EXP_MOVED
TEST_4_DX0:
        CMP      DX,0               ; Test for negative exponent
        JE       DX_ISZERO         ; Go to DX = 0 processing
; If not zero, treat number as integer. Adjust exponent
        INC      DX
        JMP      NO_POINT
;*******************
;    DX = 0
;*******************
; Possible cases:
; nonzero -->    000.002345
; nonzero -->    .2345
;    zero -->    0.00
;    zero -->    .0
; Count decimal digits to normalized position, that is, following
; the first nonzero digit
; DX is used as counter
; SI --> decimal point
DX_ISZERO:
        INC      SI                ; Skip decimal point
        INC      DX                ; Count one digit
NORM_SIGNF:
        CMP      BYTE PTR ES:[SI],'0'   ; Test for zero
        JE       ZERO_DIGIT
        JB       NUM_ISZERO
; If not equal or less, it must be larger
        JMP      OK_SIGNF          ; Normalized position found
ZERO_DIGIT:
        INC      SI                ; Bump pointer
        INC      DX                ; and digits counter
        JMP      NORM_SIGNF
;*******************
;   input string = 0
;*******************
NUM_ISZERO:
; Zero is the default floating-point value in the buffer,
; but exponent may have been changed
        MOV      SI,ENTRY_DI       ; SI --> start of output buffer
        ADD      SI,22             ;       --> first character after E
; DS:SI --> position for exponent sign in output buffer
        MOV      BYTE PTR ES:[SI],'+'   ; Sign must be +
        INC      SI
        MOV      BYTE PTR ES:[SI],'0'   ; Set zero exponent
        POP      SI
        JMP      A2FP_EXIT         ; Exit conversion
OK_SIGNF:
; Test for an invalid digit indicating a zero input
        POP      AX                ; Discard old pointer in stack
```

```
            PUSH    SI                  ; Save pointer to first nonzero
                                        ; digit
            MOV     SI,ENTRY_DI         ; SI --> start of output buffer
            ADD     SI,22               ;     --> first character after E
; DS:SI --> position for exponent sign in output buffer
            MOV     BYTE PTR ES:[SI],'-'    ; Sign must be -
            JMP     CONV_EXPONENT
.********************
;
; string is integer
;********************
;
NO_POINT:
; Exponent of integer is positive
            MOV     SI,ENTRY_DI         ; SI --> start of output buffer
            ADD     SI,22               ;     --> first character after E
; DS:SI --> position for exponent sign in output buffer
            MOV     BYTE PTR ES:[SI],'+'    ; Sign must be +
            INC     SI
; String has no decimal point. DX = exponent plus 2
            DEC     DX
            DEC     DX
CONV_EXPONENT:
            LEA     DI,EXP_BUFFER           ; Buffer for conversion
            CALL    BIN_TO_ASC          ; Binary in DX to a 5-digit
                                        ; ASCII in EXP_BUFFER
            MOV     SI,ENTRY_DI         ; SI --> start of output buffer
            ADD     SI,23               ;     --> first character after
                                        ; exponent sign
; Caller's string pointer in stack
; DI --> first nonzero ASCII digit in conversion buffer
; Move exponent digits from conversion buffer into output buffer
TO_OUTPUT_BUF:
            MOV     AL,[DI]             ; Get character
            CMP     AL,0                ; Test for end of buffer
            JE      EXP_MOVED           ; Exponent digits have been moved
            MOV     ES:[SI],AL          ; Place digit in output buffer
            INC     SI                  ; Bump pointers
            INC     DI
            JMP     TO_OUTPUT_BUF
EXP_MOVED:
            POP     SI                  ; Pointer to first nonzero digit
                                        ; in the caller's input
.********************
;
;   move up to 18
;      digits
;********************
;
            MOV     DI,ENTRY_DI         ; Start of output buffer
            INC     DI                  ; Skip sign of significand
; Move one digit preceding the decimal point. Caller's string
; will have at least one digit at this point
            MOV     AL,ES:[SI]          ; Get digit
; Test for invalid values
            CMP     AL,'0'              ; Lower limit
            JAE     VALID_1             ; Go if OK
            JMP     NUM_ISZERO          ; Force zero if invalid digit
VALID_1:
            CMP     AL,'9'              ; Upper limit of digit
            JBE     VALID_2             ; Go if OK
            JMP     NUM_ISZERO          ; Force zero if invalid digit
VALID_2:
            MOV     ES:[DI],AL          ; Move to buffer
            INC     DI                  ; Bump buffer pointers
            INC     SI
            INC     DI                  ; Skip decimal point in buffer
```

```
            MOV     CX,17               ; Load digits counter
UPTO_17:
            MOV     AL,ES:[SI]          ; Get digit
            CMP     AL,'.'              ; Test for period symbol
                                        ; in caller's string
            JE      SKIP_SYMBOL         ; Skip it
            CMP     AL,','              ; and for commas
            JE      SKIP_SYMBOL
            CMP     AL,' '              ; Test for terminator symbol
            JB      A2FP_EXIT           ; Go if less than 20H
; Test for invalid values
            CMP     AL,'0'              ; Lower limit
            JAE     VALID_3             ; Go if OK
            JMP     NUM_ISZERO          ; Force zero if invalid digit
VALID_3:
            CMP     AL,'9'              ; Upper limit of digit
            JBE     VALID_4             ; Go if OK
            JMP     NUM_ISZERO          ; Force zero if invalid digit
VALID_4:
            MOV     ES:[DI],AL          ; Move digit into buffer
            INC     DI                  ; Bump pointers
            INC     SI
            LOOP    UPTO_17
            JMP     A2FP_EXIT
; Skip period without decrementing character counter
SKIP_SYMBOL:
            INC     SI
            JMP     UPTO_17

;*******************|
; restore and exit
;*******************|
A2FP_EXIT:
            POP     DI                  ; Restore caller's data registers
            POP     SI
            POP     DX
            POP     BX
            POP     AX
            POP     ES                  ; and segment registers
            POP     DS
            RET

ASCII_TO_FPD    ENDP

;
;*******************************|
;           INPUT_NDP
;*******************************|
INPUT_DDP       PROC    FAR
; On entry:
;     DS:DX points to the caller's buffer which holds an ASCII
;     decimal number formatted in floating-point decimal notation:
;
;               sm.mmmmmmmmmmmmmmmmmm ESeeee
; where
; s = sign of number (blank = +)
; m = up to 18 significand digits. Extra digits are ignored
; . = decimal point following the first significand digit.
;     If no decimal point in string, it is assumed
; E = explicit letter E (or e) to signal start of exponent
; S = + or - sign of exponent. If no sign, positive is assumed
; e = up to four exponent digits. The numerical value of the
;     exponent cannot exceed +/- 4932
```

```
; One or more spaces can be used to separate the last digit of
; the significand and the start of the exponent
;
; Examples of input:
;                         1.781252345E-1
;                         -3.14163397  E+0
;                         1.2233445566778899 e1387
;
; On exit:
;               a. If carry flag clear
;                     Input number is loaded into NDP stack top register
;                     Previous values in the stack are pushed down one
;                     register
;                     AL = 0 (no error)
;
;               b. If carry flag set
;                     AL holds error code
;                     AL = 1 for no E or e symbol in the caller's string
;                          NAN encoding is loaded into ST(0)
;                     AL = 2 for exponent exceeds valid range
;                          Overflow - positive infinity is loaded into ST(0)
;                          Underflow - negative infinity is loaded into ST(0)
;                     AL = 3 for invalid character in caller's string
;                          NAN encoding is loaded into ST(0)
;
;               AX is destroyed. All other registers are preserved.
;               The caller's NDP environment is also preserved, except
;               the stack top register.
;
;*******************
;   save caller's
;      segments
;*******************
          PUSH      DS
          PUSH      ES
; Set ES --> caller's data
          PUSH      DS
          POP       ES
; Set DS to --> routine's data
          MOV       AX,ROUT_DATA
          MOV       DS,AX
          ASSUME    DS:ROUT_DATA
;*******************
; save NDP caller's
;   environment and
;      registers
;*******************
          FSAVE     STATE_8087
          FWAIT
          PUSH      CX                    ; Save registers used by routine
          PUSH      DX
          PUSH      SI
          PUSH      DI
;*******************
; clear BCD signif.
;      buffer
;*******************
          LEA       DI,PACKED_SIG
          MOV       CX,10                 ; Bytes in buffer
CLEAR_10:
          MOV       BYTE PTR [DI],0       ; Clear with zero
          INC       DI                    ; Bump pointer
          LOOP      CLEAR_10
```

```
;*******************
; clear work buffer
;*******************
        LEA     DI,WORK_BUF
        MOV     CX,18
CLEAR_18:
        MOV     BYTE PTR [DI],0      ; Clear byte
        INC     DI
        LOOP    CLEAR_18
;*******************
; move digits into
;    WORK_BUF
;*******************
; DS:DX --> caller's buffer with ASCII decimal number in
; floating-point decimal notation
        MOV     SI,DX               ; Copy source to SI
        LEA     DI,WORK_BUF         ; Destination
        MOV     CX,18               ; Maximum digits to move
MOVE_18:
        MOV     AL,ES:[SI]          ; Get character from user buffer
        INC     SI                  ; Bump source pointer
        CMP     AL,'.'              ; Do not move decimal point
        JE      MOVE_18
        CMP     AL,'+'              ; or + and - signs
        JE      MOVE_18
        CMP     AL,'-'
        JE      MOVE_18
        CMP     AL,' '              ; Skip spaces
        JE      MOVE_18
; Test for E or e field terminators
        CMP     AL,'E'              ; Start of exponent
        JE      END_MOVE_18         ; End move if E
        CMP     AL,'e'              ; Lowercase e also allowed
        JE      END_MOVE_18         ; End move if e
; Test for invalid digit, larger than ASCII 9 or smaller than
; ASCII 0
        CMP     AL,'9'              ; High limit
        JA      BAD_ASCII           ; Exit if larger than 9
        CMP     AL,'0'              ; Low limit
        JB      BAD_ASCII
; Value is in legal range
OK_ASCII:
        MOV     [DI],AL             ; Place ASCII in buffer
        INC     DI
        LOOP    MOVE_18
        JMP     END_MOVE_18
;*******************
;     illegal
;    character
;*******************
BAD_ASCII:
        MOV     AL,3                ; Error code for illegal character
                                    ; in caller's string
        JMP     INPUT_ERROR
;*******************
; sign of number
;*******************
END_MOVE_18:
; BCD significand is to be formatted as follows:
;           s0|dd|dd|dd|dd|dd|dd|dd|dd|dd
; where
; s = sign of significand. 1000 if number is negative
;                          0000 if number is positive
```

```
; d = 18 significand digits in packed BCD format
; 0 = required zero
;
; Set up buffer pointers
        MOV     SI,DX                   ; Caller's input buffer
        LEA     DI,PACKED_SIG           ; Output buffer
        ADD     DI,9                    ; Point to sign byte
        MOV     AL,ES:[SI]              ; Get sign of number
        CMP     AL,'-'          ; Test for negative
        JNE     POS_NUMBER      ; Go if not negative
        MOV     BYTE PTR [DI],80H       ; Set sign byte
POS_NUMBER:
        DEC     DI                      ; Point to byte number 8
;********************|
; corvert ASCII to   |
;    packed BCD      |
;********************|
        LEA     SI,WORK_BUF     ; Significand's digits
CONVERT_8:
        MOV     AH,[SI]         ; Get ASCII digit
        CMP     AH,0            ; All characters read ?
        JE      FIND_E          ; Exit if zero
                                ; Nothing to store at this point
        INC     SI              ; Bump pointer to next digit
        SUB     AH,30H          ; Convert to binary
        MOV     CL,4            ; Set up shift counter
        SHL     AH,CL           ; Shift bits to high nibble of AL
; High-order BCD digit now in AH
        MOV     AL,[SI]         ; Get ASCII digit
        CMP     AL,0            ; All characters read ?
        JNE     OK_DIGIT        ; Continue if not
; There is a valid digit in AH which must be stored
        MOV     [DI],AH         ; Store it
        JMP     FIND_E          ; and exit routine
OK_DIGIT:
        SUB     AL,30H          ; Convert to binary
        OR      AL,AH           ; Pack BCD digits in AL
        MOV     [DI],AL         ; Place in significand's buffer
        INC     SI              ; Point to next character
        DEC     DI              ; Bump pointers
        JMP     CONVERT_8
;********************|
;  find start of     |
;   exponent         |
;********************|
FIND_E:
        MOV     SI,DX           ; Caller's input buffer
        MOV     CX,22           ; Maximum character count
                                ; preceding the E symbol
SEARCH_4_E:
        MOV     AL,ES:[SI]      ; Get character
        CMP     AL,'E'
        JE      VALID_EXP       ; Valid symbol
        CMP     AL,'e'
        JE      VALID_EXP       ; Also valid
        INC     SI              ; Bump buffer pointer
        LOOP    SEARCH_4_E
; No E or e in caller's input string
        MOV     AL,1            ; Error code number 1
;********************|
;   input ERROR      |
;********************|
INPUT_ERROR:
```

```
            FRSTOR    STATE_8087         ; Restore environment
            FWAIT
            FLD       NAN_CODE           ; Load Not-a-number code
ERROR_RETURN:
            STC                          ; Error
            JMP       RESTORE_EXIT
;*******************|
; convert exponent  |
;*******************|
VALID_EXP:
            INC       SI                 ; Point to exponent sign or
                                         ; to first exponent digit

;*******************|
; sign of exponent  |
;*******************|
            MOV       SIGN_OF_EXP,0      ; Assume positive
            MOV       AL,ES:[SI]         ; Get sign of exponent
            CMP       AL,'-'             ; Test for negative
            JNE       POS_EXPON          ; Go if not negative
            MOV       SIGN_OF_EXP,1      ; Code for negative exponent
            INC       SI
            JMP       READ_EXP
POS_EXPON:
            CMP       AL,'+'             ; Test for explicit positive
            JNE       READ_EXP           ; Pointer is OK
            INC       SI                 ; Skip + sign
;*******************|
; convert digits to |
;       binary      |
;*******************|
READ_EXP:
            CALL      ASC_2_BIN          ; Convert to binary (in DX)
            MOV       BINARY_EXP,DX
;*******************|
; test for exponent |
;   out of range    |
;*******************|
; Absolute value of exponent cannot exceed the limit of the NDP
; long real format.
            CMP       DX,4933            ; Test for limit
            JB        EXPONENT_OK        ; Go if smaller than 4933
;*******************|
;      encode       |
;  + or - infinity  |
;*******************|
; Restore caller's environment
            FRSTOR    STATE_8087         ; Restore environment
            FWAIT
            MOV       AL,2               ; Exit code for this error
; Exponent is out of range. Determine if underflow or overflow
            CMP       SIGN_OF_EXP,1      ; Test for negative
            JE        UNDERFLOW          ; Encode negative infinity
; Overflow. Encode positive infinity
            FLD       INF_POSITIVE       ; Load code for positive infinity
            JMP       ERROR_RETURN
UNDERFLOW:
            FLD       INF_NEGATIVE       ; Load code for negative infinity
            JMP       ERROR_RETURN
            MOV       AL,2               ; Error code number 2
            JMP       INPUT_ERROR
```

```
;*******************
;      load BCD
;    significand
;*******************
EXPONENT_OK:
        FBLD    TEN_TO_17       ;  10^17    | EMPTY   |
        FBLD    PACKED_SIG      ;   sig     | 10^17   | EMPTY   |
        FDIV    ST,ST(1)        ; sig/10^17 | 10^17   | EMPTY   |
        FXCH    ST(1)           ;  10^17    | SIG     | EMPTY   |
        FSTP    ST(0)           ;   SIG     | EMPTY   |
;*******************
; select conversion
;     option
;*******************
; Option 1: if exponent = 0, then significand remains unchanged
; Option 2: if exponent is negative (SIGN_OF_EXP = 1), then divide
;             significand by 10^exponent
; Option 3: if exponent is positive (SIGN_OF_EXP = 0), then
;             multiply significand by 10^exponent
;
; DX holds binary exponent
        CMP     DX,0            ; Test option no. 1
        JNE     TEST_EXP_POS    ; Test for positive if not zero
        JMP     EXPONENT_ZERO
TEST_EXP_POS:
        CMP     SIGN_OF_EXP,0   ; Exponent positive ?
        JNE     EXPONENT_NEG
        JMP     EXPONENT_POS    ; Exponent must be positive
;*******************
; negative exponent
;    (option 2)
;*******************
EXPONENT_NEG:
;                               | SIG     | EMPTY   |
        FILD    BINARY_EXP      ;  exp     | SIG     | EMPTY   |
        CALL    TEN_2_X         ; 10^exp   | SIG     | EMPTY   |
        FDIVP   ST(1),ST        ; number   | EMPTY   |
        JMP     EXIT_INPUT_87
;*******************
; positive exponent
;    (option 3)
;*******************
EXPONENT_POS:
;                               | SIG     | EMPTY   |
        FILD    BINARY_EXP      ;  exp     | SIG     | EMPTY   |
        CALL    TEN_2_X         ; 10^exp   | SIG     | EMPTY   |
        FMULP   ST(1),ST        ; number   | EMPTY   |
        JMP     EXIT_INPUT_87
;*******************
; exponent = 0
;   (option 1)
;*******************
EXPONENT_ZERO:
        JMP     EXIT_INPUT_87

;*******************
;   restore NDP
;   environment
;*******************
EXIT_INPUT_87:
        FSTP    TEMP_REAL       ; Save numbers in memory
        FRSTOR  STATE_8087      ; Restore original NDP environment
        FWAIT
```

```
        FLD      TEMP_REAL       ; Load number into NDP stack
        CLC                      ; No error
        MOV      AL,0            ; Error code zero
RESTORE_EXIT:
        POP      DI              ; Restore caller's registers
        POP      SI
        POP      DX
        POP      CX
        POP      ES
        POP      DS
        RET
INPUT_NDP        ENDP
;
;
;**********************************
;             OUTPUT_NDP
;**********************************
;
OUTPUT_NDP       PROC    FAR
; Operation:
;           Converts the value in the top register of the NDP
; stack into an ASCII decimal number in scientific notation
;
; On entry:
;           DS:DX points to an unformatted caller's buffer area
;           with minimum space for 25 bytes of storage
;
; On exit:
;           a. Carry flag clear
;           The caller's buffer will contain the ASCII decimal
;           representation of the number at the NDP stack top
;           register, formatted in scientific notation, as follows:
;
;                   sm.mmmmmmmmmmmmmmmmm ESeeee
; where
; s = sign of number (blank = +)
; m = 18 significand digits
; . = decimal point following the first significand digit
; E = explicit letter E to signal start of exponent
; S = + or - sign of exponent
; e = up to four exponent digits
;
; Examples of output:
;                   1.78125234500000000 E-12
;                   -3.14163397000000000 E+0
;                   1.22334455667788998 E+1388
;
;           b. Carry flag set (invalid value in top of stack)
;           Error code in AL
;               AL = 1 for nonnormal real numbers
;                   Buffer message = NONNORMAL
;               AL = 2 for infinity
;                   Buffer message = INFINITY
;               AL = 3 for not a number
;                   Buffer message = NOT-A-NUMBER
;               AL = 4 for empty register
;                   Buffer message = EMPTY
;
;           Zero is reported as   0.00000000000000000 E+0
;
;           AX is destroyed. All other registers and the caller's
;           environment are preserved
;
```

```
;********************|
;    save caller's   |
;      segments      |
;********************|
          PUSH    DS
          PUSH    ES
; Set ES --> caller's data
          PUSH    DS
          POP     ES
; Set DS to --> routine's data
          MOV     AX,ROUT_DATA
          MOV     DS,AX
          ASSUME  DS:ROUT_DATA
;********************|
;    examine ST(0)   |
;********************|
; Get condition codes for stack top register and store for later
; reference
          FXAM                        ; Examine condition codes
          FWAIT
          FSTSW   STATUS_WORD         ; Store status word in memory
          FWAIT
;********************|
; save caller's NDP  |
;  environment and   |
;     registers      |
;********************|
          FSTP    TEMP_REAL           ; Save stack top in memory
          FLD     TEMP_REAL           ; Restore stack top value
          FSAVE   STATE_8087
          FWAIT
          FLD     TEMP_REAL           ; Restore stack top value
          PUSH    CX                  ; Save registers used by routine
          PUSH    DX
          PUSH    SI
          PUSH    DI
;********************|
; test for invalid   |
;      values        |
;********************|
          MOV     AX,STATUS_WORD             ; Status word to AX
; Clear all noncondition code bits
          AND     AH,01000111B               ; Mask to clear bits
; Condition code settings:
;   AH bits: 7  6  5  4  3  2  1  0
;            3           2  1  0
;            |_____|__|__|____ Condition code settings:
;                                   0001 - 0011 = NAN
;                                   0101 - 0111 = INFINITY
;                       0000 - 0010 - 1100 - 1110 = NONNORMAL
;                       1001 - 1011 - 1101 - 1111 = EMPTY
;                                   1000 - 1010 = ZERO
;                                   0100 - 0110 = NORMAL
; Test for normal
          CMP     AH,00000100B
          JE      NORMAL
          CMP     AH,00000110B
          JE      NORMAL
          JMP     TEST_4_NAN
;********************|
;      normal        |
;********************|
```

```
NORMAL:
        JMP        GET_EXPONENT
TEST_4_NAN:
        CMP        AH,00000001B
        JE         IS_NAN
        CMP        AH,00000011B
        JE         IS_NAN
        JMP        TEST_4_INF
.********************
;    Not-A-Number
.********************
IS_NAN:
        LEA        SI,ERROR_AL3
        CALL       FILL_CALLERS
        MOV        AL,3                    ; Error code for NAN
.********************
;    output ERROR
.********************
ERROR_EXIT:
        FRSTOR     STATE_8087              ; Restore original NDP environment
        FWAIT
; Restore registers
        POP        DI
        POP        SI
        POP        DX
        POP        CX
        POP        ES
        POP        DS
        STC                                ; Set carry flag
        RET
TEST_4_INF:
        CMP        AH,00000101B
        JE         IS_INFINITY
        CMP        AH,00000111B
        JE         IS_INFINITY
        JMP        TEST_4_NON
.********************
;    infinity
.********************
IS_INFINITY:
        LEA        SI,ERROR_AL2
        CALL       FILL_CALLERS
        MOV        AL,2                    ; Error code for INFINITY
        JMP        ERROR_EXIT
TEST_4_NON:
        CMP        AH,00000000B
        JE         NON_NORMAL
        CMP        AH,00000010B
        JE         NON_NORMAL
        CMP        AH,01000100B
        JE         NON_NORMAL
        CMP        AH,01000110B
        JE         NON_NORMAL
        JMP        TEST_4_ZERO
.********************
;    nonnormal
.********************
NON_NORMAL:
        LEA        SI,ERROR_AL1
        CALL       FILL_CALLERS
        MOV        AL,1                    ; Error code for NONNORMAL
        JMP        ERROR_EXIT
TEST_4_ZERO:
```

```
                CMP     AH,01000000B
                JE      IS_ZERO
                CMP     AH,01000010B
                JE      IS_ZERO
.*******************⊼*|
;      empty          |
.*******************⊼*|
                LEA     SI,ERROR_AL4
                CALL    FILL_CALLERS
                MOV     AL,4                    ; Error code for EMPTY
                JMP     ERROR_EXIT
.*******************⊼*|
;      zero           |
.*******************⊼*|
IS_ZERO:
                LEA     SI,NUMBER_0
                CALL    FILL_CALLERS
                MOV     AL,0            ; No error
                FRSTOR  STATE_8087      ; Restore original NDP environment
                FWAIT
; Restore registers
                POP     DI
                POP     SI
                POP     DX
                POP     CX
                POP     ES
                POP     DS
                CLC                     ; No error
                RET
.*******************⊼*|
;  compute exponent   |
.*******************⊼*|
GET_EXPONENT:
                FSTCW   USERS_CW        ; Save caller's control word
                FWAIT
                FLDCW   DOWN_CW         ; Force rounding down
;                               |   ST(0)   |   ST(1)   |   ST(2)   |
                FLD     ST(0)   ;       #   |     #     |   EMPTY   |
                FABS            ;     |#|   |     #     |   EMPTY   |
                FLD1            ;       1   |    |#|    |     #     |
                FXCH    ST(1)   ;     |#|   |     1     |     #     |
                FYL2X           ;  Log2-X   |                       |
                FLDL2T          ;  Log2-10  |  Log2-X   |     #     |
                FXCH    ST(1)   ;  Log2-X   |  Log2-10  |     #     |
                FDIV    ST,ST(1);   exp     |  Log2-10  |     #     |
                FXCH    ST(1)   ;  Log2-10  |    exp    |     #     |
                FSTP    ST(0)   ;   exp     |     #     |   EMPTY   |
                FRNDINT         ;   EXP     |     #     |   EMPTY   |
                FLD     ST(0)   ;   EXP     |    EXP    |     #     |
;
                FBSTP   PACKED_EXP      ;   EXP   |     #     |   EMPTY   |
                FISTP   BINARY_EXP      ;    #    |   EMPTY   |
;
                FLDCW   USERS_CW        ; Restore original control word
;
; Routine from Sargent & Shoemaker
.*******************⊼*|
;     compute         |
;     significand     |
.*******************⊼*|
;                               |   ST(0)   |   ST(1)   |   ST(2)   |
;                               |     #     |   EMPTY   |   EMPTY   |
                FLD     ST(0)
```

```
        FLD     ST(0)                ;  #   |   #   |   #   |
; Round and store significand, just in case number is an integer
MANTISSA:
        FRNDINT
        FBSTP   PACKED_SIG           ;  #   |   #   | EMPTY |
                                     |  #   |   #   | EMPTY |
;
; Test for BCD digits number 18 not zero
        FWAIT
        LEA     SI,PACKED_SIG
        ADD     SI,8                 ; To most significand BCD byte
        MOV     AL,[SI]
        CMP     AL,OFFH              ; Integer is too large to test
        JE      TOO_LARGE
        AND     AL,11110000B         ; Mask to clear bits 0 to 3
        JNZ     END_MANTISSA
        FILD    TEN
        FMULP   ST(1),ST
        FLD     ST(0)
        JMP     MANTISSA
TOO_LARGE:
        FILD    TEN
        FDIVP   ST(1),ST
        FLD     ST(0)
        JMP     MANTISSA
END_MANTISSA:
        FSTP    ST(0)

;********************|
;  restore NDP       |
;  environment       |
;********************|
        FRSTOR  STATE_8087           ; Restore original NDP environment
        FWAIT
;********************|
; format caller's    |
;     buffer         |
;********************|
        LEA     SI,FPD_MES                     ; Blank message
        CALL    FILL_CALLERS
;********************|
;  build decimal     |
;    number          |
;********************|
; The decimal number is built from the data stored in the buffers
; PACKED_SIG and PACKED_EXP. The number is formatted in
; floating-point decimal notation in the user's buffer
        LEA     SI,PACKED_SIG        ; Significand source
        ADD     SI,9                 ; To sign byte of BCD
        MOV     DI,DX                ; User's buffer area
        MOV     AL,[SI]              ; Get sign byte from BCD
        CMP     AL,0                 ; Zero is positive
        JE      POS_SIGNIF           ; Significand is positive
        MOV     BYTE PTR ES:[DI],'-'    ; Set negative sign
POS_SIGNIF:
        INC     DI                   ; Bump decimal buffer pointer
        DEC     SI                   ; and BCD significand pointer
; Move digit preceding the significand's decimal point
        MOV     AL,[SI]              ; Get packed BCD digits into AL
        CALL    NIBBS_2_DEC          ; Decimal digits in AH and AL
        MOV     ES:[DI],AH           ; Set first decimal digit
        INC     DI                   ; Skip decimal point
        INC     DI
        MOV     ES:[DI],AL           ; Set second digit
```

```
            INC     DI                  ; Bump pointer
; Move next seven BCD digit pairs as a block
            DEC     SI                  ; Point to next BCD pair
            MOV     CX,8                ; Digits to move
MOVE_8_DIGITS:
            MOV     AL,[SI]             ; Get packed BCD digits into AL
            CALL    NIBBS_2_DEC         ; Decimal digits in AH and AL
            MOV     ES:[DI],AH          ; Set first digit
            INC     DI                  ; Bump decimal digits pointer
            MOV     ES:[DI],AL          ; Place second digit
            INC     DI                  ; Bump pointer
            DEC     SI                  ; Source pointer to next BCD pair
            LOOP    MOVE_8_DIGITS
            ADD     DI,2                ; Bump to exponent sign position
;*********************
;   sign of exponent
;*********************
            LEA     SI,PACKED_EXP       ; Exponent BCD storage
            ADD     SI,9                ; To sign byte of BCD
            MOV     BYTE PTR ES:[DI],'+'    ; Assume positive exponent
            MOV     AL,[SI]             ; Get sign byte from BCD
            CMP     AL,0                ; Zero is positive
            JE      POS_EXPONENT        ; Significand is positive
            MOV     BYTE PTR ES:[DI],'-'    ; Set negative sign
POS_EXPONENT:
            INC     DI                  ; Bump decimal buffer pointer
;*********************
; 4 exponent digits
;*********************
            LEA     SI,PACKED_EXP       ; Reset pointer
            INC     SI                  ; to first BCD digit pair of
                                        ; exponent
; Move 4 exponent digits, skipping leading zeros
; BL = 0 if first nonzero digit not yet found
            MOV     BL,0                ; Switch for first nonzero
            MOV     CX,2                ; Counter for 2 packed BCDs
MOVE_2_DIGITS:
            MOV     AL,[SI]             ; Get packed BCD digits into AL
            CALL    NIBBS_2_DEC         ; Decimal digits in AH and AL
            CMP     BL,0                ; Execute leading zero test ?
            JNE     NO_LEAD_TEST1       ; Switch OFF, skip test
; Test for leading zero
            CMP     AH,'0'              ; Zero ASCII digit ?
            JE      SKIP_LEAD0_1        ; Skip leading zero
; Valid no zero digit, reset lead zero test switch
            MOV     BL,OFFH             ; BL not zero
NO_LEAD_TEST1:
            MOV     ES:[DI],AH          ; Set first decimal digit
            INC     DI                  ; Bump buffer pointer
SKIP_LEAD0_1:
; Second test for leading zeros
            CMP     BL,0                ; Execute test ?
            JNE     NO_LEAD_TEST2       ; Switch OFF, skip test
            CMP     AL,'0'              ; Zero ASCII digit ?
            JE      SKIP_LEAD0_2
NO_LEAD_TEST2:
            MOV     ES:[DI],AL          ; Set second digit
; Valid no zero digit, reset lead zero test switch
            MOV     BL,OFFH             ; BL not zero
            INC     DI                  ; Bump buffer pointer
SKIP_LEAD0_2:
            DEC     SI                  ; To next BCD digit pair
            LOOP    MOVE_2_DIGITS
```

```
;********************|
; test for all 0s    |
;********************|
; If exponent is all zeros, the leading zero switch will be set
        CMP     BL,0            ; Is exponent all zeros?
        JNE     EXIT_OUTPUT     ; No, exit
; Set a zero digit in the exponent
        MOV     BYTE PTR ES:[DI],'0'
;********************|
; restore and exit   |
;********************|
EXIT_OUTPUT:
        POP     DI
        POP     SI
        POP     DX
        POP     CX
        POP     ES              ; Restore caller's registers
        POP     DS
        CLC                     ; No error exit
        RET
OUTPUT_NDP      ENDP
;
;**********************************************************************
;*                       auxiliary procedures
;**********************************************************************
;********************************|
;           10 to a power        |
;********************************|
TEN_2_X         PROC    NEAR
;                               |  ST(0)  | ST(1) |  ST(2) |
        FLDL2T                  ; Log2-10 |   #   | EMPTY  |
        FMULP   ST(1),ST        ;E=#*L2-10| EMPTY |
;**********************************************************************
; Set control word rounding control to - infinity
        FSTCW   USERS_CW        ; Store caller's control word
        FLDCW   DOWN_CW         ; Temporary control word for
                                ; rounding down
;**********************************************************************
        FLD1                    ;    1    |   E   | EMPTY  |
        FCHS                    ;   -1    |   E   | EMPTY  |
        FLD     ST(1)           ;    E    |  -1   |   E    |
        FRNDINT                 ; INT(E)  |  -1   |   E    |
        FLDCW   USERS_CW        ; Restore caller's control word
        FXCH    ST(2)           ;    E    |  -1   | INT(E) |
        FSUB    ST,ST(2)        ; F = E-1 |  -1   |   I    |
        FSCALE                  ;   F/2   |  -1   |   I    |
        F2XM1                   ;F/2^2-1  |  -1   |   I    |
        FSUBRP  ST(1),ST        ;2 ^F/2   |   I   | EMPTY  |
        FMUL    ST,ST(0)        ; 2 ^F    |   I   | EMPTY  |
        FSCALE                  ; 2 ^(1+F)|   I   | EMPTY  |
        FXCH    ST(1)           ;    I    | 2 ^(1+F)| EMPTY |
        FSTP    ST(0)           ; 2 ^(1+F)| EMPTY |
        RET                     ; 10 ^X   |
TEN_2_X         ENDP
;
ASC_2_BIN       PROC    NEAR
; Convert an ASCII number to binary
; On entry:
;               SI --> start ASCII buffer
; On exit:
;               DX = binary number (range 0 to 65535)
;
```

```
              MOV      DX,0               ; Clear binary output
     ASCO:    MOV      AL,ES:[SI]         ; Get ASCII digit
              INC      SI                 ; Bump pointer to next digit
              SUB      AL,30H             ; ASCII to decimal
              JL       EXASC              ; Exit if invalid ASCII
              CMP      AL,9               ; Test for highest value
              JG       EXASC              ; Exit if larger than 9
              CBW                         ; Extend to AX
              PUSH     AX                 ; Save digit in stack
              MOV      AX,DX              ; Move into output register
              MOV      CX,10              ; Decimal multiplier
              MUL      CX                 ; Perform AX = AX * 10
              MOV      DX,AX              ; Move product to output register
              POP      AX                 ; Restore decimal digit
              ADD      DX,AX              ; Add in digit
              JMP      ASCO               ; Continue
     EXASC:   RET
     ASC_2_BIN    ENDP
     ;
     ;
     BIN_TO_ASC       PROC     NEAR
     ; Convert a 16-bit binary in the DX register to an ASCII decimal
     ; number
     ; On entry:
     ;                 DX = binary source
     ;                 DS:DI --> 5-byte output buffer
     ;
     ; Clear the buffer with blanks
              PUSH     DI                 ; Save buffer start
              MOV      CX,5               ; Five digits to clear
              MOV      AL,' '             ; Blank character
     CLEAR_5:
              MOV      [DI],AL            ; Clear digit
              INC      DI                 ; Bump pointer
              LOOP     CLEAR_5            ; Repeat for 5 digits
              DEC      DI                 ; Adjust buffer pointer to last
                                          ; digit
     ;
              MOV      CX,0               ; Clear counter
     BINAO:   PUSH     CX                 ; Save count
              MOV      AX,DX              ; Add in numerator
              MOV      DX,0               ; Clear top half
              MOV      CX,10              ; Enter decimal divisor
              DIV      CX                 ; Perform division AX/CX
              XCHG     AX,DX              ; Get quotient
              ADD      AL,30H             ; Make digit ASCII
              MOV      [DI],AL            ; Store digit in buffer
              DEC      DI                 ; Bump destination pointer
              POP      CX                 ; Restore counter
              INC      CX                 ; Count the digit
              CMP      DX,0               ; Test for end of binary
              JNZ      BINAO              ; Continue if not end
     ;
              POP      DI                 ; Restore pointer to start of
                                          ; buffer
     ; Skip leading blanks in buffer
     BUF_BLANK:
              MOV      AL,[DI]            ; Get buffer digit
              CMP      AL,' '             ; Test for ASCII blank
              JNE      NOT_BLANK          ; Exit if not leading blank
              INC      DI
              JMP      BUF_BLANK
     ; ES:DI --> first nonzero digit in buffer
```

```
NOT_BLANK:
        RET
BIN_TO_ASC      ENDP
;
;
NIBBS_2_DEC     PROC    NEAR
; Convert binary value in low and high nibble of AL into two ASCII
; decimal digits in AH and AL
; On entry:
;       AL holds two packed BCD digits in the range 0 to 9
;
; On exit:
;       AH = high-order ASCII digit (from AL bits xxxx ????)
;       AL = low-order ASCII digit (from AL bits ???? xxxx)
;
        PUSH    CX              ; Preserve entry register
        MOV     AH,AL           ; Copy AL in AH
        MOV     CL,4
        SHR     AH,CL           ; Isolate high nibble
        ADD     AH,30H          ; Convert to ASCII
;
        AND     AL,0FH          ; Isolate low nibble
        ADD     AL,30H          ; Convert to ASCII
        POP     CX
        RET
;
NIBBS_2_DEC     ENDP
;
FILL_CALLERS    PROC    NEAR
; Fill caller's buffer by DS:DX with 27-byte message by ES:SI
        MOV     DI,DX           ; Set up destination pointer
        MOV     CX,27           ; Characters to clear
CLEAR_26:
        MOV     AL,[SI]         ; Character from source
        MOV     ES:[DI],AL      ; Into buffer area
        INC     DI              ; Bump pointers
        INC     SI
        LOOP    CLEAR_26
        RET
FILL_CALLERS    ENDP
;
;
CODE    ENDS
        END
```

Appendix B

Keyboard Enhancer Utility for the PC and PC XT

```
;*****************************************************************
;                          FASTKBD.ASM
;*****************************************************************
; This program is compatible with the IBM PC, XT, AT, and all the
; models of the IBM PS/2 line. It will also operate on most
; IBM-compatible hardware. It is not compatible with the IBM
; PCjr.
; Its main use is in systems that do not have programmable
; keyboard hardware, such as the PC and PC XT.
;
;*******************|
;    description    |
;*******************|
; A TSR routine for speeding the execution of programs that use
; the arrow keys to move the cursor or to scroll the text file
; and the <Del> key for deleting a character.
;
;*******************|
;    operation      |
;*******************|
; The program installation routine reads the DOS command tail to
; install a delay (in clock cycles) and to speed up the system
; timer. The first single-character parameter in the command tail
; is the delay factor and the second one the clock speedup.
; For example, the command:
;                       FASTKBD 8,4
; introduces a delay of 8 time cycles and speeds up the system
; timer by a factor of 4. Valid input for the delay are the
; numbers 2 to 9 and the letters A to H. Valid input for the
; clock speedup factors are the values 2, 4, 6, and 8. The
; default values are 8, 2.
;
; Actions performed by the INT 09H intercept:
; (Receives control every time a key is pressed)
;       1. If scan code is a make for a keypad arrow key or for the
;          <Del> key, the code is stored in the variable KEY_CODE
;          and the interrupt is discarded.
;       2. If not, FFH is stored in variable KEY_CODE and execution
;          is restored to the original handler.
;
; Actions performed by the INT 08H intercept:
; (Receives control with every tick of the system timer)
;       1. If the variable KEY_CODE holds a scan code for a keypad
;          arrow key or for the <Del> key, the key code is placed
;          in the BIOS keyboard buffer.
;       2. If the <left><shift> key is pressed, the code is stored
;          twice in order to increase the speed.
```

```
;       3. If the variable KEY_CODE holds the value FFH, the
;          intercept routine does nothing.
;       4. Execution is returned to the original INT 08H handler
;          maintaining the original clock rate of 18.2 ticks per
;          second.
;
;********************|
;     structure     |
;********************|
;
; The program is structured as a .COM-type executable file.
;
; DOS commands for creating the run file:
;       1. MASM FASTKBD;
;       2. LINK FASTKBD;
;       3. EXE2BIN FASTKBD.EXE FASTKBD.COM
;       4. ERASE FASTKBD.EXE
;
; Note: These commands can be included in a batch file.
;
;
;****************************************************************|
;               equates for BIOS keyboard data                 |
;****************************************************************|
BUFFER_HEAD     EQU     001AH   ; Pointer to head of buffer
BUFFER_TAIL     EQU     001CH   ; Pointer to tail
;
KB_BUFFER       EQU     001EH   ; Offset of buffer start
KB_BUFFER_END   EQU     003EH   ; Offset of buffer end
;
KB_CONTROL      EQU     0017H   ; 1st keyboard status byte
;
;****************************************************************|
;                         c o d e                              |
;****************************************************************|
;
CODE    SEGMENT
;
        ORG     0100H           ; COM file forced origin
;
        ASSUME  CS:CODE,DS:CODE,ES:CODE,SS:CODE
;
ENTRY:
;
        JMP     INSTALL
;
;****************************************************************|
;               INT 09H intercept routine                      |
;                  keyboard interrupt                          |
;****************************************************************|
;
HEX09_INT:
;*****************|
; get scan code   |
;*****************|
        PUSH    AX              ; Save accumulator
        PUSHF                   ; and flags
        IN      AL,60H          ; Read scan code at port 60H
;
;*******************|
;  test for keypad  |
;  arrows and <Del> |
;*******************|
```

```
;          Keypad keys:                      Scan codes:
;                                            make/break
;        7      8      9            47H/C7H    48H/C8H    49H/C9H
;        Home   ^      PgUp
;
;        4      5      6            4BH/CBH    4CH/CCH    4DH/CDH
;        <-            ->
;
;        1      2      3            4FH/CFH    50H/D0H    51H/D1H
;        End    |      PgDn
;
;                      <Del>                             53H/D3H
;
; Test for keypad arrow keys make codes or for the <Del> key
         CMP      AL,4BH
         JE       STORE_SCAN_CODE
         CMP      AL,48H
         JE       STORE_SCAN_CODE
         CMP      AL,4DH
         JE       STORE_SCAN_CODE
         CMP      AL,50H
         JE       STORE_SCAN_CODE
;********************|
;     <Del> key      |
;********************|
         CMP      AL,53H
         JNE      EXIT_VIA_09           ; Go if not <Del> key
; Test for CTRL-ALT-DEL reset sequence
         PUSH     AX                ; Save accumulator
         PUSH     ES                ; and ES
         MOV      AX,0040H          ; Segment for BIOS data area
         MOV      ES,AX             ; To ES
         MOV      AL,ES:KB_CONTROL       ; Keyboard flag
         TEST     AL,00001100B      ; ALT_CTRL keys pressed
         POP      ES                ; Restore registers
         POP      AX
         JZ       STORE_SCAN_CODE ; Recognize <Del> key if CTRL+ALT
                                   ; not pressed
;********************|
;  exit via INT 09H  |
;********************|
EXIT_VIA_09:
; Store FFH in KEY_CODE variable and return control to the
; original INT 09H handler in BIOS
         MOV      AL,0FFH           ; Break code for intercept
                                    ; routine
         MOV      CS:KEY_CODE,AL    ; stored in variable
         POPF                       ; Restore flags
         POP      AX                ; and accumulator
; No data in buffers. Transfer execution to original vector
; The code can safely assume a valid vector at INT 09H
         JMP      DWORD PTR CS:OLD_VECTOR_09
;
;********************|
; send acknowledge   |
;    to 8048 chip    |
;********************|
STORE_SCAN_CODE:
         MOV      CS:KEY_CODE,AL
         IN       AL,61H            ; Read control port
         MOV      AH,AL             ; Save value in port 61H
         OR       AL,80H            ; Set keyboard acknowledge bit
         OUT      61H,AL            ; Send to control port
```

```
        XCHG    AH,AL                   ; Restore original control
        OUT     61H,AL                  ; Send to controller
;*******************|
;  discard key      |
;*******************|
; Discard this keystroke by exiting interrupt
        CLI                             ; Turn off interrupts
        MOV     AL,20H                  ; Send EOI code
        OUT     20H,AL                  ; to interrupt controller
        POP     AX                      ; Discard flags
        POP     AX                      ; Restore AX
        IRET
;
;*****************************************************************|
;                   INT 08H intercept routine                   |
;                     for the system timer                      |
;*****************************************************************|
HEX08_INT:
; Save registers
        PUSH    AX
        PUSH    BX
        PUSH    SI
        PUSH    ES
;
        MOV     AL,CS:KEY_CODE
        CMP     AL,0FFH                 ; Last keypad scan code
                                        ; was FFH?
        JNE     KP_MAKE                 ; No
; Reset delay counter and exit
        MOV     AL,CS:DELAY
        MOV     CS:DELAY_COUNT,AL
        JMP     EXIT_TIMER              ; Yes, exit
KP_MAKE:
; Test for initial delay exhausted or for first iteration
        MOV     AL,CS:DELAY_COUNT
        CMP     AL,0                    ; Delay exhausted
        JE      EXECUTE_KEY
; Decrement delay counter
        DEC     CS:DELAY_COUNT
; Test for first iteration exception
        CMP     AL,CS:DELAY             ; AL = delay count on
                                        ; entry
        JE      EXECUTE_KEY             ; Execute first iteration
        JMP     NORMAL_KEY
;
EXECUTE_KEY:
; Set ES to BIOS data segment base at 40H
        MOV     AX,0040H
        MOV     ES,AX
; Set repetition factor by testing for <left><shift> and
; <Ctrl> keys pressed
        MOV     AL,ES:KB_CONTROL        ; Keyboard status byte
        MOV     CS:REPEAT,2             ; Assume 2 repetitions
        TEST    AL,00000010B            ; <left><shift> key
        JNZ     REPEAT_KEY
        MOV     CS:REPEAT,1             ; Ship code once
REPEAT_KEY:
; Load scan code for keypad key into AH and clear AL
        MOV     AH,CS:KEY_CODE
        MOV     AL,0
;*******************|
;  store in buffer  |
;*******************|
```

```
            MOV     BX,ES:BUFFER_TAIL       ; [0040:001CH]
            MOV     SI,BX                   ; Save pointer in SI
; Bump buffer pointer to next available storage
            INC     BX
            INC     BX
            CMP     BX,KB_BUFFER_END        ; End of buffer?
            JNE     NOT_AT_END
; If at end of buffer, reset pointer to start of buffer
            MOV     BX,KB_BUFFER            ; Reset to buffer start
; Test for buffer wraparound
NOT_AT_END:
            CMP     BX,ES:BUFFER_HEAD       ; Buffer full condition
            JE      EXIT_TIMER              ; Do not store
            MOV     ES:[SI],AX              ; Store code in buffer
; Bump buffer tail
            MOV     ES:BUFFER_TAIL,BX
;********************
; test repetitions
;********************
            DEC     CS:REPEAT
            JZ      EXIT_TIMER              ; Go if last repetition
            JMP     REPEAT_KEY

;********************
;    exit routine
;********************
; If the count is a multiple of the speedup factor, execution is
; transferred to the original handler. This ensures that the BIOS
; INT 08H routine receives control 18.2 times per second.
EXIT_TIMER:
            DEC     CS:TIMER_COUNT
            JZ      EXIT_TO_08
; Bypass BIOS INT 09H (time-of-day) service
            CLI
            MOV     AL,20H                  ; End-of-interrupt code
            OUT     20H,AL                  ; to interrupt controller
; Restore entry registers
            POP     ES
            POP     SI
            POP     BX
            POP     AX
            IRET
;
EXIT_TO_08:
; Restore timer count from RATE variable
            MOV     AL,CS:RATE
            MOV     CS:TIMER_COUNT,AL
NORMAL_KEY:
; Restore entry registers
            POP     ES
            POP     SI
            POP     BX
            POP     AX
            STC                             ; Continue processing
            JMP     DWORD PTR CS:OLD_VECTOR_08
;
;
;****************************************************************
;                     code segment data
;****************************************************************
OLD_VECTOR_09   DD      0   ; Pointer to original 09H
                            ; interrupt
OLD_VECTOR_08   DD      0   ; Pointer to original 08H
```

```
                                ; interrupt
;
KEY_CODE        DB      OFFH    ; Last keypad keystroke received
                                ; or FFH
REPEAT          DB      1       ; Switch for left-shift key
                                ; and left-ctrl key iteration
                                ; Holds 1, 2 or 4 accordingly
;
TIMER_COUNT     DB      2       ; Counter for timer pulses
;
DELAY_COUNT     DB      8       ; Counter for first-key delay
;
; Typematic parameters. Can be modified in the command tail
DELAY           DB      8       ; Initial delay period is of 8 clock
                                ; ticks.
RATE            DB      2       ; Speedup factor for the typematic
                                ; rate as a function of the orginal
                                ; system clock rate of 18.2 cps.
                                ; The default value of 2 generates a
                                ; rate of 36.4 cps
;
;**********************************************************************
;                        Installation Routine
;**********************************************************************
;
INSTALL:
;*******************|
; read command tail |
;*******************|
; Test for input parameters in the program's command tail at
; offset 0080H of the PSP
                MOV     DI,80H          ; Use DI as pointer into PSP
                MOV     AL,DS:[DI]      ; Get command tail character
                CMP     AL,0            ; count. 0 = no command tail
                JE      NO_TAIL         ; Execute with default values
; Read command tail parameters into variables
                ADD     DI,2            ; Skip space
                MOV     AL,DS:[DI]      ; Delay factor (2 to H)
                SUB     AL,30H          ; Convert to binary
                MOV     CS:DELAY,AL     ; Store in program variables
                MOV     CS:DELAY_COUNT,AL
                ADD     DI,2            ; Skip comma
                MOV     AL,DS:[DI]      ; System clock speedup factor
                SUB     AL,30H          ; To binary range
                MOV     CS:RATE,AL      ; Store in program variables
                MOV     CS:TIMER_COUNT,AL
;
;*******************|
;                   |
;install new INT 09 |
;*******************|
NO_TAIL:
; Interrupts off while changing the vector table
                CLI
; Uses DOS service 35H of INT 21H to obtain original vector for
; INT 09H from the vector table.
                MOV     AH,35H          ; Service request code
                MOV     AL,09H          ; Code of vector desired
                INT     21H
;
; ES --> Segment address of installed interrupt handler
; BX --> Offset address of installed interrupt handler
                MOV     SI,OFFSET CS:OLD_VECTOR_09
; Offset of foward pointer in 16-byte structured table
                MOV     CS:[SI],BX      ; Save offset of original handler
```

```
            MOV     CS:[SI+2],ES    ; and segment
;
; Uses DOS service 25H of INT 21H to set address of new service
; routine in the vector table
            MOV     AH,25H      ; Service request code
            MOV     AL,09H      ; Interrupt code
; Set DS to CS for DOS service
            PUSH    CS
            POP     DS
            MOV     DX,OFFSET CS:HEX09_INT  ; Offset of service rtn
            INT     21H
;*******************|
;  speedup system
;     timer
;*******************|
; Speed up timer channel 0 by the value in the RATE variable
; Suppose RATE = 10, then:
; Original divisor = 65,535
; New divisor 65,535/10 = 6,555
            MOV     AL,00110110B    ; 00xx xxxx = channel 0
                                    ; xx11 xxxx = write LSB then MSM
                                    ; xxxx 011x = mode 3
                                    ; xxxx xxx0 = binary system
            OUT     43H,AL
;
            MOV     AX,65535    ; Original divisor
            MOV     CL,CS:RATE
            MOV     CH,0        ; Clear high byte of divisor
            MOV     DX,0        ; and dividend
            DIV     CX          ; AX = new divisor
;
            OUT     40H,AL      ; Send LSB
            MOV     AL,AH
            OUT     40H,AL      ; Send MSB
;*******************|
;install new INT 08 |
;*******************|
; Uses DOS service 35H of INT 21H to obtain original vector for
; INT 08H from the vector table.
            MOV     AH,35H      ; Service request code
            MOV     AL,08H      ; Code of vector desired
            INT     21H
;
; ES --> Segment address of installed interrupt handler
; BX --> Offset address of installed interrupt handler
            MOV     SI,OFFSET CS:OLD_VECTOR_08
; Offset of foward pointer in 16-byte structured table
            MOV     CS:[SI],BX      ; Save offset of original handler
            MOV     CS:[SI+2],ES    ; and segment
; Take over timer tick at INT 08H
; Using DOS service 25H of INT 21H
            MOV     AH,25H
            MOV     AL,08H          ; Interrupt code
; DS already set to ES
            MOV     DX,OFFSET CS:HEX08_INT
            INT     21H
            STI                     ; Reenable interrupts
;*******************|
;   terminate and
;   stay resident
;*******************|
; Exit to DOS protecting the service routine above the label
; INSTALL
```

```
          MOV      DX,OFFSET CS:INSTALL
          INC      DX                ; One more byte
          INT      27H
;
;
CODE      ENDS
          END      ENTRY
```

Appendix C

Interrupt-Driven
Serial Communications Program

```
;*******************************************************************
;                         TERM232.ASM
;*******************************************************************
; Terminal-to-terminal communications programs using the serial
; line. Operates as follows:
;        1. Interrupt driven
;        2. Simultaneous reception and transmission
;        3. Set up and display of RS-232-C protocol

;*******************************************************************
;                          s t a c k
;*******************************************************************
STACK   SEGMENT stack
;
        DB      400 DUP ('?')
;
STACK   ENDS

;*******************************************************************
;                          d a t a
;*******************************************************************
DATA    SEGMENT
;
;******************
;    messages
;******************
MENU_MS DB      '     ** PROGRAM MENU **',0DH,0AH
        DB      ' <F1> = Redisplay this MENU',0DH,0AH
        DB      ' <F2> = Set RS-232-C protocol',0DH,0AH
        DB      ' <F3> = Display RS-232-C protocol installed',0DH,0AH
        DB      '<Esc> = EXIT TERM232',0DH,0AH,0DH,0AH
        DB      ' BACKGROUND OPERATIONS:',0DH,0AH
        DB      ' Characters typed on the keyboard are'
        DB      ' automatically transmitted',0DH,0AH
        DB      ' Characters received through the serial line are'
        DB      ' automatically displayed',0DH,0AH
        DB      0DH,0AH,'$'
;
PROT_MS DB      ' * Installed communications protocol *',0DH,0AH
        DB      '        Baud rate: '
BAUD%   DB      '2400',0DH,0AH
        DB      '          Parity: '
PAR%    DB      'even',0DH,0AH
        DB      '       Stop bits: '
STOP%   DB      '1',0DH,0AH
        DB      '     Word length: '
WORD%   DB      '8',0DH,0AH,0AH,'$'
```

475

```
;
BAUD$$    DB        '110 150 300 600 1200240048009600'
PAR$$     DB        'odd noneeven'
;
BAUD_MENU           DB        ODH,OAH,' ** New communications paramete'
          DB        'rs input **',ODH,OAH
          DB        ' Baud rates:',ODH,OAH
          DB        ' 1 = 110',ODH,OAH
          DB        ' 2 = 150',ODH,OAH
          DB        ' 3 = 300',ODH,OAH
          DB        ' 4 = 600',ODH,OAH
          DB        ' 5 = 1200',ODH,OAH
          DB        ' 6 = 2400',ODH,OAH
          DB        ' 7 = 4800',ODH,OAH
          DB        ' 8 = 9600 ',ODH,OAH
          DB        '          Select: $'
;
DIVISOR DW          417H      ; 110 Bd
        DW          300H      ; 150 Bd
        DW          180H      ; 300 Bd
        DW          OCOH      ; 600 Bd
        DW          60H       ; 1200 Bd
        DW          30H       ; 2400 Bd
        DW          18H       ; 4800 Bd
        DW          OCH       ; 9600 Bd
;
DIV_JR  DW          3F9H      ; 110 Bd
        DW          2EAH      ; 150 Bd
        DW          175H      ; 300 Bd
        DW          OBAH      ; 600 Bd
        DW          5DH       ; 1200 Bd
        DW          2FH       ; 2400 Bd
        DW          17H       ; 4800 Bd
        DW          OCH       ; 9600 Bd          (NOT RECOMMENDED)
;
PAR_MENU            DB        ODH,OAH,' Parity:',ODH,OAH
          DB        ' 1 = odd',ODH,OAH
          DB        ' 2 = none',ODH,OAH
          DB        ' 3 = even',ODH,OAH
          DB        '          Select: $'
;
STOP_MENU           DB        ODH,OAH,' Stop bits:',ODH,OAH
          DB        ' 1 = 1 stop bit',ODH,OAH
          DB        ' 2 = 1.5 or 2 stop bits',ODH,OAH
          DB        '          Select: $'
;
WORD_MENU           DB        ODH,OAH,' Word length:',ODH,OAH
          DB        ' 1 = 7 bits',ODH,OAH
          DB        ' 2 = 8 bits',ODH,OAH
          DB        '          Select: $'
;
;
ERR1_MS DB          ODH,OAH,' *** cannot transmit *** ',ODH,OAH
;********************|
;    parameters      |
;  and variables     |
;********************|
PORT_BASE           DW        03F8H    ; Base address of serial port
;
; Communications interrupt number:
;                 PCjr ........ IRQ3 ........ OBH
;             All others ......... IRQ4 ........ OCH
```

```
        INT_NUM DB       0CH       ; Offset in BIOS table as follows:
                                   ; PC & PS/2- IRQ4 - 0CH * 4 = 30H
                                   ; PCjr       IRQ3 - 0BH * 4 = 2CH
        ;
        SET_UP_BYTE      DB       0BBH    ; Default value
        ;
        ; Original interrupt vector address to restore on exit
        O_INT_SEG        DW       0000H   ; Segment
        O_INT_OFF        DW       0000H   ; Offset
        ;
        ;****************
        ;    buffers     |
        ;****************
        CIRC_BUF         DB       20 DUP (00H)   ;Circular buffer
                         DW       0
        DATA_IN          DW       0       ; Input pointer
        DATA_OUT         DW       0       ; Output pointer
        ;
        ;
        DATA    ENDS
        ;
        ;********************************************************************
        ;                          c o d e
        ;********************************************************************
        CODE    SEGMENT
                ASSUME  CS:CODE
        ;
        START:
        ; Establish addressability of the program's data segment
                MOV     AX,DATA
                MOV     DS,AX
                ASSUME  DS:DATA
                MOV     ES,AX
                ASSUME  ES:DATA
        ;****************
        ; display MENU   |
        ;****************
                MOV     DX,OFFSET MENU_MS      ; Message
                CALL    SHOW_MESSAGE
        ;****************
        ;   determine    |
        ; system hardware|
        ;****************
        ; Examine RAM location F000:FFFE to get IBM system code
                PUSH    DS                     ; Save program DS
                MOV     DX,0F000H
                MOV     DS,DX
                MOV     AL,DS:[0FFFEH]  ; System ID code in AL
        ; Get base address of serial port from BIOS data area
                MOV     DX,0            ; BIOS data area segment
                MOV     DS,DX           ; Data segment to BIOS area
                MOV     CX,DS:0400H     ; Offset of card 1
                POP     DS              ; Restore program DS
                MOV     PORT_BASE,CX    ; Store serial port base address
        ; Determine interrupt number:
        ;       0CH...........IRQ3 ............. PCjr
        ;       0BH ..........IRQ4 ............. all other hardware
                CMP     AL,0FDH         ; System ID code for PCjr
                JNE     PC_SYSTEM
        ;****************
        ; set PCjr values|
        ;****************
```

```
            MOV     INT_NUM,0BH      ; Interrupt number for PCjr
; Move PCjr baud rate divisor into divisor table
            LEA     DI,DIVISOR       ; Divisor table
            LEA     SI,DIV_JR        ; Values for PCjr
            MOV     CX,8             ; 8 words to move
            CLD                      ; Forward
REP         MOVSW                    ; Move them
;*****************
; save old vector
;*****************
; Obtain and save the segment/offset of the original communications
; interrupt installed on entry
; Uses DOS service number 53 of INT 21H
PC_SYSTEM:
            MOV     AH,53            ; DOS service request number
            MOV     AL,INT_NUM       ; Interrupt number (0BH or 0CH)
            INT     21H
; ES:BX = segment/offset of original handler
            MOV     O_INT_SEG,ES     ; Save segment
            MOV     O_INT_OFF,BX     ; and offset
;*******************
;   install new
;   interrupt
;*******************
; Enter address of the communications interrupt service routine
; in the interrupt vector table
; Uses DOS service number 37 of INT 21H.
            MOV     AH,37            ; DOS service request number
            MOV     AL,INT_NUM       ; Machine interrupt number
            MOV     DX,OFFSET CS:RS232_INT
            PUSH    DS               ; Save program data segment
            PUSH    CS
            POP     DS               ; Set DS to segment base of
                                     ; interrupt service routine
            INT     21H
            POP     DS               ; Restore program's DS
;*******************************
;   set default communications
;          protocol
;*******************************
;   Baud = 2400 (divisor at offset 10 in divisor table)
;
; Bit pattern for line control register
;   x x x 1 1 x x x  ......... Parity = enabled/even
;   x x x x x 0 x x  ......... Stop bits = 1
;   x x x x x x 1 1  ......... Word length = 8
;   0 0 0 1 1 0 1 1 = 1BH
;
            MOV     SET_UP_BYTE,1BH  ; Bit map for LCR
            LEA     SI,DIVISOR       ; Pointer to divisor table
            ADD     SI,10            ; Add offset for 2400 Bd
            MOV     AX,[SI]          ; Get divisor word
            CALL    SET_PROTOCOL     ; Procedure to set protocol
;
            CALL    COMM_ON
            CALL    FLUSH            ; Flush keyboard buffer
;
;*****************************************************************
;               send and receive characters
;               monitor function keys
;*****************************************************************
MONITOR:
            MOV     AH,1             ; Code for read keyboard status
```

```
            INT     16H             ; BIOS service
            JZ      SER_IMP         ; Nothing in keyboard buffer
            JMP     CHAR_TYPED      ; Character in keyboard buffer
;
; Delay loop to allow interrupt to occur
SER_IMP:
            STI                     ; Interrupts on
            MOV     CX,50
DELAY:      NOP
            NOP
            LOOP    DELAY
;*****************
; test for new
; data received
;*****************
            CLI                     ; Interrupts off while reading
                                    ; pointer
            MOV     BX,DATA_OUT     ; Compare pointers
            CMP     BX,DATA_IN
            JNE     NEW_DATA        ; New data item or items
            STI                     ; Interrupts on
            JMP     MONITOR         ; Repeat cycle
;*******************************
;     character was typed
;*******************************
; Retrieve character from keyboard buffer.
CHAR_TYPED:
            MOV     AH,0            ; Code for read keyboard char.
            INT     16H             ; BIOS service
;
; Test for <F1>, <F2>, <F3>  and <F9> keys
            CMP     AX,3B00H        ; <F1>
            JNE     TEST_F2
            JMP     SHOW_MENU       ; <F1> key pressed
TEST_F2:
            CMP     AX,3C00H        ; <F2>
            JNE     TEST_F3
            JMP     SET_RS232C      ; <F2> key pressed
TEST_F3:
            CMP     AX,3D00H        ; <F3>
            JNE     TEST_F9
            JMP     SHOW_PROTOCOL   ; <F3> key pressed
TEST_F9:
            CMP     AX,011BH        ; <Esc>
            JE      DOS_EXIT
            JMP     SHOW_AND_SEND   ; Display and send character
;*******************************
;            exit
;*******************************
DOS_EXIT:
; Communications interrupts OFF
            CALL    COMM_OFF
; Restore original interrupt vector for communications interrupt
            MOV     AH,37           ; DOS service request number
            MOV     AL,INT_NUM      ; Machine interrupt number
            MOV     DX,O_INT_OFF    ; Offset to DX
            MOV     AX,O_INT_SEG    ; Segment
            MOV     DS,AX           ; to DS
            INT     21H
;
; Exit
            MOV     AH,76           ; DOS service request number
            MOV     AL,0            ; No return code
```

```
            INT     21H                 ; Exit to DOS
;********************************|
;    redisplay MENU             |
;********************************|
SHOW_MENU:
            MOV     DX,OFFSET MENU_MS
            CALL    SHOW_MESSAGE    ; Display message routine
            JMP     MONITOR

;********************************|
;    new data in circular buffer|
;********************************|
NEW_DATA:
            LEA     SI,CIRC_BUF      ; Circular buffer address
            MOV     BX,DATA_OUT      ; Output pointer
            ADD     SI,BX            ; Buffer start + displacement
            MOV     AL,BYTE PTR [SI]
                                     ; Get character
; Update output pointer
            INC     BX               ; Bump
            CMP     BX,20            ; Pointer overflows buffer ?
            JNE     OK_OUT_PTR
            MOV     BX,0             ; Reset to start of buffer
;
OK_OUT_PTR:
            MOV     DATA_OUT,BX      ; Update
;
; Display byte taken from buffer
            STI
            CALL    TTY
            JMP     MONITOR
;********************************|
;    set new RS-232-C protocol   |
;********************************|
SET_RS232C:
; The individual submenus for selection of BAUD RATE, PARITY,
; STOP BITS, and WORD LENGTH are posted. The value entered is
; tested for validity and then ORed into the setup byte.
; Selected values are also inserted into the parameters area
; for display.
;
; Interrupts off while resetting protocol
            CALL    COMM_OFF
;******************|
;    baud rate     |
;******************|
BAUD_RATES:
            MOV     DX,OFFSET BAUD_MENU
            CALL    SHOW_MESSAGE
            CALL    GET_KEY          ; Get single key input in AL
; Display input at cursor
            CALL    TTY
            PUSH    AX               ; Save input
            MOV     AL,0DH
            CALL    TTY              ; Execute carriage return
            MOV     AL,0AH
            CALL    TTY              ; Execute line-feed
            POP     AX
; Valid range is "1" to "8"
            CMP     AL,'1'           ; Carry set if less than 1
            JC      BAUD_RATES       ; Repeat selection
            CMP     AL,'9'           ; No carry if larger than 8
```

```
            JNC      BAUD_RATES
; Input is in valid range.
            SUB      AL,30H        ; ASCII to binary
            SUB      AL,1          ; To range 0 to 7
;********************|
;   select and set   |
; baud rate message  |
;********************|
; Select 4-byte baud rate message and place in protocol message
; area for display of installed parameters
            PUSH     AX            ; Save for control byte
; Multiply binary code by 4 to compute displacement into table
            MOV      CL,4
            MUL      CL            ; AL is now in range 0 to 28 (offset)
            MOV      SI,OFFSET BAUD$$
                                   ; SI --> baud rates message
            MOV      AH,0          ; For addition of AL displacement
            ADD      SI,AX         ; SI --> 4 ASCII characters of
                                   ; baud rate message
; Move baud rate message into protocol display area
            MOV      DI,OFFSET BAUD%
                                   ; Destination message area
            MOV      CX,4          ; 4 bytes to move
            CLD                    ; Forward
            PUSH     DS
            POP      ES
REP         MOVSB                  ; Move them
; Message moved to display area
            POP      AX            ; Restore control byte
;********************|
;    get baud rate   |
;       divisor      |
;********************|
; AL holds offset of selected baud rate in table. Offset 0
; corresponds to 110 Bd. Offset 8 to 9600 Bd. Use offset
; to obtain baud rate divisor from divisor table.
            LEA      SI,DIVISOR    ; Pointer to divisor table
            ADD      AL,AL         ; Double AL for word offset
            MOV      AH,0          ; Clear high byte for addition
            ADD      SI,AX         ; Add offset to base address
            MOV      AX,[SI]       ; Get divisor word
            PUSH     AX            ; Save divisor in stack
;********************|
;        input       |
; parity, word length |
;     and stop bits   |
;********************|
PARITY:
            MOV      SET_UP_BYTE,0 ; Clear line control register
                                   ; set up byte
            MOV      DX,OFFSET PAR_MENU
            CALL     SHOW_MESSAGE
            CALL     GET_KEY       ; Single key input in AL
            CALL     TTY           ; Display input at cursor
; Valid input range is "1" to "3"
            CMP      AL,'1'        ; Carry set if less than 1
            JC       PARITY        ; Repeat selection
            CMP      AL,'4'        ; No carry if larger than 3
            JNC      PARITY
; Input is in valid range
            SUB      AL,30H        ; ASCII to binary in range 1 to 3
            PUSH     AX            ; Save control bits
; Select 4-byte parity message and place in display area
```

```
        SUB     AL,1                ; To range 0 to 2
        MOV     CL,4
        MUL     CL                  ; Multiply to obtain offset
        MOV     SI,OFFSET PAR$$
                                    ; SI --> parity messages
        MOV     AH,0                ; For addition of displacement
        ADD     SI,AX               ; SI --> ASCII characters for
                                    ; parity
        MOV     DI,OFFSET PAR%
                                    ; DI --> destination of message
        MOV     CX,4                ; Byte to move
        CLD                         ; Forward
        PUSH    DS
        POP     ES
REP     MOVSB                       ; Move them
;
        POP     AX                  ; Restore control bits
        MOV     CL,3                ; Shift bit counter
        SHL     AL,CL               ; Shift left 3 bits
        OR      SET_UP_BYTE,AL      ; OR with stored baud rate
;
STOP_BITS:
        MOV     DX,OFFSET STOP_MENU
        CALL    SHOW_MESSAGE
        CALL    GET_KEY             ; Get single key input in AL
        CALL    TTY                 ; Display input
; Valid input range is "1" or "2"
        CMP     AL,'1'              ; Carry set if less than 1
        JC      STOP_BITS           ; Repeat selection
        CMP     AL,'3'              ; No carry if larger than 2
        JNC     STOP_BITS
; Input is in valid range. Move input digit to display area
        MOV     SI,OFFSET STOP%     ; Pointer to display area
        MOV     BYTE PTR [SI],AL
                                    ; Insert digit
; Convert input digit to binary 0 or 1
        SUB     AL,31H              ; ASCII to binary minus 1
; Shift left 2 bits
        MOV     CL,2
        SHL     AL,CL               ; Shift digits
        OR      SET_UP_BYTE,AL
                                    ; OR with stored parameters
WORD_LENGTH:
        MOV     DX,OFFSET WORD_MENU
        CALL    SHOW_MESSAGE
        CALL    GET_KEY             ; Single key input in AL
        CALL    TTY                 ; Display input
; Valid input range is "1" or "2"
        CMP     AL,'1'              ; Carry set if less than 1
        JC      WORD_LENGTH         ; Repeat selection
        CMP     AL,'3'              ; No carry if larger than 2
        JNC     WORD_LENGTH
        PUSH    AX                  ; Save input
; Input in valid range. Add 6 and move input to display area
        ADD     AL,6                ; 1 = 7 and 2 = 8
        MOV     SI,OFFSET WORD%     ; Display area
        MOV     BYTE PTR [SI],AL
        POP     AX                  ; Restore input digit
        SUB     AL,30H              ; Convert to binary 1 or 2
        INC     AL                  ; Bring to range 2 or 3
        OR      SET_UP_BYTE,AL
                                    ; OR with stored parameters
; Carriage return and line-feed
```

```
                MOV     AL,0DH
                CALL    TTY                 ; Execute carriage return
                MOV     AL,0AH
                CALL    TTY                 ; Execute line-feed
        ;**********************|
        ; install word length, |
        ;  stop bits, parity,   |
        ;    and baud rate      |
        ;**********************|
        ;
        ; Line control register bit map:
        ; 0  0  0
        ;    |  |  |
        ; 7  6  5  4  3  2  1  0
        ;             |  |  |  |_____ Word length (7 or 8 bits)
        ;             |  |  |_____ Stop bits (1 or 2)
        ;             |  |_____ Parity enable (0 = no parity)
        ;             |_____ Parity select (odd or even)
        ;
                POP     AX                  ; Recover baud rate divisor
                CALL    SET_PROTOCOL
        ;
        ; Communications interrupts on
                CALL    COMM_ON
                JMP     MONITOR
        ;
        ;*****************************|
        ;    display RS-232_C protocol |
        ;*****************************|
        SHOW_PROTOCOL:
                MOV     DX,OFFSET PROT_MS
                CALL    SHOW_MESSAGE        ; Display message routine
                JMP     MONITOR
        ;
        ;
        ;*****************************|
        ;  display and send character |
        ;*****************************|
        SHOW_AND_SEND:
        ; Send through RS-232C line
        ; Wait loop for transmitter holding register empty
                MOV     CX,2000             ; Prime wait counter
                PUSH    AX                  ; Save character to transmit
        ;
        THRE_WAIT:
                MOV     DX,PORT_BASE
                ADD     DX,5                ; Line status register
                IN      AL,DX               ; Get byte at port
                JMP     SHORT $+2           ; I/O delay
                TEST    AL,20H              ; THRE bit set ?
                JNZ     OK_2_SEND
                LOOP    THRE_WAIT
        ; Wait period timed out. Display error message and exit
                POP     AX                  ; Restore stack
                MOV     DX,OFFSET ERR1_MS
                CALL    SHOW_MESSAGE        ; Error to screen
                JMP     MONITOR
        ;
        OK_2_SEND:
                POP     AX                  ; Retrieve byte
        ; Place in transmitter holding register to send
                MOV     DX,PORT_BASE        ; THR register
                OUT     DX,AL               ; Send
```

```
        JMP     SHORT $+2        ; I/O delay
;
; Display character
        CALL    TTY
;
        JMP     MONITOR
;
;******************************************************************
;                    p r o c e d u r e s
;******************************************************************
;*****************************
;            serial line ON
;*****************************
COMM_ON          PROC    NEAR
; Set communications line for interrupt operation on received
; data
;
        CLI                     ; Interrupts off
; Reset buffer pointers to start of buffer
        MOV     DATA_IN,0
        MOV     DATA_OUT,0
;
; Set DX to base address of RS 232-C card from BIOS
        MOV     DX,PORT_BASE
;
; Initialize modem control register for data terminal ready
; (bit 0), request to send (bit 1), and OUTPUT 2 (bit 3).
; DX is still holding port address.
        MOV     DL,0FCH         ; MCR address
        MOV     AL,00001011B    ; Bits 0, 1, and 3 set
        OUT     DX,AL
        JMP     SHORT $+2
;
; Set bit 7 of the line control register (DLAB) to access
; the interrupt enable register at xF9H.
        MOV     DL,0FBH         ; xFBH = line control register
        IN      AL,DX           ; Read byte at port
        JMP     SHORT $+2       ; I/O delay
        AND     AL,7FH          ; Reset DLAB
        OUT     DX,AL           ; Write to LCR
        JMP     SHORT $+2       ; I/O delay
;
; Enable interrupts for DATA READY only
        MOV     DL,0F9H         ; Interrupt enable register
        MOV     AL,1            ; Data ready interrupt
        OUT     DX,AL
        JMP     SHORT $+2
;
; Enable communications interrupts by resetting the bits
; corresponding to the IRQ3 and IRQ4 lines on the interrupt mask
; register (port address = 21H)
        IN      AL,21H          ; Read byte at port
        JMP     SHORT $+2       ; I/O delay
        AND     AL,0E7H         ; Reset bits 3 and 4
        OUT     21H,AL
        JMP     SHORT $+2       ; I/O delay
;
; Reenable interrupts
        STI
        RET
;
COMM_ON          ENDP
;
```

```
;*******************************
;         serial line OFF
;*******************************
COMM_OFF        PROC    NEAR
; Disable communications interrupts by setting bits for IRQ3 and
; IRQ4 lines on the interrupt mask register (port address = 21H)
        IN      AL,21H
        OR      AL,18H          ; Set bits 3 and 4
        OUT     21H,AL
        JMP     SHORT $+2
        RET
;
COMM_OFF        ENDP
;
;
SHOW_MESSAGE    PROC    NEAR
; Display string --> by the DX register using DOS function 09H
        MOV     AH,9            ; Service request number
        INT     21H             ; DOS interrupt
        RET
;
SHOW_MESSAGE    ENDP
;
;*******************************
;         teletype write
;*******************************
TTY             PROC    NEAR
; Display character or control code at cursor position
TTY_ONE:
        PUSH    AX              ; Save character
        MOV     AH,14           ; BIOS service request number
                                ; for ASCII teletype write
        MOV     BX,0            ; Display page
        INT     10H             ; BIOS service request
        POP     AX
; Test for carriage return and add line-feed
        CMP     AL,0DH
        JNE     NOT_CR
        MOV     AL,0AH
        JMP     TTY_ONE
NOT_CR:
        RET
;
TTY             ENDP
;
;*******************************
;         flush buffer
;*******************************
FLUSH   PROC    NEAR
; Flush keyboard buffer of old characters
FLUSH_1:
        MOV     AH,1            ; BIOS service request code
        INT     16H
        JZ      NO_OLD_CHARS
; Flush old character
        MOV     AH,0
        INT     16H
        JMP     FLUSH_1
;
NO_OLD_CHARS:
        RET
FLUSH   ENDP
;
```

```
;******************************|
;      get keyboard input      |
;******************************|
GET_KEY             PROC    NEAR
; Read keyboard character
        MOV     AH,0              ; BIOS service request number
        INT     16H
        RET
;
GET_KEY             ENDP
;
;******************************|
;  set communications protocol |
;******************************|
SET_PROTOCOL     PROC    NEAR
;
; On entry:
;       AX holds baud rate divisor
;       The variable SET_UP_BYTE holds bit map for word length,
;       stop bits, and parity, to be set in the LCR
;
        PUSH    AX                ; Save divisor in stack
        MOV     DX,PORT_BASE      ; Address of system's serial port
        ADD     DX,3              ; Line control register is at
                                  ; base address + 3
        IN      AL,DX             ; Read contents of LC register
        JMP     SHORT $+2         ; I/O delay
        OR      AL,80H            ; To set the divisor latch access
                                  ; bit (DLAB)
        OUT     DX,AL             ; To line control register
        JMP     SHORT $+2         ; I/O delay
;
        POP     AX                ; Restore baud rate divisor to AX
        MOV     DL,0F8H           ; Address of divisor's LSB
        OUT     DX,AL             ; AL to baud rate divisor LSB
        JMP     SHORT $+2         ; I/O delay
        MOV     AL,AH             ; HOB of divisor word to AL
        MOV     DL,0F9H           ; Address of divisor's MSB
        OUT     DX,AL             ; AL to baud rate divisor MSB
        JMP     SHORT $+2         ; I/O delay
;
        MOV     AL,SET_UP_BYTE    ; Get bit pattern
        MOV     DX,PORT_BASE      ; Address of system's serial port
        ADD     DX,3              ; Line control register is at
                                  ; base address + 3
        OUT     DX,AL             ; Set-up byte to LCR
        JMP     SHORT $+2         ; I/O delay
        RET
;
SET_PROTOCOL     ENDP
;
;********************************************************************
;              i n t e r r u p t    s e r v i c e
;                         r o u t i n e
;********************************************************************
RS232_INT:
        STI                       ; Interrupts on - except for
                                  ; communications
; Save registers to be used by the service routine
        PUSH    AX                ; Registers to stack
        PUSH    BX
        PUSH    DX
```

```
                PUSH    DI
                PUSH    DS
; Set DS establish addressability of main program data
                MOV     DX,DATA
                MOV     DS,DX
                ASSUME  DS:DATA
;*******************|
;   check line      |
;*******************|
; Check line status register for reception error and data ready
DATA_CHECK:
                MOV     DX,PORT_BASE
                MOV     DL,0FDH         ; Line status register
                IN      AL,DX           ; Read port byte
                JMP     SHORT $+2       ; I/O delay
; Check for data ready on line
                TEST    AL,01H
                JNZ     DATA_READY
; Check for error codes
                TEST    AL,1EH
                JNZ     DATA_ERROR
                JMP     DATA_CHECK
;*******************|
;   error           |
;*******************|
DATA_ERROR:
                MOV     AL,'?'          ; Error symbol
                JMP     STORE_BYTE
;
; Pull data from the receiver data register and store in the
; circular buffer
DATA_READY:
                MOV     DL,0F8H         ; RDR
                IN      AL,DX           ; Get byte
                JMP     SHORT $+2       ; I/O delay
                AND     AL,7FH          ; Mask off high bit
;
;*******************|
;   byte to buffer  |
;*******************|
STORE_BYTE:
                LEA     DI,CIRC_BUF     ; Buffer pointer
                MOV     BX,DATA_IN      ; Input pointer
                ADD     DI,BX           ; Point DI to active byte
                MOV     BYTE PTR [DI],AL
                                        ; Store in CIRC_BUF
; Index input pointer. Reset if pointer overflows buffer.
                INC     BX              ; Bump pointer
                CMP     BX,20           ; Past end of buffer ?
                JNE     OK_IN_PTR
; Reset pointer to start of buffer
                MOV     BX,0
OK_IN_PTR:
                MOV     DATA_IN,BX      ; Store new pointer displacement
;
; Signal end of interrupt to the interrupt command register
                MOV     AL,20H          ; Code
                OUT     20H,AL          ; EOI port address
                JMP     SHORT $+2       ; I/O delay
;*******************|
;   restore and exit|
;*******************|
                POP     DS              ; Registers in stack
```

```
        POP     DI
        POP     DX
        POP     BX
        POP     AX
; Return from interrupt
        IRET
;
CODE    ENDS
        END     START
```

Bibliography

Angermeyer, John, and Kevin Jaeger. *MS DOS Developer's Guide*. Indianapolis: Howard W. Sams, 1986.

Bradley, David J. *Assembly Language Programming for the IBM Personal Computer*. Englewood Cliffs, N.J.: Prentice-Hall, 1984.

Brumm, Peter, and Don Brumm. *80386 A programming and Design Handbook*. Blue Ridge Summit, Pa.: Tab Books, 1987.

Chien, Chao C. *Programming the IBM Personal Computer: Assembly Language*. New York: CBS College Publishing, 1984.

Conrac Corporation. *Raster Graphics Handbook*. New York: Van Nostrand Reinhold, 1985.

Davis, William S. *Computing Fundamentals—Concepts*. 2d. ed. Reading, Mass.: Addison-Wesley, 1989.

Doty, David B. *Programmer's Guide to the Hercules Graphics Cards*. Reading, Mass.: Addison-Wesley, 1988.

Duncan, Ray. *Advanced MS DOS*. Redmond, Wash.: Microsoft Press, 1986.

——— *Advanced OS/2 Programming*. Redmond, Wash.: Microsoft Press, 1989.

Franklin, Mark. *Using the IBM PC: Organization and Assembly Language Programming*. New York: CBS College Publishing, 1984.

Freedman, Allen. *The Computer Glossary*. 4th. ed. Point Pleasant, Pa.: AMACOM, 1989.

Gofton, Peter W. *Mastering Serial Communications*. San Francisco: Sybex, 1986.

Halliday, Caroline M., and James A. Shields. *IBM PS/2 Technical Guide*. Indianapolis: Howard W. Sams, 1988.

Hogan, Thom. *The Programmer's PC Sourcebook*. Redmond, Wash.: Microsoft Press, 1988.

Hoskins, Jim. *IBM PS/2 A Business Perspective*. New York: Wiley, 1984.

Iacobucci, Ed. *OS/2 Programmer's Guide*. Berkeley, Calif.: Osborne/McGraw-Hill, 1988.

IBM Corporation. *Technical Reference, Personal Computer*. Boca Raton, Fla.: IBM, 1984.

———*Technical Reference, Personal Computer AT*. Boca Raton, Fla.: IBM, 1984.

——— *Technical Reference, Personal Computer PCjr*. Boca Raton, Fla.: IBM, 1983.

────── *Technical Reference, Personal System/2, Model 30*. Boca Raton, Fla.: IBM, 1987.

────── *Technical Reference, Personal System/2, Model 50 and 60*. Boca Raton, Fla.: IBM, 1987.

────── *Personal System/2 and Personal Computer BIOS Interface Technical Reference*. Boca Raton, Fla.: IBM, 1987.

────── *Technical Reference, Options and Adapters*, vol. 1. Boca Raton, Fla.: IBM, 1986.

────── *Technical Reference, Options and Adapters*, vol. 2. Boca Raton, Fla.: IBM, 1986.

────── *Technical Reference, Options and Adapters*. Boca Raton, Fla.: IBM, 1986.

────── *Technical Reference, Supplements for the PS/2 Model 70, Hardware Interface, and BIOS Interface Technical References*. Boca Raton,Fla.: IBM, 1988.

Intel Corporation, *iAPX 86/88, 186/188 User's Manual* (Programmer's Reference). Santa Clara, Calif.: Reward Books, 1983.

────── *iAPX 86/88, 186/188 User's Manual* (Programmer's Reference). Santa Clara, Calif.: Intel, 1987.

────── *80286 and 80287 Programmer's Reference Manual*. Santa Clara, Calif.: Intel, 1987.

────── *80386 Programmer's Reference Manual*. Santa Clara, Calif.: Intel, 1986.

────── *Memory Components Handbook*. Santa Clara, Calif.: Intel, 1986.

────── *Microprocessor and Peripheral Handbook*, vol. I: *Microprocessor*. Santa Clara, Calif.: Intel, 1988.

────── *Microprocessor and Peripheral Handbook*, vol. II: *Peripheral*. Santa Clara, Calif.: Intel, 1988.

────── *Programmable Logic Handbook*. Santa Clara, Calif: Intel, 1988.

────── *Product Guide*. Santa Clara, Calif.: Intel, 1988

Jourdain, Robert. *Programmer's Problem Solver for the IBM PC, XT & AT*. New York: Brady Communications, 1986.

Jump, Dennis N. *Programmer's Guide to MS DOS for the IBM PC*. Reston, Va.: Brady Communications, 1984.

Kliewer, Bradley Dyck. *EGA/VGA A Programmer's Reference Guide*, 2d ed. New York: McGraw-Hill, 1988.

Liu, Yu-Cheng, and Glenn A. Gibson. *Microcomputer Systems: The 8086/8088 Family*. Englewood Cliffs, N.J.: Prentice-Hall, 1984.

Money, Steve A. *Practical Microprocessor Interfacing*. New York: Wiley, 1987.

Morgan, Christopher L. *Bluebook of Assembly Language Routines for the IBM PC & XT*. New York: Waite Group, 1984.

Norton, Peter. *Inside the IBM PC. Access to Advanced Features and Programming*. Bowie, Md: Robert J. Brady Co., 1983.
────── *Peter Norton's Assembly Language Book for the IBM PC*. New York: Prentice-Hall, 1986

—— *The Peter Norton Programmer's Guide to the IBM PC*. Redmond, Wash.: Microsoft Press, 1985.

Palmer, John F., and Stephen P. Morse. *The 8087 Primer*. New York: Wiley, 1984.

Ralston, Anthony, and Chester L. Meek. *Encyclopedia of Computer Science*. New York: Mason and Charter, 1983

Rogers, David F. *Procedural Elements for Computer Graphics*. New York: McGraw-Hill, 1985.

Rosch, Winn L. *The Winn Rosch Hardware Bible*. New York: Prentice-Hall, 1989.

Royer, Jeffrey P. *Handbook of Software & Hardware Interfacing for the IBM PCs*. Englewood Cliffs, N.J.: Prentice-Hall, 1987.

Runnion, William C. *Structured Programming in Assembly Language for the IBM PC*. Boston, Mass.: PWS-Kent, 1988.

Sanchez, Julio. *Assembly Language Tools and Techniques for the IBM Microcomputers*. Englewood Cliffs, N.J.: Prentice-Hall, 1990.

—— *Graphics Design and Animation on the IBM Microcomputers*. Englewood Cliffs, N.J.: Prentice-Hall, 1990.

Seyer, Martin D. *RS-232 Made Easy*. Englewood Cliffs, N.J.: Prentice-Hall, 1984

Sargent, Richard, III, and Richard L. Shoemaker. *The IBM Personal Computer from the Inside Out*. Reading, Mass.: Addison-Wesley, 1984

Scanlon, Leo J. *Assembly Language Subroutines for MS-DOS Computers*. Blue Ridge Summit, Pa.: Tab Books, 1987.

—— *IBM PC & XT Assembly Language*. Bowie, Md.: Brady Communications, 1983.

Schatt, Stan. *Understanding Local Area Networks*. Indianapolis: Howard W. Sams, 1987.

Smith, James T. *The IBM PC AT Programmer' Guide*. New York: Waite Group, 1986.

Smith, Bud E., and Mark T. Johnson. *Programming the Intel 80386*. Glenview, Ill.: Scott, Foresman, 1987.

Stallings, William. *Handbook of Computer Communications Standards*. vols. 1–3. New York: Macmillan, 1988.

Starts, Richard. *8087 Applications and Programming for the IBM PC, XT, and AT*. New York: Brady Communications, 1985.

Vieillefond, C. *Programming the 80286*. San Francisco: Sybex, 1987.

Willen, David C. *IBM PCjr Assembler Language*. Indianapolis: Howard W. Sams, 1984.

Willen, David C., and Jeffrey I. Krantz. *8088 Assembler Language Programming: The IBM PC*. Indianapolis: Howard W. Sams, 1983.

Wilton, Richard. *Programmer's Guide to PC & PS/2 Video Systems*. Redmond, Wash.: Microsoft Press, 1987.

Woram, John. *The PC Configuration Handbook*. New York: Bantam Books, 1987.

Index

About the Authors

JULIO SANCHEZ is a professor of computer science and the author of several text and reference books in the fied of microcomputers.

MARIA P. CANTON is vice-president of a software development and consulting firm. She also serves as a documentation consultant to major software firms.